"The book reveals that reconciliation cannot materialize as long as the vulnerable, marginalized, and Indigenous nations of this world remain captive, anonymous, and subject to pseudo colonial-hegemonic groups. The authors envision, through concrete transformational praxes, to unearth historical injustices by amplifying the values of marginalized Indigenous communities and fostering societal change. May it be that the vision of Nelson Rolihlahla Mandela materializes in our age: 'Never, never and never again shall it be that this beautiful land will again experience the oppression of one by another and suffer the indignity of being the skunk of the world.'"

—GORDON ERNEST DAMES, professor of practical theology, University of South Africa

"In its investigation of the connection between reconciliation in practice and the role of truth and reconciliation commissions (TRCs), this book presents us with comparative research that is driven by leading scholars from three different continents presenting both the global North and South. It makes a vital contribution to the discourse around TRCs and whether or how their processes are successful in cultivating communities for visible transformation."

—TIANA BOSMAN, senior lecturer in religion and theology, University of the Western Cape, South Africa

"The expanding literature around the contested legacies of truth and reconciliation commissions necessitates multidimensionality. Contributions in this volume move between the domains of politics, law, philosophy, sociology, and theology, filling this lacuna through a South African–Nordic exchange, where restoration and transformation remain inseparable from the examination of colonial heritages. At once political and religious, TRCs here are subject to their inherent limitations but also creatively interpreted into new horizons of possibility. This is a significant collaborative effort and rich collection."

—CALVIN D. ULLRICH, senior lecturer in interdisciplinary theology, University of the Free State, South Africa

"This book is an important contribution to what is a new but important and growing field in the Nordic countries – truth, reconciliation, and the implication for the relationships between peoples of the north. The inclusion of several minority groups alongside the Indigenous Sámi makes the book one of special interest."

—TORJER A. OLSEN, professor of indigenous studies, UiT The Arctic University of Norway

Cultivating Transformative Reconciliation

Cultivating Transformative Reconciliation

Are TRC Processes Enough?

EDITED BY
LINE MERETHE SKUM
JOHN KLAASEN
BERND KRUPKA
RAY ALDRED

☙PICKWICK *Publications* • Eugene, Oregon

CULTIVATING TRANSFORMATIVE RECONCILIATION
Are TRC Processes Enough?

Copyright © 2024 Wipf and Stock Publishers. All rights reserved. Except for brief quotations in critical publications or reviews, no part of this book may be reproduced in any manner without prior written permission from the publisher. Write: Permissions, Wipf and Stock Publishers, 199 W. 8th Ave., Suite 3, Eugene, OR 97401.

Pickwick Publications
An Imprint of Wipf and Stock Publishers
199 W. 8th Ave., Suite 3
Eugene, OR 97401

www.wipfandstock.com

PAPERBACK ISBN: 978-1-6667-7875-5
HARDCOVER ISBN: 978-1-6667-7876-2
EBOOK ISBN: 978-1-6667-7877-9

Cataloguing-in-Publication data:

Names: Skum, Line Merethe, editor. | Klaasen, John, editor. | Krupka, Bernd, editor. | Aldred, Ray, editor.

Title: Cultivating Transformative Reconciliation : Are TRC Processes Enough? / edited by Line Merethe Skum, John Klaasen, Bernd Krupka, and Ray Aldred.

Description: Eugene, OR: Pickwick Publications, 2024. | Includes bibliographical references and index.

Identifiers: ISBN 978-1-6667-7875-5 (paperback). | ISBN 978-1-6667-7876-2 (hardcover). | ISBN 978-1-6667-7877-9 (ebook).

Subjects: LCSH: Reconciliation. | Truth commissions. | Human rights. | Indigenous peoples. | Decolonization. | Sámi (European people). | Kvens (European people).

Classification: JC580 C98 2024 (print). | JC580 (ebook).

10/29/24

Contents

Abbreviations vii

Introduction: Cultivating Transformative Reconciliation ix
    Line Merethe Skum, John Klaasen, Bernd Krupka,
    and Ray Aldred

PART ONE: TRANSFORMATIVE ISSUES IN LAW AND POLITICS

1. The Nordic Truth and Reconciliation Commissions: A New TRC Model for Resolving Historic and Ongoing Violations of Indigenous Rights?   3
Elin Skaar

2. TRC and Processes within the Church of Norway: Unequal Status of North Sámi and Kvens/Norwegian Finns in Shared Regions   30
Hans Morten Haugen

3. Untangling the Gordian Knot: Recognition of Indigenous Minorities in the Context of Truth and Reconciliation in Norway and Peru   52
Anne Margrethe Sønneland and Carola Lingaas

4. Reflections on Truth and Reconciliation Commissions in the Context of Decolonization   74
Girum Zeleke

PART TWO: UNDERSTANDING HISTORY FROM A TRANSFORMATIVE PERSPECTIVE

5   Historical Justice as a New Challenge in Historical Research: Reflections on the White Paper Project on the Historical Relations Between the Church of Sweden and the Sámi People   101
    DANIEL LINDMARK

6   Decolonizing Scandinavian Creation Theology: The Constructive Critique of Key Concepts in the Works of Sámi Theologian Tore Johnsen   119
    GYRID GUNNES

7   Truth and Reconciliation in Sápmi and Lebanon: Messianism of Decolonization   138
    HELGE HIRAM ABDELNOOR JENSEN

8   The Relation of Civil Society to the Norwegian TRC-Process in the Light of TRUCOM Research: A Reconciliation without the Majority?   173
    KJELL OLSEN

PART THREE: TRANSFORMATIVE RECONCILIATION— THE TRC PROCESSES AND BEYOND

9   Between Performance and the Absurd: Evaluating Reconciliation at the South African TRC   195
    DEMAINE SOLOMONS

10 Small Stories Challenging Large Narratives: The Contribution of Personal Accounts to Transformative Reconciliation in Post-TRC Norway   209
    TORE JOHNSEN

11 Narrative as Interlocutor of Identity and Reconciliation   244
    JOHN KLAASEN

12 Remembering: A Pathway to Unburden our Present?   260
    BONITA BENNETT

Appendix   283

Index   287

Abbreviations

ANC	African National Congress
CCN	Christian Council of Norway
CoN	Church of Norway
CoS	Church of Sweden
COVID	Coronavirus disease
CPA	The Consumer Protection Act
CPCE	Community of Protestant Churches in Europe
DRC	Dutch Reformed Church
GAA	Group Areas Act
IJR	Institute for Justice and Reconciliation
ILO	International Labor Organization
IR	International Relations
IRS	Indian Residential School
KM	Church Synod
KUN	North Norwegian Church Education Center
NGO	Non-Governmental Organization
NOU	Norwegian Official Report
NP	National Party
NRK	National Broadcasting
NRL	Sámi Reindeer Herder's Association of Norway

NSD	Norwegian Center for Research Data
NTA	Non-Territorial Autonomy
PLO	Palestine Liberation Organization
RLRA	Restitution of Land Rights Act
SABC	The South African Broadcasting Corporation
SACC	South African Council of Churches
SANKS	Sámi National Center for Mental Health Care
SCC	Sámi Church Council
SCT	Scandinavian Creation Theology
TC	Truth Commission
TRC	Truth and Reconciliation Commission
TRUCOM	Expectations, Truth and Reconciliation in a Democratic Welfare State
UCP	Ukrainian Communist Party
UNDRIP	United Nations Declaration on the Rights of Indigenous Peoples
UNESCO	United Nations Educational, Scientific and Cultural Organization
UNWGIP	UN Working Group for Indigenous Populations
UN	United Nations
VID	VID Specialized University
WCC	World Council of Churches

Introduction
Cultivating Transformative Reconciliation

LINE MERETHE SKUM
Faculty of Theology and Social Sciences,
VID Specialized University, Tromsø, Norway

JOHN KLAASEN
Faculty of Theology and Religion, University of the Free State, South Africa; Faculty of Theology and Social Sciences, VID Specialized University, Oslo, Norway

BERND KRUPKA
Faculty of Theology and Social Sciences,
VID Specialized University, Tromsø, Norway

RAY ALDRED
Vancouver School of Theology,
The University of British Columbia, Vancouver, Canada

This volume represents the second research publication of ReconTrans, an international comparative research project coordinated by Kirkelig utdanningssenter nord/Girkolaš Oahpahusguovddáš Davvin—VID Tromsø (Norway), in collaboration with the University of the Western Cape (South Africa) and Vancouver School of Theology (Canada). The project examines how and to what extent 'reconciliation' as a transformative concept and practice takes place in association with truth and reconciliation commissions (TRCs). Monitoring Norway's recently concluded TRC process that investigated the Norwegianization policy and injustices against the Sámi, Kvens, and Norwegian Finns (2018–2023), the project facilitated comparative research across the South African, Canadian, and Norwegian/Nordic TRC experiences. Despite the apparent diversity among these nations—South Africa, Canada, Norway, and Sweden—they all share a fundamental common challenge: addressing the historical injustices and enduring legacies of settler colonialism. To confront these complex issues, each of these countries has established TRCs tasked with investigating past wrongs, offering recommendations for reparations, and exploring ways for promoting reconciliation. Contributions to ReconTrans were discussed at conferences that took place at the University of the Western Cape in Cape Town, South Africa; VID Specialized University in Tromsø and Oslo, Norway; and Vancouver School of Theology in Vancouver, Canada.

Volume 1, *Trading Justice for Peace? Reframing Reconciliation in TRC Processes in South Africa, Canada and Nordic Countries,* which was published in 2021,[1] examined how reconciliation is framed and reframed before, during, and after TRCs, attentive to the risk that justice is traded for peace in pursuit of reconciliation. This first volume emerged as a direct outcome of two consultative gatherings held in Cape Town and Tromsø. Embedded in a transformative research paradigm committed to social justice and human rights, this edited volume explored the various strands and stages employed across the different countries. Within these multifaceted explorations, 'reconciliation' was conceptualized as a transformative concept aimed at addressing and renegotiating power relations. It critically acknowledged the often deeply ingrained asymmetric power relations that underlie the injustices and traumas at the heart of the political violence confronted by the TRCs. Moreover, the volume also raised pertinent questions surrounding vital issues such as identity, land, decolonization, and transformation, shaping a holistic and illuminating discourse on the subject.

The title of the current book, Volume 2, *Cultivating Transformative Reconciliation. Are TRC processes enough?* aptly captures the themes that were identified during the last two consultations in Oslo and Vancouver. The themes serve as guiding beacons, directing our focus toward perspectives on decolonization and indigenization. They contribute significantly to the emerging discourse surrounding the nature and scope of truth and reconciliation, particularly in the aftermath of assimilation

---

1. Guðmarsdóttir et al., *Trading Justice for Peace*.

policies and colonization. Additionally, they illuminate both historical and contemporary issues.

The current edited volume builds upon research questions that evolved from prior reconciliation processes, while also addressing the inherent limitations of their outcomes. The contributions assess how the TRC involves and fosters the civil society processes of 'political self-expression,' 'social reconciliation,' and 'healing' in a nation-to-nation perspective: What are the responsibilities and contributions of the church, broader civil society, research, and the political sphere in this context? How are stories shared and received in the TRC processes? And what insights can be gained from the South African and Nordic experiences?

This publication embarks on an investigation of the Norwegianization policy, a historical framework that wrought injustices upon minority groups, such as the Sámi, Kvens, and Forest Finns in Norway. Furthermore, it extends its exploration to analogous unjust policies in South Africa and various other contexts. Within the complex web of cultural, social, political, and economic struggles stemming from colonial policies, the roles of religion, politics, research institutions, and civil society are critically examined.

Part One of the book, titled Transformative Issues in Law and Politics, discusses the potential shifts in law and politics that may arise from the TRC processes. TRCs can be understood as pre-political mechanisms,[2] characterized by their extraordinary nature and time-limited existence, setting them apart from the ordinary political space. Thus, the process of implementing the transformative outcomes derived from TRC processes back into political spaces demands special consideration and attention. The implementation of these transformative outcomes can be envisioned as a continuation of impulses generated from the TRC process.

Elin Skaar, a senior researcher at the Chr. Michelsen Institute, is a member of the research group TRUCOM, dedicated to monitoring the TRC process in Norway. In Chapter 1, titled "The Nordic Truth and Reconciliation Commissions: A New TRC Model for Resolving Historic and Ongoing Violations of Indigenous Rights?," Skaar provides a comprehensive overview of the Nordic TRC processes. In this context, she asserts that the organizational structure of the Norwegian TRC inherently embodies transformative elements, which have the potential to shape and influence the broader landscape of justice and reconciliation.

2. Nordquist, *Reconciliation as Politics*.

Professor Hans Morten Haugen from the Faculty of Theology and Social Sciences at VID Specialized University examines the legal situation of the Kvens, a Finnish-speaking national minority in Northern Norway. In Chapter 2, titled "TRC and Processes within the Church of Norway: Unequal Status of North Sámi and Kvens/Norwegian Finns in Shared Regions," he details the reconciliatory processes implied by their legal status for the Church of Norway.

TRC processes have the potential to initiate changes in law and politics when previously unresolved issues come to the forefront during TRC proceedings, only to remain unaddressed. In Chapter 3, titled "Untangling the Gordian Knot: Recognition of Indigenous Minorities in the Context of Truth and Reconciliation in Norway and Peru," Senior Lecturer Anne Margrethe Sønneland and Professor Carola Lingaas, both from the Faculty of Social Studies at VID Specialized University, discuss the crucial role of political trust in shaping the outcomes of reconciliation processes. They assert that political trust relies on a shared pluralistic societal foundation that represents both minority and majority voices.

In Chapter 4, a comparative chapter titled "Reflections on Truth and Reconciliation Commissions in the Context of Decolonization," Associate Professor Girum Zeleke, from the Faculty of Theology and Social Sciences at VID Specialized University, examines the Norwegian TRC process alongside other TRC processes. In his critical assessment, he posits that TRCs may not be fully equipped to effectively address the fundamental issues of justice in a society.

Part Two of the book, Understanding History from a Transformative Perspective, explores the process of writing and rewriting history as a pivotal component of transformative reconciliation. In these processes, the writing of history is contested (cf. the chapter by Helge Hiram Abdelnoor Jensen in this volume) as a symbolic ground for claims to power and legitimacy.

Professor of Church History and History, Daniel Lindmark at the Faculty of Arts and Humanities and Umeå School of Education at Umeå University, reflects on his involvement in the Swedish White Paper Project, which focuses on the relations between the Sámi people and the Church of Sweden. In Chapter 5, titled "Historical Justice as a New Challenge in Historical Research: Reflections on the White Paper Project on the Historical Relations between the Church of Sweden and the Sámi People," he explores the challenges that arise in history-writing when viewing the past through the lens of reconciliation and decolonization processes.

In Chapter 6, titled "Decolonizing Scandinavian Creation Theology: The Constructive Critique of Key Concepts in the Works of Sámi Theologian Tore Johnsen," Associate Professor Gyrid Gunnes, at the Faculty of Theology and Social Sciences at VID Specialized University, unpacks the impact of Tore Johnsen's decolonizing theological work on Scandinavian creation theology, introducing the concept of a 'sociology of dogma.' This approach examines theological concepts and dogma not merely as theological teachings but also as artifacts within social processes, including colonization and decolonization.

Highlighting the interconnectedness of historical perspective-taking and political vision, Associate Professor Helge Hiram Abdelnoor Jensen at the Department of Organization, Leadership and Management at Inland Norway University of Applied Sciences, draws a comparison between the case of the transnational Sápmi in Northern Scandinavia and the multiethnic landscape of Lebanon. In Chapter 7, titled "Truth and Reconciliation in Sápmi and Lebanon—Messianism of Decolonization," he undertakes an analysis that uncovers common roots and interdependencies between colonial and decolonizing ideas and traditions.

Professor Kjell Olsen at the Department of Tourism and Northern Studies at UiT The Arctic University of Norway is a fellow member of the TRUCOM project. In his thought-provoking analysis of the Norwegian and other TRC processes, his contribution in Chapter 8, titled "The Relation of Civil Society to the Norwegian TRC Process in the Light of TRUCOM Research—A Reconciliation Without the Majority?," highlights the crucial importance of involving not only the perpetrators but also the silent majority who have benefited from social injustice, even if they were not directly involved in perpetrating harmful actions.

Part Three of the book, Transformative Reconciliation—TRC Processes and Beyond, focuses on transformative social processes in the wake of TRCs, potentially instilling the inherent dynamics of TRCs as permanent features within the broader society.

Associate Professor Demaine Solomons from the Department of Systematic Theology and Ecclesiology, Faculty of Theology, Stellenbosch University, South Africa, presents a profound philosophical perspective in Chapter 9, titled "Between Performance and the Absurd: Evaluating Reconciliation at the South African TRC." Within this insightful analysis, Solomons delves into the contemporary critique of unaddressed issues within the South African TRC process. Drawing on Camus and the philosophy of the absurd, Solomons intriguingly posits that intangible values such as hope and resilience emerge as the primary outcomes of TRC processes. These values, in turn, instill a sense of courage within society, motivating them to confront ongoing injustices and continue the journey of reconciliation.

In Chapter 10, titled "Small Stories Challenging Large Narratives: The Contribution of Personal Accounts to Transformative Reconciliation in Post-TRC Norway," Associate Professor Tore Johnsen, from the Faculty of Theology and Social Sciences at VID Specialized University, provides an account of the 'small stories' of colonial injustice that surfaced during the Norwegian TRC process. Shifting the victim's side of colonial processes into historical consciousness, they play a twofold role: On the one hand, once acknowledged by the TRC process, these narratives necessitate the rewriting of national history as the unveiling of the victims' perspective cannot be erased. On the other hand, they can be read as a typology of unsolved reconciliation issues, encompassing a range of concerns from identity issues such as the internalization of racist stereotypes by the victims to land-related and other economic issues.

In Chapter 11, titled "Narrative as Interlocutor of Identity and Reconciliation," Professor John Klaasen, Dean of the Faculty of Theology and Religion, University of the Free State, South Africa, underlines the importance of story and storytelling as a transformative reconciliatory practice. Klaasen's analysis centers on the South African TRC meetings, which served as a platform for victims of colonial aggression to reclaim their status as individual subjects by sharing their stories. Through this process, victims addressed the perpetrators and incorporated them into their own stories, fostering a sense of reconciliation and understanding.

Research Associate Bonita Bennett of the District Six Museum in Cape Town, South Africa, explores transformative reconciliation through a chronological lens. In Chapter 12, "Remembering: A Pathway to Unburden our Present," she underscores the significance of addressing both current and future concerns within reconciliation processes. This approach is grounded in a comprehensive understanding of the past, as exemplified by the discussion of two South African projects striving to restore certain areas to their pre-apartheid multiethnic status. Bennett argues that attempting to merely revert to a former status quo before the injustice occurred fails to rectify past wrongs in a context of historical change.

While the editors have thoughtfully organized the chapters based on their contributions to various aspects of transformative reconciliation, it is worth noting that several of them can also serve as comprehensive introductions to specific TRC processes. In this respect, the chapters authored by Haugen and Johnsen, together with Skaar's contribution, provide vital information about the Norwegian TRC process. Additionally, Klaasen and Bennett's chapters offer valuable insights into the South African TRC process, while the contributions of Sønneland and Lingaas and Zeleke also shed light on TRC processes in other countries.

The editors wish to express their sincere thanks to:

- Kirkelig utdanningssenter nord/Girkolaš Oahpahusguovddáš Davvin—VID Tromsø, and
- John Klaasen, from the University of the Free State, provided the funds in his personal capacity for this publication.

The editors further wish to express their gratitude to all those who made invaluable contributions to the processes of the ReconTrans project, and the conferences held throughout its duration, including:

- Tore Johnsen, whose tireless dedication as the project leader of the ReconTrans project was instrumental to its success.
- The Church of Norway and VID Oslo (Diakonhjemmet), along with their administrative and technical staff, for their pivotal role as co-hosts for the Oslo conference.
- Stiftelsen Diakonhjemmet and The HUMANHARM research group at VID for their generous financial contributions to the Oslo conference.
- Vancouver School of Theology for graciously hosting the Vancouver conference, and the Anglican Church of Canada for their invaluable financial support.
- Lastly, but certainly not least, we extend our gratitude to Dr. Lee-Anne Roux for her meticulous proofreading of the manuscript, which has elevated the language and clarity of expression to a level beyond the reach of most of us.

These collective efforts have greatly enriched the ReconTrans project and the discourse surrounding transformative reconciliation.

Nordquist, Kjell-Åke. *Reconciliation as Politics: A Concept and Its Practice.* Church of Sweden Research Series 13. Eugene, OR: Pickwick Publications, 2017.

Guðmarsdóttir, Sigriður, et al. *Trading Justice for Peace? Reframing Reconciliation in TRC Processes in South Africa, Canada, and Nordic Countries.* Cape Town: Aosis, 2021.

PART ONE

Transformative Issues in Law and Politics

1

The Nordic Truth and Reconciliation Commissions
A New TRC Model for Resolving Historic and Ongoing Violations of Indigenous Rights?

ELIN SKAAR

Chr. Michelsen Institute, Bergen, Norway

INTRODUCTION[1]

Truth commissions (TCs) have been established in diverse contexts and tasked with addressing a wide range of human rights violations and atrocities.[2] While this mechanism of transitional justice is usually

---

1. This chapter is based on data collected for the research project TRUCOM (project # 302041 financed by the SAMEFORSK program of the Norwegian Research Council, 2020–23). The project is a collaboration between the Arctic University of Norway and the Chr. Michelsen Institute in Bergen, Norway. See the CMI TRUCOM page at https://www.cmi.no/projects/2521-truth-and-reconciliation-in-a-democratic-welfare-state-the-indigenous-sami-and-the-kven.

2. TCs are non-judicial bodies with no prosecutorial powers, and they cannot impose criminal sanctions. Legally speaking, TCs are *ad hoc* bodies established by national institutions, such as the executive or parliament, and should thus be distinguished from international fact-finding commissions established on a regular basis by various bodies of the United Nations (Skaar, "Truth and Reconciliation Commissions"). TCs, then, are a specialized form of a commission of inquiry, commonly known as the public inquiry.

associated with political transitions following authoritarian regimes or internal armed conflict, recent years have witnessed the emergence of TCs in non-transitional contexts. More specifically, there is a growing trend of establishing TCs in democratic welfare states to investigate historical injustices committed by the state against Indigenous peoples or minority groups.

This chapter focuses on four of the most recent commissions belonging to this small group of TCs explicitly tasked with addressing historical injustices committed against the Indigenous Sámi—the only Indigenous group in Europe—and the Kvens, a cross-border minority group.[3] These injustices occurred during the period of nation building in the 1800s and early 1900s, yet their repercussions continue to reverberate in all three societies. Taking inspiration from previous truth and/or reconciliation processes worldwide, notably in Canada, Norway (2018), Sweden (2020 and 2021) and Finland (2021) have established national Truth (and Reconciliation) Commissions (TRCs) to deal with the long-term effects of the historical injustices committed against the Indigenous Sámi people and national minorities. These three Nordic countries are all well-known for their egalitarian policies and pro-human rights profiles. The call for addressing racist policies and the historical forced assimilation of Indigenous and national minority populations into mainstream culture has arisen in the global context of transitional justice and a heightened focus on decolonization. The pressure to uncover the 'truth'—or at the very least, attain a broader understanding of a shared, often violent history—is evident in all three nations. So is the need for (political) reconciliation.

Following extensive discussions within the Indigenous Sámi and Kven communities about the possibility and desirability of investigating the colonialist policies implemented by their respective states,[4] four TRCs were established. Utilizing a comparative empirical analysis based on desk research, I demonstrate that the Norwegian 'early bird' TRC has served as a source of inspiration for the commissions in neighboring Sweden and Finland. Nevertheless, notable differences exist in their approaches.

While the Norwegian TRC chose to concentrate on assimilation policies directed at three groups in its mandate—the Sámi, Kvens/Norwegian Finns, and later, also the Forest Finns—the Swedish state opted

---

For details, see Stanton, "Truth Commissions and Public Inquiries."

3. In this chapter, I use 'Kvens' as a short form for both Kvens/Norwegian Finns in Norway and for the Kvens, the Tornedalians, and the Lantalaiset in Sweden.

4. See Kuokkanen, "Reconciliation as a Threat."

for the establishment of two separate commissions: one for the Sámi and another for the Kvens, the Tornedalians, and the Lantalaiset, respectively. The TRC in Finland, where there is no Kven minority, focuses exclusively on the Sámi. The central role of the Sámi parliaments in all three countries, in conjunction with direct communication between commissioners, has led to a remarkably uniform development allowing for a range of similar—but also intentionally *dissimilar*—choices regarding the mandates, processes, and compositions of these commissions.

As a result, we may be witnessing not only the contours of a new Nordic TRC model but potentially several distinct models. Given the Nordic-specific tailoring, it remains to be seen how transferable this model is to other contexts and, thus, its potential contribution to decolonization in different parts of the world.

The structure of this chapter is as follows. Following the introductory section, the first part contextualizes the Nordic TCs within the broader global transitional justice landscape. It provides a concise overview of the existing literature on TCs. Subsequently, the focus shifts to the Nordic region, where a succinct summary is provided of the historical repression faced by Indigenous peoples and national minorities in the three countries. These historical injustices sparked demands from the Sámi and Kven communities for the redress of past wrongs. The chapter proceeds with a comparative analysis of how Nordic governments responded to these demands. It also delves into the processes leading up to the establishment of the TCs and the formulation of their mandates, with a special emphasis on the prominent role played by the Norwegian TRC. Furthermore, the chapter outlines the appointment procedures for commissioners in each country, with a particular focus on addressing issues related to representation. Finally, the concluding section offers a reflection on the exchange of ideas and procedures among the three countries and examines the unique features that distinguish the Nordic TCs from similar commissions in the Global North.

PLACING THE NORDIC TCs IN A GLOBAL CONTEXT

Significant shifts have occurred both in the *context* (i.e., the environments in which TCs are typically established) and in the *content* (i.e., the subject matters TCs address and deal with) since the first TCs emerged in response to military dictatorships in Latin America in the early 1980s.

TCs constitute one of several central pillars in what we call transitional justice, along with prosecutions, reparations, and amnesty laws.[5] What exactly is a TC then? As succinctly put by one of the authorities in the field, TCs "... provide a platform from which victims can tell their stories and have their suffering officially acknowledged. In doing so, the conventional wisdom holds that truth commissions can ultimately promote reconciliation and conflict resolution."[6] Despite conflicting evidence regarding the societal impact of TCs on measures like democracy, human rights protection, accountability, and reconciliation, the phenomenon of a TC has not lost its emotional and empirical appeal, nor its ability to generate new scholarly questions on causes, relevance, and impact.

Historically, depending on which definition one uses, somewhere between forty and seventy TCs have been established across the world after various kinds of authoritarian regimes or civil wars to address gross and systematic human rights violations.[7] These commissions have generally sought to document a wide range of human rights abuses, mainly, but not limited to, the breach of physical integrity rights, such as torture, extrajudicial executions, political exile, internal displacement, and in extreme cases of violence, genocide. In terms of timing, these TCs have been established either around the time of transition, often referred to as *transitional* commissions, or years, and in some cases decades, after the transition took place, known as *post-transitional* commissions.[8]

Over the past decade or so, we have seen the establishment of TCs in, I would argue, a radically different context. These commissions have emerged in well-established Western democracies with the primary objective of addressing various forms of repression, primarily non-physical in nature, perpetrated against Indigenous or minority populations.[9]

The TCs in the latter group are tasked with investigating a set of human rights violations that are wholly or in part distinct. These violations are not committed by the military, police, or armed opposition groups but by bureaucrats or individuals working in or on behalf of the state in

---

5. See Teitel, *Transitional Justice*.

6. See Wiebelhaus-Brahm, "Global Transitional Justice," 1.

7. Some of the most influential and most widely used definitions of TCs include, but are not limited to, those made by Bakiner, *Truth Commissions*; Freeman, *Necessary Evils*; Hayner, "Fifteen Truth Commissions" and; Hayner, *Unspeakable Truths*.

8. See Skaar, "Truth and Reconciliation Commissions."

9. For diverse perspectives on the differences between transitional, post-transitional, and non-transitional truth commissions, see Skaar, "When Truth Commission Models Travel"; and Wiebelhaus-Brahm, "Truth Commissions."

well-established democratic countries. Rather than primarily examining the violation of physical integrity rights, these new types of commissions place particular emphasis on addressing structural economic and cultural violations committed against Indigenous people and/or minority populations.[10] This type of TC, established in well-developed and stable democracies, remains relatively scarce, with only a handful in existence as of August 2024.

The 'new' type of commissions that have garnered the most scholarly attention have already completed their work and submitted their final reports. While the *Greenland* commission remains a relatively obscure and less-researched case, the TCs of *Australia,* and particularly that of *Canada,* have undergone more in-depth analysis.[11] There is also a seminal body of literature on the Nordic TRCs, even though some of these commissions have completed their work. Kuokkanen offers an interesting analysis of the discourse surrounding the advocacy for a TC in Finland,[12] while Björn and Sjögren reflect on the Swedish case, well before the TC was actually set up, highlighting the role of the Swedish Church in pushing for reconciliatory measures.[13] The commission in Norway, which delivered its report in June 2023, is coming under scrutiny by scholars from various discipline.[14]

This concern with TCs that are still in operation is relatively uncommon in a transitional justice context. Scholars usually investigate TCs long after their work has been concluded. In recent years, there has been a heightened interest in the impact of TCs,[15] as well as the relevance and importance of their recommendations.[16] To date, there has been limited systematic comparative analysis of these new types of TCs, although

10. See Skaar, "When Truth Commission Models Travel."

11. For the Greenland TC, see Andersen, "The Greenland Reconciliation"; and Thisted, "The Greenlandic Reconciliation Commission." For the Australian TC, see Short, "Reconciliation, Assimilation." For the Canadian TC, see de Costa, "Discursive institutions"; Fee, "The Truth and Reconciliation Commission"; Nagy, "The Truth and Reconciliation Commission of Canada"; Niezen, *Truth and Indignation*; and Stanton, "Canada's Truth and Reconciliation Commission".

12. See Kuokkanen, "Reconciliation as a Threat."

13. See Björn and Sjögren, "Educational History."

14. See Johnsen, "Negotiating the Meaning"; Saugestad, "Sannhetskommisjoner"; and Skaar, "When Truth Commission Models Travel."

15. See Bakiner, "Truth Commission Impact"; Brahm, "Truth and Consequences"; Brahm, "Uncovering the Truth"; and Duggan, "Show Me Your impact."

16. See Skaar, Wiebelhaus-Brahm, and García-Godos, *Exploring Truth Commission Recommendations*; Skaar, Wiebelhaus-Brahm, and García-Godos, *Latin American Experiences.*

there are a few noteworthy exceptions.[17] While there is a growing body of comparative literature on Norway and other TCs, such as those in Australia,[18] South Africa, and Canada,[19] to the best of my knowledge, no one has attempted to compare the ongoing TC processes in Sweden and Finland with those in other parts of the world.[20]

This chapter seeks to make a modest contribution to (i) the literature on TCs in operation, and (ii) the seminal comparative work on TCs in the Nordic countries. The focus on political reconciliation is a central theme for all three Nordic commissions.

COLONIZATION AND ASSIMILATION— RESISTANCE AND REPARATIONS

Historically, colonization was primarily associated with the colonization of the Global South (i.e., Africa, Latin America, and Asia) by a few European colonial powers. However, starting in the 1950s, the discourse has progressively expanded to include the colonization of Indigenous people and minorities within the borders of Western nation states. Scholarly debates on decolonization have gained momentum in recent years.[21] In the Nordic countries, the presence and active involvement of the Sámi in international organizations such as the United Nations (UN) and the International Labor Organization (ILO) played a crucial role in advancing improved rights protection for Indigenous people.[22] Concurrently, national movements advocating for the recognition of rights for the Sámi were underway in Norway, Sweden, and Finland. According to a prominent Sámi scholar, "Many Sámi agree that there is a pressing need to identify and discuss the historical and present-day wrongs by the state. These include the history of assimilation, dispossession of land and resources, legacy of residential schools, language and identity theft,

---

17. See Cassidy, "The Stolen Generations"; Szpak and Bunikowski, "Saami Truth."
18. See Griffiths, "Hegemony and Reconciling."
19. See Guðmarsdóttir et al., *Trading Justice*.
20. Note that this litterature review builds on previous published work in Skaar, "When Truth Commission Models Travel."
21. See, for example, Lehtola, "Contested Sámi Histories"; Nagy, "The Scope and Bounds"; and Regan, "Unsettling the Settler."
22. Panel conversation with Anne Julie Semb in "Samenes historie," podcast NRK Episode "Urfolk og folkerett." https://radio.nrk.no/serie/norgeshistorie/sesong/202111/KMTE87005321.

forced conversion to Christianity, destruction and defamation of Sámi spirituality and sacred sites, and active engagement in racial biology research as recently as in the late 1960s in which Sámi were measured and categorized."[23] A quick foray into history provides some context to this claim.

Nation Building and Assimilation Policies

Norway, Sweden, and Finland are all multicultural societies with two groups of cross-border people: the Sámi and the Kvens. The Sámi are an Indigenous people whose culture is based on hunting, fishing, gathering, and reindeer herding. The precise population figures for the Sámi and Kvens are widely contested as many have lost their language and cultural heritage due to assimilation policies. As a result, they may either be unaware of or deny their ethnic origins. Various sources provide estimates ranging from 80,000 to 150,000 Sámi individuals living in the Arctic regions of Finland, Sweden, Norway, and the Kola Peninsula (western Russia)—the Saami homeland collectively referred to as Sápmi.[24] The largest Sámi population is currently found in Norway. Among the Sámi, several languages are spoken, with Northern Sámi being the most widely spoken mother tongue. Notably, colonial and assimilationist practices had an impact on the Sámi but also on other minority groups, particularly the Kvens, who are sometimes referred to interchangeably with Norwegian Finns. The Kvens are a distinct group of people with close linguistic and cultural ties to Finland. They live in the northern regions of Norway, Sweden, Finland, and Russia, in an area called *Nordkalotten*. The Forest Finns, who live in the south-eastern part of Norway, were also affected by the assimilation policies.

The attempts to colonize and assimilate the Indigenous Sámi and national minorities into the mainstream culture of the three Nordic countries can be considered part of the construction of the nation state, a process that took place in Europe in the 1800s and well into the 1900s.[25] Beginning in 1846, Sweden adopted policies designed to define and

23. Kuokkanen, "Reconciliation as a Threat," 294.

24. Estimate 1: 100–150,000 (Eye on the Arctic, "Sami in Sweden").
Estimate 2: 80,000, with about 8,000 on Finnish territory (Jamet, "Sámi Rights").
Estimate 3: The Swedish Sámi population (estimated 20,000–40,000) inhabits thirty-five percent of Sweden.

25. For a classical work on nation building, see, for example, Rokkan, *State Formation*.

control its northern region, and to integrate its Sámi and Finnish populations with the Swedish nation.[26] Norway followed suit in 1851 when its Parliament adopted the *"Finnefondet"* (the Lapp Fund) "to promote the teaching of Norwegian in the transitional districts and to ensure the enlightenment of the Sámi people."[27] A commonality among the three Nordic countries was their collective endeavor to assimilate Sámi, Kvens, and other minority populations (such as the Tornedalians and the Lantalaiset in Sweden) into becoming 'mainstream citizens.' This involved stripping them of their cultural and linguistic identities and, to some extent, their traditional ways of life. Initially, these policies were racially motivated: the Sámi in particular were considered an inferior people that needed to be 'civilized.'[28] These policies aimed to teach children the national languages, including Norwegian, Swedish, and Finnish. In Sweden, this was implemented through nomadic schools, while in Norway, residential schools became prominent starting in 1905.[29] As a result of these assimilation policies, many individual Sámi, Kvens/Norwegian Finns, and Tornedalians and Lantalaiset—even entire communities—have lost their mother tongue and the connection to their cultures.

A new dimension of the colonization process was brought in with the era of industrialization, when natural resources located in the northernmost areas of the three Nordic countries (water, timber, minerals) became attractive to investors from the south. Conflicts over land and water began during this period and have persisted into the present day. This is why many scholars claim that decolonization is not just a policy of the past but an ongoing one.[30] These claims are true not only for the Sámi but also regarding the long-term consequences of assimilation policies directed at the minority groups discussed here.

---

26. Wikipedia, "Swedification." For differences in assimilation policies between the Nordic countries, see Dankertsen and Arvidsson, "Truth Commissions."

27. Minde, "Assimilation of the Sami," 12.

28. Baglo, "På ville veger?" and Niemi, *Koka Björn*.

29. For a detailed account of residential schools in Norway, see Tjelle, *Internatliv*. Please note that residential schools were also intended to provide education to children living in remote areas and to improve the living conditions, including access to food and better hygiene, for impoverished families.

30. See Kuokkanen, "Reconciliation as a Threat."

Resistance and Reparations

Mobilization against the assimilation policies implemented by the Nordic states has exhibited distinct patterns between the Indigenous Sámi and the other minority groups. In Norway, the Sámi initiated their struggle for rights and political representation in the early nineteenth century, whereas the Kvens/Norwegian Finns mobilized much later, forming their first organizations only in the 1980s. This mobilization took place in a context of increasing global concern with human rights in general after the Second World War and a particular focus on indigenous rights after the 1980s.[31]

Sámi struggles for rights and recognition have swept across the Nordic countries in several waves, beginning with a young Sámi woman named Elsa Laula Renberg who convened the first major cross-border Sámi meeting in Trondheim on February 6, 1917. However, one of the most significant waves occurred in the 1970s when young Sámi activists mobilized against state takeovers and the exploitation of natural resources. The world-famous Alta uprising in 1979, which saw Sámi activists from both the Norwegian and Swedish sides come together, prompted "political mobilization and international organization on the part of the Sámi and other Indigenous peoples over the past two decades," leading to "changes in assimilation policy in the Nordic countries."[32]

In response to the frustrations expressed by both Sámi and national minority groups within the three Nordic states, the governments took steps to rectify the wrongs of the past. These reparations were primarily symbolic in nature, although there are a few rare instances of economic compensation for historical injustices. The reparations can be divided into at least six different categories: recognition as Indigenous people, establishment of political institutions, recognition of language rights, symbolic reparations, official apologies, and economic reparations.

---

31. Although the idea of Indigenous people had been around for a while (Béteille, "The Idea") indigenous rights gained a lot of traction in the 1980s, particularly with the adoption of the Indigenous and Tribal Peoples Convention in 1989 (No. 169). See also Vik and Semb, "Who Owns the Land?"

32. Nilsen, "From Norwegianization," 163.

Reparations to the Sámi

All three states have officially recognized the Sámi as Indigenous people, with Sweden taking this step in 1977, followed by Norway in 1990, and Finland in 1995. This recognition has constitutional status in all three countries. Interestingly, Norway was the only one of the three Nordic states to ratify the 1989 ILO Indigenous and Tribal Peoples Convention the following year, thereby granting the Sámi status as Indigenous people according to international law.[33] Sámi political rights were further acknowledged through the establishment of Sámi parliaments in Norway (1989), followed by Sweden (1993) and Finland (1995). Although the Sámi parliaments are consultative bodies, they act as institutions of cultural autonomy for the Indigenous Sámi. They have been important arenas for discussing political issues and have helped advocate for Sámi political, economic, and cultural issues at the national level in all three states.[34]

Language recognition was another crucial point of contention, given the enduring adverse effects of assimilation policies enforced through the educational system on Sámi and other minority children. Sámi is acknowledged as a minority language in Norway, Sweden, and Finland and holds official language status within the Sámi administrative regions in all three countries.[35]

The Sámi National Day, celebrated on February 6, was institutionalized across the Nordic countries (presumably also in Russia) in 1993.

The age of apology[36] has also reached the Nordic countries. King Olav of Norway issued a formal apology to the Sámi for the Norwegian state's assimilation policy as early as 1997. In contrast, Sweden took a quarter of a century before the Church of Sweden (CoS) officially offered its apology on November 24, 2021.[37] Finland, however, has not taken similar actions yet. Nevertheless, on January 13, 2022, a Lutheran bishop

---

33. Semb, "Why (not) Commit?"

34. For a comparative analysis of Sámi parliaments in Norway and Sweden, see Josefsen, Mörkenstam and Saglie, "Different Institutions."

35. It is important to note that there are several Sámi languages. Among these languages, Northern Sámi is spoken and written by the majority of the Sámi population in all three countries. The standardized written language used today was collectively adopted by Norway, Sweden, and Finland in 1979.

36. See Gibney et al., *The Age of Apology*.

37. See Dankertsen and Arvidsson, "Truth Commissions."

from Finland conveyed to Pope Francis that his church intends to issue a historic apology to Europe's only Indigenous people.[38]

To the best of my knowledge, Norway is the only country that has gone beyond offering official apologies and symbolic reparations. The Norwegian Parliament established the "*Samefolkets Fond*" (The Sámi People's Fund) in 2001, which was administered by the Sámi Parliament until 2006. This fund provided collective economic compensation to the Sámi for cultural and linguistic harm suffered due to the Norwegianization policy. Between 2001 and 2014, approximately 700 Sámi received 75 million Norwegian crowns as compensation for their lack of education. Most Sámi received individual payments of 70,000 NOK.[39]

Reparations to the Kvens and Other National Minorities

The Kvens and other national minorities in the three Nordic countries in question have not been offered reparations in the same way as the Sámi. However, there have been some steps taken toward recognizing their rights in all three countries, particularly in terms of language recognition. Norway took the lead once again in 1998 when it granted the Kvens/Norwegian Finns status as a national minority, as one of five minority groups, all of whom had experienced racism and assimilation policies. The Kven language was officially recognized as its own language in Norway in 2005, and Norwegian Finns were also officially accepted in the same way as the Kvens in 2011.[40]

In Sweden, Meänkieli (Tornedal Finnish) was officially recognized as a minority language in 1999, alongside Finnish, Sámi, Romani, and Yiddish.[41] A significant stride toward redress occurred when Sweden ratified the Council of Europe's Framework Convention for the Protection of National Minorities[42] and the European Charter on Regional or Minority Languages.

---

38. See Chocteau, "Lutheran Church in Finland."
39. See Tjelle, *Internatliv—den unike historien*.
40. See Veranger Museum, "Kvensk/norskfinsk historie."
41. Wikipedia, "Official minority languages." In 2009, the Riksdag passed the Language Law ("Språklag" SFS 2009:600), which recognized Sámi languages and Meänkieli as official minority languages of Sweden.
42. Utriksdepartementet, *Sveriges Internationella överenskommelser*.

Table 1: Rights recognition and reparations for assimilation policies directed at the Sámi and national minorities in the Nordic countries

Reparations	Norway	Sweden	Finland
Sámi nationally recognized as Indigenous people	1990	1977	1995
Status of Sámi rights	Constitutional	Constitutional	Constitutional
Ratification of ILO convention	1990	Not ratified	Not ratified
Sámi Parliament	1989	1993	1995
Sámi recognized as official language	Yes	Minority language	Minority language
Official apology to the Sámi	Yes 1997 (the King)	Yes November 24, 2021 (The Church of Sweden)	No Plans for The Evangelical Lutheran Church of Finland to apologize
Economic compensation to the Sámi	2000	NA	NA
Samefolkets dag (Feb 6) institutionalized	1993	1993	1993
Kvens recognized as national minority	1998	1999	—
Kven language officially recognized	2005	1999	—

Sources: Evjen, Ryymin and Andresen, *Samenes historie*; Minde, "Assimilation of the Sami"; and a wide range of web pages and web articles.

The assimilation policies of the Nordic states, commonly known as 'Norwegianization,' 'Swedification,' and 'Finnicization,' respectively, have long since been formally abolished, and substantial efforts have been made to restore both political and cultural rights. Nevertheless, strong feelings persist in many communities. These feelings arise from the enduring impacts of these assimilation policies, which manifest, through racism against the Sámi and the national minority groups, as well as the ongoing infringement upon their traditional ways of life and rights. It is, therefore, not entirely surprising that these groups have not only mobilized on a national level but have also engaged in cross-national efforts to formulate claims for TCs before the formerly repressive states.

STATE RESPONSES TO DEMANDS FOR A TC

The Sámi Parliamentary Council (a joint body of the three Sámi Parliaments) issued a statement on the Sámi National Day February 6, 2017, encouraging the Nordic countries to establish TCs to examine Sámi-state relations.[43] At that point in time, processes to establish TCs were already underway in all three countries.

The first official demand for a TC was put forward in the Sámi Parliament in Norway by Laila Susanne Vars, the leader of a small Sámi opposition party Arja, in 2016. Initially, her initiative was met with silence, but after a series of consultations, particularly with the Board of Elders, the Sámi Parliament eventually embraced and supported the idea of a TC. The Sámi Parliament then formally approached the Norwegian Parliament with a proposal for a TC. The proposal was initially (unofficially) turned down. However, two left-wing politicians took up the cause and advocated for the establishment of a TC. After a series of public hearings, public consultations, civil society action, and several rounds of political negotiations and compromises, the Norwegian Parliament, with a narrow majority vote, finally established the 'Kommisjonen for å granske fornorskingspolitikk og urett overfor samer, kvener og norskfinner' (Sannhets- og forsoningskommisjonen) (also simply called the Truth and Reconciliation Commission) in June 2018.[44] The TRC delivered its final report to the Norwegian Parliament on June 1, 2023.

In neighboring Sweden, the Swedish Church initiated an inquiry into a reconciliation commission as early as 2006.[45] Several years later, the church embarked on the 'White Paper Project on the Church of Sweden and the Sámi,' an academic endeavor aimed at historically documenting the Swedish government's assimilation policies. The Sámi Council

---

43. Kuokkanen, "Reconciliation as a Threat," 296.

44. For a more detailed analysis, see Skaar, "When Truth Commission Models Travel." English translation: "The Commission to Investigate the Norwegianisation Policy and Injustice Against the Sámi and Kven/Norwegian Finnish Peoples" (The Truth and Reconciliation Commission). A third minority group, the Forest Finns (Skogfinnene), was later included in the mandate. See https://www.stortinget.no/no/Stortinget-og-demokratiet/Organene/sannhets—og-forsoningskommisjonen/.

45. Kuokkanen, "Reconciliation as a Threat," 293.

within the Church of Sweden (CoS) played a central role in organizing the Ságastallamat conference, held in Kiruna in 2011, which can be regarded as the national starting point of the White Paper Project.[46] This project reached its culmination with the release of a 1,200-page report in April 2019. However, in 2018, the Swedish government initially rejected the proposal to establish a TC. Nevertheless, it later agreed to engage in negotiations with the Sámi Parliament to define the parameters for the establishment of a TC.[47]

On June 13, 2019, the Sámi Parliament officially requested funds from the Swedish government to explore the possibility of establishing a TC. A year later, in June 2020, the Swedish government finally gave the green light to the Sámi Parliament to lay the groundwork for the establishment of a TC in Sweden and allocated funds to initiate the process. The following year, the Sámi Parliament in Sweden submitted their final report outlining how the TC should be structured. On November 3, 2021, the Swedish government formally established a TC to investigate the abuses suffered by the Sámi people at the hands of the Swedish state.[48] Commissioners were appointed in the spring of 2022. The commission is as of August 2024 more than half-way through it's work.

Similarly, there was an extensive discussion in Finland concerning the potential establishment of a TC. Commissioned by the Prime Minister's Office, public hearings were held in 18 Sámi communities and five cities in May and June 2018 as part of the preparatory process leading to the possible establishment of a TC in Finland.[49] In November 2019, after years of negotiations and planning in the Sámi Parliament, the Finnish government approved the formation of a TRC for the Sámi people in Finland.[50] The main Sámi political bodies also endorsed the proposal for the commission in late 2019. Due to the Covid-19 pandemic, the Sámi

46. Björn and Sjögren, "Educational History," 75, n 2. See also VK, "Samer." The original report from this conference, issued by the Church of Sweden (CoS), is publicly available: *Rapport från Ságastallamat, en koneferens om samerna och Svenska kyrkan, i Kiruna den 11–13 oktober 2011* e2c9363d-84a8-482a-98d9-99e442b28714.pdf (svenskakyrkan.se).

47. Kuokkanen, "Reconciliation as a Threat," 293–94.

48. Sametinget. "Truth Commission in Sweden." See also the Swedish government's web page at Kartläggning och granskning av den politik som förts gentemot samerna och dess konsekvenser för det samiska folket—Regeringen.se. The official document is found at kartlaggning-och-granskning-av-den-politik-som-forts-gentemot-samerna-och-dess-konsekvenser-for-det-samiska-folket-dir.-2021103.pdf (regeringen.se).

49. Kuokkanen, "Reconciliation as a Threat," 293.

50. See YLE News, "Finnish Gov Agrees."

Parliament in Finland decided to postpone the launch of the commission.⁵¹ It was formally established in October 28, 2021,⁵² with commissioners appointed in the spring of 2022. The TRC's report was supposed to be due in November 2023, but the TRC has been granted an extension until December 2025.

Notably, while the Sámi Parliaments were negotiating the establishment of TCs to specifically examine historical wrongs against the Sámi, two minority groups in Sweden were working to establish their own commission. On March 19, 2020, the Swedish government established a TRC to investigate the past treatment of Tornedalians (a minority of Finnish origin), Kvens, and Lantalaiset. The commission is formally known as 'Sannings- och försoningskommissionen för tornedalingar, kväner och lantalaiset'.⁵³ Initially, the commission was scheduled to conclude its work on May 16, 2022. However, due to delays related to the Covid-19 pandemic, the time frame for its work was renegotiated in June 2021.⁵⁴ The TRC submitted it's final report to the Swedish government on November 15, 2023.⁵⁵

A COMPARATIVE ANALYSIS OF MANDATES AND COMPOSITION

The TCs established in Norway, Sweden, and Finland share many common features. To varying degrees, they have drawn inspiration from the Canadian TRC, which operated from 2008–15 and focused on addressing the forced assimilation of Indigenous people through residential schools, as a model. Although the Canadian TRC primarily aimed to examine historical wrongs committed against its Indigenous population, it differs from the Nordic TCs in several aspects.⁵⁶ Firstly, it was established as part of the largest class-action settlement in Canadian history, which mandated apologies from the Canadian government, official church bodies, and other entities involved in the atrocities committed against its

---

51. See Eye on the Arctic, "Sami Parliament in Finland."
52. Sametinget. "Truth Commission in Sweden."
53. For the official government document, see Regeringskansliet. "Uppgörelse med historiska kränkningar."
54. Regeringskansliet. "Tilläggsdirektiv."
55. See Truth Commission in Sweden, *Som om vi aldrig funnits*.
56. For a more thorough analysis of the Canadian TRC and its role as a model for the Norwegian TRC, see Skaar and Spitzer, "Conceptualizing the Legitimacy."

Indigenous population.⁵⁷ The settlement recommended policy changes, provided economic compensation (ca. $2 billion) to Indian Residential School (IRS) system survivors, and, in 2008, led to the creation of the TRC. Secondly, the Canadian TRC had a remarkably narrow mandate, explicitly focusing on Canada's IRS system, which was considered one of the country's most shameful legacies.⁵⁸ Thirdly, it opted for a very small commission, consisting of only three commissioners, who were supported by a very large secretariat.⁵⁹

The Head of the Norwegian TRC has frequently emphasized the significance of the Canadian TRC as a source of inspiration for the Norwegian TRC. Similarly, Sweden has also looked to Canada as a model when establishing its TC for the Sámi.⁶⁰ Yet, the Nordic countries have made a series of choices that distinguish their TCs from Canada's TRC. First, the three Nordic TCs focusing on indigenous rights were established in direct response to demands from the Sámi parliaments, i.e., through a political route rather than via the courts. Importantly, their establishment was preceded by consultations with the Sámi communities and national minorities. This means that the affected communities had a say in whether a commission should be established at all.

Second, in contrast to the Canadian case, once the decision to establish TCs had been made, consultative processes with the affected communities were carried out in all three Nordic countries in connection with the formulation of mandates. Furthermore, unlike Canada, the Nordic countries granted their commissions broader mandates.

Third, the Nordic countries opted for larger commissions, where consultations with affected communities were used to identify suitable commissioners.

The Norwegian TRC, which is the 'early bird' among the four, has arguably served as a more direct role model, though not as a blueprint, as the following discussion illustrates. Notably, already prior to its establishment, one of the main points in the Swedish Sámi commission was to

---

57. See *Indian Residential Schools Class Action Settlement-Settlement Agreement (residentialschoolsettlement.ca)*.

58. See *"What Are the Truth & Reconciliation Commission's 94 Calls to Action & How Are We Working Toward Achieving Them Today? (reconciliationeducation.ca)."*

59. For the background to the Canadian TRC and its operations, see, for example, Fee, "The Truth and Reconciliation"; MacDonald, "Canada's Truth and Reconciliation Commission"; Nagy, "The Truth and Reconciliation Commission"; and Stanton, "Canada's Truth and Reconciliation Commission."

60. White, "Sweden Looks to Canada."

ensure "That cross-border exchanges of experience be continuous with the process in Norway and Finland."[61] This is reflected in the mandates of the commissions.

Mandates

The Norwegian TRC's mandate is threefold, namely, to: (1) Conduct a historical survey to map the Norwegian authorities' policy and activities towards the Sámi and Kvens/Norwegian Finns locally, regionally, and nationally; (2) Undertake an investigation of the effects of the Norwegianization policy;[62] and (3) Propose measures aimed at contributing to further reconciliation.[63] Although the mandate did not specify a fixed time period for the investigation, the Norwegian commission effectively covered the time period from the mid-1850s (or even earlier) till the TRC submitted its final report.

While difficult to prove, the Norwegian TRC's challenges stemming from its exceptionally broad mandate might provide some insight into why Sweden chose to divide the investigation into assimilation policies between two separate commissions. In Sweden, the mandate of the TC focusing on the Sámi is threefold, namely, to: (1) Document and analyze the politics that was carried out against the Sámi and identify the actors who were responsible for the policy; (2) Disseminate knowledge to enhance public understanding of Sámi history and the conditions necessary for the Sámi to pass this knowledge on to future generations; and (3) Propose recommendations aimed at rectifying past wrongs, contributing to reconciliation and a healthy Sámi society.[64]

The TRC for the Tornedalians, Kvens and Lantalaiset was tasked with several key objectives, including: (1) Map and review the assimilation policy and its consequences for the minority, specific groups within the minority, and individuals; (2) Disseminate information to increase

---

61. Library of Congress, "Sweden: Government Announces."

62. The commission was tasked with evaluating how the Norwegianization policy has affected the attitudes of the majority population towards the Sámi and Kvens/Norwegian Finns and would investigate the consequences of Norwegianization up to the present day.

63. See the Norwegian TRC, https://www.stortinget.no/no/Stortinget-og-demokratiet/Organene/sannhets—og-forsoningskommisjonen/.

64. For more details, see Sametinget. "Truth Commission." See also Regeringskansliet, "Kartläggning och granskning."

knowledge about the minority and its historical experiences; and (3) Submit proposals for additional initiatives aimed at addressing past injustices and fostering reconciliation.[65] Initially, the commission was scheduled to complete its work no later than May 16, 2022. However, on January 26, 2023, its mandate was extended for an additional six months, now concluding on November 15, 2023.[66]

The purpose of the Finnish TRC is to: (1) Identify and assess instances of discrimination against the Sámi people and historical as well as present violations of their rights, including assimilation policies; (2) Conduct research on how these policies continue to affect the Sámi and their community in the present day; (3) Present proposals on how to facilitate interaction between the Sámi people and the Finnish state, as well as between different Sámi groups; and (4) Raise awareness in the country about the Sámi people's status as Finland's Indigenous population.[67] The deadline for the commission to deliver its final report to the Finnish government, the Sámi Parliament, and the Skolt Village Assembly was initially December 31, 2023.[68] The final submission date has been extended until December 31, 2025.

In summary, all four commissions, while concentrating on assimilation policies directed at various segments of their populations, essentially share a tripartite mandate to: (i) Investigate historical wrongs; (ii) Assess the continuing repercussions of past injustices; and (iii) Recommend measures for reconciliation.

THE COMPOSITION OF THE TRCs

The size of the four commissions analyzed here varies considerably, as do their appointment procedures.

---

65. See Regeringskansliet, "Uppgörelse med historiska"; Regeringskansliet, "Kartläggning och granskning."
66. See Kvaner Lantalaiset Tornedalingar, "Truth and Reconciliation Commission."
67. See Truth and Reconciliation Commission Concerning the Sámi People, "Mandate."
68. See Hofverberg, "Finland: Sami Truth."

Norway's TRC (on the Sámi, Kvens/Norwegian Finns, and Forest Finns)

The Norwegian TRC was composed of twelve members, including the head of the commission. The commissioners were selected through a thorough consultative process. Following a series of hearings involving various interest organizations, the final list of commissioners consisted of seven men and five women:[69] Ivar Bjørklund (Professor, Tromsø), Håkon Hermanstrand (PhD candidate, Kolvereid), Per Oskar Kjølaas (Bishop Emeritus, Tromsø), Pia Lane (Professor, Oslo), Anne Kalstad Mikkelsen (Senior Advisor, Hamarøy), Marit Myrvoll (Researcher, Tromsø), Einar Niemi (Professor Emeritus, Vadsø), Anne Julie Semb (Professor, Oslo), Liv Inger Somby (College Lecturer, Kautokeino), Aslak Syse (Professor Emeritus, Oslo), and Ketil Zachariassen (Associate Professor, Tromsø).

All commissioners were appointed by the Norwegian Parliament. Notably, the commission was composed almost exclusively of academics, with the addition of a retired bishop. While efforts were made to appoint people with competence relevant to the commission's work, there was also consideration for a certain level of representativeness. There were at least four Sámi and one (or two) Kven on the TRC. It is noteworthy to point out that no South Sámi individuals were appointed to the TRC in Norway, only North Sámi and Lule Sámi. Additionally, there were no Norwegian Finns among the commissioners, which sparked some criticism.

Sweden's TC (on the Sámi)

The commissioners of the Swedish TC are Kerstin Calissendorff (Justitieråd, Head of the Commission), Anna-Lill Drugge (Fil. Dr.), Gunlög Fur (Professor), Marie B Hagsgård (International Expert), Patrik Lantto (Professor), Marianne Liliequist (Professor Emerita), Britta Marakatt-Labba (Artist), Bertil Marklund (Fil. Dr.), Jonas Monié-Nordin (Docent), Ulf Mörkenstam (Professor), Mikael Svonni (Professor Emeritus), Eivind Torp (Docent), and Laila Susanne Vars (Fil. Dr.).

Similar to the Norwegian TRC, the Swedish commission also chose a predominantly academic composition, with the notable addition of a prominent artist, Labba. Moreover, it has included several Sámi among

---

69. The commisioners were presented with short biographies on the TRC's home page during the operation of the commission. However, the home page was taken down after the TRC concluded its work on June 1, 2023, and can no longer be accessed.

its commissioners, including a prominent former Sámi politician from Norway: Laila Susanne Vars.[70] Her role as the initiator of the TC process in Norway adds a fascinating dimension to her appointment.

Sweden's TRC (on the Tornedalians, Kvens, and Lantalaiset)

The TRC consisted of a chairperson, seven members, and a secretariat. The individuals holding these positions were as follows: The chairperson, Elisabet Fura (lawyer and judge), Hanna Aili (Cultural Heritage Officer), Malin Arvidsson (historian), Lars Elenius (Professor Emeritus in History), Kenneth Hyltenstam (Professor Emeritus in Multilingualism), Klas-Göran Karlsson (Professor of History), Bengt Niska (former Chairperson of the National Association of Swedish Tornedalians), and Kaisa Syrjänen Schaal (Docent in International Law). The secretariat consisted of seven persons.[71]

Finland's TRC (on the Sámi)

The Finnish TRC operates independently of the Finnish government, the Sámi Parliament, and the Skolt Sámi Village. Unlike in Norway and Sweden, the members of the commission are appointed by different bodies. The commissioners are: Heikki J. Hyvärinen (Doctoral student and Master of Law, appointed by the Finnish Sámi Parliament), Miina Seurujärvi (Master of Philosophy, appointed by the Finnish Sámi Parliament), Irja Jefremoff (Master of Administration, appointed by the Skolt Sámi Village Administration Assembly), Kari Mäkinen (Archbishop Emeritus and Doctor of Theology, appointed by the Finnish government), and Hannele Pokka (Professor of Working Life and Doctor of Law, appointed by the Finnish government). Both the Sámi Parliament and the Skolt Village Assembly confirmed the two members appointed by the Finnish government.[72] Initially, there were Sámi appointed to the commission, but they withdrew early.[73] Its secretariat, though, is largely Sámi. Based on anec-

70. For details, see the TRC's home page at https://sanningskommissionensamer.se/

71. Information was taken from the Swedish TRC's home page which is no longer in operation.

72. See Library of Congress, "Finland." See the official government document at Perma | valtioneuvosto.fi.

73. See Truth and Reconciliation Commission Concerning the Sámi People. https://sdtsk.fi/en/home/.

dotal evidence, it appears that there has been considerable disagreement between the commissioners and the secretariat. This discord has reportedly hampered the progress of the commission during its initial stages.[74]

In summary, the commissioners of the four TCs have been appointed through somewhat different procedures, and the commissions vary in size. Norway and Sweden chose relatively large commissions with twelve and thirteen members, respectively, while the Swedish TRC for the Tornedalians, Kvens, and Lantalaiset had seven members, and the Finnish TRC has only five. While the Norwegian commission remained unchanged since its inception, the Swedish commission had two commissioners resign early in the process. The Finnish commission has also suffered internal disagreements that have impeded its progress.

Since the commissioners in Sweden and Finland had only quite recently started their work when this chapter was written, it was a bit premature to comment on their work. The Norwegian TRC has since completed its mandate. It has undertaken archival and documentary research; conducted a series of open hearings/meetings; collected life stories and testimonies from individuals belonging to target groups all over the country; and engaged in numerous public meetings.

While the Norwegian TRC was still operating, direct communication occurred between the Norwegian TRC, primarily facilitated by the Head of the Commission, Dagfinn Høybråten, and the Head of the Secretariat, Liss-Ellen Ramstad, and the two other TCs. Although most of this communication was conducted privately and therefore not subject to public analysis, there are some concrete examples of dialogue between the commissions. For example, on May 5, 2022, Høybråten met with the Finnish Ambassador to Norway, Antell. Also present at this meeting, held at the Ambassador's residence, was the Head of the Secretariat of the Norwegian TRC.

A second example involved one of the regular commission meetings of the Norwegian TRC, which occurred approximately every two months and were not open to the public. On August 17, 2022, such a meeting was held in Finland. Additionally, there were webinars featuring Høybråten and commission members from the Swedish TC. Presumably, these meetings took place to facilitate the transfer of knowledge and experience between the Norwegian TRC and the other two TCs. While the exchanges of ideas help elucidate the potential similarities and differences in the TC processes,

---

74. Information provided by Veli-Pekka Lehtolan in a TRUCOM project meeting, 02/22/2023.

they also highlight the extent of the cross-border communication that has transpired since the idea of TCs was first launched in the Nordic countries.⁷⁵

CONCLUDING REMARKS

In this chapter, a comparative analysis was conducted of four non-transitional TRCs established in Norway, Sweden, and Finland. These commissions were tasked with investigating historical wrongs committed against their Indigenous Sámi population and national minority groups. The analysis has identified a number of similarities, but also significant differences. Notably, the Norwegian state decided to establish a single commission for both the Sámi and national minorities, whereas Finland established one commission exclusively focused on the Sámi. In contrast, the Swedish government established two separate commissions, one for the Sámi and another for the national minorities.

Although these TCs have drawn inspiration from other truth-finding processes, notably the Canadian TRC, they have by no means replicated their models. Instead, as demonstrated in this chapter, the lessons drawn from the Canadian TRC have been adapted to fit the Nordic context. This is due to three main factors: First, in distinction from the Canadian TRC and the majority of other TCs established in democratic welfare states, the Nordic TCs originated in response to a shared cross-border initiative from the Sámi Council and national minority groups. Second, the Nordic governments extensively employed consultative processes when determining whether to establish a TC. Consultative procedures were also widely applied in all three countries during the formulation of their mandates and the selection of commissioners after the decision to establish a commission was made. Third, the mandates of all these commissions extend well beyond the narrow focus on assimilation through residential schools and cover large historic time periods.

There was a close dialogue between the Norwegian TRC, which was the 'early bird' established in 2018, and the TCs established later in Sweden (in 2020 and 2021) and Finland (in 2021). How this learning process will take place in the mandate period of the Swedish and Finnish commissions remains to be seen. Nevertheless, there is a strong likelihood that cross-border sharing and learning will continue to be a part of these ongoing TC processes. This may also serve as inspiration when the

---

75. See Skaar, "When Truth Commission Models Travel."

time comes to draft recommendations and transfer the responsibility for implementing measures to enhance political reconciliation to the respective governments and parliaments.

As argued by Paulette Regan, the Canadian TRC aimed to transition towards an indigenous-centered TRC.[76] The Nordic TCs are following the same path: the Sámi and national minorities were part of the negotiations setting up the commission; they are at the core of the mandates; and they are represented either among commissioners or the secretariats, or both. Indigenous people and national minorities are therefore at the core of these Nordic commissions. This in itself may be interpreted as a step towards decolonization. The ultimate goal is to reshape societal structures by bolstering indigenous rights and enhancing rights protection for these vulnerable groups. However, ongoing conflicts over land and water rights, including disputes over issues like windmills, between Indigenous groups and the states pose a significant threat to the project of decolonization.

To effectively contribute to the broader project of decolonization, it is crucial for the TCs to be regarded as fair and legitimate throughout their work. Their reports and recommendations should address the issues that the target groups consider most urgent and important. These recommendations should not favor one target group over another. Furthermore, it is essential for the commissions to disseminate their reports widely, ensuring that the majority populations also have the opportunity to engage with the findings and recommendations.[77][78]

BIBLIOGRAPHY

Andersen, Astrid N. "The Greenland Reconciliation Commission: Moving Away From a Legal Framework." *The Yearbook of Polar Law Online* 11 (2020) 214–44.

Baglo, Cathrine. "På ville veger? Levende utstillinger av samer i Europa og Amerika." PhD diss., University of Tromsø, 2011.

Bakiner, Onur. "Truth Commission Impact: An Assessment of How Commissions Influence Politics and Society." *International Journal of Transitional Justice* 8 (2014) 6–30.

———. *Truth Commissions: Memory, Power, and Legitimacy*. Philadelphia: University of Pennsylvania Press, 2016.

---

76. See Regan, "Canada's TRC."

77. Lessons drawn from the experiences of thirteen TCs in Latin America, see Skaar et al., *Exploring Truth Commission Recommendations*.

78. See Appendix, 281–84.

Béteille, André. "The Idea of Indigenous People." *Current Anthropology* 39 (1998) 187–92.

Björn, Norlin, and David Sjögren. "Educational History in the Age of Apology: The Church of Sweden's "White book" on Historical Relations to the Sami, the Significance of Education and Scientific Complexities in Reconciling the Past." *Educare- Vetenskapliga Skrifter* (2019) 69–95.

Brahm, Eric. "Truth and Consequences: The Impact of Truth Commissions in Transitional Societies." PhD diss., University of Colorado, 2006.

———. "Uncovering the Truth: Examining Truth Commission Success and Impact." *International Studies Perspectives* 8 (2007) 16–35.

Cassidy, Julie. "The Stolen Generations—Canada and Australia: The Legacy of Assimilation." *Deakin Law Review* 11 (2006) 131–77.

Chocteau, Anaëlle. "Lutheran Church in Finland to Apologize to Sámi People." *LA Croix International* (January 2022). https://international.la-croix.com/news/religion/lutheran-church-in-finland-to-apologize-to-smi-people/15508.

Dankertsen, Astri, and Malin Arvidsson. "Truth Commissions in the Nordic States: Who is to be Reconciled with Whom?" https://www.justiceinfo.net/en/85028-truth-commissions-nordic-states-who-is-to-be-reconciled-with-whom.html.

de Costa, Ravi. "Discursive Institutions in Non-Transitional Societies: The Truth and Reconciliation Commission of Canada." *International Political Science Review* 38 (2017) 185–99.

Duggan, Colleen. "'Show Me Your Impact': Evaluating Transitional Justice in Contested Spaces." *Journal of Planning and Program Evaluation* 35 (2010) 199–205.

Evjen, Bjørg, et al., eds. 2021. *Samenes historie fra 1751 til 2010*. 2 vols. Oslo: Cappelen Damm Akademisk.

Eye on the Arctic. "Sami in Sweden Start Work on Structure of Truth and Reconciliation Commission." https://thebarentsobserver.com/en/life-and-public/2020/06/sami-sweden-start-work-structure-truth-and-reconciliation-commission.

———. "Sami Parliament in Finland agrees More Time Needed for Truth and Reconciliation Commission Preparation." https://thebarentsobserver.com/en/arctic/2021/02/sami-parliament-finland-agrees-more-time-needed-truth-and-reconciliation-commission.

Fee, Margery. "The Truth and Reconciliation Commission of Canada." *Canadian Literature* 215 (2012) 6–10.

Freeman, Mark. *Necessary Evils. Amnesties and the Search for Justice*. New York: Cambridge University Press, 2009.

Gibney, Mark, et al. *The Age of Apology: Facing Up to the Past*. University of Pennsylvania Press, 2008.

Griffiths, Kate. "Hegemony and Reconciling Indigenous–State Relations A Discourse Analysis of Truth Commission Debates in Australia and Norway." Master's thesis, Universitetet i Sørøst-Norge, 2018.

Guðmarsdóttir, Sigríður, et al., eds. *Trading Justice for Peace? Reframing Reconciliation in TRC Processes in South Africa, Canada and Nordic Countries*. Cape Town: AOSIS, 2021.

Hayner, Priscilla B. "Fifteen Truth Commissions—1974 to 1994: A Comparative Study." *Human Rights Quarterly* 16 (1994) 597–655.

———. *Unspeakable Truths: Transitional Justice and the Challenge of Truth Commissions*. 2nd ed. London and New York: Routledge, 2011.

Hjelm, Jonny. "Samer, kyrkan och staten—sanningssökandets utmaningar." *Västerbottens-Kuriren* (May 30, 2020). https://www.vk.se/2020-05-30/samer-kyrkan-och-staten-sanningssokandets-utmaningar?fbclid=IwAR2_VqNbJseqTj1Lx9rDMvQ_gVMHboxNGDISVmRoG3iyOAgXbwd_M7w6YAo

Hofverberg, Elin. "Finland: Sami Truth and Reconciliation Commission Established." Finland: Library of Congress, 2021.

Jamet, Églantine, and Sámi Rights. "Self-Determination of the Only Indigenous People in Europe." https://www.humanrightspulse.com/mastercontentblog/smi-rights-self-determination-of-the-only-indigenous-people-in-europe.

Johnsen, Tore. "Negotiating the Meaning of 'TRC' in the Norwegian Context." In *Trading Justice for Peace? Reframing Reconciliation in TRC Processes in South Africa, Canada and Nordic Countries*, edited by Sigríður Guðmarsdóttir et al. Cape Town: AOSIS, 2021.

Josefsen, Eva, et al. "Different Institutions Within Similar States: The Norwegian and Swedish Sámediggis." *Ethnopolitics* 14 (2015) 32–51.

Kuokkanen, Rauna. "Reconciliation as a Threat or Structural Change? The Truth and Reconciliation Process and Settler Colonial Policy Making in Finland." *Human Rights Review* 21 (2020) 293–312.

Kväner Lantalaiset Tornedalingar. "Truth and Reconciliation Commission for Tornedalians, Kvens and Lan-tallaiset." https://komisuuni.se/en/start-en/.

Lehtola, Veli-Pekka et al. "Contested Sámi Histories in Finland." In *Sámi Research in Transition*, edited by Laura Junka-Aikio et al., 51–70. Routledge, 2021.

Library of Congress (Finland). "Finland: Sami Truth and Reconciliation Commission Established." https://www.loc.gov/item/global-legal-monitor/2021-11-18/finland-sami-truth-and-reconciliation-commission-established/.

Library of Congress (Sweden). "Sweden: Government Announces Truth Commission at Sami Repatriation Ceremony Following Official Sami Request." https://www.loc.gov/item/global-legal-monitor/2019-12-12/sweden-government-announces-truth-commission-at-sami-repatriation-ceremony-following-official-sami-request/.

MacDonald, David B. "Canada's Truth and Reconciliation Commission: Assessing Context, Process, and Critiques." *Griffith Law Review* 29 (2020) 1–24.

Minde, Henry. "Assimilation of the Sami—Implementation and Consequences." *Gáldu Čála, Journal of Indigenous Peoples Rights* 3 (2005) 1–33.

Nagy, Rosemary. "The Truth and Reconciliation Commission of Canada: Genesis and Design." *Canadian Journal of Law & Society/La Revue Canadienne Droit et Société* 29 (2014) 199–217.

———. "The Scope and Bounds of Transitional Justice and the Canadian Truth and Reconciliation Commission." *International Journal of Transitional Justice* 7 (2012) 52–73.

Niemi, Mikael. *Koka björn*. Piratförlaget, 2017.

Niezen, Ronald. *Truth and Indignation: Canada's Truth and Reconciliation Commission on Indian Residential Schools*. University of Toronto Press, 2017.

Nilsen, Ragnar. "From Norwegianization to Coastal Sami Uprising." In *Indigenous Peoples. Resource management and Global rights*, edited by Svein Jentoft et al. Eburon Academic, 2013.

Regan, Paulette. "Canada's TRC: An "Unsettling" Indignous-Centered Relational Justice and Reconciliation Model." In *Trading Justice for Peace*, edited by Sigríður Guðmarsdóttir et al., 41–61. Cape Town: AOSIS, 2021.

———. "Unsettling the Settler Within: Canada's Peacemaker Myth, Reconciliation, and Transformative Pathways to Decolonization." PhD diss., University of Victoria, Canada, 2005.

Regeringskansliet. "Kartläggning och granskning av den politik som förts gentemot samerna och dess konsekvenser för det samiska folket." https://regeringen.se/rattsliga-dokument/kommittedirektiv/2021/11/dir.-2021103/.

———. "Tilläggsdirektiv till Sannings- och försoningskommissionen för tornedalingar, kväner och lantalaiset." https://regeringen.se/rattsliga-dokument/kommittedirektiv/2023/02/dir.-202315.

———. "Uppgörelse med historiska kränkningar och övergrepp mot tornedalingar, kväner och lantalaiset." https://regeringen.se/rattsliga-dokument/kommittedirektiv/2020/03/dir.-202029.

Rokkan, Stein. *State Formation, Nation-Building, and Mass Politics in Europe*. Oxford University Press, 1999.

Sametinget (Sweden). "Truth Commission in Sweden." https://www.sametinget.se/truth-commission.

Sanningskommissionen för det samiska folket. "Sanningskommissionen för det samiska folket." https://sanningskommissionensamer.se/.

Saugestad, Sidsel. "Sannhetskommisjoner. Om institusjonalisert kunnskap, kritisk distanse og andre antropologiske utfordringer." *Norsk Antropologisk Tidsskrift* 30 (2019) 7–19.

Semb, Anne J. "Why (not) Commit?–Norway, Sweden and Finland and the ILO Convention 169." *Nordic Journal of Human Rights* 30 (2012) 122–47.

Short, Damien. "Reconciliation, Assimilation, and the Indigenous Peoples of Australia." *International Political Science Review* 24 (2003) 491–513.

Skaar, Elin. "When Truth Commission Models Travel: Explaining the Norwegian Case." *International Journal of Transitional Justice* 17 (2023) 123–40.

———. "Truth and Reconciliation Commissions (TRCs)." In *Elgar Encyclopedia of Human Rights*, edited by Manfred N. C. Binder et al., Edward Elgar Publishing, 2022.

———. "When Truth Commission Models Travel: Explaining the Norwegian Case." *International Journal of Transitional Justice* 17 (2023) 123–40.

Skaar, Elin and Aaron J. Spitzer. "Conceptualizing the Legitimacy of Non-Transitional Truth Commissions: Norway and Canada Compared." *Nordic Journal of Human Rights*, open access (2024), 1–26.

Skaar, Elin, Eric Wiebelhaus-Brahm, Jemima García-Godos. *Exploring Truth Commission Recommendations in a Comparative Perspective: Beyond Words*. Transitional Justice Series. 1 vol. Uitgevers NV: Intersentia/Cambridge University Press, 2022a.

———, eds. *Latin American Experiences with Truth Commission Recommendations: Beyond Words*. Transitional Justice Series. 2 vols. Uitgevers NV: Intersentia/Cambridge University Press, 2022b.

SOU 2023:68a. *Som om vi aldrig funnits: exkludering och assimilering av tornedalingar, kväner och lantalaiset. Slutbetänkande av Sannings- och försoningskommissionen för tornedalingar, kväner och lantalaiset*. https://www.regeringen.se/rattsliga-dokument/statens-offentliga-utredningar/2023/11/sou-202368/

Stanton, Kim. "Canada's Truth and Reconciliation Commission: Settling the Past?" *International Indigenous Policy Journal* 2 (2011) 1–18.

———. "Truth Commissions and Public Inquiries: Addressing Historical Injustices in Established Democracies." PhD diss., University of Toronto, 2010.

Svenska Kyrkan. "Rapport från Ságastallamat, en koneferens om samerna och Svenska kyrkan, i Kiruna den 11–13 oktober 2011." https://docplayer.se/19479461-Rapport-fran-sagastallamat-en-konferens-om-samerna-och-svenska-kyrkan-i-kiruna-den-11-13-oktober-2011.html.

Szpak, Agnieszka, and Dawid Bunikowski. "Saami Truth and Reconciliation Commissions." *International Journal of Human Rights* 26 (2021) 306–31.

Teitel, Ruti. *Transitional Justice*. New York: Oxford University Press, 2000.

Thisted, Kirsten. "The Greenlandic Reconciliation Commission: Ethnonationalism, Arctic Resources, and Post-Colonial Identity." In *Arctic Environmental Modernities*, edited by Lill-Ann Körber et al., 231–46. Springer, 2017.

Tjelle, Ingjerd. *Internatliv—den unike historien om skoleinternatene i Finnmark*. Karasjok: CálliidLágádus, 2022.

Truth and Reconciliation Commission Concerning the Sámi People. "Comission." https://sdtsk.fi/en/commission/.

———. "Mandate. Establishing a truth And Reconciliation Commission Concerning the Sámi People." n.d. https://sdtsk.fi/en/mandate/.

Utriksdepartementet, *Sveriges Internationella överenskommelser*, 2002. https://www.regeringen.se/contentassets/02b946ed1ee747a1a7bf4874fd8d3633/ramkonvention-om-skydd-for-nationella-minoriteter/.

Varanger Museum. "Kvensk/norskfinsk historie." https://www.varangermuseum.no/fagomrader/kvener-norskfinner/.

Vik, Hanne H., and Anne J. Semb. "Who Owns the Land? Norway, the Sami and the ILO Indigenous and Tribal Peoples Convention." *International Journal on Minority and Group Rights* 20 (2013) 517–50.

White, Patrick. "Sweden Looks to Canada as It Launches Truth Commission into Treatment of Indigenous People." *The Globe and Mail*, January 9, 2023.

Wiebelhaus-Brahm, Eric. "Global Transitional Justice Norms and the Framing of Truth Commissions in the Absence of Transition." *Negotiation and Conflict Management Research* 14 (2020) 170–86.

———. "Truth Commissions in Non-Transitional Contexts: Implications for Their Impact and Legacy." In *The Legacies of Truth and Reconciliation Commissions*, edited by Jeremy Sarkin. Cambridge: Internsentia. 2019.

Wikipedia, "Official Minority Languages of Sweden." https://en.wikipedia.org/wiki/Official_minority_languages_of_Sweden

Wikipedia. "Swedification." https://en.wikipedia.org/wiki/Swedification

YLE News, "Finnish Gov Agrees to Formation of Sámi Truth and Reconciliation Commission." https://thebarentsobserver.com/en/life-and-public/2019/11/finnish-gov-agrees-formation-sami-truth-and-reconciliation-commission/.

2

TRC and Processes within the Church of Norway

Unequal Status of North Sámi and Kvens/Norwegian Finns in Shared Regions

HANS MORTEN HAUGEN

Faculty of Theology and Social Sciences,
VID Specialized University, Oslo, Norway

INTRODUCTION

The Sámi and the Kvens/Norwegian Finns have distinct statuses in Norway and varying levels of international influence.[1] Nonetheless, both groups share the experience of colonization. The Church of Norway (CoN) has, at different times and with varying degrees of intensity, played a role in implementing the government's forced assimilation policies, particularly during the period covered by the Norwegian Truth and Reconciliation Commission (TRC), which spans from approximately 1800 to the present day.

---

1. On the various international influences exercised by the Sámi and Kven, see Haugen, "Any Role," 209–11.

Although the TRC includes Forest Finns, this chapter will not cover Forest Finns living in southern Norway. Norway is home to three other national minorities: Jews, Rom, and Romani, primarily living in southern Norway. Furthermore, Norway is a party to two European treaties: The Framework Convention for the Protection of National Minorities and The European Charter for Regional or Minority Languages.[2] Among the Sámi, only the North Sámi will be included, as they traditionally reside in the same areas as the Kvens/Norwegian Finns in Troms and Finnmark, Northern Norway.

The term Sápmi denotes the region spread across four states (Norway, Sweden, Finland, Russia), which has traditionally been inhabited by the Sámi. The Sámi hold official recognition as Indigenous peoples and have been enshrined in the Norwegian Constitution since 1988, alongside receiving legal acknowledgment through various other avenues. Notably, in 2021, a significant amendment was introduced to the Sámi Act, establishing a brand-new chapter that focuses on consultations between the Sámi Parliament and political authorities at the national, regional, and local levels.[3]

Since 1992, the CoN has had a Sámi Church Council (SCC), leading to a gradual increase in recognition and visibility.

Some regions traditionally inhabited by the North Sámi, the largest linguistic group among the Sámi people, have also been home to the Kvens/Norwegian Finns. As will be explored further below, the term 'Kvenland' had historical usage dating back to the first millennium. Although an exact historical account of the Kven presence in what is today Norway is difficult, an overview will be provided. It is essential to note that tracing the history of the Kvens/Norwegian Finns in Norway does not grant them indigenous status; instead, they hold the status of a national minority, officially recognized in 1998. Furthermore, the Kven language received recognition as a minority language in 2005; prior to that, it was considered a Finnish dialect.

---

2. Article 3(1) in the Framework Convention reads: "Every person belonging to a national minority shall have the right freely to choose to be treated or not to be treated as such and no disadvantage shall result from this choice or from the exercise of the rights which are connected to that choice," see Council of Europe, "Framework Convention."

3. The updated Act is not translated into English, see: https://lovdata.no/dokument/NL/lov/1987-06-12-56?q=sameloven; for an updated version of the 2005. Consultation Agreement between the Sámi Parliament and the Norwegian Government, see Norwegian Government, "Procedures for Consultations."

Within the CoN, two consecutive four-year plans, effective from 2015–2018 and 2019–2022, featured the statement: "Kven language and culture is fostered in the church services and in Christian education."[4] The implementation will be reviewed below.

The next section briefly describes the church and theoretical contexts. Recognizing the limited historical knowledge concerning the Kvens/Norwegian Finns, this chapter places particular emphasis on Kven history. This focus arises from the resolution of debates surrounding Sámi history in both the north and the south, including the debunking of the 'immigration thesis' in the north and the 'expansion thesis' in the south, as Sámi presence has been increasingly documented.[5] The chapter also includes a discussion of criteria for indigenousness, and whether the Kvens/Norwegian Finns meet these. This is followed by a brief overview of the CoN's historical relationships with the Sámi and the Kvens and their languages, respectively, starting in the mid-nineteenth century. The chapter then reviews the tensions arising from 2015 to 2021 concerning the implementation of the CoN Synod decisions[6] in 2014 and 2018, along with new initiatives that emerged outside of the CoN. Finally, an evaluation is conducted to determine whether the SCC can play a role in what could be termed a reconciliation process between the Kvens/Norwegian Finns and the CoN.

The research question that this chapter seeks to answer is: How did the CoN relate to the Sámi and the Kvens/Norwegian Finns historically? What are the recent experiences in the encounter between the CoN and, in particular, the Kvens/Norwegian Finns? Can the CoN and its Sámi Church Council accommodate the expectations of the Kvens/Norwegian Finns?

The first two components of the research question are addressed by drawing upon prior studies and CoN documents. In contrast, the third aspect of the research question is addressed through the collection of responses to specific inquiries from four CoN leaders possessing pertinent

---

4. CoN, "KM 07/18," CoN, "KM 07/14." The current eight-year plan (2022–2029) has a different structure and is much shorter.

5. See Norwegian Supreme Court, "Selbu judgement," which represents the main shift in this understanding.

6. All Church of Norway Synod decisions (except for the 1997 decision) are available at: https://kirken.no/nb-NO/om-kirken/slik-styres-kirken/kirkemotet/dokumentervedtak.

expertise in Sámi-related matters. This segment of data collection received approval from NSD, the Norwegian Center for Research Data.[7]

CHURCH AND THEORETICAL CONTEXTS

The Church of Norway (CoN), the majority church in Norway, achieved formal independence in 2017 while still relying on the Norwegian authorities for church tax collection and funding. Its role in various forms of dialogue is characterized by building a common platform for conviviality—or living together rather than imposing its positions—leading to accusations of being too soft or too leftist.[8] The CoN has been an active member of relevant ecumenical and confessional bodies since its founding, with the exception of the Community of Protestant Churches in Europe (CPCE, earlier known as Leuenberg), which it joined in 2000, several decades after the CPCE's establishment.

The CoN's role within the ecumenical community concerning social-ethical matters is characterized by three key features: (i) The CoN actively engages with and contributes to various programs of the World Council of Churches (WCC); (ii) It maintains a positive stance toward liberation theology; and (iii) The CoN actively advocates for and promotes the core messages of the WCC and other church bodies to Norwegian authorities.[9] Additionally, the Mission from the Margins (formerly known as Just and Inclusive Communities) Program of the WCC, which includes the Ecumenical Disability Advocates Network, Ecumenical Indigenous Peoples Network, and Migration and Multicultural Ministry, has become part of the CoN's agenda in various ways.[10]

The CoN has initiated reconciliation processes with the Sámi, marking four significant milestones: (i) The establishment of the SCC in 1992; (ii) In 1997, the CoN Synod prioritized Indigenous peoples in

---

7. From January 1, 2022 NSD changed name to Sikt—Norwegian Agency for Shared Services in Education and Research.

8. Listhaug, "Der andre tier," 146–54; NTB, "Listhaug"; the interview was made just after her appointment as Norwegian Minister for Immigration and Integration; Listhaug is now chairperson of the Norwegian Progress Party.

9. This is most evident regarding immigration issues, see CoN, "Den norske kirkes arbeid." Several of the documents by the WCC are published by the Christian Council of Norway (CCN), see CCN, "Andre publikasjoner."

10. As an example, for persons with disabilities, see CoN, "Kirken oppretter råd."

the global church, centered on Sámi church life[11]; (iii) In 2011, the CoN Synod approved an eight-year Strategy for Sámi church life[12]; and (iv) Subsequently, another eight-year strategy gained approval from the CoN Synod in 2019.[13]

While no churches in Norway operated boarding schools, the Norwegian Sámi Mission owned one boarding school for South Sámi pupils, which imposed strict restrictions on speaking Sámi. Additionally, there was a boarding school (secondary) for North Sámi students that actively promoted the Sámi language.[14] Subsequently, the latter was turned into the Sámi Folk High School. The predominance of Sámi language instruction in this institution prompted discussions about potentially replacing it with a state-owned or "state-controlled" folk high school.[15] Furthermore, no organization was devoted to mission efforts among the Kvens/Norwegian Finns.

It is pertinent to note that the CoN has previously initiated reconciliation processes with another Norwegian national minority. The Romani people, who have resided in Norway since the sixteenth century, experienced severe treatment, including corporal punishment for their 'leaders,' as documented in Christian Vs "Norske Lov" of 1687.[16] In the same section, it was stipulated that Jews captured without an official permit could face fines equivalent to over 700,000 euros in present-day value.[17] A public commission was established to investigate Norwegian policies and consider the apologies extended by the CoN.[18]

11. CoN, "KM 13/97."

12. CoN, "KM 08/11."

13. CoN, "KM 14/19." In the 2019 strategy, there are two references to Kvens/ Norwegian Finns: one regarding "internal church dialogue" and the other concerning Kven psalms in the CoN's Psalms book; please refer to the details below.

14. The South Sámi school at Havika, located near Namsos, was operational from 1910 to 1951. During its initial three years, the school had two different owners; see Andresen et al., *Samenes historie*, 172, 327; the North Sámi school was established in 1938; for other institutions owned by the Norwegian Sámi Mission, see Andresen et al., *Samenes historie*, 186–87. In 1913, the Norwegian Sámi Mission adopted Basic Rules, expressing that its work shall "in no regard be in contradiction to state efforts in school and church"; see Andresen et al. *Samenes historie*, 185.

15. Lund, "Folkehøgskolen."

16. Book 3, Section 22, paragraph 3 is on Romani («Tater») and Jews; see Christian V, "Chr. Vs NORSKE LOV."

17. Christian V, "Chr. Vs NORSKE LOV," paragraph 1. The calculation of 1,000 Riksdaler is done here: https://www.norges-bank.no/tema/Statistikk/Priskalkulator.

18. See "NOU 2015:7," 43–72; 86–87 (the latter on the CoN's two apologies, in

The absence of the CoN's involvement in boarding schools or similar institutions sets it apart from experiences in countries such as Canada and Australia. Nevertheless, during the era of Norwegianization, the CoN played a central role as a representative of Norwegian public authorities. There are several ways authorities from the dominant culture can impose subordination, lack of self-respect, and psychological wounds on persons of all ages belonging to non-dominant cultures. In all reconciliation processes, at least three phases must be acknowledged by the non-dominant party in any asymmetrical relationship: (i) *Recognition*, which entails the expression of a shared basic understanding; (ii) *Repentance*, involving the expression of an apology, without necessarily expecting forgiveness; and (iii) *Restoration,* which necessitates at least the repeal of discriminatory laws and the implementation of new policies and priorities.[19] Additionally, a fourth phase, (iv) *forgiveness*, has been introduced in later discussions.[20] However, it can be argued that a unilateral expression of apology might be better than a call for forgiveness, with an implicit expectation of being granted such forgiveness, as not everyone might be prepared to grant this.[21]

HISTORY OF THE KVENS/NORWEGIAN FINNS

The fact that there are three organizations for Kvens/Norwegian Finns, all being founded in the 1980s/1990s, has more to do with differing contemporary strategies than with diverse perspectives on history.[22] Nonetheless,

---

1998 and 2000). The forced assimilation of the Romani was facilitated by priests who were obligatory members of the municipal Child Protection Boards, and priests who held leadership positions in a diaconal organization that runs institutions for children, single men, and families. In 1986, this organization was relieved of its previous public mandate, and in 1987, it transformed into a diaconal foundation with a new mandate. It is currently known as Crux.

19. Johnsen, *Jordens barn*, 103–10.
20. Johnsen, "Acknowledged History," 111–14.
21. Haugen, "Den vanskelige forsoningen," 245–46.
22. The largest organization seeks to strengthen the status of Kvens/ Norwegian Finns without explicit criticism of the privileged status of the Sámi; for its statutes, see: https://kvener.no/om-oss/vedtekter; the second largest organization seeks to promote the interests of the Finns recently settled in Norway; for its statutes, see: https://www.klubbinfo.no/finskforb/vedtekter-norsk.html; the smallest organization promotes the wider Finnish-Ugric perspectives and is explicitly critical of the privileged status of the Sámi; its purpose is available at https://kvenfinn.no/medlem/; see also https://www.ruijan-kaiku.no/likestilling-mellom-kvener-norskfinner-og-samer; and https://

there are distinctions among them. The smallest organization of Kvens/ Norwegian Finns, which is the most critical of the privileged status afforded to the Sámi, asserts that the long history of Finnish-speaking individuals in Norway allegedly predates the presence of the Sámi, a claim that is incorrect.[23] Nevertheless, the history of the Kvens/Norwegian Finns in what is today Norway remains relevant.

The term 'Kvenland' is used in the Norwegian mythical foundation story, *Fundinn Nóregr*, where a king named Fornljot is said to have ruled over Kvenland in what is purportedly the sixth century.[24] More reliable historical accounts come from the sailor Ottar, who referred to "Cwenas" and "Cwenland" when he visited the English King Alfred around 890.[25] The use of the term "East" in *Fundinn Nóregr* and the mention of "mountains" in Ottar's accounts suggest that this area corresponds to the region around the northern part of the Bothnian Sea, which encompasses present-day Northern Finland and Northern Sweden.[26]

The beginnings of the Finnish-speaking presence in what is now Norway are somewhat uncertain, particularly regarding permanent settlement. However, they were included in Danish/Norwegian taxation, at the very least, from the sixteenth century onwards.[27] Finnish-speaking traders had arrived on the coasts of present-day Norway in earlier periods.[28] Swedish expansion and taxation became more pronounced in the thirteenth and fourteenth centuries. In 1328, an agreement was signed with the so-called 'Birkarls,' who were defined by their occupation rather

kvenfinn.no/author/admin/page/2. The information on size is from Norwegian Government, "White Paper 12 (2020–2021)," 18–20.

23. Seppola, "E-post fra Kvenlandsforbundet," 15; the wording is "at least as old"; Dervo, "Ivar Dervos brev." The term "Finns" was the earliest name used for the Sámi people, but it was later replaced by the term "Lapps."

24. Codex Flatöiensis, "Fundinn Nóregr." The text is located at the beginning of the Orknøyingenes saga. The last individual mentioned in the text is Ragnvald Earl, who lived around 830–900 (some accounts suggest 892). He is situated 12 generations after Fornjot, who is referred to as the king of Jotland and Kvenland.

25. Ottar of Hålogaland, retold by King Alfred, see Thorpe, *The Life and Works* 247, 251.

26. For a relevant map, see Hansen and Olsen, *Samenes historie*, 134.

27. Niemi ("Kvenene og staten," 13) writes that "many" Kven were subject to Danish/Norwegian taxation in the sixteenth century. Information about arrivals in the sixteenth century is also conveyed by NRK, "Kvenenes historie."

28. Guttormsen, "Spor," 28–29; see also Hansen and Olsen, *Samenes historie*, 149–50 and 226.

than their ethnicity.[29] The agreement was sanctioned on March 16, 1340, by the Swedish-Norwegian king Magnus Eriksson. The birkarls were given monopoly on trade and taxation in the northern parts of Sweden and Finland, whereas the local inhabitants' property rights were guaranteed if they consented to come under the King's tax jurisdiction. The scope of trade and tax jurisdictional authority might not have perfectly aligned with geographical areas, and political borders were not firmly established until 1751. In preceding centuries, four agreements delineated territories for taxation, even designating specific areas as eligible for taxation by both states.[30] The intensification of taxation and the risk of being taxed twice by different state representatives were genuine concerns. Finnish-speaking individuals and families opted to settle further north, in what is now present-day Norway, to ensure that they remained beyond the reach of Swedish tax collectors.

March 16 is the official Kven people's day. The date is chosen to commemorate the approval of the taxation agreement in 1340. The choice of this date is intriguing for several reasons. On the one hand, it marks the first occasion when an agreement pertaining to 'Kvenland'—a region that had previously not fallen under the jurisdiction of any state, with the legal recognition of the property rights of its inhabitants—was endorsed by a sovereign ruler. On the other hand, it signifies the formal colonization of the Kvens, who had previously existed without being under the sovereignty of a single state but were subject to taxation jurisdiction by both Sweden and Novgorod.

More Kven-speaking individuals migrated to present-day Norway in the decades following 1751. Some of these migrations were prompted by the hardships endured during the Great Nordic War (1700–1721).

---

29. The 1328 Agreement is known as "Täljestadgan"; see Hansen and Olsen, *Samenes historie*, 151; see also 152, 161 and 226 for more on the ethnic composition of the Birkarls, being mainly Swedes in the South and mainly Kven in the North. There are two opposing views on the Birkarls' origin; one identifying Pirkkala/Birkala, Southern Finland; see Bergman, *Kulturarv*, 58; see also Kalberg, "Svenskehandelen." For an alternative origin, emphasizing the term "karl" as a "free man" loyal to the Swedish king and thus rewarded with privileges, see Vahtola, "Birkarlaproblemet"; see also Guttormsen, "Spor," 19. It is therefore wrong that a Birkarl was always a Kven, as alleged by the smallest organization for Kvens/ Norwegian Finns; see https://kvenfinn.no/historie/1250–1450-senmiddelalder.

30. For the 1323 Sweden-Novgorod and the 1326 Norway-Novgorod agreements, see map in Hansen and Olsen, *Samenes historie*, 145; for the 1595 Sweden-Russia and the 1613 Denmark/Norway-Sweden/Finland agreements, see maps in Hansen and Olsen, *Samenes historie*, 248.

Various other factors contributed to people moving in the subsequent centuries. By the year 1900, approximately twenty-five percent of the population in Finnmark and eight percent of the population in Troms were Kvens/Norwegian Finns.[31]

The visibility of the Kvens/Norwegian Finns in the political sphere and within the CoN has fluctuated over the centuries. It will be shown later that the Kvens/Norwegian Finns and their language have, at least in principle, been considered important by the priests in the CoN. One article, available in the Norwegian Research Ethics Library, discusses historical injustice against the Sámi and Kvens/Norwegian Finns, arguing that efforts were made to render the Kvens/Norwegian Finns invisible in order to "avoid competition in minority policy."[32] This phenomenon is associated with the 1980s and the establishment of the first (and largest) organization for Kvens/Norwegian Finns. From the context, it appears that it was the (North) Sámi who sought to "avoid competition" and, as a result, have endeavored to keep the Kvens/Norwegian Finns invisible. This accusation against the (North) Sámi is not substantiated by sources, unlike the arguments pertaining to how researchers have also played a role in perpetuating the 'hierarchization' that impacts Norwegian policy.

APPLYING 'INDIGENOUS PEOPLES' CRITERIA TO NORWAY

There is no universally accepted, legally binding definition of 'Indigenous peoples.' However, there are lists of characteristics and elements that are central to the classification of a group as 'indigenous.' The 2007 UN Declaration on the Rights of Indigenous Peoples (UNDRIP) contains five preambular paragraphs that highlight several important characteristics of Indigenous peoples:

> (i) "suffered from historic injustices. . ."; (ii) "the inherent rights . . . derive from their political, economic and social structures. . .": (iii) "rights . . . affirmed in . . . arrangements with States"; (iv) "organizing themselves for political, economic, social and cultural enhancement. . ."; and (v) "control . . . to maintain and strengthen their institutions, cultures and traditions. . ."[33]

---

31. Niemi, "Kvenene," 14.
32. Niemi and Semb, "Forskningsetisk kontekst."
33. UN General Assembly, *A/RES/61/295, Annex*, preambular paras. 6–10.

We see that the characteristics emphasize 'self-organizing' in the last four of these characteristics.

Own customs or traditions, own institutions, and historical continuity from pre-colonial or pre-establishment of modern states are also emphasized in Article 1 of the 1989 ILO Convention 169 on Indigenous and Tribal Peoples in Independent States (ILO 169).

Similar emphasis is found in the four elements that constitute the first definition of Indigenous peoples made by a UN-mandated expert, from 1986: (i) have historical continuity with pre-invasion and pre-colonial societies; (ii) consider themselves distinct; (iii) are non-dominant; and (iv) "are determined to preserve, develop and transmit to future generations their ancestral territories, and their ethnic identity . . ., in accordance with their own cultural patterns, social institutions, and legal system."[34]

Another definition, from 1996, mirrors these, but applies the term "earliest presence" in addition to "own . . . social institutions and legal system," emphasizing "perpetuation in upholding characteristics."[35] The 1996 report later paved the way for the UNDRIP.

We see that the UNDRIP is *less* explicit than the two reports, which require "own . . . legal systems" in order to be considered indigenous. On the other hand, by specifying "political . . . structures" and institutions, the UNDRIP is more demanding than the ILO 169, which requires "customs or traditions," in addition to institutions and continuity, as well as self-identification, to be considered indigenous.

Regardless of one's perspective on Norwegian colonial expansion in the north and the question of who settled there first, there is no basis to dispute the presence of Kvens/Norwegian Finns predating the drawing of the border in 1751. Hence, the first element of historical continuity, 'pre-colonial,' must be considered as fulfilled. Additionally, the attributes of distinctness and non-dominance are applicable to the Kvens/Norwegian Finns.

Elements that relate to self-organizing are, however, more challenging. While Kven villages may have been "organizing themselves for political, economic, social and cultural enhancement," the requirements for broader "political . . . structures" do *not* apply to the Kvens/Norwegian Finns. If this element is interpreted to include wider institutions for the

---

34. UN Special Rapporteur, "Study," para. 379.
35. UN Working Group on Minorities, "Report," para. 70.

purpose of solving conflicts or making collective demands, such institutions have not existed.

Therefore, when applying the five characteristics outlined in the UNDRIP, it becomes apparent that the Kvens/Norwegian Finns have largely been unorganized throughout most of their history. The Kvens/Norwegian Finns were not part of any collective mobilization until the 1980s. Additionally, it is challenging to identify the fulfillment of the customs and institutions requirement as stipulated by ILO 169, as historically, there were no overarching institutions established by them.

The delayed collective mobilization among Kvens/Norwegian Finns can be partly attributed to the forced assimilation policies imposed upon them. Norwegian authorities did not promote self-organization and were tardy in recognizing both the Kvens/Norwegian Finns as a national minority (in 1998) and the Kven or Finnish language (in 2005). However, when considering the five characteristics outlined in the UNDRIP or the four characteristics specified by ILO 169, it appears challenging to assert that the Kvens/Norwegian Finns meet the criteria for being classified as Indigenous peoples.

CoN'S ROLE IN THE FORCED ASSIMILATION OF THE SÁMI AND KVENS/NORWEGIAN FINNS

The history of CoN bishops, deans, priests, and the Norwegian Sámi Mission in relation to both the Sámi and the Kvens/Norwegian Finns must consider the role of priests as enforcers of various public policies. They often served as the primary representatives of Norwegian authorities in local communities. Three distinct epochs are particularly noteworthy: the mid-nineteenth century during the early stages of the Norwegianization policy, the turn of the twentieth century at the height of the Norwegianization policy, and the mid-twentieth century marked by new challenges.

In 1848, Nils Vibe Stockfleth—a priest who taught Sámi and Kven at the University of Oslo, translated the New Testament, and wrote Sámi grammar—succeeded in his advocacy efforts for a Royal Decree. It specified that all priests who were to serve in Sámi and Kven areas had to take exams in Sámi and gain knowledge in Kven.[36] A subsequent Royal Decree

36. The actual knowledge of Kven in the nineteenth century was limited, with one priest taking the exam, and interpretation being the preferred solution; see Maliniemi, *Arkivdokumentene*, 28. The requirements regarding exams were specified in the subsequent Royal Decree of 6 October 1848; see: https://lovdata.no/dokument/SFO/

from July 4, 1859, used the term "obligation" for the Kven language,[37] and the same term was used by the bishop of Tromsø in a 1903 instruction.[38]

It is important to note that these developments took place during the most intensive phase of the Norwegianization policy. During this period, there were comprehensive language instructions issued in 1898,[39] and in 1902, a prohibition was enacted against selling land to individuals who did not speak or write Norwegian. This prohibition also mandated that properties must have Norwegian names.

The name of the diocese was changed from Tromsø to Hålogaland in 1918. During his tenure as Bishop from 1928 to 1937, Eivind Berggrav, who later became the Bishop of Oslo and a central figure in the CoN's resistance against the Nazi regime, considered the Kven population to be a national security risk. He instructed all priests to report any instances of "Finnish-cultural agitation"[40] to him. Additionally, he expressed concerns that priests from Finland might be involved in "propaganda."[41]

During the mid-twentieth century, the decision-makers within the CoN were hesitant to challenge the Norwegianization policy. While the first President of the Sámi Parliament acknowledged the CoN's opposition to Norwegianization at the beginning of the twentieth century, he went on to state that: "The 1940s and 1950s were characterized by inaction. Most tragic were the 1960s and 1970s. Leading churchmen, priests and Sámi missionaries, stood passive and even opposed the 'Sámi activists.'"[42]

It is evident that there were certain ambitions for language competence among priests in both Sámi and Kvens,[43] as observed in the mid-nineteenth century and at the dawn of the twentieth century. Despite

---

forskrift/1848-10-06-1.

37. Maliniemi, *Arkivdokumentene*, 80.

38. Maliniemi, *Arkivdokumentene*, 75, n 32 and accompanying text; see also Haugen, "Any Role," 216, n 38 and accompanying text.

39. The responsible minister, Wilhelm A. Wexelsen (minister 1891–1893 and 1898–1903) became bishop in 1905; see Haugen, "Any Role," 216, n 37 and accompanying text.

40. Eriksen and Niemi, *Den finske fare*, 222. On Berggrav's role, specifying that he also asked teachers to report to him, see Norwegian Truth and Reconciliation Commission, "Sannhet og forsoning," 243, 255, 503.

41. Eriksen and Niemi, *Den finske fare*, 226; for a softer position, not approving of restricting the possibility of priests from Finland to use church buildings in Norway, see Eriksen and Niemi, *Den finske fare*, 225.

42. Magga, "Samene."

43. For a historical and contemporary account of the Kven language, see Räisänen and Kunnas, *The Kven language*.

the instructions, little effort seems to have been made to facilitate such competence. As the CoN was—and still is—highly dependent on Norwegian authorities for funding for any additional efforts, the lack of interest in these languages until rather recently among Norwegian authorities appears to be a relevant explanation. The twentieth century witnessed the emergence of new 'lay church' initiatives aimed at strengthening the Sámi language. However, there were no similar efforts in the case of the Kvens, except for general instructions to conduct a specific number of church services annually in Kven in certain parishes. Instead, Johan Arnt Beronka, the dean of Eastern Finnmark (Varanger, 1924–1930), who spoke Kven, Sámi, and Russian and published language books, was ignored and suspected of holding 'non-Norwegian attitudes' due to his use of and promotion of Kven and Finnish.[44] In 1930, he accepted a new position in southern Norway, where he lived for the rest of his life.

In summary, while it is not possible to provide a comprehensive account of the various decision-makers within the CoN for the two northern counties of Norway, a concise summary can be provided. First, there was verbal resistance to the Norwegianization policy combined with accommodation for the use of Sámi and, to a lesser extent, Kven in some church services in certain churches. Second, there were no organized and consistent efforts to substantively challenge the Norwegianization policies; instead, only individual efforts were made, and these individuals often found themselves isolated and without support.

CONTEMPORARY INITIATIVES FOR KVEN LANGUAGE AND CHURCH LIFE BY CoN AND OTHERS

The initial institutional response, following the first mention of the Kvens in a CoN multi-year strategy, was the establishment of a Commission on Kven Church Life in 2015 under the Diocese of Nord-Hålogaland. This initiative was initially well received by the largest Kven organization.[45]

The Kvens/Norwegian Finns have subsequently voiced their dissatisfaction primarily regarding two issues. The first issue concerned the CoN's lack of national responsibility, which they suggested should be addressed through the establishment of a national Kven Church Council,[46]

---

44. Niemi, "Johan Beronka."
45. Norske Kveners Forbund, "Kvensk satsing."
46. Nord-Hålogaland Diocese Commission for Kven Church Life, "Ny

similar to the SCC, which celebrated its thirtieth anniversary in 2022. In 2017, the Nord-Hålogaland Diocese Council requested that the CoN central office take on a greater national responsibility for Kven church life.[47] Additionally, the Bishop of Nord-Hålogaland has requested funding for a position at the Diocese office dedicated to Kven issues.[48] In response to the demands, the CoN central office has, since 2021, appointed a member to the Nord-Hålogaland Diocese Commission for Kven Church Life. Furthermore, in 2022, the CoN National Council decided to mandate a working group, which includes members from all three Kvens/Norwegian Finns organizations, to prepare for the establishment of a national body and diocesan bodies for Kven church life.[49]

The second issue revolved around the challenges encountered during the publication of a Kven psalm booklet by the CoN. There were negative reactions regarding the *proposed* decision in 2020—that was revised in a meeting—of not proceeding with the printing of the booklet.[50] A meeting held two months later reaffirmed its importance and emphasized the need for continuity in membership when establishing a committee with a new mandate. This committee was tasked with securing funding and creating a detailed plan for publishing a Kven psalm booklet.[51] Ultimately, the Kven Psalm booklet was launched on June 11, 2022.[52] It is worth noting that the regular CoN psalm book contains fifteen psalms in the Kven language.[53]

---

kirkeordning." For similar positions by its subsequent leaders, see Lanes, "Kirkerådet." For positions of some of the 21 bodies supporting the inclusion of Kvens in the CoN's overall structure, see Lanes, "Kirka."

47. Nord-Hålogaland Diocese Council, "Decision 28/17." The wording was: "Nord-Hålogaland bispedømmeråd mener det er et klart behov for sentralkirkelig ivaretakelse av Kvensk kirkeliv."

48. Lanes, "Biskopen."

49. CoN National Council, "Decision 75/22."

50. For the decision made, see Nord-Hålogaland Diocese Council, "Decision 37/20." For the proposed decision and the report from the Kven Psalms Committee, see Lanes, "Bispekontoret." The Norwegian Truth and Reconciliation Commission, "Sannhet og forsoning," 504 is incorrect in claiming that a decision was made that the Kven Psalm book project "should end"; this is not correct, as the Diocese Council made another decision than the proposal from the secretariat.

51. Nord-Hålogaland Diocese Council, "Decision 58/20."

52. *NRK*, "Kvensk salmehefte."; Nord-Hålogaland Diocese Office, "Ønsker du."

53. The register of Kven psalms is found at 1422 in the CoN Psalms book.

A third issue, although it has not caused similar tensions, is the absence of any parts of the Bible translated into Kven. However, CoN liturgical resources are available in the Kven language.[54]

In 2021, the largest Kven organization, Norske Kveners Forbund, called for a reconciliation process due to what was perceived as an inadequate implementation of the 2014 and 2018 decisions.[55] Hence, they are urging for more specific measures to be taken by the CoN.

There are four examples of recent recognition of Kvens, in addition to Sámi, that are relevant for the CoN. First, the larger trade union for priests has outlined specific strategies in its 2021–2024 plan, including: (i) Engaging in dialogue with Sámi and Kven church life; (ii) Focusing on the conditions for ministry in Sámi and Kven areas; (iii) Increasing the visibility of Sámi and Kven church life within the entire CoN; (iv) Emphasizing the role of priests in the Norwegianization processes in relation to the Norwegian TRC; and (v) Establishing a project group to implement these efforts.[56]

Second, the smaller trade union for priests has appointed a contact person for Kven church life,[57] who is acknowledged by the CoN.[58]

Third, a Christian education project centered on Sámi and Kven psalms is being developed through a partnership between VID Specialized University and a CoN congregation.[59] This project explicitly outlines its plans to expand implementation to neighboring municipalities. Furthermore, its goal is to create a booklet for use in Christian education. It is evident that this initiative complements the Kven Psalms project and has the potential to reach a broader Kven-speaking audience.

Fourth, a Study Plan in practical theology has seven references to Kven and Sámi church life and Christian education, treating them on an *equal* footing in the Norwegian context.[60] Although there are more references to the Sámi in the Study Plan, they primarily relate to a wider

54. Available in CoN, *Gudstjenestebok*, 283–86; see also Nord-Hålogaland Diocese Office, "Liturgiske ledd på kvensk." For recorded liturgical elements, see CoN, "Hyvvää."

55. Norske Kveners Forbund, "Ord over grind -Vil kirken komme kvenene i møte?" [Words over the gate—Will CoN meet the Kvens?]; available via Lanes, "Kirkerådet."

56. Presteforeningen, "Samisk og kvensk."

57. TeoLOgene, "Arne Skare."

58. CoN, "Hyvvää"; Skare was also one of the panelists at a panel on the Norwegian TRC at the biannual Theology Days, see CoN, "Program."

59. Nordreisa Municipal Church Council, "Prosjektsamarbeid."

60. VID Specialized University, "Programme Description."

geographical context, the diversity within the Sámi people, and existing liturgical sources and academic literature. While other study plans may lack explicit wording like this, the awareness demonstrated in the three previous examples suggests a growing recognition of these issues.

Therefore, although it may not be possible to meet the expectations of the Kvens/Norwegian Finns representatives entirely, there are significant new initiatives that deserve recognition.

FOSTERING RECONCILIATION BETWEEN THE KVENS/NORWEGIAN FINNS AND THE CoN: POSSIBLE STEPS AND PROGRESS

The Sámi and the Kvens/Norwegian Finns have both experienced colonization. As mentioned in the introductory section, four informants, all of whom are CoN leaders with specialized competence in Sámi issues, were contacted via email and responded in writing to four questions. It was made clear that the questions were not focused on Sámi–Kven/Norwegian Finn reconciliation but instead aimed to explore whether influential CoN leaders could provide "seeds" for *possible* CoN decisions involving communication by its highest body, the Synod.

In addition to the four questions, some background information was specified, including the trade unions' initiatives as mentioned above and certain efforts by CoN bodies addressing decolonization. However, it is important to note that as of early April 2022, I had no information about the processes within the CoN National Church Council. Nonetheless, I did obtain more specific information in early May 2022.[61] The four questions asked were: (i) "Aware of recent initiatives, do you want *additional* priority of and visibility for Kven church life in CoN?" (ii) "If yes, how could this best be achieved, specifically regarding new organizational solutions?" (iii) "If yes, do you consider that any form of cooperation, institutional or ad hoc, could be foreseen to jointly promote Sámi church life and Kven church life, by the Sámi Church Council and the Nord-Hålogaland Diocese?" and (iv) "If your response to Question 1 is no, please provide reasons for your answer."

---

61. The former (now retired) Deputy Director of CoN National Church Council, Gerd Karin Røsæg provided me with the information on the process leading to the CoN National Council, "Decision 75/22," on May 2, 2022.

The term 'reconciliation' was omitted from the questions. In addition to the importance of the questions being open, they sought to identify shared perceptions that could potentially serve as a basis for action by the CoN, acknowledging that reconciliation processes are complex and time-consuming.

Since all informants responded affirmatively to the first question, the last question is not relevant.

Two informants outlined strategies for increasing the visibility of Kven church life, which were contingent on input from the Kvens/Norwegian Finns. One informant emphasized the need for assistance from the CoN's central office. The proposed measures focused on the actual use of the Kven language in church life in regions with "roots and connection to the Kven." In these regions, the Bishop of Nord-Hålogaland has encouraged the use of Kven in services, similar to the use of Sámi. Specific initiatives mentioned included the Kven Psalm book, enhanced training for CoN staff, and a greater role taken on by the CoN's central office. One informant also noted that the initial outcomes of the Nord-Hålogaland Diocese assuming national responsibility have been positive for the church life of Kvens/Norwegian Finns within the CoN.

One informant pointed out that "placing responsibility with a staff person in CoN centrally" was identified as a positive step. This staff member is an ordinary member of the Nord-Hålogaland Diocese Commission for Kven Church Life, as specified above. Another informant suggested the establishment of a national *body* for Kven church life that reports to the CoN central office. Note that the non-specific term 'body' is used here to avoid implying a council on the same level as the SCC. This choice is made to acknowledge that the status of the Sámi as Indigenous peoples necessitates unique considerations, unlike those for national minorities.[62]

The SCC was noted for its expertise in "how to work with the wider community," and one informant emphasized that cooperation with the SCC was crucial for the success of increasing the visibility of Kven church life. Additionally, the organizations of the Kvens/Norwegian Finns and their cultural actors were generally regarded as relevant. Two informants highlighted ongoing dialogue in shaping Sámi–Kven cooperation.

This concise survey confirms that there are tangible measures and a willingness to take further steps in promoting Kven church life within

---

62. Lanes, "Kirkerådet," interviewed Kvens/Norwegian Finns who opposed this view. Similar positions as those expressed by the CoN Director have been conveyed to the author from other central persons in the CoN.

the CoN. The crucial role of the SCC in sharing experiences is acknowledged, and the proposal to establish a national body for Kven church life in the CoN, which was not endorsed by the CoN National Council Director in 2021,[63] will most likely be the outcome when deciding on recommendations in a report submitted in 2024.[64] This decision, along with the publication of the Kven Psalms booklet, increased visibility of Kven liturgical elements, and the initiatives of *Presteforeningen* (Clergy Association), represent measures that could provide important foundations for a potential process of reconciliation between the CoN and Kvens/Norwegian Finns.

CONCLUSION

The CoN has played a significant role in supporting the WCC's efforts concerning Indigenous peoples. The influential position of the SCC within the CoN's central structure has served as a model of influence for the WCC's broader work on indigenous issues. In this context, the CoN's engagement with the Kvens/Norwegian Finns, who inhabit regions overlapping with those of the North Sámi, is noteworthy.

It is evident that while the (North) Sámi and the Kvens/Norwegian Finns have different formal statuses in Norway, a distinction supported by historical and factual arguments, the CoN is demonstrating a growing commitment to promoting Kven church life. The TRC's report should serve as a catalyst for the CoN to introduce new initiatives concerning the church life of both the Sámi and the Kvens/Norwegian Finns.

The history of the Kven language within the CoN has been marked by unfulfilled promises. Meeting the full expectations of the Kvens/Norwegian Finns may prove challenging, and many have expressed their disappointment with CoN processes and decisions. However, recent developments within the CoN and actions taken by other stakeholders provide a foundation for future collaborative efforts.

---

63. Lanes, "Kirkerådet."

64. CoN Working Group, «Utredning og innstilling» (currently on hearing; a majority proposes that two members shall be appointed by the largest Kven organisation and the two smaller organisations appoint one member each; a minority proposes that each Kven/Norwegian Finns organisation appoints one member each).

BIBLIOGRAPHY

Andresen, Astri et al. *Samenes historie fra 1751 til 2010* [The History of the Sámi 1751–2010]. Oslo: Cappelen Damm, 2021.

Bergman, Ingela. *Kulturarv, landskap och identitetsprocesser i Norra Fennoskandien 500–1500 e.Kr. Slutrapport från ett forskningsprogram* [Cultural Heritage, Landscapes and Identity Processes in Northern Fennoscandia 500–1500 AD]. Gothenburg: Makadam, 2018.

CCN. "Andre publikasjoner." https://norgeskristnerad.no/andre-publikasjoner.

Christian V. "Chr. Vs Norske Lov." https://www.hf.uio.no/iakh/tjenester/kunnskap/samlinger/tingbok/lover-reskripter/chr5web/chr5_03_22.html/.

Codex Flatöiensis. "Fundinn Nóregr." http://www.heimskringla.no/wiki/Norge_blir_funnet.

CoN. Den norske kirkes arbeid med migrasjon, asylpolitikk og solidaritet med mennesker på flukt [CoN's Work on Migration, Asylum Policy and Solidarity with Refugees]. Oslo: CoN, 2021.

———. *Gudstjenestebok for Den norske kirke. Hovedgudstjeneste*. Bergen: Eide, 2020.

———. "Hyvvää kvääninkansan päivä!—Gratulerer med kvenfolkets dag!" [Congratulations on the Kven Peoples' Day!]. https://kirken.no/nb-NO/om-kirken/for-medarbeidere/nyheter/nyhetsartikler/kvenfolkets-dag/?fbclid=IwAR3vUuAFEg67diakwpbS8IVd46Gyk7ak9oyuMUIcgjj7GhZ1m8T2hT7-z5I.

———. "Kirken oppretter råd for personer med funksjonsnedsettelse" [CoN Establishes Council for Persons with Disabilities]. https://www.kirken.no/nb-NO/om-kirken/aktuelt/kirken%20oppretter%20r%C3%A5d%20for%20personer%20med%20funksjonsnedsettelse.

———. "KM 07/18, Visjonsdokument 2019–2022."

———. "KM 07/14, Visjonsdokument 2015–2018."

———. "KM 08/11, Strategic Plan for Sámi Church Life." https://www.kirken.no/globalassets/kirken.no/samisk-kirkeliv/dokumenter/samisk-strategiplan/strategiplan_samisk_krkliv_engelsk.pdf

———. "KM 13/97, Indigenous Peoples in the Worldwide Church Based on Sámi Church Life." https://kirken.no/globalassets/kirken.no/migrering/km_1997_sak_13_vedtak.pdf.

———. "KM 14/19, Strategic Plan for Sámi Church Life." https://kirken.no/globalassets/kirken.no/samisk-kirkeliv/dokumenter/strategiplan%202019-2028/strategiplan%20for%20samisk%20kirkeliv%202019-2027_bokm%C3%A5l.pdf.

———. National Council. "Decision 75/22: Kvensk kirkeliv." https://kirken.no/nb-NO/om-kirken/slik-styres-kirken/kirkeradet/saksdokumenter-og-vedtak/september-2022

———. "Program for Teologidagene 2022." https://kirken.no/nb-NO/om-kirken/slik-styres-kirken/bispemotet/prestetjeneste/om-teologidagene-2018/teologidagene%202022/program%20teologidagene%202021.

Council of Europe. Framework Convention for the Protection of National Minorities and Explanatory Report. https://rm.coe.int/16800c1ocf

CoN Working Group, «Utredning og innstilling fra Arbeidsgruppe med mandat til å fremme forslag til Kirkerådet om oppgaver og sammensetning av et nasjonalt organ for kvensk kirkeliv (Kirkerådssak 75/22)» [Assessment and recommendations from the Working Group with a mandate to submit proposals to the Church

Council regarding the tasks and composition of a national body for Kven church life] (available from the author), 2024.

Dervo, Ivar. "Ivar Dervos brev." https://kvenfinn.no/ivar-dervos-apne-brev-til-sannhets-og-forsoningskommisjonen-for-samer-og-kvener.

Eriksen, Knut E., and Einar Niemi. *Den finske fare. Sikkerhetsproblemer og minoritetspolitikk i nord 1860–1940* [The Finnish Danger. Security Problems and Minority Policy in the North 1860–1940]. Oslo: Universitetsforlaget, 1981.

Guttormsen, Helge. "Spor etter eldre kvensk bosetting i Nord-Troms og Finnmark." In *Kvenenes historie og kultur: Seminarrapport,* edited by Helge Guttormsen, 13–34. Storslett: Nord-Troms Historielag, 1998.

Hansen, Lars I. and Bjørnar Olsen. *Samenes historie fram til 1750* [The History of the Sámi until 1750]. 2nd ed. Oslo: Cappelen Damm, 2022.

Haugen, Hans M. "Any Role for Human Rights in the Norwegian Truth and Reconciliation Commission Addressing Forced Assimilation?" *International Journal of Minority and Group Rights* 29 (2022) 205–29.

———. "Den vanskelige forsoningen: Den norske kirke, Kirkens Sosialtjeneste og romanifolket/taterne" [The Challenging Reconciliation: The Church of Norway, Kirkens Sosialtjeneste and the Norwegian Romani/tater]. *Teologisk Tidsskrift* 6 (2017) 242–61.

Johnsen, Tore. "Acknowledged History and Renewed Relationships. Perspectives on Reconciliation Work between the Church and the Sami People." In *The Sami and the Church of Sweden. Results from a White Paper Project,* edited by Daniel Lindmark and Olle Sundström, 97–124. Möklinta: Gidlunds förlag, 2018.

———. *Jordens barn, solens barn, vindens barn: kristen tro i et samisk landskap* [Children of the Earth, Children of the Sun, Children of the Wind: Christian Faith in a Sámi Landscape]. Oslo: Verbum, 2007.

Kalberg, Torbjørn. "Svenskehandelen som tok slutt" [The Swedish Trade that Ended]. *Heimen* 54 (2017) 43–61.

Lanes, Laila. "Biskopen om kvensk-kritikk: Vi har mye å gjøre og lære" [The Bishop on Kven Criticism: We Have a lot to Do and Learn]. NRK, 2020.

———. "Bispekontoret beskyldt for å være "fornorskere"" [The Diocese Office Accused of "Norwegianization"]. NRK, 2020.

———. "Kirka tar ikke kvenene inn i ny kirkeordning" [CoN Does Not Include the Kven in New Church Structure for CoN]. NRK, 2019.

———. "Kirkerådet vil ha dialog, men ikke om et kvensk kirkeråd" [The National Church Council Wants Dialogue, But Not About a Kven Church Council]. NRK, 2021.

Listhaug, Sylvi. *Der andre tier* [Where Others Stay Quiet]. Oslo: Kagge, 2018.

Lund, Svein. "Folkehøgskolen og samane" [The Folk High School and the Sámi People]. http://skuvla.info/skolehist/fhs-n.htm.

Magga, Ole H. "Samene og den flerkulturelle kirke," quoted on 3 in Tore Johnsen. "Samisk kirkeråd. Et historisk tilbakeblikk og veien framover." https://www.kirken.no/globalassets/kirken.no/samisk-kirkeliv/dokumenter/samisk_kirkeraad_tilbakeblikk_2012_johnsen.pdf/.

Maliniemi, Kaisa J. *Arkivdokumentene forteller. To kommuner—to typer minoritetspolitikk, ABM Skrift 65* [Archive Documents. Two Municipalities—Two Types of Minority Policy]. Oslo: ABM Utvikling, 2010.

Niemi, Einar. "Johan Beronka." *Store norske leksikon.* https://nbl.snl.no/Johan_Beronka.

———. "Kvenene og staten—et historisk riss." In *Rapport fra seminaret Kvenene—en glemt minoritet?*, edited by Anne Torekoven Strøm, 13–29. Tromsø: Universitetet i Tromsø/Tromsø museum, 1994.

Niemi, Einar and Anne Julie Semb. "Forskningsetisk kontekst: Historisk urett og forskning som overgrep." https://www.forskningsetikk.no/ressurser/fbib/bestemte-grupper/samisk-forskning-historisk-urett-og-forskning-som-overgrep/.

Nord-Hålogaland Diocese Commission for Kven Church Life. "Ny kirkeordning for Den norske kirke. Høringsinnspill fra medlemmene i Utvalg for kvensk kirkeliv." [Response to New Church Structure for CoN]. https://kirken.no/globalassets/kirken.no/om-kirken/slik-styres-kirken/kirkeradet/2018/horinger-i-kirkeradets-regi/horingssvar—-kirkeordning/org-utvalg-for-kvensk-kirkeliv.pdf.

Nord-Hålogaland Diocese Council. "Decision 28/17: Kvensk kirkeliv" [Kven Church Life]. https://kirken.no/globalassets/bispedommer/nord-halogaland/dokumenter/bispedommeradet/f%C3%B8r%202020/protokoll—-mote-i-nord-halogaland-bispedommerad-11-12.05.2017.pdf/.

———. "Decision 37/20: Kvensk salmeprosjekt—sluttrapport" [Kven Psalms Project—Final Report]. https://kirken.no/globalassets/bispedommer/nord-halogaland/dokumenter/bispedommeradet/protokoll%20nord-h%C3%A5logaland%20bisped%C3%B8mmer%C3%A5d%2022.04.2020.pdf/.

———. "Decision 58/20: Kvensk salmeprosjekt." https://kirken.no/globalassets/bispedommer/nord-halogaland/dokumenter/bispedommeradet/protokoll%20fra%20m%C3%B8te%2019.06.2020.pdf/.

Nord-Hålogaland Diocese Office. "Liturgiske ledd på kvensk" [Liturgical elements in Kven]. https://kirken.no/nb-NO/bispedommer/nord-haalogaland/tema/kvensk-kirkeliv/liturgiske%20ledd.

———. "Ønsker du å kjøpe Kväänin virsihäfti?" [Do you want to purchase the Kven Psalm booklet?]. https://kirken.no/nb-NO/bispedommer/nord-haalogaland/aktuelt/kvensk%20salmehefte2.

Nordreisa Municipal Church Council. "Prosjektsamarbeid om sangressurser for kvensk og samisk trosopplæring." https://nordreisasokn.no/Artikler/Artikkeldetaljer/ArticleId/89/Prosjektsamarbeid-om-sangressurser-for-kvensk-og-samisk-trosoppl-230-ring/.

Norske Kveners Forbund. "Kvensk satsing i Den Norske Kirke." https://kvener.no/2015/05/kvensk-satsing-i-den-norske-kirke.

Norske Kveners Forbund, "Ord over grind -Vil kirken komme kvenene i møte?" https://kvener.no/2021/02/forbundet-sendte-et-apent-brev-til-kirkeradet/.

Norwegian Government. "Procedures for Consultations Between State Authorities and the Sami Parliament [Norway]." https://www.regjeringen.no/en/topics/indigenous-peoples-and-minorities/Sami-people/midtspalte/PROCEDURES-FOR-CONSULTATIONS-BETWEEN-STA/id450743/.

———. "White Paper 12 (2020–2021) National Minorities in Norway—A comprehensive policy (2020)." https://www.regjeringen.no/en/dokumenter/white-paper-no.-12-20202021/id2814676/.

Norwegian Supreme Court. "Selbu judgement" [Plenary], Rt. 2001 s. 769.

NOU 2015:7, Assimilering og motstand—Norsk politikk overfor taterne/romanifolket fra 1850 til i dag. Via: https://www.regjeringen.no/no/dokumenter/nou-2015-7/id2414316

[for an English short version, see https://www.regjeringen.no/contentassets/7fc9dff997e34dafba07fa095ef632dc/nou-2015_7_summary.pdf/].
NRK. "Kvenenes historie kjapt forklart." https://www.nrk.no/video/kvenenes-historie-kjapt-forklart_fa3396ba-5b48-4372-86c5-90e0f41cf31a/.
———. "Kvensk salmehefte lanseres endelig" [Kven Psalms Booklet Finally Launched]. https://www.nrk.no/tromsogfinnmark/kvensk-salmehefte-lanseres-endelig-1.15985539.
NTB. "Listhaug:—Kirken er gjennomsyret sosialistisk" [Church of Norway is Infused With Socialism]. *NRK*, 2015.
Presteforeningen. "Samisk og kvensk kirkeliv" [Sámi and Kven Church Life; Part of Overall Work Plan 2021–2024]. https://www.prest.no/seksjon/samisk-og-kvensk-kirkeliv/.
Räisänen, Anna K., and Niina Kunnas. *The Kven Language: An Overview of a Language in Context. Working, Papers in European Language Diversity 15*. Mainz: European Language Diversity for All, 2012. https://phaidra.univie.ac.at/open/o:105485/.
Seppola, Bjørnar. "E-post fra Kvenlandsforbundet v/leder Bjørn Seppola vedrørende kommisjon om fornorskingspolitikk og urett begått mot det samiske og kvenske folk i Norge. Høringsuttalelse fra Kvenlandsforbundet, datert 30. april 2018" [E-mail Regarding Commission on Norwegianization Policy and Injustice Committed Against the Sámi and Kven People in Norway], 13–25, in "Innst. 408 S (2017–2018) Innstilling til Stortinget fra Stortingets presidentskap."
TeoLOgene, "Arne Skare. Kontakt og ressursperson teoLOgene på Kvensk kirkeliv." https://www.fagforbundet.no/a/361982/yrke/teologene/aktuelt/arne-skare.-kontakt-og-ressursperson-teologene-kvensk-kirkeliv/?fbclid=IwAR2mrchL8J-bU7_Op77fUuDeApoB2lhTgV3TY3cUqQeCYJ6envxks30J148/.
Thorpe, Benjamin. "King Alfred's Anglo-Saxon Version of the History of Paulus Orosius." In *The Life and Works of King Alfred,* trans. Benjamin Thorpe. London: Bell, 1902.
Truth and Reconciliation Commission in Norway. "Sannhet og forsoning—grunnlag for et oppgjør med fornorskingspolitikk og urett mot samer, kvener/norskfinner og skogfinner. Rapport til Stortinget fra Sannhets- og forsoningskommisjonen, Dokument 19 (2022–2023)." [Truth and Reconciliation—Basis for a Settlement with Norwegianization Policies and Injustice against Sami, Kvens/Norwegian Finns and Skog Finns].
United Nations General Assembly. "A/RES/61/295, Annex, United Nations Declaration on the Rights of Indigenous Peoples."
United Nations Special Rapporteur of the Sub-Commission on the Promotion and Protection of Human Rights, Jose Martinez Cobo. "E/CN.4/Sub.2/1986/7 Add.1–4. Study of the Problem of Discrimination against Indigenous Populations."
United Nations Working Group on Minorities. "E/CN.4/Sub.2/1996. Report of the Working Group on Minorities on its first session."
Vahtola, Jouko. "Birkarlaproblemet" [The Birkarl Problem]. *Studia Historica Septentrionalia* 14 (1987) 328–37.
VID Specialized University. "Programme Description for Studies in Practical Theology 1, KUN 30 ECTS." https://www.vid.no/site/assets/files/15369/studieplan-for-praktisk-teologisk-utdanning-for-prester-vid-1.pdf?3ry024/.

3

Untangling the Gordian Knot
Recognition of Indigenous Minorities in the Context of Truth and Reconciliation in Norway and Peru

ANNE MARGRETHE SØNNELAND
AND CAROLA LINGAAS
Faculty of Social Studies, VID Specialized University, Oslo, Norway

INTRODUCTION

The recent political crisis and protests in Peru show that the report of a Truth and Reconciliation Commission (TRC) alone does not provide reconciliation. Peru's TRC submitted its report in 2003, after a twenty-year period of internal armed conflict and authoritarian rule. While the reality and the crimes addressed in the report of the Peruvian commission are very different from those addressed by the Norwegian TRC, several insights may prove useful: Firstly, for the report to become a common understanding of the past, there is a need for a process following the publication of a report by a TRC. Second, truth in itself is important, but not sufficient, for any kind of reconciliation. In this chapter, we argue that in processes where the truth addressed is linked to processes of discrimination and assimilation policies, the aspect of marginalization in a wide sense of the term must be given particular attention. We also assert that in contexts where the population targeted has been (and is) considered less than human, truth commissions (TCs) may raise expectations of being recognized as equal partners in social interactions[1] and as persons who matter,[2] primarily as citizens of the state. One aspect of such recognition is related to the use of land and water, which we will discuss from a Norwegian perspective.

In Norway, the focus of the currently ongoing reconciliation process has mainly been on the assimilation policies themselves and on the cultural and linguistic consequences of these policies.[3] One of the tasks in the TRC's mandate is the investigation of "the consequences of Norwegianization up until the present day" for the Sámi, Kvens, and Forest Finns.[4] The commission interpreted this task to include the examination of the

> repercussions of the Norwegian policy today, predominantly connected to the Sámi and Kven/Finnish language and culture in today's society, as well as any material, social, health-related or identity-related impacts of the Norwegianization policy, both for groups as a whole and for individuals. The commission shall further investigate the repercussions of Norwegianization in society in forms such as hate crimes and discrimination.[5]

This chapter claims that we should place a particular emphasis on historic and contemporary forms of marginalization that emanate as a direct consequence of the assimilation policies themselves. We underscore the need for increased focus and research on the socio-economic, political, social, and legal marginalization of the victims of assimilation policies. As argued elsewhere, we highlight the pivotal role of the majority population's engagement in fostering substantive discussions on reconciliation and marginalization.[6]

The term 'Gordian Knot' is a proverbial expression used to describe an intricate and complex problem that can only be solved through bold and decisive action. According to the story, the knot was so difficult to untangle that it ultimately had to be cut. In this chapter, we use this

1. Fraser, "On Justice," 41–51.
2. Sennett, *Respect.* 2003
3. Vars, "Samene i Norge."
4. Truth and Reconciliation Commission Concerning the Sámi People, Mandate."
5. Truth and Reconciliation Commission, "Mandate," 2–5.
6. Sønneland and Lingaas, "Righting Injustices towards the Sámi."

metaphor as an image of the challenges faced by societies that are dealing with and trying to overcome conflicts, assimilation, and marginalization. The chapter provides comparative aspects of and insights into the reconciliation processes in Norway and Peru. It argues that the untangling of the difficult societal problems that originate in situations of colonial and post-colonial domination requires perspectives 'outside of the box.' The work, efforts, and reports of the TRCs of Norway and Peru cannot be expected to solve all problems. Instead, to achieve success, these reports should be viewed as just one steppingstone on a much longer path toward reconciliation. In this context, the process of reconciliation is the proverbial Gordian Knot that requires broader and bolder approaches, including genuine recognition of Indigenous groups. The chapter adopts a mixed sociological and legal approach to reconciliation in Peru and Norway, with a particular focus on the situation of the Sámi Indigenous people in Norway.

DEALING WITH A HISTORY OF MISRECOGNITION

The TRCs in Norway and Peru address histories of misrecognition and the imperative need to recognize the segments of the population that have endured past wrongs. Axel Honneth distinguishes between three kinds of misrecognition or disrespect, namely:[7] (i) Maltreatment, which involves forcibly depriving a person of any opportunity to have control over their own body. (ii) Legal misrecognition, which is related to structural exclusion from the possession of certain rights within a society. Legal recognition, on the other hand, implies that an individual is entitled to rights and is recognized as a member of a collective. In this context, 'rights' refers to the individual claims that a person, as a participant in the institutional order of a community, can legitimately expect to have fulfilled socially. The denial of such rights signifies that a person is not accorded the same degree of moral responsibility as other members of society. (iii) Evaluative disrespect involves the denigration of individual or collective ways of life. When the hierarchy of values is structured in a manner that devalues individual or collective forms of life and belief systems as inferior or deficient, the individuals in question will be unable to attribute social value to their own abilities.

---

7. Honneth, *The Struggle for Recognition*.

According to Nancy Fraser, the status of individual group members as full partners in social interaction is contingent on their recognition.[8] Therefore, misrecognition means subordination in the sense of being prevented from participating as a peer in social life. When certain actors are characterized as inferior, excluded, considered 'other,' or made invisible, it results in misrecognition and status subordination. Being misrecognized is not only to be thought ill of or looked down upon; it means being denied the status of a full partner in social interactions due to institutionalized patterns that depict a person as comparatively unworthy of respect or esteem. Misrecognition can be formal, such as being institutionalized in government policies, administrative codes, or professional practice. It can also manifest informally. Regardless of its form, wherever misrecognition occurs, there is a need for recognition.[9] Redressing injustices requires policies of recognition that are specifically designed to overcome subordination and (re)establish those who have been misrecognized as full members of society, enabling them to participate on equal terms with others.[10] Since the injustices faced by subaltern collectivities tend to be both of a socio-economic and cultural-symbolic nature, there is a need for programs that address both redistribution and recognition.[11]

YOU WILL KNOW THE TRUTH, AND THE TRUTH WILL SET YOU FREE?

TCs seek to transform societies and deter future human rights violations.[12] By entering a contentious space where multiple narratives dominate, they have the potential to construct a complex truth and challenge the myths that aggressors or perpetrators have successfully established.[13] This section discusses the aims, components, and types of TRCs.

TCs can be broadly categorized into two types: The traditional version is established after the transition to democracy from a period of authoritarian rule or armed conflict. These commissions explore and

8. Fraser, "Rethinking Recognition," 107–20.
9. Fraser, "Rethinking Recognition," 107–20.
10. Fraser, "Rethinking Recognition," 107–20.
11. Fraser, *Justice Interruptus*; Woolford, "Negotiating Affirmative Repair," 111–44.
12. Wiebelhaus-Brahm et al., "Examining Compliance, 4.
13. Langer, "Conclusions," 229.

address violations committed by the previous regime. For example, the Peruvian TRC falls into this category. It documented violations that occurred during the internal armed conflict in the 1980s and early 1990s, as well as during the authoritarian regime of Alberto Fujimori in the 2000s. The commission's report includes chapters that provide a chronological overview of the violence, identify individual and collective victims, and ascertain the group membership of the perpetrators. Additionally, it delves into the root causes of the internal armed conflict.[14] The Norwegian TRC does not fall into the same category as the Peruvian TRC. Instead, it belongs to a newer group of TCs that have been established without a preceding change of regime, operating within the context of a settler democracy with a history of racism.[15] In this regard, the Norwegian TRC belongs to the same group as the Canadian and the Greenlandic TRCs, all of which focus on addressing harms committed against Indigenous peoples, often through welfare or educational systems.

Priscilla Hayner outlines five essential characteristics that must be present for an entity to be considered a TC: (1) TCs are temporary bodies; (2) their aim is the publication of a report; (3) they are authorized by the very state that is the subject of the investigation; (4) they search for patterns rather than single events; and (5) they actively engage with individuals who were targeted or affected by the actions of state authorities, collecting information about their experiences.[16]

The Peruvian TRC fulfills all these aspects:[17] (1) It was temporary (from 2001–2003); (2) it published an 8,000-page report in August 2003; (3) it was initiated by the interim president Valentin Paniagua in 2000 and inaugurated in 2001, after President-elect Alejandro Toledo took office; (4) its mandate was to analyze why the violence occurred, determine the scale of victimization, assess responsibility, propose reparations, and recommend preventative reforms. The Peruvian TRC also fulfills the fifth requirement: (5) it collected nearly 17,000 testimonies and held twenty-seven public hearings, featuring testimonies from 422 Peruvians regarding 318 separate allegations of human rights abuses.[18]

By comparison, the Norwegian TRC was also a temporary body (2018–2023); it had the objective of producing and publishing a

14. CVR: *Informe Final*.
15. Skaar, "When Truth Commission Models Travel."
16. Hayner, *Unspeakable Truths*.
17. CVR, *Informe Final*.
18. Heilman, "Truth and Reconciliation Commission."

comprehensive report, which was completed and released in June 2023; and it was established by the Norwegian Parliament, not the government, and examined the individual and collective consequences of the Norwegian authorities' policy and activities towards the Sámi, Kvens, and Forest Finns. Furthermore, similar to the Peruvian TRC, the Norwegian TRC organized thirty-seven open meetings and so-called coffee meetings, participated in 156 different events and meetings across the country, and collected more than 650 testimonies.[19]

TCs have several aims. They originate from the idea that victims need to know the truth about what has happened, but also that the society at large must be aware of former harms and violations in order to continue as a society.[20] In several Latin American countries, TRCs were considered necessary to expose the hidden truth, since the systems of abuse, including forced disappearances, in these countries had been designed to hide the facts.[21] In other countries where TRCs were considered or established, there was no hidden truth but rather multiple, contesting, and conflicting 'truths,' often connected to and propagated by an ethnic and/or national group.[22] The cases of Bosnia and Herzegovina and Serbia exemplify such instances.

After a TC has issued a report, it is difficult to deny systematic violations of human rights.[23] In contrast to cases in Latin America or Bosnia where TRCs were established to urgently uncover the truth about relatively recent events, in Norway, historical facts—the 'truth'—are to a significant extent already well-established and widely recognized.[24] Nevertheless, Láilá Susanne Vars argues that most state abuses remains undocumented, highlighting an ongoing need for further documentation.[25] In the case of injustices against the Sámi, the TRCs of Norway,

19. Høybråten, "Kommisjonslederens julehilsen"; Muotka, "Sametingspresidentens Nyttårstale."

20. Aldana, "A Victim Centred Reflection"; Hayner, *Unspeakable Truths*; Klikner and Davis, *The Right to Truth*.

21. Kritz and Finci, "A Truth and Reconciliation Commission in Bosnia," 50.

22. Kritz and Finci, "A Truth and Reconciliation Commission in Bosnia," 50. Clark, "Does Bosnia Need a Truth and Reconciliation Commission?," 225–46; Dragovic-Soso, "History of a Failure," 292–310.

23. Ignatieff, "Articles of Faith."

24. See, for example, the recent two-volume publications: Hansen and Olsen, *Samenes historie fram til 1750*; Andresen, Evjen, and Ryymin, *Samenes historie fra 1751 til 2010*.

25. Vars, "Samene i Norge," 178.

Sweden, and Finland share a common aim to spread knowledge about and raise awareness of Sámi history, and how historical abuses continue to affect the Sámi today.[26] The Norwegian TRC considers its most important task to "research and describe the policy and activities carried out by the Norwegian authorities against the Sámi (. . .) from around 1800 until today."[27] Despite Dagfinn Høybråten, the leader of the Norwegian TRC, emphasizing in his end-of-year speech that the commission works "to bring out the real truth," asserting that "the truth will set you free,"[28] and Vars highlighting the need for documentation, the Norwegian TRC does not arise from the same sense of urgency in finding the truth.

HEARING THE VOICE OF THE VICTIMS

There are some possible advantages of TCs over trials and other truth-finding mechanisms. The first point relates to listening to those who are often not heard. TCs mainly listen to victims, thereby giving a voice to those who have suffered harm.[29] Unlike courtroom testimonies, individuals who share their stories with a TRC can speak in their own words and emphasize what they consider important. The majority of TRC testimonies occur privately, and even in cases of public hearings,[30] TRCs do not adhere to the same level of formalism and protocol as courts. Additionally, the narrators are not subjected to harsh questioning or have their credibility questioned.[31]

TRCs offer victims a platform to share their stories, even without public hearings. This provides individuals who have experienced injustices, and who are often excluded or marginalized, with an opportunity to be recognized by the state as citizens and equal rights holders.[32] By listening to the victims, TRCs have the potential to challenge the discourse

---

26. Järvensivu, Pohjola, and Romakkaniemi, "Locating Sámi Social Work in Finland," 600–13.

27. Truth and Reconciliation Commission Concerning the Sámi People, "Mandate."

28. Høybråten, "Kommisjonsleder Dagfinn."

29. Langer, "Conclusions," 229.

30. Office of the United Nations High Commissioner for Human Rights, "Rule-of-Law Tools."

31. See Herman, 'The Mental Health."

32. Stephen, 'Testimony and Human Rights Violations," 52–58; de Greiff, "Truth without Facts?," 282.

of the aggressors or perpetrators,[33] and new understandings of the past can be negotiated.[34] Such a new understanding of the past is currently underway in Norway, as the leader of the Norwegian TRC suggests that new insights are challenging the image of Norway as a democracy with a strong human rights record.[35]

It is often assumed that testifying in TCs has positive or healing effects for victims. However, experiences with testifying in TCs vary. In earlier TRCs, most victims felt respected and recognized; their experiences and narratives were valued. At the same time, many reported mental health problems after testifying, and others expressed a wish for the perpetrators to take responsibility for their crimes or for justice through trials.[36] The strain of testifying is implicitly acknowledged in the Norwegian and the recently established Finnish TRC. In Norway, two-and-a-half positions are dedicated to support for persons who testify before the TRC.[37] The Finnish TRC has allocated special funds for psychosocial support for victims testifying before the commission. Its mandate explicitly states that psychosocial support must be an integral part of the process.[38] Thus, while TCs provide a platform for victims to tell their stories and be heard by state representatives, it is a space that comes with a request or an expectation to share painful stories. It thereby places responsibility with those who have been victimized. A participant in a meeting in Troms (Norway) aptly describes the courage required from those who testify: "You won't get anywhere if you don't dare, there are some bad things you have to dare to talk about — and that's part of reconciliation."[39]

EXPECTATIONS OF TRCs

The work and reports of TRCs come with inherent expectations. When individuals who have suffered human rights violations provide their

---

33. Langer, "Conclusions," 229.
34. Burchianti, "Building Bridges of Memory."
35. Høybråten, "Kommisjonsleder Dagfinn."
36. Doak, "Therapeutic Dimension"; Backer, "The Human Face"; Espinoza Cuevas, Ortiz Rojas, and Rojas Baeza, *Comisiones de La Verdad*; Hamber, Nageng, and O'Malley, "Telling It like It Is. . ."; Hayner, *Unspeakable Truths*.
37. Sannhets- og forsoningskommisjonen, "Krise- og støttesamtaler."
38. Truth and Reconciliation Commission Concerning the Sámi People, "Mandate," Section 3.5.
39. Høybråten, "Kommisjonsleder Dagfinn."

testimony, they may expect something in return. In the case of the Peruvian TRC, for instance, there were expectations of economic reparations, especially among the rural, impoverished population who had been victims of violence.[40] However, the reparation policies that were implemented failed to meet these expectations and fell short of the expectations of being treated as respected citizens. The victims were not involved in the design of the reparation schemes, and the individual economic reparations were so meager that many perceived them as yet another form of disrespect.[41]

TRCs often put forth recommendations, and the Norwegian TRC is no different in this regard. Such recommendations can include legal reforms, reparations to victims, memorials, or the prosecution of perpetrators. The recommendations will inevitably raise expectations, both for increased knowledge about the wrongs committed in society at large[42] and for measures like reparations.[43] Still, recommendations by TRCs encounter numerous impediments.[44] In a study of Latin American TRCs, Wiebelhaus-Braun and colleagues found that the fewer recommendations a TRC makes, the higher the chance of their implementation.[45] As TRCs by nature are temporary and follow-up mechanisms are not necessarily put in place, the transformative character is often limited and dependent on political goodwill.[46] Even when there is ample political will, there may not always be sufficient institutional capacity or funding to fully implement all of a TRC's recommendations.[47] Despite these difficulties, the official recognition of a TRC's mandate, work, report, and recommendations by a country's executive and legislative branches represents a significant step on the path toward long-term reconciliation. If official state institutions do not engage in discussions about the findings of a report, it becomes easier for violators to perpetuate their discourse without hindrance. Consequently, both public and official debates about the findings of TRCs are of paramount importance.

40. Laplante and Theidon, "Truth with Consequences."
41. Sønneland, "These Trials Are Not Easy," 342–57.
42. Sametinget, "Sametingets innspill."
43. Laplante and Theidon, "Truth with Consequences."
44. Wiebelhaus-Brahm et al., "Examining Compliance."
45. Wiebelhaus-Brahm et al., "Examining Compliance," 5.
46. Langer, "Conclusions."
47. Office of the United Nations High Commissioner for Human Rights, "Truth Commissions," 36.

TCs can also generate broader expectations of change, especially with regards to diminishing the stigma linked to victimhood resulting from state-inflicted harm or violence, recognizing victims as individuals of significance and as citizens with equal worth and rights, or ushering in more profound societal transformations. These expectations are considerably more challenging to fulfill and measure than simply publishing a TRC report. Both the Norwegian and the Peruvian TRCs address questions of marginalization and recognition, which are topics that require more extensive structural measures than a TRC alone is able to address, let alone improve or repair. On a general level, such expectations have a long-term perspective, since they involve multi-generational improvements of living conditions, including access to health care, jobs, education, and infrastructure, as well as participation and equal opportunities to be heard in the same manner as other citizens. In other words, there may be an expectation of recognition, following Fraser's definition of the term. In sum, TCs may raise expectations of remedies for the injustices experienced. When important aspects of TRCs are linked to discrimination and marginalization, wider and more fundamental changes might be anticipated.

ENDING MARGINALIZATION THROUGH TRUTH?

Much can be said about the political crisis in Peru from December 2022, a conflict related both to deep structural injustices in Peruvian society as well as to a dysfunctional political system. This section will focus on some aspects that can be linked to the TRC and its report, emphasizing the significance of complementing TCs with programs aimed at recognition. The Peruvian TRC conducted remarkable work in its pursuit of truth. In a mere two years, it compiled a 12-volume report detailing the perpetrated violations, identifying the victims, estimating the number of casualties, disappearances, and various forms of violence, and pinpointing the armed forces, police, and multiple armed groups responsible for these acts. The TRC's report underscored the ongoing marginalization of Indigenous populations and the unequal distribution of wealth, political influence, and symbolical power. It also highlighted that the impact of the violence differed across regions and groups, with the majority of those killed or disappeared living in impoverished conditions and having

Quechua as their first language.[48] Despite the efforts of the commission, the report continues to be contested: it is not accepted as 'truth' by the society at large.[49] Even though the report clearly identified the victims of state violence, there is still a stigma with being a victim.[50]

The Peruvian state and the upper and middle classes in Lima have long disregarded the existence of marginalized and subordinated Indigenous populations.[51] They have exhibited evaluative disrespect towards these groups, characterized by the denigration of their collective ways of life.[52] In essence, life in the Andes appears to be assigned less value, and the sentiment prevails that "there is no justice for the poor."[53] These feelings of depreciation permeate the reconciliation process: the pain of being ignored and of having one's worth diminished persists if one's very existence is not acknowledged. This symbolic devaluation is seen as a lack of respect and a form of misrecognition.[54]

There are significant differences between the harms that require remedy, the mandates, and the contexts addressed by the Peruvian and Norwegian TRCs. One notable distinction is the considerably more violent treatment and more brutal marginalization experienced by the Indigenous population in Peru. However, a commonality is their examination of the effects and consequences stemming from the portrayal of certain groups as inferior, resulting in marginalization at individual, group, and societal levels. In both countries, the Indigenous population was perceived as 'others' of lesser worth. Aguiar and Halseth describe a

> [d]eep shame that is felt by many Aboriginal people is rooted first and foremost in the processes of colonialism, which denigrated Aboriginal culture and values leaving many with a poor sense of self-worth. The effects of this are acutely felt by individuals, families, communities and nations, and play out through all facets of life.[55]

48. CVR, *Hatun Willakuy*, 14, 22–23, 337.
49. García-Godos and Reátegui, "Peru."
50. Sønneland, "'These Trials Are Not Easy.'"
51. García-Godos and Reátegui, "Peru."
52. Honneth, *Disrespect*; Honneth, *The Struggle for Recognition*.
53. Sønneland, "'These Trials Are Not Easy.'"
54. Haldemann, "Another Kind of Justice," 692.
55. Aguiar and Halseth, *Aboriginal Peoples*, 25.

Descendants of individuals who endured the harsh Norwegianization policies can attest to the shame and denial of their Sámi heritage and culture. This enduring shame, often handed down from one generation to the next, is what Minde refers to as the "Sámi pain."[56] Until recently, many considered it shameful to be Sámi-speaking.[57] TCs established in contexts of denigration of collective ways of life must confront and address these feelings of shame.

The marginalization remains apparent: in Norway and Peru, indigenous languages and cultures remain depreciated.[58] In Peru, there is a higher level of poverty among the Indigenous population.[59] In both countries, there are conflicts over land and water that originate in historical legislation and/or jurisprudence on ownership and citizenship, which in turn built on a marginalized and discriminatory understanding of the Indigenous population. While the Norwegian TRC has decided that conflicts over land and water are indeed relevant for the mandate of the TRC, they are only treated implicitly in the Peruvian report. We argue that there is a need to address not only the loss of language and cultural assets, but also any remaining differences in education and standard of living, as well as the question of ownership of land and water. The discussions will focus on the latter issue.

LEGAL BATTLES OVER INDIGENOUS LAND AND OWNERSHIP

In Norway and Peru, there are ongoing conflicts regarding land and water, especially linked to mining and the use of land for energy purposes. Who should decide on natural resources, and how does this matter connect to TRCs? In Norway, the use of indigenous land for the construction of big windmill parks, dams, and mines has caused tensions between the Sámi people and the implementing government agencies and companies. The leader of the Norwegian Commission, Høybråten, recently raised the question of how the Norwegian state aims to ensure the human rights of the Sámi, particularly in the case of the windmill park in Fosen. He

---

56. Minde, "Assimilation," 29.
57. Larsen and Tronsen, "Oppgjørets Time."
58. Theidon, *Intimate Enemies*; Josefsen, "Selvopplevd diskriminering."
59. Clausen and Trivelli, "Explorando La Pobreza"; Cecchini et al., "Caja de herramientas."

suggested that the conflict surrounding these windmills could erode trust within the Sámi population regarding the authorities.[60] In doing so, he highlights that trust is an essential requirement for achieving reconciliation between the government and the Sámi.

The Norwegian Supreme Court judgment in the *Fosen* case concerned the use of natural resources and the so-called green transition that will make the Norwegian society less oil-dependent. In 2016, a windmill park consisting of 151 windmills was erected on the Fosen peninsula despite protests from reindeer herders, environmentalists, and Sámi activists.[61] The wind farms were erected on the winter pastures of the local Sámi reindeer herders. Ever since, the reindeer have avoided the turbine park, and the pastures became unusable. The Supreme Court conceded that the area is lost to traditional reindeer husbandry.[62] In the process of granting concession licenses to a partially state-owned power company, the Sámi were not consulted, potentially violating their right to free, prior, and informed consent.[63]

On October 11, 2021, the Grand Chamber of the Supreme Court ruled that the licenses for wind power development in Fosen were invalid because they violated the Sámi people's right to culture as protected under Article 27 of the International Covenant on Civil and Political Rights.[64] The judgment was a long-awaited and significant success for the Sámi community. It was celebrated as a historic milestone by the Sámi Parliament, Sámi, lawyers, human rights and environmental organizations, as well as activists, among others.[65]

The initial joy over the legal victory, however, quickly subsided. Now, in fall 2023, the windmills in Fosen continue to generate power and revenues, much to the dismay of the Sámi, who expected the demolition of the park. The unchanged situation is viewed as an ongoing human rights violation by the Sámi, lawyers, and activists.[66] The Sámi find sup-

60. Adresseavisen, "Vil vite hvordan"; Ballovara, "Vindkraftdom."

61. Lingaas, "Wind Farms"; Larsen and Holth, "Vindkraftutbygging," 88–94.

62. Supreme Court of Norway, *Fosen*, paras. 79, 84 and 91.

63. For a discussion of the case, see Ravna, *SP artikkel 27*, 440–58. For a comparative analysis, see Allard, "The Rationale," 25–43; Jääskeläinen, "The Sámi Reindeer Herders," 52.

64. Supreme Court of Norway, *Fosen*.

65. Skaar, "When Truth Commission Models Travel," 5; Ravna, "Sameretten"; Kolsrud, "Storkammerdom"; Aftenposten, "Folkebevegelse."

66. Ravna, "Sameretten"; Norsk institusjon for menneskerettigheter, "Ett år"; Stranden, "Sterk uenighet."

port from the Church of Norway (CoN)[67] and, notably for this chapter, the Norwegian TRC.

The Ministry of Petroleum and Energy was surprised to receive a letter from Høybråten in which he reminded the authorities of their legal obligation based on the *Fosen* judgment. Høybråten also cautioned that in an ongoing reconciliation process, mutual trust between citizens and the government was crucial, which *Fosen* risks undermining.[68] The Sámi directly affected by *Fosen* consider that their entire existence has, for time immemorial, been about fighting for their legal rights.[69] Although the recent Sámi discourse is very noticeably focused on legal rights, there remains distrust in the Sámi population towards the judiciary and the effective implementation of their (human) rights.[70]

The failure to implement the unanimous judgment by the Grand Chamber of the Norwegian Supreme Court, in our view, serves as another illustration of evaluative disrespect and a lack of recognition of the legal rights of the Sámi. The dispute over the windmills in Fosen is just one of several ongoing conflicts, which revolve around the ever-growing demand for green energy on the one hand, and the Sámi way of life, culture, belief systems, and traditions on the other. The problem, as other legal scholars have pointed out, is that the transition to cleaner energy and the associated exploitation of the land (all too often) happen on the traditional territories of Indigenous peoples.[71] Similar conflicts are also found in Peru, where there are legal battles about who the legitimate owners of the land are as well as over the use of land and water.[72]

In comparison to its Nordic neighbors, Norway stands out as the state with a Sámi Indigenous population that has granted the most rights and has made significant efforts to provide them with legal protection. Legal scholars agree that the Sámi's rights today are best protected in Norway.[73] Nevertheless, this comparison overlooks the fact that it should

67. Tveit and Eira, "Høyesterettsdom."
68. Ballovara, "Vindkraftdom."
69. Bjørnback, "Maja Kristine."
70. Ravna, "Indigenous Peoples," 1–3; Ravna, "Sameretten"; Eriksen, et al., "Den norske rettsstaten."
71 Gilbert, *Natural Resources*; Cambou, "Uncovering Injustices," 310–33; Lawrence and Larsen, "Politics of Planning," 1164–80; Lawrence, "Internal Colonisation," 1036–53.
72 Spiegel, "Climate Injustice," 1–14; Domínguez and Luoma, "Decolonising Conservation Policy," 1–22; Townsend and Townsend, "Epistemic Injustice," 147–59.
73. Labba, "The Characteristics," 495 and 497; Ravna, "Norwegian Courts," 179.

not be the Sámi who must be granted rights. Instead, as an Indigenous people, they arguably possessed all rights long before the Norwegian state actively colonized the heartland areas of *Sápmi* and imposed its domestic laws onto the Sámi. In Norway, as in other states, indigenous law is subordinate to state-based laws."¹ Thus, from a decolonial perspective, the Sámi laws and legal traditions, which resisted Norwegian assimilation and still exist, should be fully reinstated and equally respected by the Sámi and the majority population. In the context of the exploitation of Sámi land, this perspective would entail prioritizing Sámi laws and ownership rules necessitating corresponding adjustments by the Norwegian state.

Moreover, legal scholars have repeatedly affirmed that the legal systems of Indigenous people are inherently more respectful of nature, the environment, and the biosphere. This applies not only to Peruvian Indigenous peoples but also to the Sámi.[75] Indigenous laws are founded on a deep respect for the surroundings and especially for nature, rather than on the dominance of a supreme authority from whom one receives rights and duties. In times of climate and security emergencies as the ones we currently live in, adopting a more respectful and reconciliatory approach to our living surroundings, like the Sámi indigenous worldviews, would mitigate conflicts and promote a more peaceful coexistence.[76] Embracing a respectful approach to nature, based on Sámi traditions and customary laws, would likely avoid the irrevocable destruction of indigenous lands through the construction of dams, mines, and windmill parks, among others. These projects, authorized by the majority government, not only impact the cultural practices of the Sámi but also threaten the sustainability of land use and the harmonious relationship between humans and nature. Consequently, they contribute to conflicts and undermine mutual trust, factors that must be carefully considered within the context of a reconciliation process.

74. Labba, "The Characteristics," 503.

75. Åhrén, "Indigenous People," 63–112; Redvers et al., "Indigenous Natural and First Law," 1–12.

76. Jääskeläinen, "The Sámi Reindeer Herders," 50; Toivanen and Fabritius, "Artic Youth Transcending Notions," 58.

CONCLUDING REMARKS

A TRC can acknowledge past harms, how they impacted those who have suffered them, and it can contribute towards a common understanding of the past. Yet, the creation of a TRC and the publication of its report are only the beginning of a long process of constructing an equitable society, where those who have been wronged are recognized as fully equal partners in social interactions.[77] TRCs are typically created where a state is responsible for inflicting harm on parts of the population, and where there is a need to restore the trust between the state and the targeted population. If trust is, as Waldron and Haldemann theorize, taken as the foundation of a decent society,[78] then the state must put all its efforts into rebuilding it. Mutual trust becomes, as such, the primary goal after the TRC publishes its report.

A successful reconciliation goes beyond legal justice; it necessitates the acknowledgment of the particular truth and the recognition of the victims' experiences, grievances, shame, and their subjective sense of endured injustice as both individuals and members of a collective, rather than merely as abstract rights bearers.[79] A successful reconciliation also demands that the state must evaluate current situations where the rights of an already marginalized group are still curtailed for the benefit of the majority. In situations of competing rights, building trust might entail the foregrounding of the rights of the Indigenous minority group at the expense of the majority society.[80]

The Norwegian TRC will inevitably "fall short of offering meaningful avenues for rectifying ongoing injustices centered on land dispossession."[81] This holds especially true if the exploitation of indigenous lands is perceived as an ongoing injustice rather than isolated acts of wrongdoing.[82] The unresolved *Fosen* case shows that Norwegian positive law perpetuates this injustice through legal title and ownership rights that do not respect Sámi legal traditions and worldviews. The legal system can

---

77. Fraser, "On Justice."

78. Waldron, "Redressing Historic Injustice," 140; Haldemann, "Another Kind of Justice," 690–93.

79. Haldemann, "Another Kind of Justice," 705.

80. Similarly, Åhrén, "Indigenous People," 112. The issue of trust is also mentioned in the case of the Finnish TRC, see Kuokkanen, "Reconciliation as a Threat," 303.

81. Corntassel and Holter, "Who's Sorry Now?," 466.

82. Waldron, "Redressing Historic Injustice," 147.

rectify this injustice by recognizing traditional, pre-colonial land ownership and returning ownership to those from whom the land was taken. In cases where there are latent or ongoing conflicts over rights related to the use of natural resources, such as land and water, the need for redistribution, in line with Fraser's theories, becomes apparent. Therefore, reconciliation should include a just re-distribution of resources, along with the full recognition of legal and moral rights.

How, then, can the Gordian Knot of historic marginalization be untangled? Jeremy Waldron holds that a well-ordered society and state should be built on shared fundamental understandings and beliefs, much like the foundations of human rights. A state should, at a minimum, be based on mutual trust.[83] However, cases of historic (and ongoing) injustice, such as the Norwegianization of the Sámi or the marginalization of the Peruvian Indigenous population, erode the basis for trust. Untangling the Gordian Knot involves the reestablishment of mutual trust among different societal groups. While the responsibility for rebuilding trust lies with all involved parties, a significant portion arguably rests with the state, given its direct involvement in historic injustices. Erik Pozo-Buleje, a Peruvian anthropologist, suggests that there is a need to imagine a different kind of state.[84] Mere reform and strengthening of the state are insufficient; instead, there is a necessity for a state that is co-constructed by marginalized populations. The challenge is that historically excluded groups have not participated in shaping the framework of participation.

BIBLIOGRAPHY

Adresseavisen. "Vil vite hvordan menneskerettighetene i Fosen-saken skal ivaretas." *Adresseavisen*, 2022.
Aftenposten. "Folkebevegelse krever at 151 vindturbiner rives etter Fosen-dom." *Aftenposten*, 2021. https://www.aftenposten.no/norge/politikk/i/28qdzv/folkebevegelse-krever-at-151-vindturbiner-rives-etter-fosen-dom.
Aguiar, William, and Regine Halseth. *Aboriginal Peoples and Historic Trauma: The Processes of Intergenerational Transmission*. Prince George: National Collaborating Centre for Aboriginal Health, 2015.
Aldana, Raquel. "A Victim Centred Reflection on Truth Commissions and Prosecutions as a Response to Mass Atrocities." *Journal of Human Rights* 5 (2006). https://doi.org/10.1080/14754830500485916

---

83. See discussion in Waldron, "Redressing Historic Injustice," 140 et seq.
84. Erik Pozo, "De Campesino a Indígena?"

Allard, Christina. "The Rationale for the Duty to Consult Indigenous Peoples: Comparative Reflections from Nordic and Canadian Legal Contexts." *Arctic Review on Law and Politics* 9 (2018) 25–43.

Andresen, Astri, et al. *Samenes historie fra 1751 til 2010*. Oslo: Cappelen Damm akademisk, 2021.

Åhrén, Matthias. "Indigenous Peoples' Culture, Customs, and Traditions and Customary Law—The Saami People's Perspective." *Arizona Journal of International and Comparative Law* 21 (2004) 63–112.

Backer, David. "The Human Face of Justice: Victims' Responses to South Africa's Truth and Reconciliation Commission Process." Phd diss., University of Michigan, 2004.

Ballovara, Mette. "Vindkraftdom kan ødelegge for forsoningsarbeid.." https://www.nrk.no/sapmi/fosen-dom-kan-odelegge-for-forsoningsarbeid-1.16229769.

Bjørnback, June Grønnvoll, et al. "Maja Kristine tror hennes kampvilje ligger i blodet." NRK, 25th of August 2021. https://www.nrk.no/sapmi/maja-kristine-jama-tror-hennes-kampvilje-ligger-i-blodet-1.15623001.

Burchianti, Margaret. "Building Bridges of Memory: The Mothers of the Plaza de Mayo and the Cultural Politics of Maternal Memories." *History and Anthropology* 15 (2004) 133–50. https://doi.org/10.1093/ijtj/ijq015.

Cambou, Dorothée. "Uncovering Injustices in the Green Transition: Sámi Rights in the Development of Wind Energy in Sweden." *Arctic Review on Law and Politics* 11 (2020) 310–33.

Cecchini, Simone, et al. *Caja de Herramientas. Promoviendo la Igualdad: el Aporte de Las Políticas Sociales en América Latina y el Caribe. Introducción a la desigualdad de los pueblos indígenas*. Santiago: Comisión Económica para América Latina y el Caribe (CEPAL), 2021. https://igualdad.cepal.org/sites/default/files/2022-02/DB_intro_indigenas_es.pdf.

Clark, Janine N. "Does Bosnia Need a Truth and Reconciliation Commission? Some Reflections on its Possible Design." *Ethnopolitics* 12 (2016) 225–46.

Clausen, Jhonatan and Carolina Trivelli. "Explorando La Pobreza Multidimensional Rural: Una Propuesta Comprehensiva y Sensible al Contexto Peruano." Lima: Instituto de Estudios Peruanos, 2019.

Comisión de la Verdad y Reconciliación (CVR). *Hatun Willakuy: Versión Abreviada del Informe Final de la Comisión de la Verdad y Reconciliación—Peru*. Lima: Comisión de la Verdad y Reconciliación, 2008.

———. *Informe Final Comisión de la Verdad y Reconciliación*. Lima: Comisión de la Verdad y Reconciliación, 2003. http://www.cverdad.org.pe/ifinal/index.php.

Corntassel, Jeff, and Cindy Holter. "Who's Sorry Now? Government Apologies, Truth Commissions, and Indigenous Self-Determination in Australia, Canada, Guatemala, and Peru." *Human Rights Review* 9 (2008) 465–89.

Cuevas, Espinoza, et al. *Comisiones de La Verdad. Un Camino Incierto? Estudio Comparativo de Comisiones de La Verdad En Argentina, Chile, El Salvador, Guatemala y Sudáfrica Desde Las Victimas y Las Organisaciones de Derechos Humanos*. Santiago de Chile: CODEPU, 2003.

Doak, Jonathan. "The Therapeutic Dimension of Transitional Justice: Emotional Repair and Victim Satisfaction in International Trials and Truth Commissions." *International Criminal Law Review* 11 (2011) 263–98.

Domínguez, Lara, and Colin Luoma. "Decolonising Conservation Policy: How Colonial Land and Conservation Ideologies Persist and Perpetuate Indigenous Injustices at the Expense of the Environment." *Land* 9 (2020) 1–22.

Dragovic-Soso, Jasna. "History of a Failure: Attempts to Create a National Truth and Reconciliation Commission in Bosnia and Herzegovina, 1997–2006." *International Journal of Transitional Justice* 10 (2016) 292–310.

Eriksen, Gunnar, et al. "Den norske rettsstaten er ignorant overfor internasjonale menneskerettigheter." https://khrono.no/den-norske-rettsstaten-er-ignorant-over for-internasjonale-menneskerettigheter/627678.

Fraser, Nancy. *Justice Interruptus: Critical Reflections on the 'Postsocialist' Condition*. London: Routledge, 1997.

———. "On Justice." *New Left Review* 74 (2012) 41–51.

———. "Rethinking Recognition." *New Left Review* 3 (2000) 107–20.

García-Godos, Jemima, and Félix Reátegui. "Peru." In *Transitional Justice in Latin America: The Uneven Road towards Accountability*, edited by Elin Skaar, et al. New York: Routledge/ GlassHouse, 2016.

Gilbert, Jérémie. *Natural Resources and Human Rights: An Appraisal*. Oxford: Oxford University Press, 2018.

Greiff, Pablo de. "'Truth without Facts?': On the Erosion of the Fact-Finding Function of Truth Commissions." In *The Transformation of Human Rights Factfinding*, edited by Philip Alston and Sarah Knuckey. Oxford: Oxford University Press, 2016.

Haldemann, Frank. "Another Kind of Justice: Transitional Justice as Recognition." *Cornell International Law Journal* 41 (2008) 75–737.

Hamber, Brandon, et al. "'Telling It like It Is. . .': Understanding the Truth and Reconciliation Commission from the Perspective of Survivors." *Psychology in Society* 26 (2000) 18–42.

Hansen, Lars I., and Bjørnar Olsen. *Samenes historie fram til 1750*. Oslo: Cappelen Damm akademisk, 2022.

Hayner, Priscilla. *Unspeakable Truths: Transitional Justice and the Challenge of Truth Commissions*. 2nd ed. New York: Routledge, 2011.

Heilman, Jaymie. "Truth and Reconciliation Commission of Peru." https://oxfordre.com/latinamericanhistory/display/10.1093/acrefore/9780199366439.001.0001/acrefore-9780199366439-e-495.

Herman, Judith L. "The Mental Health of Crime Victims: Impact of Legal Intervention." *Journal of Traumatic Stress* 16 (April 2003) 159–66.

Honneth, Axel. *Disrespect: The Normative Foundations of Critical Theory*. Cambridge: Polity, 2007.

———. *The Struggle for Recognition: The Moral Grammar of Social Conflicts*. Cambridge: Polity, 1995.

Høybråten, Dagfinn. "Kommisjonsleder Dagfinn Høybråtens julehilsen: en rapport som skal legge grunnlag for et oppgjør." https://uit.no/kommisjonen/presse/artikkel_en?p_document_id=798854.

Ignatieff, Michael. "Articles of Faith." *Index on Censorship* 25 (1996) 110–22.

Jääskeläinen, Tiina. "The Sámi Reindeer Herders' Conceptualizations of Sustainability in the Permitting of Mineral Extraction—Contradictions Related to Sustainability Criteria." *Current Opinion in Environmental Sustainability* 43 (2020) 49–57.

Järvensivu, Linda, et al. "Locating Sámi Social Work in Finland: Meanings Produced by Social Workers in Working with Sámi People." *International Social Work* 59 (2016) 600–13. https://doi.org/10.1177/0020872816646817.

Josefsen, Eva. *Selvopplevd diskriminering blant samer i Norge*. Alta: Kommunal- og regionaldepartementet, 2006.

Kolsrud, Kjetil. "Storkammerdom: Vindkraftkonsesjon er ugyldig—krenket urfolkrettigheter." https://rett24.no/articles/storkammerdom-vindkraftkonsesjon-er-ugyldig—krenket-urfolkrettigheter.

Klikner, Melanie, and Howard Davis. *The Right to Truth in International Law: Victims' Rights in Human Rights and International Criminal Law*. London: Routledge, 2019.

Kritz, Neil, and Jakob Finci. "A Truth and Reconciliation Commission in Bosnia and Herzegovina: An Idea Whose Time Has Come." *International Law FORUM du Droit International* 3 (2001) 50–58.

Kuokkanen, Rauna. "Reconciliation as a Threat or Structural Change? The Truth and Reconciliation Process and Settler Colonial Policy Making in Finland." *Human Rights Review* 21 (2020) 293–312.

Labba, Kristina. "The Characteristics and Legal Status of Sámi Legal Tradition and Law." In *The Sámi World*, edited by Sanna Valkonen et al. Abingdon: Routledge, 2022.

Langer, Johannes. "Conclusions." In *Get the Truth out of Truth Commissions: Lessons Learned from Five Case Studies*, edited by Johannes Langer. Bogotá: Editorial Bonaventura, 2018.

Laplante, Lisa, and Kimberly Theidon. "Truth with Consequences: Justice and Reparations in Post-Truth Commission Peru." *Human Rights Quarterly* 29 (2007) 228–50.

Larsen, Hanne, and Jo H. Tronsen. "Oppgjørets time: Det var en skam å være samisktalende." https://www.nrk.no/tromsogfinnmark/sannhets—og-forsoningskommisjonen-henter-historier-fra-dem-som-ble-berort-av-fornorskningspolitikken-1.15170198.

Larsen, Ingrid W., and Fredrik Holth. "Vindkraftutbygging på Fosenhalvøya og samiske rettigheter etter SP artikkel 27." *Kart og Plan* 115 (2022) 88–94.

Lawrence, Rebecca. "Internal Colonisation and Indigenous Resource Sovereignty: Wind Power Developments on Traditional Saami Lands." *Society & Space* 32 (2014) 1036–53.

Lawrence, Rebecca, and Rasmus K. Larsen. "The Politics of Planning: Assessing the Impacts of Mining on Sami Lands." *Third World Quarterly* 38 (2017) 1164–180.

Lingaas, Carola. "Wind Farms in Indigenous Areas: The Fosen (Norway) and the Lake Turkana Wind Project (Kenya) Cases." https://opiniojuris.org/2021/12/15/wind-farms-in-indigenous-areas-the-fosen-norway-and-the-lake-turkana-wind-project-kenya-cases/.

Minde, Henry. "Assimilation of the Sami: Implementation and Consequences." *Gáldu Čála—Journal of Indigenous Peoples Rights* 3 (2005) 1–33.

Muotka, Silje K. "Sametingspresidentens Nyttårstale." https://sametinget.no/politikk/taler-og-innlegg/sametingspresidentens-nyttarstale.23234.aspx/.

Norsk institusjon for menneskerettigheter. "Ett år siden Fosen dommen falt." https://www.nhri.no/2022/ett-ar-siden-fosen-dommen/.

Office of the United Nations High Commissioner for Human Rights. *Rule-of-Law Tools for Post-Conflict States. Truth Commissions*. United Nations, 2006. https://www.ohchr.org/Documents/Publications/RuleoflawTruthCommissionsen.pdf/q.

Pozo, Erik. "De Campesino a Indígena?" *Revista Ideele* 221 (2012). https://www.revistaideele.com/2023/02/13/de-campesino-a-indigena/.

Ravna, Øyvind. "Indigenous Peoples' Rights and the Norwegian Courts Moving into 2021." *Arctic Review on Law and Politics* 12 (2021) 1–3.

———. "Norwegian Courts and Sámi Law." *Arctic Review on Law and Politics* 12 (2021) [illegible].

———. "Sameretten etter Fosen-dommen." https://juridika.no/innsikt/sameretten-etter-fosen-dommen/.

———. "SP artikkel 27 og norsk urfolksrett etter Fosen-dommen." *Lov og Rett* 61 (2022) 440–58.

Redvers, Nicole, et al. "Indigenous Natural and First Law in Planetary Health." *Challenges* 11 (2020) 1–12. https://doi.org/10.3390/challe11020029.

Sametinget. "Sametingets innspill til mandat for sannhetskommisjonen." Sametinget, sak 17/2805–432, May 2018.

———. "Truth Commission in Sweden," 2021. https://www.sametinget.se/truth-commission.

Sannhets- og forsoningskommisjonen. "Krise- og støttesamtaler." https://uit.no/kommisjonen/sanks.

Sannhets- og forsoningskommisjonen. "Sannhets- og forsoningskommisjonens mandat." https://www.stortinget.no/no/Stortinget-og-demokratiet/Organene/sannhets—og-forsoningskommisjonen/sannhets—og-forsoningskommisjonens-mandat/

Sennett, Richard. *Respect: The Formation of Character in an Age of Inequality*. London: Penguin, 2003.

Skaar, Elin. "When Truth Commission Models Travel: Explaining the Norwegian Case." *International Journal of Transitional Justice* 17 (2023) 123–40.

Sønneland, Anne M. "These Trials Are Not Easy, Because They Are Against the State." PhD diss., University of Oslo, 2021.

Sønneland, Anne M., and Carola Lingaas, "Righting Injustices Towards the Sámi: A Critical Perspective on the Norwegian Truth and Reconciliation Commission." *International Journal of Minority and Group Rights* 30 (2023).

Spiegel, Samuel. "Climate Injustice, Criminalisation of Land Protection and Anti-Colonial Solidarity: Courtroom Ethnography in an Age of Fossil Fuel Violence." *Political Geography* 84 (2021) 1–14.

Stephen, Lynn. "Testimony and Human Rights Violations in Oaxaca." *Latin American Perspectives* 38 (2011) 52–58.

Stranden, Ingrid L. "Sterk uenighet om utbygging er pågående menneskerettighetsbrudd." https://wws.nrk.no/trondelag/stat-og-jurister-svaert-uenige-om-vindkraftanlegg-pa-fosen-er-et-menneskerettighetsbrudd-1.16170690.

Supreme Court of Norway. "HR-2021–1975-S, 11th of October 2021." https://www.domstol.no/globalassets/upload/hret/decisions-in-english-translation/hr-2021-1975-s.pdf.

Theidon, Kimberly. *Intimate Enemies: Violence and Reconciliation in Peru*. Philadelphia: University of Pennsylvania Press, 2013.

Toivanen, Reetta, and Nora Fabritius. "Arctic Youth Transcending Notions of 'Culture' and 'Nature': Emancipative Discourses of Place for Cultural Sustainability." *Current Opinion in Environmental Sustainability* 43 (2020) 58–64.

Townsend, Dina L., and Leo Townsend. "Epistemic Injustice and Indigenous Peoples in the Inter-American Human Rights System." *Social Epistemology* 35 (2021) 147–59.

Truth and Reconciliation Commission. "Mandate." https://www.stortinget.no/no/Stortinget-og-demokratiet/Organene/sannhets—og-forsoningskommisjonen/

Truth and Reconciliation Commission Concerning the Sámi People. "Mandate: Establishing a Truth and Reconciliation Commission Concerning the Sámi People." https://sdtsk.fi/en/mandate/.

Tveit, Olav F., and Sara E. A. Eira. "Høyesterettsdommen i Fosen-saken må respekteres." https://www.nrk.no/ytring/hoyesterettsdommen-i-fosen-saken-ma-respekteres-1.16267440.

Vars, Láilá S. "Samene i Norge: Fra fornorsking til forsoning?" In *Nasjonale minoriteter og urfolk i norsk politikk fra 1900 til 2016*, edited by Nik Brandal et al., 177–99. Oslo: Cappelen Damm, 2017.

Waldron, Jeremy. "Redressing Historic Injustice." *University of Toronto Law Journal* 52 (2002) 135–60.

Wiebelhaus-Brahm, Eric, et al., "Examining Compliance with Domestic Human Rights Bodies: The Case of Truth Commission Recommendations." *Journal of Human Rights* (2022) 1–19. https://doi.org/10.1080/14754835.2022.2111657.

Woolford, Andrew. "Negotiating Affirmative Repair: Symbolic Violence in the British Columbia Treaty Process." *Canadian Journal of Sociology* 29 (2004) 111–44.

4

Reflections on Truth and Reconciliation Commissions in the Context of Decolonization

GIRUM ZELEKE

*Faculty of Theology and Social Sciences,
VID Specialized University, Stavanger, Norway*

INTRODUCTION

The extensive history of violence and wrongdoing in human society highlights the need for Truth and Reconciliation Commissions (TRCs). Examining the historical records of numerous nations reveals that many were founded on violence, inequality, and conflict, with the colonization of Indigenous peoples' lands as a prime example.[1] Colonialism has left its mark on society, and it is necessary to recognize and face these effects to rectify the injustices and power dynamics they have created. A TRC is an important step towards acknowledging and addressing historical injustices. Beyond acknowledging the wrongs that these indigenous communities have endured, there is a need to reverse the new order through the

---

1. Bacchiocchi, Sant, and Bates, "Energy Justice."

decolonization of these nations. Decolonization is the process of undoing colonial impacts, challenging oppressive structures, and restoring agency to colonized peoples.[2] Decolonization involves acknowledging past injustices and taking concrete steps to restore Indigenous peoples' control over their traditional lands, resources, and cultural traditions.

The decolonization of knowledge and education is part of a larger process of emancipation from colonialism at both the physical and mental levels. Restoring Indigenous peoples' control over their traditional lands, resources, and cultural traditions is also an essential part of the decolonization process. Generally, TRCs do not have an explicit mandate to decolonize nations. However, by discussing TRCs and decolonization together, we can better understand the interconnectedness of these processes and the importance of a holistic approach to the healing and restoration of indigenous communities.

A TRC is a body established to address the historical injustices faced by Indigenous peoples, particularly due to colonial policies and practices. From a governmental perspective, TRCs are typically established during periods of conflict or when democratic rule is threatened. However, the Canadian TRC came into existence at the behest of Canada's indigenous communities, specifically the survivors of the Indian Residential Schools (IRS). Similarly, the TRCs in Norway and Sweden were initiated by Sámi politicians. They were established to investigate human rights violations that occur during conflict or periods of violence, provide victims with a platform to share their experiences, address past human rights abuses, promote forgiveness and healing, and foster social and political reconciliation.

The primary objective of a TRC is to document and acknowledge past wrongs, facilitate dialogue between affected communities and the broader society, and promote healing and reconciliation. TRCs often involve collecting testimonies from survivors, researching the impact of past actions, and recommending measures to address the ongoing consequences of these actions.

Several key features define truth commissions (TCs). According to Gilbert, TCs focus on patterns of abuse over time rather than on individual events.[3] Their objective is to provide a comprehensive overview of human rights violations and legal abuses within a specified timeframe.

2. Coulthard, *Red Skin, White Masks*.
3. Gilbert, "Impact, Legitimacy, and Limitations."

TCs generally operate for a predetermined period and are dissolved upon completing their mandate, often accompanied by the submission of a report on their findings.[4] Additionally, TCs are typically granted authority, which also allows them access to official information,[5] and they are officially empowered or authorized by the state in which they are reviewed.[6]

It is worth noting that TCs do not have the power to prosecute or punish those who have committed human rights violations or make binding legal rulings. They also lack the authority to enforce or require enforcement of their recommendations. Hayner offers an in-depth examination of the role and effectiveness of forty different TCs, as well as a comparative analysis of their impacts.[7]

The design and purpose of TCs vary greatly depending on the country, the events that led to their establishment, as well as their mandate, composition, and duration. Interest in TCs has grown for various reasons, such as the universal recognition that past human rights abuses must be addressed during democratic transitions and the need to establish similar bodies in conflict zones.[8] Brahm also views TCs as a significant aspect of transitional justice, promoting healing for victims and their families, fostering peaceful coexistence, and establishing a new democratic order based on respect for human rights and the rule of law.[9]

Despite their well-intentioned nature, TRCs have encountered criticism from various quarters. They have been faulted for their inability to catalyze decolonization and substantial transformation, deliver justice, or offer victims sufficient compensation for their losses. This critique emanates from the constrained power and resources at the disposal of TRCs, which can pose challenges in accomplishing these objectives.[10] Critics contend that TRC processes can be superficial, focusing on symbolic gestures rather than tackling structural issues that underlie historical injustices. Additionally, some argue that TRCs prioritize the narrative of reconciliation over justice, which can lead to a lack of accountability for those responsible for past wrongs. Furthermore, TRC processes may

4. Hayner, *Unspeakable Truths*, 215.
5. Hayner, *Unspeakable Truths*, 227.
6. Hayner, *Unspeakable Truths*, 210.
7. Hayner, *Unspeakable Truths*.
8. Hayner, *Unspeakable Truths*, 7.
9. Brahm, "Uncovering the Truth," 17.
10. Avruch, "Truth and Reconciliation Commissions," 33.

not always adequately address the full scope of decolonization processes, which requires a more comprehensive approach.

According to a definition by an esteemed Japanese legal adviser, Usami, TRCs can be understood as short-term neutral entities established to investigate human rights violations during specific periods of suppression or conflict.[11] This compelling idea offers a concise and well-structured perspective of the role and function of TRCs in addressing historical injustices.

The primary goals of TRCs are to collect data about the hardships endured by those impacted by injustice, conduct inquiries, present findings about these events, provide recommendations for compensation, and offer measures to avoid future mistreatment.[12] Several nations have established commissions to address historical injustices and promote healing in societies affected by conflict and violence. These commissions aim to heal the lasting impact of civil wars and promote peace by bridging cultural and linguistic divisions.[13]

However, TRCs are not always equipped to decolonize and bring about significant changes in power structures and institutions, partly because decolonization has not been explicitly part of the mandates of TRCs. While some TRCs have made efforts to address historical injustices and human rights violations, their primary focus has been on truth-seeking, reconciliation, and accountability rather than undertaking comprehensive decolonization processes. Consequently, the effectiveness of TRCs in decolonizing nations remains a subject for further examination. This chapter discusses the role of TRCs in Canada, South Africa, and Norway. The effectiveness of TRCs in achieving these aims of decolonization is a topic of ongoing academic research and debate.

TRC IN CANADA

Canada has a troubling history of perpetrating injustices against its Indigenous populations. In the 1860s, the country implemented a policy of Indian Residential Schools (IRSs) to assimilate the First Nations of Canada, the Inuit, and the Métis into Canadian culture. Religious denominations established residential schools long before Canada was a

11. Usami, "Defining Truth Commission," 58.
12. Usami, "Defining Truth Commission," 58.
13. Guðmarsdóttir et al., "Trading Justice for Peace?," 2.

nation. With schools becoming an official policy in Canada around 1868, the government took a more active role, partnering with the church in the running of schools. Indigenous parents were either persuaded or coerced into sending their children to residential schools, or in some cases, the children were forcibly taken from their families and sent to these institutions. Within these schools, children frequently endured physical, sexual, and emotional abuse, and were systematically stripped of their cultural heritage. The students in these schools often had to contend with overcrowded living conditions, which facilitated the spread of infectious diseases and tragically contributed to a high mortality rate among the students.

The Indian Residential Schools Settlement Agreement, considered the largest settlement in Canadian history, encompasses distinctive non-financial measures. These measures comprised the establishment of the TRC, which was responsible for crafting the Calls to Action currently under evaluation, as well as the provision of funds for commemoration projects aimed at memorializing the impact of residential schools. Additionally, the agreement allocated funds to provide mental health support to all the plaintiffs included in the settlement.[14] However, the IRS settlement negotiations focused primarily on the First Nations; consequently, many Métis and Inuit were excluded from the discussions.[15] Research suggests that the design of the TRC did not fully embody the intended principles of restoration, as the negotiations were dominated by the government and were limited in scope.[16] The TRC focused solely on IRSs.[17] This narrow focus meant that the commission could not provide a full picture of the broader systemic issues affecting Indigenous peoples and communities, and limited its potential for real reconciliation.

In addition, rather than serving as an impartial mediator, the settlement mediator advocated for the federal government's interests, tipping the scales in their favor.[18] Despite the presence of high-ranking church leaders and government officials in these negotiations, the perpetrators of residential school abuse have not been engaged despite the TRC's extensive consultation with a wide range of stakeholders, including survivors, experts on TCs, and federal and indigenous leaders. Perpetrators

14. Truth and Reconciliation Commission of Canada, *Honoring the Truth*, 130.
15. Miller, *Residential Schools*, 348.
16. Petoukhov, "An Evaluation," 87–88.
17. Petoukhov, "An Evaluation," 114.
18. Petoukhov, "An Evaluation," 87–88.

may be reluctant to speak up for fear of facing criminal charges, even if they were not formally accused of a crime before TRC talks began. As a result, perpetrators may continue to dispute their culpability, contradicting the premise that they should own up to wrongdoing. According to Nagy, many culprits in the residential school system have died since its abolition.[19] For many reasons, this is a barrier that talks are unlikely to overcome.

During the TRC process, there were difficulties ensuring that survivors had unrestricted access to public forums where they could share their experiences.[20] While the TRC has concluded its work, it is essential to continue efforts to provide ongoing opportunities for truth-telling. Initiatives such as ongoing dialogue sessions can be instrumental in addressing these challenges, allowing women and young people to share their experiences in a supportive and inclusive manner. Another significant limitation of the TRC is its lack of binding power. The commission did not have the power to enforce its recommendations, and many of them are yet to be fully implemented.[21] This lack of enforcement mechanisms has been criticized as a major barrier to real reconciliation, as it has meant that the injustices documented by the commission have gone unaddressed.

Additionally, the TRC has faced scrutiny for its lack of inclusion and representation of indigenous perspectives.[22] Indigenous peoples were notably underrepresented by the commission's staff, and many indigenous communities felt that the commission's process was not sufficiently inclusive. Furthermore, the TRC has come under fire for its focus on individual rather than systemic responsibility. This individualized approach has been condemned as a means of deflecting accountability away from the government and other institutions that facilitated and perpetuated abuse.[23]

The Canadian government has also faced criticism for its lack of action in terms of reparations. While the TRC recommended a range of measures to support healing and reconciliation, the government has faced backlash for not taking substantial steps to address the material harm

19. Nagy, "Settler Witnessing," 222.
20. Petoukhov, "An Evaluation," 111.
21. Regan, "Canada's TRC," 56.
22. Reed et al., "Indigenizing Climate Policy," 1–2.
23. Henkeman, "Reconciliation as an Outcome," 88–89.

suffered by Indigenous people.²⁴ This lack of action on reparations has been seen as a failure to address past injustices and support reconciliation.

In discussions responding to the TRC's call to action, Canadian universities intend to close the gap between Indigenous and non-Indigenous students by committing to a set of Principles on Indigenous Education aimed at decolonizing Canadian campuses and integrating Indigenous perspectives into Canadian scholarship and learning.²⁵ Almeida and Kumalo argue that Indigenous bodies and scholarship in Canadian universities are consumed to affirm institutional pride and innocence.²⁶ Decolonization has authorized fragmented forms of inclusion, voice, and scholarship, and reinforced colonial thinking and white supremacy in Canadian institutions.²⁷ The discourse on decolonization reinforces colonialist thinking and decolonization, as discourse underwrites and recycles colonialist and nationalist thinking in educational institutions while claiming to unsettle it.²⁸ While there remains no way to discuss these issues without foregrounding them in these institutions of learning, it appears that this step is better than doing nothing.

The TRC played a crucial role in acknowledging and addressing injustices of the IRS system. It served as an important platform for truth-telling and reconciliation, and the individuals involved in the TRC worked diligently to fulfill its mandate. However, the TRC had various flaws that limited its potential for reconciliation, including limited scope, lack of binding power, focus on individual responsibility, and failure to address reparations. While the TRC itself was not directly part of the Canadian government, its recommendations and calls for action were directed towards the government for implementation. It is important to recognize that the government of Canada's response to the TRC's recommendations has not always been adequate, and further efforts are needed to ensure full implementation and support to achieve meaningful reconciliation.

---

24. Guðmarsdóttir et al., "Trading Justice for Peace?," 7.
25. Almeida and Kumalo, "(De)coloniality through Indigeneity," 13.
26. Almeida and Kumalo, "(De)coloniality through Indigeneity," 14.
27. Almeida and Kumalo, "(De)coloniality through Indigeneity," 14.
28. Almeida and Kumalo, "(De)coloniality through Indigeneity," 15.

TRC IN SOUTH AFRICA

In South Africa, the TRC was formed in 1995 after the end of the apartheid era by legislation passed by the South African parliament to investigate gross human rights violations committed by both the apartheid government and the liberation movement. The commission's mandate was to provide victims of human rights violations with the opportunity to share their stories and for perpetrators to confess their crimes. The TRC aimed to foster national unity and reconciliation in a post-apartheid society, which had been deeply divided along racial lines for decades.

The TRC allowed those responsible for human rights violations to apply for amnesty and provided a platform for victims to share their experiences. The commission listened to both sides of the argument and suggested moving forward in the apartheid era. Over the course of 140 public hearings throughout the country, thousands of victims and perpetrators from diverse backgrounds were examined. Victims and perpetrators testified to their experiences, and the commission subsequently compiled an extensive report.

The TRC also invited various organizations and groups, including academic institutions, correctional services, lawyers, political parties, media outlets, medical professionals, and religious communities, to attend special sessions. The role of religious communities was particularly important, as they were closely connected to both victims and perpetrators of apartheid, and their perspective was crucial in discussions of forgiveness and reconciliation. The TRC's work contributed to the establishment of a culture of human rights in South Africa and facilitated the country's transition from apartheid to democracy.

However, critics have pointed out several flaws in the TRC. One critique is that the commission failed to hold high-ranking officials accountable for gross human rights violations, including apartheid-era President P.W. Botha. Some argue that the TRC's focus on reconciliation undermines the importance of justice in dealing with past atrocities. As Balint notes, the dominant narrative established by organizations such as the TRC does not necessarily bring about enduring change[29] but rather serves to elucidate what transpired and the suffering inflicted, providing a solid foundation for reconciliation.

Furthermore, the TRC exposed uncomfortable truths about the past, enhancing public understanding and creating a new discourse in

---

29. Balint, "Justifying the Means."

which denying crimes was no longer an option. In addition, the TRC did not address economic and social inequalities. Thus, it failed to challenge the underlying power structures that had created and sustained apartheid, making it difficult for meaningful decolonization to occur in the years following the TRC's work. To move forward, the TRC will need to hold more high-ranking officers accountable for their actions while simultaneously devising solutions that might impact the economic and social status of Indigenous people.

As the discussion on the TRC continues, a new field of study has emerged, focusing on settler colonialism, and this perspective has been integrated into the field of transitional justice.[30] According to Park, South Africa's TRC has not been thoroughly examined through the lens of settler-colonialism.[31] Traditionally, settler colonialism in South Africa has been seen as a historical phase, and recent scholarship has highlighted its ongoing presence.[32] Research has shown that a settler colonial perspective is relevant for understanding the South African TRC, especially regarding the settler colonialism of apartheid.[33] However, the TRC's Report acknowledges settler colonialism while simultaneously advancing a series of denials, leading to what is termed 'ambivalent denial'.[34] This ambivalent denial has implications for democratization without addressing decolonization, as it enables settler denial and fails to address settler colonial structures.[35] Although transitional justice in South Africa might have contributed to democratization, it fell short of promoting decolonization.[36] By combining settler colonialism with paradigmatic transitional justice, it becomes apparent that the latter cannot effectively address settler colonialism. Both paradigms are built upon liberal teleology, characterized by 'linear progressivism' and the ultimate goal of liberalism.[37]

30. Balint, "Justifying the Means," 1.
31. Park, "Settler Colonialism."
32. Park, "Settler Colonialism."
33. Grey and James, "Truth, Reconciliation, and 'Double Settler Denial,'" 5.
34. Park, "Settler Colonialism."
35. Grey and James, "Truth, Reconciliation, and 'Double Settler Denial,'" 5.
36. Park, "Settler Colonialism."
37. Park, "Settler Colonialism."

TRC IN NORWAY

Norway established a TRC to investigate Norwegianization politics and injustices towards the Sámi people, Kvens/Norwegian Finns, and Forest Finns. In my interpretation, the TRC was formed to document the human rights violations and atrocities committed during the protracted conflict between the government and Indigenous Sámi community, and I will focus on the process of the Sámi. The commission's core mandate was to offer a platform for both victims and perpetrators to share their testimonies regarding their experiences and, in doing so, facilitate understanding and forgiveness. Through this meticulous process, the country aspired to achieve reconciliation and move toward a future characterized by greater peace and inclusivity. While the TRC model may not be universally applicable to every country, Norway's example illustrates the significance of acknowledging past wrongs and actively working towards reconciliation as a means to construct a more just and harmonious society.

As noted by Kuokkanen, the TRC was established in Norway to examine the historical wrongdoings of the state against the Sámi and Kven communities.[38] The Norwegian government implemented a policy aimed at forcing ethnic minorities, specifically the Sámi, to embrace the Norwegian culture and language. During the 'Norwegianization' period, the Sámi and Kvens/Norwegian Finns were provided instructions on social norms to integrate them into Norwegian society. Tore Johnsen states that the ethnic groups were depicted as being intellectually inferior.[39] The Norwegianization campaign sought to erase the Sámi and Kven identities along with their languages, customs, and ways of life. Communities were forced to abandon their traditional lifestyles because of the implementation of this policy. Sámi children were separated from their families, forbidden from using their language, and sent to boarding schools to assimilate and become familiar with the Norwegian language and culture.[40] In exchange, the government granted the Sámi the rights of modern society, including the ability to own property, start a business, pay taxes, and work for a living.[41] However, these communities continued to be discriminated against because of their appearance, language, and dress.

38. Kuokkanen, "Reconciliation as a Threat," 296.
39. Johnsen, "Negotiating the Meaning," 18.
40. Zdeněk, "Norway's Indigenous People."
41. Johnsen, "Negotiating the Meaning," 34–35.

There were serious repercussions for minority groups because of Norwegianization. These groups had to fight for basic rights such as recognition and property ownership. According to Zdeněk, the Norwegian state monopolized agriculture, communication, media, and the military to stamp out the minority's way of life.[42] Furthermore, Hansen and colleagues discovered that ethnic bullying and discrimination against Sámi and Kven people are common. Truth and reconciliation with minorities are essential components of the Norwegian TRC.[43] According to Kuokkanen, the TRC investigated the effects of past and present discrimination on minorities, including government assimilation policies and rights abuses.[44]

The TRC in Norway was assigned the responsibility of examining the impact of the country's Norwegianization program on the ability of the Sámi and Kvens/Norwegian Finns to preserve and advance their language, culture, and traditional economic practices.[45] According to the TRC mandate in Norway, the TRC has implemented three key initiatives.[46] The first one was to compile a comprehensive timeline of Sámi and Kven history. This was achieved by investigating and documenting Norwegianization policies and actions implemented by Norwegian authorities at the local, regional, and national levels between 1800 and the present. The next step was to analyze the current impact of these policies on minority languages and cultures. The TRC also evaluated the effects of the policies on social, economic, and health aspects, as well as the sense of self of the Sámi and Kven people.[47] Finally, the commission was tasked with proposing methods for ongoing reconciliation to achieve true equality between majority and minority populations.[48] The TRC in Norway was established with the support of the Norwegian government and includes representatives from the Sámi parliament, the Skolt Sámi village council, and the Finnish government.

The TRC also investigated the effects of the Norwegianization strategy on the majority population's perceptions, the changes it brought to the Sámi and Kvens/Norwegian Finns' own culture, language, and

42. Zdeněk, "Norway's Indigenous People."
43. Hansen et al., "Ethnic Discrimination," 100.
44. Kuokkanen, "Reconciliation as a Threat," 294.
45. Kuokkanen, "Reconciliation as a Threat," 295.
46. UiT.no., "The Commission to Investigate."
47. UiT.no., "The Commission to Investigate."
48. UiT.no., "The Commission to Investigate."

identity, and its present-day effects on the two groups and individuals, including through hate crimes and discrimination.

The TRC proposed reconciliation initiatives, including educating the public about the Sámi and Kven/Norwegian Finnish cultures and histories, as well as evaluating ongoing reconciliation efforts. The commission's findings were disseminated through various channels, including online and digital media, with the aim of fostering a shared understanding of the past and increasing awareness of our collective history.

Kvittingen and Nuse,[49] along with Kristiansen,[50] cited historical evidence pertaining to the Sámi's participation in the 1852 Kautokeino revolt. According to their research, thirty-five adults and twenty-two youths took part in the uprising, which tragically led to the deaths of local shopkeepers and a sheriff. Furthermore, the villagers faced imprisonment and endured abuse, with the priest even being subjected to whipping. These accounts significantly contribute to the existing body of research on this subject.

Kvittingen and Nuse's findings also shed light on the fact that the Sámi people engaged in the Laestadian revival movement to protest the non-Sámi people's sale of alcohol to locals, which resulted in addiction, bankruptcy, and the subsequent forcible confiscation and slaughter of reindeer.[51] This event also hindered the economic incorporation of the Sámi and Kven people into Norwegian society. Unlike its counterparts in Canada and South Africa, the TRC in Norway has not yet established any evidence of Norwegianization-related deaths, leading others to wonder if the Norwegian TRC is only lip service meant to put Norway in a better light worldwide on matters of human rights and democracy.

EFFICIENCY OF THE TRC IN CANADA

The misrecognition that Indigenous people in Canada have endured for a long time may become more apparent to non-Indigenous Canadians through the TRC as they learn about the past and grow to appreciate the variety of Indigenous traditions. The TRC has the potential to lay the groundwork for teaching future generations of Canadians about Indigenous languages, traditions, and customs. It underscores the importance

---

49. Kvittingen and Nuse, "Why Did Some."
50. Kristiansen, "The Kautokeino Rebellion."
51. Kvittingen and Nuse, "Why Did Some."

of these cultural aspects in creating a diverse nation that is characterized by equality rather than the dominance of one group over another by combating racist stereotypes and attitudes.

The TRC has had an enormous impact on Indigenous people, and it can be improved by exposing the public to the truth regarding residential schools.[52] The TRC's affirmation of the Indigenous people's equality and worth is crucial to repairing their identities and promoting recognition of the harm that has occurred.[53] During the TRC's first national event, many survivors highlighted the importance of finding their true selves again. The TRC's overarching goal is to put an end to centuries of discrimination against Indigenous people through the promotion of mutual understanding between them and the wider society.[54] As Ross notes, the TRC has been attempting to correct "historical misperceptions of cultural inferiority."[55] This process of survivors sharing their experiences is called settler witnessing. According to Nagy, 'settler witnessing' refers to the role and responsibility of non-Indigenous people in acknowledging and bearing witness to the injustices inflicted upon Indigenous peoples, including the trauma stemming from the IRS system.[56] His concept acknowledges that non-Indigenous people bear a unique responsibility to actively engage with the enduring legacy of colonialism and to contribute to the reconciliation process between Indigenous and non-Indigenous peoples.

Despite the TRC's report and the recommendations it provided, which illuminated the violence and trauma endured by Indigenous children in residential schools, the efficiency of the 94 Calls to Action[57] has been limited. In the years following the closure of the commission, both the government and the broader public largely failed to adequately address these Calls to Action. Even six years after Trudeau's commitment to implementing the Calls to Action, many of them remain unfulfilled,

52. Konstantin, "An Evaluation."
53. Nagy, "Settler Witnessing," 222.
54. Truth and Reconciliation Commission of Canada, *Honoring the Truth*.
55. Ross, "Telling Truths," 15.
56. Nagy, "Settler Witnessing," 223.
57. 94 Calls to Action refers to the recommendations from the Canadian TRC to all levels of government to work together to repair the harm caused by residential schools and begin the process of reconciliation.

indicating that significant work is still required for the TRC's efforts to achieve their intended impact in Canada.[58]

EFFICIENCY OF THE TRC IN SOUTH AFRICA

The establishment of the TRC was a collaborative effort between the South African government, civil society, and religious leaders.[59] Support for the TRC came from various sources, including legislators, Nelson Mandela, international experts such as Kader Asmal, and religious leaders such as Archbishop Desmond Tutu. The TRC, formed in 1995, was widely acknowledged as one of the most influential commissions ever established. Its primary objectives were to address human rights violations, advocate for victims, and oversee amnesty requests from offenders.[60]

The TRC marked its first significant achievement by conducting an extensive investigation into a complex and contentious history, without compromising the stability of the new democratic system. The TRC's emphasis is on a 'forward-looking' approach to justice, with the intention of creating a clear separation between a tumultuous past marred by violence and the potential for a peaceful future. Central to this message was the commission's focus on breaking the cycle of violence. This mindset, championed by leaders like Nelson Mandela and Archbishop Desmond Tutu, and reflected in the TRC's deliberations, underscored the paramount importance of approaching others with empathy and a shared aspiration for peace.

Consequently, the TRC played a crucial role in reducing the risk of communities growing apart and fostering a sense of hope and optimism.[61] In addition, the TRC's promotion of a normative framework is firmly rooted in respect for human rights. Equal treatment of all individuals and groups exemplifies the notion that human rights belong to all humans, and the organization's desire to uphold this value is vital in demonstrating the type of culture it envisioned. Thus, the TRC marked a decisive transition away from an era of conflict and impunity towards a future founded on the rule of law and respect for human rights. The TRC played an indispensable role in signaling a turning point in South African

58. Nardi, "Much Work Remains."
59. Rose, "Twenty Years," 65.
60. Rose, "Twenty Years," 65.
61. Lindahl, "Restricted Reconciliation," 35.

history and in raising awareness of the harm inflicted by the apartheid regime. Similar to other TCs, the TRC was responsible for rewriting the country's official history and creating a shared historical memory that incorporated difficult and traumatic events.

The TRC allowed millions of people in South Africa to listen to the experiences of others for the first time, increasing their understanding and shaping collective memories. It played a pivotal role in uncovering the truth about the past through the accounts of perpetrators who confessed their crimes. One such confession, made by a member of the security force, revealed the widespread use of torture techniques, leaving the nation stunned. Through the mechanism of public hearings and by offering a physically and symbolically inclusive space for all South African citizens to share their stories and experiences, the TRC crafted a new narrative about apartheid violence and resistance to oppressive rule. The posters and banners at the hearing locations reassured the public that they were in a secure and official environment controlled by the commission.

The TRC brought about a transformative shift in how marginalized communities were both perceived and treated in South Africa. It provided them with a formal platform to share their stories and gain recognition. For the first time, black women and other previously excluded groups could hear their voices and acknowledge their contributions, which helped to alter the nation's official history. The TRC demonstrated respect for diversity by allowing testimony to be given in any language, which was especially significant for black women facing racial and gender discrimination. The commission's decision to provide a safe and secure space for victims to share their stories was a powerful statement that recognized the importance of their contributions and their existence as legitimate citizens. It can be argued that the TRC helped reduce inequality by giving previously marginalized communities a voice in official discourse and a place in traditional national institutions.

Expanding upon Verwoerd's critique of a reductionist 'materialist' understanding of social justice,[62] I propose that the TRC's success in confronting unjust conditions can be measured by its impact on the psychological and social well-being of marginalized groups. The TRC addressed the unequal distribution of power by providing previously unheard groups with a platform to share their stories. Moreover, it championed the

---

62. Verwoerd, "Individual and/or Social Justice," 116.

democratization of the power to produce knowledge by challenging the former regime's monopoly on official truth and allowing ordinary South Africans to participate in constructing a new official account of the past. The TRC brought about a significant positive change by shedding light on private rituals and expressions of emotions, such as grief, rage, apologies, and regrets. Unlike in a courtroom, TRC members could give lengthy, personal testimonies without fear of being interrupted by rules or judges. The emotionally charged testimonies of victims astonished, touched, and elicited empathy from the wider South African audience. Many victims finally received the much-needed recognition they had longed for, while offenders had the opportunity to hear about the impact of their actions. The process facilitated a deeper understanding of the seriousness of their mistakes, and public shaming made them feel accountable. Additionally, victims' experiences were amplified into a powerful message of shared suffering and injustice.

The TRC victim hearings and the testimonies of victims remain memorable events for many South Africans. The entire nation bore witness to the collective expression of grief and not just private sorrow. The TRC's greatest success was fostering a sense of shared humanity and compassion among its members and the public. It went beyond examining past acts of violence and fostered a deeper understanding of the truth. The TRC, along with those who testified before it, placed past conflicts under a glaring spotlight by humanizing suffering and exposing the personal tragedies of murder, torture, and rape.

The TRC received testimonies from various entities, including businesses, churches, and non-governmental organizations (NGOs), to gain insight into their perspectives. Although many entities profited from apartheid, they were not responsible for government policies. Critics argue that the TRC placed more blame on private organizations and companies than on the National Party (NP), which played a significant role in the discriminatory practices of the apartheid system. By focusing on the actions of private entities, the TRC allegedly shifted its blame away from the NP and onto company executives who continued to support the government's policies. This move was seen as erasing the unique horror of apartheid, which was systematic and sanctioned the ill treatment of black individuals by the state and society.[63] The TRC had a mandate biased against the then-current NP government. It primarily focused on

---

63. Cottle and Thapa, "The Role of Truth and Reconciliation," 222.

political crimes while overlooking the daily, non-political atrocities endured by millions of South Africans over decades. This narrow focus of the TRC has reduced the prospects for reconciliation.

Individuals were free to participate in the TRC, but this was not mandatory. Some powerful political figures either declined to participate or feigned ignorance of the crimes committed under their supervision. For instance, the former NP President and 'engineer' of apartheid, Frederik Willem de Klerk, claimed that he was unaware of apartheid crimes. In contrast, the former Minister of Law and Order, Adriaan Vlok, showed "selective amnesia" and refused to accept responsibility for the atrocities committed against the people.

EFFICIENCY OF THE TRC IN NORWAY

The TRC in Norway was established in 2018 and has the potential to stimulate discussions on the significance of TCs for the rights of Indigenous and minority groups in the country's well-established democracies. The TRC adopted an innovative approach that incorporates on-site observations, hearings, interviews, and surveys involving key stakeholders. While the primary focus of the establishment of the TRC was not human rights, integrating human rights principles offers essential guidance for its efforts, providing a normative foundation for mobilization, inclusive decision-making, and ensuring high-quality implementation. However, it is important to note that definitive assessments of the TRC's effectiveness at this early stage may require further evaluation and consideration. The incorporation of human rights principles into reconciliation processes, including the TRC, has the potential to empower and bring about transformative outcomes, but its overall impact will necessitate careful observation and analysis in the subsequent stages of its implementation.[64]

CHALLENGES FACED BY TRCs

Colonialism has spawned an economic system primarily geared toward serving the interests of the colonizing power. This frequently entails the extraction of natural resources and the exploitation of local labor, resulting in the underdevelopment of the local economy and the establishment of a dependent relationship between the colony and the colonizing power.

---

64. Haugen, "Any Role."

In the aftermath of colonialism, most Indigenous people continue to experience persistent economic underdevelopment, low levels of investment, and a lack of diversification in their economies. TRCs have been established in Canada, South Africa, and Norway to address the impact of colonialism on Indigenous peoples. Despite the positive intentions behind these initiatives, evidence from other TRCs suggests that TRCs are in no position to decolonize Indigenous peoples in these countries. TRCs typically work within the confines of established political systems, some of which may have been shaped by colonial influences. This context can sometimes hinder their ability to scrutinize and bring about changes to these systems. Despite the progress made by these countries in addressing the wrongdoings of the past, the results have not been sufficient to completely decolonize the Indigenous people in these countries.

TRCs faced various challenges that hindered them from achieving their goals. One such challenge was that TRCs were funded by the same governments that were complicit in the actions being investigated. Additionally, some key players were excluded from the process and survivors were not given adequate opportunities to share their experiences. For example, in Canada, survivors were not allowed to directly name their perpetrators, many of whom held high-ranking positions or had affiliations with government officials.

TRCs typically focus on documenting human rights abuses and providing recommendations for reconciliation. However, they lack the authority to enforce their recommendations or bring about significant structural changes. Many of the recommendations put forth by TRCs have yet to be implemented. The execution of these recommendations is left in the hands of government officials, who often compromise perpetrators of past wrongdoings. For instance, in South Africa, recommendations against apartheid have not been fully implemented due to government collaboration. The relationship between majority law and Sámi Indigenous customary law is still evolving in Norway. While the majority's legal system is the state's primary legal system, Sámi customary laws hold a subordinate place.[65] TRCs are limited in their ability to address the systemic and ongoing impact of colonialism on Indigenous peoples, such as the loss of land, culture, and sovereignty.

---

65. Lingaas, "Indigenous Customary Law," 19.

The gendered component of colonial harm[66] was largely overlooked by the South African and Canadian TRCs, leading to an incomplete understanding of the full extent of these harms. The commissions portrayed colonialism as having had minor negative effects on Black and Indigenous peoples, while bringing about indirect and convoluted benefits for settlers. TRCs missed the opportunity to address gendered injustices and inequities. A reconciliation based on gender considerations would have set a standard for how transitional justice is considered and applied to settler-colonial governments.[67]

The state co-opted the TRCs as a tool for reconciliation without accountability. TRCs are often viewed as a way for governments to move from the legacy of colonialism without taking concrete action to address the ongoing injustices. This can result in the state using TRCs to avoid accountability for past and present wrongs while continuing to perpetuate colonial policies and structures.

TRCs are often dominated by state actors and representatives of the dominant culture rather than by Indigenous peoples. This has resulted in a situation where Indigenous perspectives and experiences are marginalized or even ignored, reinforcing colonial power dynamics. The capacity of TRCs to address persistent systemic problems, such as institutional racism and economic inequality that sustain colonialism and the marginalization of Indigenous peoples, may also be constrained. TRCs do not tackle the root causes of colonial violence or oppression. They primarily focus on documenting and acknowledging past wrongs but do not address the ongoing systemic and structural factors contributing to colonial violence and oppression. Therefore, TRCs are unlikely to result in meaningful and lasting changes for Indigenous people.

The decolonization of Indigenous peoples is a complex and challenging process that requires genuine reconciliation, meaningful dialogue, and tangible actions, rather than solely commissioning investigations and making recommendations. These actions should include reparations to Indigenous peoples in the form of financial compensation, land restitution, self-determination, and other measures that recognize the sovereignty of Indigenous peoples and restore their human rights. The successful decolonization of Indigenous peoples will necessitate collective efforts from all stakeholders to empower Indigenous peoples

---

66. Grey and James, "Truth, Reconciliation, and 'Double Settler Denial,'" 323.
67. Grey and James, "Truth, Reconciliation, and 'Double Settler Denial,'" 324.

to live in dignity and exercise self-determination within their ancestral lands and territories.

ALTERNATIVES FOR TRCs

Considering the inadequacies of TRCs in decolonization, alternative approaches that prioritize the perspectives and experiences of Indigenous peoples and focus on systemic and structural changes are necessary. These approaches might include the recognition of indigenous sovereignty, restoration of Indigenous land rights, and the implementation of self-determination policies.

Decolonization must extend beyond the mere attainment of political independence by the colonized and encompass the restoration of Indigenous peoples' sovereignty, control over their lands and resources, and cultural and spiritual practices. Thus, the true goal of decolonization is to revitalize Indigenous cultures and reestablish the connections between Indigenous peoples and their lands. Ultimately, decolonization must involve a fundamental shift in the relationships between Indigenous peoples and the state, along with a recognition of the ongoing legacy of colonialism.

There is a need for more attention from courts and legal research to address the rights of Indigenous peoples to maintain their customary laws in the domestic legal system. I argue for a structure that provides more legal autonomy to Indigenous people, as the coexistence of two legal systems within the same state raises questions about historical injustice, assimilation, and the supremacy of majority laws.

RECOMMENDATIONS FOR FUTURE TRCs

Significant lessons for future TRCs can be learned from the setbacks of these commissions. The South African TRC has identified its limitations in terms of time and scope, hindering its effectiveness. Future TRCs should be given more resources to avoid similar setbacks, including time and flexibility, to conduct thorough investigations and yield more comprehensive outcomes. However, as Taylor-Smith highlights, success is not just dependent on these factors but also requires political support, resources, and a safe environment in which to work.[68]

---

68. Taylor-Smith, "The Truth and Reconciliation Commission."

In Canada's situation, for example, the government had strong motives to sabotage the TRC's efforts because they posed a potential risk of revealing unethical conduct by certain former government officials and church leaders. Considering this, future TRCs would benefit from being autonomous of the state, where they would not be subject to arbitrary interference or interference in terms of funding and security.

Studies have also shown that TRCs are often tasked with incompatible duties. To address these incompatibilities arising from competing interests, TRCs require additional time, personnel, and resources to fulfill every aspect of their mandate effectively. Empowering TRCs with the authority to implement certain recommendations could demonstrate that their work is meaningful and not in vain.

CONCLUSION

In conclusion, TRCs have emerged as significant instruments in several countries to address the impacts of colonization and advance decolonization efforts. They play a critical role in unearthing historical injustices, amplifying the voices of marginalized Indigenous communities, and fostering societal dialogue. However, despite their success in promoting understanding and reconciliation, achieving true decolonization has been exceedingly challenging.

The commitment to truth-seeking and complete transparency is commendable. They delve into history, confront the past, and reveal the hidden aspects of the colonial era. However, despite their efforts to address historical injustices, the legacies of colonialism are difficult to completely dismantle due to the enduring structures of colonial power and influence. Moreover, transitional justice practices fall short of addressing all facets of past human rights abuses and advancing accountability, restitution, and healing. The shortcomings of transitional justice in fully acknowledging the enduring effects of colonialism and its neglect of Indigenous peoples' perspectives have attracted criticism.

Transitional justice contributes to the creation of spaces where the voices of Indigenous people can be heard and acknowledged, thereby facilitating decolonization. However, the effectiveness of TRCs in decolonization is determined by their ability to fulfill their mandate, the implementation of their recommendations, and their willingness to address current inequalities. Learning from past experiences and genuinely incorporating diverse perspectives can pave the way for a transformative path that prioritizes reconciliation and justice.

While TRCs have made significant strides in documenting historical injustices and fostering societal dialogue, more needs to be done to address the present-day inequalities and systemic challenges rooted in colonial legacies. This requires a commitment to go beyond the documentation of past injustices and to actively work towards dismantling structures that perpetuate inequality and marginalization. It also necessitates a shift in focus from the past to the present and future, with an emphasis on tangible actions that can bring about real changes in the lives of Indigenous people.

In essence, while TRCs have played a crucial role in the decolonization process, their effectiveness is contingent on their ability to adapt and respond to the evolving needs and realities of the communities they serve. This includes not only acknowledging and addressing historical injustices, but also working towards creating a future that is characterized by justice, equality, and self-determination. By doing so, TRCs can contribute to a transformative path that prioritizes genuine reconciliation and justice, thereby playing a more effective role in the decolonization process.

BIBLIOGRAPHY

Almeida, Shana, and Siseko H. Kumalo. "(De)coloniality through Indigeneity: Deconstructing Calls to Decolonize in the South African and Canadian University Contexts." *Education as Change* 22 (2018) 1–15.
Avruch. Kevin, "Truth and Reconciliation Commissions: Problems in Transitional Justice and the Reconstruction of Identity." *Transcultural Psychiatry* 47 (2020) 33. https://doi.org/10.1177/1363461510362043.
Bacchiocchi, Eana, et al. "Energy Justice and the Co-opting of Indigenous Narratives in U.S. Offshore Wind Development." *Renewable Energy Focus* 41 (2022) 133–42.
Balint, Jennifer. "Justifying the Means: The Law as Accomplice in Crimes Against Humanity, African Truth and Reconciliation Commission." *European Journal of Development Research* 11 (2011) 115–40.
Brahm, Eric. "Uncovering the Truth: Examining Truth Commission Success and Impact." *International Studies Perspectives* 8 (2007) 16–35.
Cottle, Drew, and Sunil Thapa. "The Role of Truth and Reconciliation Commission in Peace Building: Nepal." *People: International Journal of Social Sciences* 3 (2017) 218–38.
Coulthard, Glen. *Red Skin, White Masks: Rejecting the Colonial Politics of Recognition*. Minneapolis: University of Minnesota Press, 2014.

Gilbert, Danielle. "Impact, Legitimacy, and Limitations of Truth Commissions." *Democracy and Security* 15 (2019) 408–10. doi:10.1080/17419166.2019.1672292.

Grey, Sam, and James Alison. "Truth, Reconciliation, and 'Double Settler Denial': Gendering the Canada-South Africa Analogy." *Human Rights Review* 17 (2016) 303–28. doi:10.1007/s12142-016-0412-8.

Hansen, Ketil L., et al. "Ethnic Discrimination and Bullying in the Sami and Non-Sami Populations in Norway: the SAMINOR study." *International Journal of Circumpolar Health* 67 (2008) 99–115. doi:10.3402/ijch.v67i1.18243.

Haugen, Hans M. "Any Role for Human Rights in the Norwegian Truth and Reconciliation Commission Addressing Forced Assimilation?" *International Journal on Minority and Group Rights* 29 (2022) 1–25. doi:10.1163/15718115-bja10059/.

Hayner, Priscilla. *Unspeakable Truths: Facing the Challenge of Truth Commissions*. 2nd ed. New York, NY: Routledge, 2011.

Henkeman, Stanley. "Reconciliation as an Outcome Rather than an Intention." In *Trading Justice for Peace? Reframing Reconciliation in TRC Processes in South Africa, Canada, and Nordic Countries*, edited by Sigríður Guðmarsdóttir et al., 1–16. Cape Town: AOSIS, 2021.

Johnsen, Tore. "Negotiating the Meaning of 'TRC' in the Norwegian Context." In *Trading Justice for Peace? Reframing Reconciliation in TRC Processes in South Africa, Canada and Nordic Countries*, edited by Sigríður Guðmarsdóttir et al., 17–40. Cape Town: AOSIS, 2021.

Kristiansen, Roald E. "The Kautokeino Rebellion 1852." http://www.laits.utexas.edu/sami/dieda/hist/kautokeino.htm.

Krog, Antjie. *Country of My Skull: Guilt, Sorrow, and the Limits of Forgiveness in the New South Africa*. New York: New York Times/Random House, 1998.

Kuokkanen, Rauna. "Reconciliation as a Threat or Structural Change? The Truth and Reconciliation Process and Settler Colonial Policy Making in Finland." *Human Rights Review* 21 (2020) 293–312. doi:10.1007/s12142-020-00594-x.

Kvittingen, Ida, and Ingrid P. Nuse. "Why Did Some of the Indigenous Sami People Revolt in 1852? Two of the Rebels Tell Their Stories in a New Book." https://sciencenorway.no/cultural-history-history-sami/why-did-some-of-the-indigenous-sami-people-revolt-in-1852-two-of-the-rebels-tell-their-stories-in-a-new-book/1629700.

Lindahl, Amanda. "Restricted Reconciliation: Limitations of the Truth and Reconciliation Commission of South Africa." PhD diss., University of Wisconsin, 2010.

Lingaas, Carola. "Indigenous Customary Law and Norwegian Domestic Law: Scenes of a (Complementary or Mutually Exclusive) Marriage?" *Laws* 11 (2022) 19. doi:10.3390/laws11020019.

Miller, J. R. *Residential Schools and Reconciliation: Canada Confronts Its History*. University of Toronto Press, 2017.

Nagy, Rosemary. "Settler Witnessing at the Truth and Reconciliation Commission of Canada." *Human Rights Review* 21 (2020) 222.

Nardi, Christopher. "Much Work Remains on the Truth and Reconciliation Commission's 94 Calls to Action." https://nationalpost.com/news/much-work-remains-on-the-truth-and-reconciliation-commissions-94-calls-to-action.

Park, Augustine. "Settler Colonialism and the South African TRC: Ambivalent Denial and Democratisation Without Decolonisation." *Social and Legal Studies* 31 (2021) 216–37. doi:10.1177/09646639211022786.

Petoukhov, Konstantin. "An Evaluation of Canada's Truth and Reconciliation Commission (TRC) through the Lens of Restorative Justice and the Theory of Recognition." Master's thesis, University of Manitoba, 2011. https://www.collectionscanada.gc.ca/obj/thesescanada/vol.

Reed, Graeme, et al. "Indigenizing Climate Policy in Canada: A Critical Examination of the Pan-Canadian Framework and the ZéN RoadMap." *Frontiers in Sustainable Cities* 3 (2021) 1–12. doi:10.3389/frsc.2021.644675.

Regan, Paulette. "Canada's TRC: An 'Unsettling' Indigenous-Centred Relational Justice and Reconciliation Model." In *Trading Justice for Peace? Reframing Reconciliation in TRC Processes in South Africa, Canada, and Nordic Countries*, edited by Sigríður Guðmarsdóttir et al.,1–16. Cape Town: AOSIS, 2021.

Rose, Evelyne. "Twenty Years Since Democracy in South Africa: Reconsidering the Contributions of the Truth and Reconciliation Commission." *Melbourne Journal of Politics* 37 (2015) 61–77.

Ross, Rupert. "Telling Truths and Seeking Reconciliation: Exploring the Challenges." In *From Truth to Reconciliation: Transforming the Legacy of Residential Schools*, edited by M. Castellano et al., 143–59. Ottawa: AHF, 2008.

Solomons, Demaine, et al. "Trading Justice for Peace? Perils and Possibilities." In *Trading Justice for Peace? Reframing Reconciliation in TRC Processes in South Africa, Canada, and Nordic Countries*, edited by Sigríður Guðmarsdóttir et al., 1–16. Cape Town: AOSIS, 2021.

Taylor-Smith, Rodmire N. "The Truth and Reconciliation Commission and traditional methods of reconciliation in Sierra Leone." Master's thesis, University of Tromsø, 2009. ahttps://hdl.handle.net/10037/2085

Truth and Reconciliation Commission of Canada. *Honoring the Truth, Reconciling for the Future: Summary of the Final Report of the Truth and Reconciliation Commission of Canada*. Ottawa: Truth and Reconciliation Commission of Canada, 2015.

UiT.no. "The Commission to Investigate the Norwegianization Policy and Injustice Against the Sámi and Kven/Norwegian Finnish Peoples (The Truth and Reconciliation Commission)." https://uit.no/kommisjonen/mandat_en.

Usami, Makoto. "Defining Truth Commission." *Research & Reviews: Journal of Social Sciences* 2 (2016) 56–61.

Verwoerd, Wilhelm. "Individual and/or Social Justice after Apartheid? The South African Truth and Reconciliation Commission." *The European Journal of Development Research* 11 (1999) 115–40. doi:10.1080/09578819908426741.

Zdeněk, Lyčka, "Norway's indigenous people: From Assimilation to Recognition—Arctic Festival." https://arktickyfestival.cz/en/2020/09/09/norways-indigenous-people-from-assimilation-to-recognition/

PART TWO

Understanding History from a Transformative Perspective

5

Historical Justice as a New Challenge in Historical Research
Reflections on the White Paper Project on the Historical Relations between the Church of Sweden and the Sámi People

DANIEL LINDMARK

Faculty of Arts and Humanities and Umeå School of Education, Umeå University, Umeå, Sweden

INTRODUCTION

When, in early spring 2012, I was asked to direct the White Paper Project on the historical relations between the Church of Sweden (CoS) and the Sámi, I was faced with a dilemma: How could I simultaneously make the results of the project scientifically reliable *and* practically usable in the reconciliation process between the CoS and the Sámi people? Would the project be able to establish a scientific use of history, or would the project's results be disregarded as a moral or ideological use of history? Leading the project entailed navigating different expectations of the academic community, the CoS, and the Sámi people, respectively. If the project were to make a difference, it was imperative that its results not be questioned.

This chapter addresses some of the problems that can occur when historians contribute their research work to processes aimed at establishing historical justice. Drawing from my experience with 'The Church of Sweden and the Sámi—a White Paper Project,' I explore these issues, offering insights into strategies employed to secure the project's scholarly integrity. Additionally, I share my personal reflections on writing for the project. Rather than presenting my experiences as exemplary, I acknowledge that, in the White Paper Project, I was compelled to adopt a more traditional approach to history writing. For a similarly transformative example, I refer to Paulette Regan's classic book *Unsettling the Settler Within*, which describes a path towards a decolonizing engagement with the history of the oppressed.[1] Nonetheless, my own experiences serve to illustrate the challenges historians may confront and the strategies they can employ when they are engaged in processes for historical justice.

Some of the challenges I was confronted with in the White Paper Project are similar to those that arise in most kinds of commissioned research. Often, conflicting interests must be dealt with, including tensions between the wishes of the principal, on the one hand, and the professionalism and integrity of the researcher, on the other. However, the challenges that the White Paper Project gave rise to were more complicated than a mere conflict of interests. First, the principal was divided across several conflicting interests that were also represented in the project's steering group. Second, the project was situated in a reconciliation process characterized by an ideological or moral agenda.

In general, work for historical justice entails overcoming challenges that cannot be covered in this article, for example, the fact that previous research, sources, and theories are impregnated by the power position of Western civilizations and majority societies. To a large extent, the work for historical justice involves deconstructing such perspectives and narratives.

Another problem associated with work for historical justice for the Sámi people concerns the risk of emphasizing or even reinforcing a victim's perspective that does not take the Sámi people's agency into account. Were the Sámi people merely powerless victims of state and church policies? There is a Swedish term, *tvångskristnandet,* which means 'forced conversion to Christianity.' If we employ this term, we tend to forget that the Sámi people, to some extent, could choose which religious worldview and practice they wanted to follow and how they could relate to the Christian

---

1. Regan, *Unsettling*.

faith. Closely connected to this perspective is the risk of homogenizing and stereotyping the Sámi people and their cultural expressions.

HISTORICAL JUSTICE AS RESEARCH AND PRACTICE

Historical justice is both a research field and an area of practical measures. Regarding the latter, various types of historical wrongs, from genocide and war crimes to colonial oppression and discrimination, are dealt with practically. Historical justice includes various elements or steps, including documentation, information, and reparation. Several typologies relevant to historical justice have been developed by scholars and practitioners. For example, one approach in this field is to distinguish between transitional practices, reconciliatory practices, apologizing practices, and communicative practices.[2]

My first contact with the research field and the practice of historical justice was concerned with communicative practices, specifically *educational practices*. Between 2008 and 2012, I directed an international research project concerned with the international revision of history textbooks.[3] The project focused on an educational practice initiated in 1919 by the Norden Association in Norway. In the 1920s, this practice was adopted by the League of Nations, and after World War II, it was employed by several transnational organizations, including the United Nations Educational, Scientific and Cultural Organization (UNESCO). Today, some twenty bilateral and regional commissions remain engaged in negotiating national histories and purging history textbooks from expressions of militarism, nationalism, and prejudiced descriptions of neighboring countries' people, culture, and history. The purpose of this practice is to contribute to peace, international understanding, and even reconciliation. The reconciliatory aspect is evident when societies have been at war with each other, for example, in the Balkans and Southeast Asia.

HISTORIANS AND HISTORICAL JUSTICE

Historians have come to play an essential role in the pursuit of historical justice. For instance, they have frequently contributed important knowledge concerning historical abuses. However, on occasion, historians have

2. Torpey, "Introduction"; Sjögren, "Att göra upp."
3. Åström Elmersjö, "History."

been criticized for pursuing specific political causes in their contribution of historical knowledge to processes aimed at establishing historical justice. However, historian Klaus Neumann holds the view that the contributions made by historians are significantly broader than that. He highlights five areas where historians have made significant contributions with critical and nuanced perspectives:

> [1] They have provided critical analyses of processes of memorialising and historicising historic wrongs, [2] highlighted silences and absences in representations of past injustices, [3] drawn attention to pasts that have been largely forgotten, [4] engaged with seemingly unbidden intrusions of the past into the present and [5] identified and analysed the motives and desires of individual actors.[4]

These contributions refer to research fields that have grown from strength to strength in recent decades and include areas where not only historians have been active, for instance, research on historical culture, the use of history, cultural memory, and historical justice, the latter often referred to as *transitional justice*. Take note that historical justice has become a growing field of research. In a variety of ways, historians have thus contributed with a critical approach to practices in the field of historical justice.

It should be noted that many historians who have contributed historical knowledge to processes aimed at establishing historical justice have also engaged in research and reflection on these processes. Among Swedish historians, Malin Arvidsson, Björn Norlin, and David Sjögren have this double experience.[5] I claim membership in this category of historians.[6] For example, when I was responsible for the White Paper Project, I also directed a research project on the use of history in similar processes.[7] After the White Paper Project concluded, I continued to engage in research on historical justice processes.[8] The reflections I share in

---

4. Neumann, "Historians," 145.

5. Arvidsson, *Att ersätta*; Norlin and Sjögren, "Educational History"; Norlin and Lindmark, "Generating."

6. Lindmark, "Historiebruk."

7. I was in charge of the research project "Sami Voices and Sorry Churches: Use of History in Church-Sami Reconciliation Processes," funded by the Swedish Research Council Formas (2012–2015).

8. I have been involved in two research projects: "ReconTrans: Trading Justice for Peace? Reconciliation as a Transformative Concept in TRC Processes," directed by Tore Johnsen at VID Specialized University, Tromsø, Norway (2019–2023), and "TRiNC: Truth & Reconciliation in the Nordic Countries," directed by Astrid Andersen at the

this chapter are thus based on experiences from my double approach to the field of historical justice.

THE WHITE PAPER PROJECT ON THE CoS AND THE SÁMI PEOPLE

In November 2012, the White Paper Project on the CoS and the Sámi people began. At the Ságastallamat conference in Kiruna, October 2011, representatives of the Sámi people argued that a continued reconciliation process between the CoS and the Sámi people required documentation of the historical abuse that the CoS had committed against the Sámi people. The White Paper Project was thus considered a prerequisite for a continued reconciliation process. At the same time, it was part of a reconciliation process that, inspired by the international ecumenical work, had been ongoing since the 1990s. Reconciliation services were held, the Sámi Council of the Church of Sweden was established, Sámi working groups were formed in the northern dioceses, the South Sámi parish newspaper *Daerpies Dierie* was launched, and commissions were established. In 2006, an investigation resulted in a report on Sámi issues in the CoS.[9] Among other actions, a hearing was proposed, which came to fruition in 2011 in the form of the Ságastallamat conference, where the desire for a white paper project was articulated.[10]

After the Ságastallamat conference, the CoS's Theological Committee was commissioned to develop an action plan with the Sámi Council of the Church of Sweden. The plan contained eight items, two of which were documentation projects. First, the Nomad School's activities would be documented through interviews with former students. The Nomad School was instituted in 1913 as a segregated, residential school system for children of nomadic Sámi people who practiced reindeer herding. The school aimed to offer its pupils a restricted curriculum that did not expose the Sámi children to the lure of Western civilization but kept them faithful to their traditional culture and business practices. Second, the proposed white paper project would document historical abuses against the Sámi people. The action plan also proposed that a compilation be made concerning what was known about the two periods when the

---

Danish Institute for International Studies, Copenhagen, Denmark (2021–2023).

9. Ekström and Schött, *Samiska frågor*.

10. For more details, see Lindmark and Sundström, "The Church of Sweden."

repression against the Sámi people had been at its strongest, namely: (i) the period of "the witchcraft trials" of 1680–1730, and (ii) the period of racial biology policies that took place around the turn of the twentieth century. This compilation was supplemented with an inventory expressing the need for further research.

The CoS's Central Board decided to implement the action plan, and the CoS's Research Department was commissioned to finance the White Paper Project. The project was located at Umeå University under my leadership, and in November 2012, the first steering group meeting took place. The steering group included representatives of Umeå University and some of the most relevant central bodies of the CoS, including the Theological Committee, the Research Department, and the Sámi Council. The steering group was dominated by Sámi people who participated in developing the project plan, which was completed in August 2013.

The White Paper Project resulted in two publications. In April 2016, the 'scientific anthology' was published.[11] This comprehensive collection of academic articles in two volumes, to which more than thirty scholars had contributed, is often referred to as the "White Paper," even though these words are not included in the document's title. In February 2017, the project concluded with the publication of the popular science version of the "scientific anthology."[12] After the project's formal conclusion, the editors produced an extended and updated English version of the popular science publication.[13]

Whilst the project aimed to produce scientific knowledge, we ask: How would it be possible to safeguard the project's scientific integrity? After all, the project was part of an ideologically driven reconciliation process, and in the project's mandate, it was assumed that the church had committed wrongdoings against the Sámi people. Would it be possible to turn such an ideologically driven project into a scientific enterprise? I made several efforts to safeguard the scientific independence of the project. Thus, in retrospect, it is apparent that I had engaged in *academic boundary work*.[14] This term is used in the sociology of science and refers to strategies scientists use to draw a rhetorical line between their research and activities not

11. Lindmark and Sundström, *De historiska relationerna*.
12. Lindmark and Sundström, *Samerna och Svenska kyrkan*.
13. Lindmark and Sundström, *The Sami and the Church of Sweden*. The three publications are freely available on the Internet: https://www.svenskakyrkan.se/samiska/vitboken.
14. Lindmark, "Historiebruk."

characterized by the qualities that should distinguish scientists, their methods, and claims. The most well-known representative of this theory, Thomas F. Gieryn, states that academic boundary work is most conspicuous when researchers explain their science to the public.[15] "Protection of autonomy" is a primary strategy used in boundary work, which I duly invoked in my efforts to defend the scientific integrity of the project.

Protecting the Scientific Independence of the White Paper Project

1. The project adopted a free and independent approach to its mandate. On its own initiative, the steering group decided to expand the scope and goals of the project from compiling information about what was known about two (limited) periods (when the actions of the church had been most problematic) to covering the entire historical period from the Middle Ages to the 1900s.

2. In order to protect the professional integrity of the researchers involved in the project, the scholars were granted the freedom to choose their own research problems and perspectives within a thematically defined area. The researchers were free to draw any conclusions that they found scientifically justified.

3. Each researcher individually stood for their own text and was not expected to take responsibility for the entire project. Furthermore, each researcher could freely decide whether they wished to refer to the present-day situation and the reconciliation process in their text. It transpired that most of the participating scholars preferred to write purely historically.

4. The scientific contributions to the "scientific anthology" underwent a peer review process. For this task, the project engaged scholars who possessed eminent knowledge of the research field. Furthermore, the anthology was published in an academic book series that required peer review to be considered for publication. The peer review process was thus used to strengthen the academic standard of the publication.

5. The distinction between (a) historical research produced by academic scholars and (b) the more ideological texts aimed at inspiring

---

15. Gieryn, "Boundary-Work"; Gieryn, *Cultural Boundaries*.

action was maintained in the division of the project's output into two different publications, namely the peer-reviewed 'scientific anthology' of 1,135 pages published in two volumes,[16] and the 228-page popular science book with the subtitle *Basis for Church Reconciliation Work*.[17]

6. In the popular science book that was published in 2017, a distinction was made between academic research and political action in the form of two sections. One main section included a summary of the scientific anthology and one shorter section included texts representing perspectives on reconciliation theology, reconciliation ethics, and reconciliation politics.

7. The project refrained from presenting a formal action plan or roadmap toward reconciliation by referring to Tore Johnsen's reconciliation theology,[18] which emphasizes the idea that reconciliation is a process between two parties. This policy also drew a clear demarcation between academic research and political action. The popular science book concluded with an article by Sylvia Sparrock, then chair of the Sámi Council in the Church of Sweden and a member of the project's steering group.[19] Sparrock articulated several demands in her article, but they reflected the author's perspective and did not represent the views of the entire project and its steering group. However, whilst representing a Sámi voice, Sparrock's article can be regarded as the starting point of a dialogue between the Sámi people and the CoS based on the results of the White Paper Project.

8. The distinction between academic research and political action was also manifested in restrictions that I imposed on myself in my contact with the media. The White Paper Project attracted no small amount of interest in the media, and I was repeatedly interviewed

16. Lindmark and Sundström, *De historiska relationerna*.

17. Lindmark and Sundström, *Samerna och Svenska kyrkan*. This strategy of distinguishing between "research" and "policy" was influenced by experiences from the State of Sweden's White Paper on abuse against the Roma people, which was published in 2014 (Ministry of Culture Sweden, *Dark Unknown History*). The White Paper Committee commissioned research by a number of researchers, but the researchers' voices were not heard. Instead, their results were incorporated—without references—into the politically-controlled text that resulted from the project. I deliberately chose a different path. I wanted to keep research and politics separate, or in other words, I chose to distinguish between a scientific and ideological use of history.

18. Johnsen, "Erkänd historia"; Johnsen, "Acknowledged History."

19. Sparrock, "Vägar framåt"; Sparrock, "Ways Forward."

on television and for the newspapers. During these interviews, I avoided responding to questions concerning the reconciliation process. Instead, I directed the media's focus on the White Paper Project, its assignment, the working process, and its expected outcomes.

9. The ambition to safeguard the scientific quality of the project also entailed that I reflected on the boundaries between historical science, on the one hand, and the users' expectations, on the other. These reflections included questions about truth, ethics, and responsibility but also encompassed issues concerning the crucial link between the past and the present.[20]

VARIOUS USES OF HISTORY AND TRUTH CLAIMS

One particular challenge in historical research that takes place within the framework of a reconciliation process is a consequence of the fact that so many different expectations are inevitably tied to the results of such research. These expectations can be interpreted in terms of different uses of history. The Swedish historian, Klas-Göran Karlsson, has constructed a typology of uses that includes, among other things, the scientific, political, ideological, moral, and existential use of history.[21]

In the field of historical justice, different kinds of uses of history can be linked to different truth claims. For example, the South African Truth and Reconciliation Commission (TRC) pointed out in a 1998 report that various truths or truth claims can make the work of historical justice a complicated task. These various truths include:

1. "factual or forensic truth," meaning that evidence was obtained and corroborated through reliable procedures;
2. "personal and narrative truth," based upon the many stories that individuals told about their experiences under apartheid;
3. "social or 'dialogue' truth," established through interaction, discussion and debate; and
4. "healing and restorative truth," referring to the truth that places facts and their meaning within the context of human relationships.[22]

20. Lindmark, "Historiebruk."
21. Karlsson, *Historia som vapen*; Karlsson, "Historia."
22. Truth and Reconciliation Commission of South Africa, *Report*, 110.

The list of different conceptualizations of truth can be made considerably longer by including, for example, moral truth, political truth, and communicative truth, the latter referring to a 'truth' that can be communicated to the general public. Consequently, in the context of a white paper project or a truth commission (TC), the truth can be of many different kinds and represent a wide range of interests and ways of approaching and using the past. In the following section, I present my own encounter with the truth claims of the principal and stakeholders of the White Paper Project.

TRUTH CLAIMS AND THE LAPP SCHOOL SYSTEM

The fact that historians often shy away from the concept of 'truth' is a particular problem. Traditionally, historians have held the view that their work involves an objective search for truth, an exposition of the past "just as it was" (*wie es eigentlich gewesen*), as Leopold von Ranke put it. However, in recent decades, this objectivist view has been challenged by more constructivist conceptions of historical truth that note that the past is always viewed and told from a particular perspective.

Constructivist conceptions of historical truth are difficult to reconcile with concepts of truth that a stakeholder might express in their expectations of the outcome of a TRC, for example. In the case of the White Paper Project, conceptualizations of an absolute, objective truth became visible when authoritative representatives of the CoS expressed their views. For instance, then Archbishop Anders Wejryd argued that "the truth must come to light" and Bishop Karl-Johan Tyrberg argued that "truth and reconciliation belong together."[23] In these utterances, we find the expression of an absolute, objective truth, arguably with an additional theological nuance conveying something along the lines of "the truth shall set you free."[24]

My research for the White Paper Project was concerned with the church's teaching efforts in the Swedish part of Sápmi in the early modern period, especially the so-called "Lapp School."[25] The Lapp School was a residential school system instituted by the Diet of 1723. By the middle of the century, all the parishes in Swedish Sápmi had one school each. These schools were designed to teach reading and religion to six pupils for two

---

23. Lindmark, "Historiebruk."
24. John 8:32.
25. Lindmark, "Svenska undervisningsinsatser."

years. The schools were co-educational institutions. From 1744, the most talented students could be hired as catechists, i.e., itinerant auxiliary teachers, usually after spending an extra year at school.[26]

Prior to my contribution to the White Paper Project, I had written articles about the Lapp School system from a critical postcolonial perspective. This was especially the case in one article on 'Pietism and Colonialism,'[27] which was quite an argumentative piece of research. The article aimed to prove that early modern Sámi schools displayed the same characteristics as the Catholic priest seminaries in twentieth-century Congo, according to Valentin Mudimbe's postcolonial analysis.[28] These two school systems shared the principles of isolation, domestication, and acculturation in their operations. In the above-mentioned article, I also referred to Richard Gawthrop's indoctrination analysis of the Pietist *Anstalten* in eighteenth-century German Halle.[29]

However, in the White Paper Project, I found it difficult to use the theoretical framework I had applied in my previous articles, even though a postcolonial perspective should have been a good fit since it very clearly highlighted the oppression that took place in the Lapp School system. The stance that I adopted was quite confusing to me, and I will share some explanations as to why this was the case. Had I arrived at the conclusion that postcolonial theory no longer represented cutting-edge research? For some years, there had been a shift from theories that reinforced notions of "victimhood" to theories that focused on a sense of agency. Given the context, this explanation would not be particularly far-fetched. Or was I just uncomfortable with the possibly speculative, hazardous, and potentially anachronistic parallels I had drawn between different school system initiatives? As a matter of fact, I had previously discussed some of the weaknesses of my approach in a lecture on problems in educational history research.[30] Consequently, my critical view of my earlier research could have impacted my position when I began work on the White Paper Project. Other possible explanations regarding my theoretical position take into consideration the fact that the White Paper Project can be characterized as "commissioned research." Did I adjust my approach to the overarching reconciliation agenda by downplaying my

26. Lindmark, "Sámi Schools."
27. Lindmark, "Utbildning och kolonialism"; Lindmark, "Pietism and Colonialism."
28. Mudimbe, *The Idea of Africa*.
29. Gawthrop, *Pietism*.
30. Lindmark, "History of Education."

critical perspective? Or did I merely adopt the concept of "truth" then prevalent among the principal and stakeholders, i.e., an absolute, objective truth that existed beyond any theoretical perspective?

The approach to the work that I eventually chose entailed that I applied no explicit theory at all. Instead, I presented the empirical 'truth' of the eighteenth-century school system of Swedish Sápmi. In doing so, I approached an objectivist concept of truth that I did not really advocate for in my profession as a historian. I think my approach can be explained as an attempt to respond to the demands and expectations placed on the White Paper Project. I did not want to expose myself to criticism for making moral, ideological, or political use of the past. Consequently, I tried to stay as neutral as possible and write as nuanced as possible. However, I was not the only historian who had decided to write 'purely' empirically; a large majority of the scholars engaged in the project also chose the same path. I suggest that this move the other scholars made was a consequence of the genre and the truth claims linked to it.

CONNECTING THE PAST TO THE PRESENT

In my contribution to the White Paper Project, I also refrained from making connections between the past and present, something I had previously done when writing from a postcolonial perspective.[31] This, too, may seem contradictory. The White Paper Project was, after all, concerned with producing historical knowledge aimed for present-day use. On this point, I adopted a more traditional historian's ideal. Generally, historians speak only about the past and refrain from commenting on the consequences a particular history may have on the present. Moreover, even if the study of history at school is often motivated by its usefulness for understanding the present, history students receive very limited training on how to connect the past to the present, even candidate history teachers.

Of course, reflections on the link between the past and present are not entirely lacking. In this context, consider the research fields of the use of history, history culture, and cultural memory, which are devoted to this phenomenon. However, research in these fields is subject to several limitations since it is usually restricted to examining how individuals, groups, and organizations connect the past to the present whilst omitting to recommend how these connections should be made.

31. Lindmark, "Utbildning och colonialism."

However, some historians have appeared in defense of the otherwise hateful concept of 'presentism,' which refers to the problematic intrusion of the present into the study of the past, i.e., a source of anachronism. As a rule, historians are perceived to "reconstruct the past without the distorting effects of the present" to avoid anachronism or presentism.[32] As demonstrated by historian David Armitage and others,[33] various types of presentism exist. Notwithstanding this, some aspects of presentism are not only acceptable but also quite necessary. For example, consider the most obvious link between the past and the present, namely the historians themselves. Historians choose their topics according to their current interests, and their arguments concerning relevance and urgency relate to present-day discussions that take place among historians. Historical research is generally characterized by a constant negotiation between the past and present.

The moral use of history can illustrate one problem concerning the connection between the past and the present. In many ways, the White Paper Project, like TRCs in general, can be considered as exercising a moral use of history. The search for historical justice is concerned with establishing who can be held morally responsible for what happened in the past and what demands can be made with regard to moral responsibility. The practices of historical justice usually have a strong moral dimension, including the exhortation to commit to the victim of abuse, to document the abuse, and to restore the victim in some way.

Nevertheless, it can be challenging to reconcile academic historical research with a moral use of history. Historians receive no training in making moral judgments but are taught to refrain from such things because of the risk of making the present a norm for the past, thus allowing presentism or anachronism to color their work. However, in recent years, historians have debated how moral issues in historical research should be dealt with.[34] I argue that historians' engagement in practices of historical justice can contribute to this debate.

---

32. Armitage, "In Defense of Presentism" (2020).

33. Armitage, "In Defense of Presentism" (2023); Loison, "Forms of Presentism"; Tosh, "Anachronism."

34. See, for instance, Wiklund, *I det modernas landskap*.

ATTEMPTS AT EXPLORING THE LINK BETWEEN THE PAST AND PRESENT

My work on the White Paper Project intensified my reflections on the links between the past and present, including various types of presentism. In the years following the project's conclusion, I developed several strategies that can be employed to deal with the connection between the past and present in a more conscious and systematic way than before. I will briefly mention three initiatives in this area that are, to some degree, conflicting. First, I returned to the topic of the Lapp School system of the eighteenth century and wrote a piece on physical abuse in the system *without using present-day concepts*, thereby minimizing the intrusion of the present into the past.[35]

Second, I reflected on the possibility of developing more systematic approaches to the application of historical knowledge in contemporary society. In my research field, I proposed a form of applied history of education. Under the leadership of Johannes Westberg, this idea was further developed into a platform for a national graduate school involving four Swedish universities.[36] This enterprise aims to provide doctoral candidates with the theoretical and methodological tools they need to contribute historical knowledge that benefits the present-day school system.

Third, I explored the link between historical justice and history education. With colleagues at Umeå University, I organized an international conference on this theme in June 2019, resulting in an edited volume.[37] This publication includes both empirical studies and more conceptual pieces of work. The chapters provide examples of the process of *educationalization*, i.e., the process by which knowledge generated from historical justice practices is made relevant and useful in educational settings.[38] Not only do the contributions in the anthology emphasize the necessary link between the past and present in history education by

---

35. Lindmark, "Att undersöka."

36. "Schooling in perspective: A graduate school in applied history of education" is directed by Johannes Westberg and funded by the Swedish Research Council (2020–2024). Ten doctoral candidates are financed by the graduate school, and another four are affiliated to the graduate school, albeit with alternative sources of funding. Westberg has published an article in which he further elaborates on the usefulness of educational history (Westberg, "What We Can Learn").

37. Keynes et al., *Historical Justice*.

38. See, for instance, Norlin and Lindmark, "Generating."

applying the concept of 'historical consciousness,'[39] but they also provide history teachers with several tools and recommendations for teaching about historical abuses.[40]

CONCLUDING REFLECTIONS

I have addressed some of the challenges that historians can be confronted with when their research contributes to processes for historical justice. Drawing on my experience from 'The Church of Sweden and the Sámi—a White Paper Project,' I have presented the strategies that were employed to protect the scientific autonomy of the project. In addition, I have discussed my reactions to the contribution of my research to the project. After providing a general discussion concerning the links between the past and present in historical research, I presented a number of initiatives that can be used to explore these links further in educational history and history education research.

Historical justice is, indeed, a challenge for historians, and I must admit that I hesitated somewhat when I was asked to organize and direct the White Paper Project. Notwithstanding my initial hesitancy, I am glad that I rose to the challenge. The task proved to be very rewarding, not only in terms of its significance for the continued reconciliation process but also regarding my own professional development. The project provoked reflections on how one can make the past relevant in the present and how to make the competencies that historians possess relevant to contemporary issues without jeopardizing their professional integrity. As revealed above, these reflections have continued even after the project's conclusion.

BIBLIOGRAPHY

Armitage, David. "In Defense of Presentism." https://scholar.harvard.edu/files/armitage/files/in_defence_of_presentism.pdf.

———. "In Defense of Presentism." In *In History and Human Flourishing*, edited by Darrin M. McMahon, 59–84. Oxford: Oxford University Press, 2023.

Arvidsson, Malin. *Att ersätta det oersättliga: Statlig gottgörelse för ofrivillig sterilisering och vanvård av omhändertagna barn*. Örebro: Örebro University, 2016.

---

39. See, for instance, Robinson, "Developing."
40. See, for instance, Bermudez, "Narrative Justice?"

Bermudez, Angela. "Narrative Justice?: Ten Tools to Deconstruct Narratives about Violent Pasts." In *Historical Justice and History Education*, edited by Matilda Keynes et al., 269–89. London: Palgrave Macmillan, 2021.

Ekström, Sören, and Marie Schött. *Samiska frågor i Svenska kyrkan*. Stockholm: Church of Sweden, 2006.

Åhlmersjö, Henrik A. "History Beyond Borders. Peace Education, History Textbook Revision, and the Internationalization of History Teaching in the Twentieth Century." *Historical Encounters: A Journal of Historical Consciousness, Historical Cultures, and History Education* 1 (2014) 62–74.

Gawthrop, Richard L. *Pietism and the Making of Eighteenth-Century Prussia*. Cambridge: Cambridge University Press, 1993.

Gieryn, Thomas F. "Boundary-Work and the Demarcation of Science from Non-Science: Strains and Interests in Professional Ideologies of Scientists." *American Sociological Review* 48 (1983) 781–95.

———. *Cultural Boundaries of Science: Credibility on the Line*. Chicago: Chicago University Press, 1999.

Johnsen, Tore. "Acknowledged History and Renewed Relationships: Perspectives on Reconciliation Work between the Church and the Sami People." In *The Sami and the Church of Sweden: Results from a White Paper Project*, edited by Daniel Lindmark and Olle Sundström, 97–124. Möklinta: Gidlunds förlag, 2018.

———. "Erkänd historia och förnyade relationer: Perspektiv på försoningsarbetet mellan kyrkan och samerna." In *Samerna och Svenska kyrkan: Underlag för kyrkligt försoningsarbete*, edited by Daniel Lindmark and Olle Sundström, 101–30. Möklinta: Gidlunds förlag, 2017.

Karlsson, Klas-Göran. "Historia, historiedidaktik och historiekultur—teori och perspektiv." In *Historien är närvarande: Historiedidaktik som teori och tillämpning*, edited by Klas-Göran Karlsson and Ulf Zander, 13–89. Lund: Studentlitteratur, 2014.

———. *Historia som vapen: Historiebruk och Sovjetunionens upplösning 1985–1995*. Stockholm: Natur och kultur, 1999.

Keynes, Matilda, et al., eds. *Historical Justice and History Education*. London: Palgrave Macmillan, 2021.

Lindmark, Daniel. "Att undersöka historiska övergrepp: Arjeplogs lappskola vid 1800-talets början." In *Vardagsliv i kåta och stuga: Bidrag från Vilhelminabiennalen 23–24 september 2019*, edited by Susanne Haugen and Robert Eckeryd, 191–212. Umeå: Johan Nordlander-sällskapet, 2021.

———. "Historiebruk i retrospektiva praktiker: Historikers bidrag till försoning." In *Gränsöverskridande kyrkohistoria: De språkliga minoriteterna på Nordkalotten*, edited by Daniel Lindmark, 115–42. Umeå: Religious History of the North, 2016.

———. "History of Education, Truth and Reconciliation: The Case of Sami Educational History." Unpublished plenary lecture at the EERA Histories of Education Summer School Conference, Umeå University, 12–15 June 2014.

———. "Pietism and Colonialism: Swedish Schooling in Eigthteenth-Century Sápmi." *Acta Borealia: Nordic Journal of Circumpolar Societies* 23 (2006) 116–29.

———. "Sámi Schools, Female Enrolment, and the Teaching Trade: Sámi Women's Involvement in Education in Early Modern Sweden." In *Sámi Educational History in a Comparative International Perspective*, edited by Otso Kortekangas et al., 13–26. London: Palgrave Macmillan, 2019.

———. "Svenska undervisningsinsatser och samiska reaktioner på 1600- och 1700-talen." In *De historiska relationerna mellan Svenska kyrkan och samerna: En vetenskaplig antologi*, edited by Daniel Lindmark and Olle Sundström, 341–69. Skellefteå: Artos, 2016.

———. "Utbildning och kolonialism: Svensk skolundervisning i Sápmi på 1700-talet." *Tidskrift för lärarutbildning och forskning* 11 (2004) 13–31.

Lindmark, Daniel, and Olle Sundström. "The Church of Sweden and the Sami—a White Paper Project: Background, Assignment and Organisation." In *The Sami and the Church of Sweden: Results from a White Paper Project*, edited by Daniel Lindmark and Olle Sundström, 9–20. Möklinta: Gidlunds förlag, 2018.

Lindmark, Daniel, and Olle Sundström, eds. *De historiska relationerna mellan Svenska kyrkan och samerna: En vetenskaplig antologi*. Skellefteå: Artos, 2016.

———. *Samerna och Svenska kyrkan: Underlag för kyrkligt försoningsarbete*. Möklinta: Gidlunds förlag, 2017.

———. *The Sami and the Church of Sweden: Results from a White Paper Project*. Möklinta: Gidlunds förlag, 2018.

Loison, Laurent. "Forms of Presentism in the History of Science: Rethinking the Project of Historical Epistemology." *Studies in History and Philosophy of Science* 60 (2016) 29–37.

Ministry of Culture Sweden. *The Dark Unknown History: White Paper on Abuses and Rights Violations against Roma in the 20th Century*. Stockholm: Fritzes, 2014.

Mudimbe, Valentin Y. *The Idea of Africa*. Bloomington: Indiana University Press, 1994.

Neumann, Klaus. "Historians and the Yearning for Historical Justice." *Rethinking History* 18 (2014) 145–64.

Norlin, Björn, and Daniel Lindmark. "Generating and Popularising Historical Knowledge in a Reconciliation Process: The Case of the Church of Sweden and the Sami." In *Historical Justice and History Education*, edited by Matilda Keynes et al., 131–51. London: Palgrave Macmillan, 2021.

Norlin, Björn, and David Sjögren. "Educational History in the Age of Apology: The Church of Sweden's 'White Book' on Historical Relations to the Sami, the Significance of Education and Scientific Complexities in Reconciling the Past." *Educare* 14 (2019) 69–95.

Regan, Paulette. *Unsettling the Settler Within: Indian Residential Schools, Truth Telling, and Reconciliation in Canada*. Vancouver: University of British Columbia Press, 2010.

Robinson, Natasha. "Developing Historical Consciousness for Social Cohesion: How South African Students Learn to Construct the Relationship between Past and Present." In *Historical Justice and History Education*, edited by Matilda Keynes et al., 341–63. London: Palgrave Macmillan, 2021.

Sjögren, David. "Att göra upp med det förflutna: Sanningskommissioner, officiella ursäkter och vitböcker i ett svenskt och internationellt perspektiv." In *De historiska relationerna mellan Svenska kyrkan och samerna: En vetenskaplig antologi*, edited by Daniel Lindmark and Olle Sundström, 123–152. Skellefteå: Artos, 2016.

Sparrock, Sylvia. "Vägar framåt: Från kolonisering till försoning." In *Samerna och Svenska kyrkan: Underlag för kyrkligt försoningsarbete*, edited by Daniel Lindmark and Olle Sundström, 157–183. Möklinta: Gidlunds förlag 2017.

———. "Ways Forward: From Colonisation to Reconciliation." In *The Sami and the Church of Sweden: Results from a White Paper Project*, edited by Daniel Lindmark and Olle Sundström, 149–178. Möklinta: Gidlunds förlag, 2018.

Torpey, John. "Introduction: Politics of the Past." In *Politics and the Past: On Repairing Historical Injustices*, edited by John Torpey, 1–36. Lanham, MD: Rowman & Littlefield, 2003.

Tosh, Nick. "Anachronism and Retrospective Explanation: In Defense of a Present-Centred History of Science." *Studies in History and Philosophy of Science* 34 (2003) 647–59.

Truth and Reconciliation Commission of South Africa. *Report*. 1 vol. 1998. https://www.justice.gov.za/trc/report/finalreport/Volume%201.pdf.

Westberg, Johannes. "What We Can Learn from Studying the Past: The Wonderful Usefulness of History in Educational Research." *Encounters in Theory and History of Education* 22 (2021) 227–48.

Wiklund, Martin. *I det modernas landskap: Historisk orientering och kritiska berättelser om det moderna Sverige mellan 1960 och 1990*. Eslöv: Östlings bokförlag Symposion, 2006.

6

Decolonizing Scandinavian Creation Theology

The Constructive Critique of Key Concepts in the Works of Sámi Theologian Tore Johnsen

GYRID GUNNES

*Faculty of Theology and Social Sciences,
VID Specialized University, Oslo, Norway*

INTRODUCTION

In her book *The Lords Sent Us Here*,[1] Elin Anna Labba, a North Sámi writer, discusses multiple consequences of the forced deterritorialization of the Sámi people from the Troms region during the early and mid-twentieth century. She concludes her narration by noting the striking absence of the Sámi people's stories from the master narratives of the Scandinavian nation states. One way of engaging the emotional, political, and epistemological work of decolonization is to transform such absence into presence in these master narratives. Labba argues that the metaphor of the *void* left by the oblivion of Indigenous people should give way to a different metaphor: the *weaving of a fabric*. To decolonize is to weave

---

1. Labba, *Herrene sendte oss hit*, hereafter *The Lords Sent Us Here*.

patterns of stories of Sámi lives into the fabric of the national master narratives "with a voice which those who went before us never had."[2]

As a native of the Tromsø region, Labba's book compellingly exposes a truth I must humbly acknowledge with a sense of shame—the stark absence of Sámi voices, not only within the national narrative but also in very local narratives. Even though I received all my elementary and college education from Tromsø, as well as my university degree in theology and comparative religion from the University of Tromsø, the stories of the forced deterritorialization of the Sámi people from the island of Kvaløya and the intergenerational trauma that followed in its wake were unfamiliar to me until the publication of Labba's book in 2021. Her book gives potent examples showing that colonization is an epistemological issue tied to the production of knowledge. Decolonization necessitates recognizing colonization not only as an outcome of policies enacted and subsequently implemented by the state governance in the past. When viewed through an epistemological lens, colonization becomes a script deeply embedded in the prevailing ignorance held by the majority population of what it means to be subjected to, among other evils, forced deterritorialization. Sámi voices thus summoned the Norwegian majority population to a *metanoia from the ignorance enabled by majority privilege* to a state of self-reflexivity and even repentance.

This process needs to be understood as a continuous hermeneutical process. It must never be subcontracted to the individual believer and transformed into a matter of the personal piety and emotional constitution of the individual. Rather, this *metanoia* needs to happen on the institutional level as a calling to those who, in one way or another, hold the power to speak publicly and shape the conceptual contours of the conversation—in other words, those who partake in professional theological discourse.

Following Labba's call to examine the absence of Sámi patterns in the fabric of Scandinavian theological master narratives and to articulate the responsibility of professional theological and religious institutions, a key question arises: *What would a fabric of Scandinavian master narratives that consists of both minority and majority voices look like in theological discourse?* In this chapter, the aim is to answer this question, with particular attention paid to certain aspects of the work of Sámi-Norwegian theologian Tore Johnsen. My argument is that the inclusion

---

2. Labba, *The Lords Sent Us Here*, 188.

of Sámi voices in the master narratives of Scandinavia is an epistemologically complex matter. It demands attention to the epistemological agentic status of Indigenous people today in different kinds of institutions, such as the church. Additionally, it necessitates a critical examination of the theological traditions of the majority populations, including those aspects of these traditions that may not initially appear relevant to discourses of colonization.

WHAT DOES IT MEAN TO BE INCLUDED IN THE FABRIC OF THE SCANDINAVIAN MASTER NARRATIVE?

One way of conceptualizing a fabric of Scandinavian master narratives that consists of both minority and majority voices as a theological discourse would be to enlarge such master narratives with stories that point to the agency of colonized peoples. Using the metaphor of 'fabric,' one could argue that this would imply making the pattern of the fabric more complicated by including elements of Sámi voices. Empirically speaking, this points to the establishment of Sámi ecclesial structures within the Scandinavian Lutheran churches, such as the Sámi Church Council (SCC) within the Church of Norway (CoN). Other examples are the employment of Sámi-speaking priests and Sámi-language confirmation classes across the borders of the nation states of Scandinavia. Furthermore, it encompasses the creation of Sámi contextual theology, such as the Sámi catechism *Jordens Barn, Solens Barn, Vindens Barn* by Tore Johnsen and contributions by Line Skum.[3]

All of these vital efforts may be seen as examples of turning absence into presence by weaving Sámi patterns into the fabric of theological national master narratives. This may entail a movement toward theological, ecclesial, and ritual justice for the Sámi citizens of Scandinavia. They give Sámi members of the Lutheran churches of Scandinavia what is rightfully theirs as baptized members. Furthermore, they are practices of decolonization because they affirm and embody the Sámi people's self-evident membership and epistemic agency in a mainline ecclesial institution.

These efforts may be classified as examples of the established and growing global literature and ecclesial practice of contextual theological enterprise within the overall framework of theologies of liberation.

3. Johnsen, *Jordens barn*; Skum, "En åpen kirke"; Skum, "Diakoni."

Theologies of liberation are found in various forms, but they share a common commitment to validating human experience in theological discourse. They insist on a more complex hermeneutics to establish normativity in theological discourse by attentively considering the lived experiences of previously subjugated social groups. The examples of inclusion described above represent the Sámi contribution to the global repertoire of theologies of liberation. In doing so, they bear witness to the vitality and ethical significance of the discourse on theologies of liberation and the discourse within the Northern Hemisphere.

However, Argentinian postcolonial and queer theologian Marcella Althaus-Reid highlights the ambivalence of contextuality as a strategy for decolonization and emancipation for marginalized social groups. In the impactful and semi-ethnographic introduction to her book *Indecent Theology*, Althaus-Reid writes:

> My purpose of this book is not to demolish Liberation theology a la European (in a European academic fashion), but to explore the contextual hermeneutical circle of suspicion in depth by questioning the traditional liberationist context of doing theology . . . I still emphatically affirm the validity of Liberation theologies as crucial in processes of social transformation and superior to idealistic North Atlantic theologies. However, Liberation Theology needs to be understood as a continuing process of re-contextualization, a permanent exercise of serious doubting in theology. By serious doubting, *I do not mean adding new contextual perspectives,* such as the ones provided by the living metaphors of God and sexuality in the image of lemon vendors to an established theological discourse . . . Serious doubting as a theological method re-contextualizes Liberation Theology by questioning those very hermeneutical principles that led liberationists to be indifferent to the reality of lemon vendors in the first place.[4]

To Althaus-Reid, this ambivalence is so pronounced that she is reluctant to label her indecent theology a 'contextual theology.' She argues that while 'contextual theology' may seem like a theological strategy for liberation, as it may create a space for previous unheard voices, it does not necessarily change the differentiation and asymmetrical power balance between center and periphery in theological discourse. In this framework, someone may speak, but there may not be anyone who truly listens, reads, or cites.

4. Althaus-Reid, *Indecent Theology*, 5.

In light of Althaus-Reid's warning, it is of great importance that Sámi theological contributions be understood not only as Sámi contextual theology in the form of various dialogues between indigenous Sámi life experiences and Lutheran theology, such as Johnsen's catechism, *Jordens Barn, Solens Barn, Vindens Barn*, and his dissertation "The Contribution of North Sámi Everyday Christianity to a Cosmologically-Oriented Christian Theology,"[5] which serve as notable examples. According to Althaus-Reid, theologians whose works emerge from individual and collective experiences of diverse forms of subjugation, such as colonization, need not settle for "adding new contextual perspectives." Instead, these theologians ought to engage in an examination of the theological and epistemological production of discourses of theological 'normality' and normativity, while also scrutinizing the relationship between these discourses and the process of colonization. These are politically and theologically far more dangerous issues than to settle for bringing 'new contextual perspectives'[6] to an already established theological discourse. Rather, such issues destabilize the relationship between what is regarded as center and periphery by deconstructing what is seen as 'normal' and what is seen as 'other,' while also shedding light on the varying degrees of power access that this naturalization harbors. In other words, the theological tradition of the majority population is not granted the role of the benevolent includer of 'new contextual perspectives' but is itself under scrutiny. Althaus-Reid's name for this is "indecent theology."

An example of interrogating the relationship between theological normativity and the construction of the 'contextual' is Tore Johnsen's theological engagement with one trajectory of the theological tradition of the Scandinavian majority population, namely, Scandinavian creation theology (SCT). I have elsewhere called SCT "contextual Scandinavian theology."[7] In the following, I want to examine Tore Johnsen's Sámi critique of SCT, particularly his emphasis on the problematic notion of 'folk' and the idea of the universality of the creation. In Johnsen's work, key SCT terms like 'folk' are examined from the theological perspectives of persons who have been socially produced as unstable or dubious participants in the 'folk' of the nation state, namely persons with indigenous identity. One may call such issues an "indecenting" of the SCT. Johnsen's project implies to frame the politics of contextual theology not as

5. Johnsen, "The Contribution."
6. Althaus-Reid, *Indecent Theology*, 5.
7. Gunnes, "*Hvem Skjuler*," 165–84.

a straightforward process: to work contextually as a theologian implies to give voice to, in theological discourse, human experiences that have not been heard. However, of equal importance is to insist on and *actually treat* discourses which have not been labeled as or understood themselves as 'contextual,' as situated knowledge traditions. Only when these two processes happen in tandem, normativity in theological discourse is destabilized.

By addressing such issues, Johnsen accomplishes two things. First, his work on SCT may be understood as a theological program for decolonizing aspects of SCT. This is a novel and uncomfortable aspiration: for centuries, the ecclesial and theological discourse in Scandinavia has been the all-too-familiar ecclesial-popular script of "folk-church/SCT versus pietistic revival church." In this discourse, SCT ends up as the open-minded and culture-affirming party of the two. Thus, Johnsen's decolonization of SCT suggests the possibility of the implication of *liberal* theological agents, scripts, and resources in the colonization of Sámi people. It is important to recognize the politically controversial nature of Johnsen's work: he summons those of us with self-images as liberal and open-minded to serious and uncomfortable self-reflexivity. Johnsen's work thus questions the all-too-familiar discourse of "conservative versus liberal regarding questions of gender and sexuality" as the only possible structuring principle in Scandinavian theology. He does so not by reducing the validity or importance of this discourse but by canvassing a richer and thicker picture of what is at stake politically in the Scandinavian theological scene.

Second, Johnsen's interrogation of key SCT terms not only creates a space for Sámi spirituality and theological contextualization but also interrogates the theological legacy of the majority. By doing so, he destabilizes the relationship between the center and periphery by treating SCT as a contextual theology that has emerged in a specific time and place, motivated by the creation of political and cultural interests, along with providing religious legitimation for these interests. Although Johnsen—to my knowledge—does not identify as an "indecent theologian," one may say that Johnsen undertakes an 'indecent' reading of key SCT. In the following, I will demonstrate how Johnsen's decolonizing reading deploys tools that resonate with Althaus-Reid's indecent theology by destabilizing SCT as 'normal theology' and treating the theology of the majority population—SCT, and not the Sámi contribution—as the *contextual party*.

DECOLONIZING ASPECTS OF SCANDINAVIAN FOLK CHURCH ECCLESIOLOGY AND SCT IN TORE JOHNSEN'S WORK

The relationship between SCT, folk church ecclesiology, colonialism, and postcolonialism is complex. This complexity is not fueled primarily by the general complexity of writing history when the subject matter—the events of the past—is submerged in questions of unequal access to self-presentation in historical written texts. This general complexity applies to any historian working with social groups where questions of marginality and discrimination are at stake, such as the history of disability or women's history.

Such general questions of representation do, of course, apply with full force to the history of the relationship between the Sámi people and concepts emerging from the Scandinavian majority culture, such as the notion of *folk* as an ecclesiological term. However, the complexity of the intersection between SCT, folk church ecclesiology, and colonialism is not only related to the political-methodological issues of history as an academic discipline. The complexity of the matter is heightened by the success of Norway, Sweden, and Denmark in presenting self-images as nations that protect and honor human rights and minority rights, in contrast to the colonial legacies of grand nations like England and France. For this reason, the history of these countries has, for a surprisingly long time, been seen in research as immune to criticism for having a colonial past.[8] One of the reasons for the success of this self-image is that the forced deterritorialization of the Sámi people and discrimination against the Sámi language and culture did not fit into the traditional definition of colonialism as something that took place geographically *outside* the homeland of the colonizer.

In contrast, the forced deterritorialization and discrimination against the Sámi language and culture happened in temporal and geographical tandem with the establishment of the political boundaries between Denmark and Norway post 1814 and between Norway and Sweden in 1905, when Norway broke out of the union with Sweden. This means that in a Scandinavian context, the colonizer and colonized were not separated by geography. However, in recent scholarship, the traditional understanding of colonialism has given way to a more nuanced and 'thicker' understanding that also includes the geographical collocation of colonizer and

---

8. Höglund and Burnett, "Introduction," 4; Fur, "Colonial Fantasies," 11.

colonized.[9] This makes room for radical new perspectives on the role of the Nordic nation states in relation to the Sámi people.

The inclusion of the spatial copresence of colonizer and colonized also enriches the postcolonial analytic apparatus. It points to the importance of the social production of the imaginations of the difference between 'us' and 'them' in the colonial project. However, the importance of the production of such imaginations is radicalized when there is little or no geographical boundary between those human beings who are discursively assessed as 'us' and those assessed as 'them.' In a context in which physical distance does not guarantee this discursive difference, the potential for transgressive behavior between the 'us' and 'them' categories needs to be policed by imaginations differently than if the 'them' are located far away. Thus, imaginations of who legitimately belongs to the 'folk,' what constitutes the 'folk,' and notions of what a proper 'folk' should look like become practical-political categories for handling transgressive behavior across categories. Thus, one may argue that in the context of the Nordic countries, entrepreneurs of imaginations—like religious agents—were vital to the colonizing project. The social construction of a 'folk' (the colonizers) in opposition to the (colonized) folk served as a structure of legitimization for structural difference in access to legal, political, and economic power and resources. To articulate a decolonized theology and ecclesiology in a context in which the colony and the 'motherland' are geographically intertwined is thus a process that demands a high degree of epistemological and conceptual awareness with regard to the social production of imaginations. This awareness points to the pivotal role of entrepreneurs of imaginations—like religious agents—in the process and maintenance of such imaginations.

DECOLONIZING SCT: WHAT DOES IT MEAN TO BE "HUMAN" AND "CHRISTIAN"?

SCT is a theological trajectory emerging from the Nordic countries, exerting significant influence in Norway, Sweden, and Denmark. It is firmly rooted in Lutheran theology and legacy, interpreted by the influential Danish writer, theologian, priest, and hymnal writer, poet Nikolai Fredrik Grundtvig (1783–1872), and further developed in the twentieth century by theologians like the Dane Knut Løgstrup (1905–1981) and

---

9. Fur, "Colonial Fantasies," 11.

the Swede Gustav Wingren (1910–2000). The core of SCT is an affirmative and positive attitude toward human and common culture. This is grounded in the first article of faith—God as Creator—as the epistemological starting point and the structuring hermeneutical key to the other two articles: Christ had to be born as Mary's son in order to become the Messiah.

Despite its name as a creation theology, SCT is thus not foremost a theology concerned with ecology and the relationship between the human and nonhuman worlds, as in various forms of ecotheology or process theologies (e.g., Sallie McFague and Catherine Keller). Discursively, SCT derives its normative horizon and epistemological traditions not from global theologies of liberation but rather from the inner-Scandinavian Lutheran adaption and negotiation of the Lutheran heritage of the region. 'Creation' in SCT discourse refers to 'the common' or 'the secular,' the part of the world that is not part of the empirical church, rather than to nature or the nonhuman. It holds that God reveals herself in and through common culture and human works. SCT should be understood as a theological tradition that theologizes on the relationship between the common culture and the empirical church rather than a theological tradition that theologizes on the nonhuman or nature. Creation in SCT is thus conceptualized as something not static but evolving and in continual interaction with cultural change. In contrast to SCT's discursive antagonist—the revival movements—SCT theology understands the ontological and theological distinction between the 'the saved Christian' versus 'the sinful and unsaved worldly human' as a theological construction of little or no theological interest.

A key element in Johnsen's critique of SCT implies a location in the historical context of perhaps the most famous theological motive and maxim of SCT, formulated by Grundtvig himself: the development of a theological anthropology that does not understand the Christian and the human as moral or ontological competitors: "The Christian is first and foremost a human, then Christian." This implies that the very context of Christian identity and discourse is human culture. When used by Lutheran theologians in a contemporary context, the term 'human' is understood as a politically and racially innocent term. 'Human' means everybody everywhere. 'First human, then Christian' indicates a theological affirmation of the value of what is socially regarded as non-Christian, secular, 'profane' or 'heathen.'

Johnsen places the sentence in a historical context—not the latter half of the twentieth century, but the original historical context. By doing so, he teases out different and highly problematic aspects of the maxim compared to how it has been used and is used in contemporary liberal theological discourse. Johnsen thus exposes how the maxim is historically embedded in discourses on racism—who gets to count as 'human' and whose culture is regarded as 'civilized.'[10] Statistically, the 'universal' human was far from being universal; instead, it exemplified specific features of whiteness and Western European culture, shaped from its inception by racist notions regarding who should be considered part of the universal category. Grundtvig's theological negotiation between the specific religious and the general common occurred within an intellectual framework deeply influenced by conceptual racism. Johnsen points out a contradiction in Grundtvig's thinking: on the one hand, he asserts the constructive 'spirit of the people' of all humans and committed to a discourse of the ideals of the French Revolution: freedom, equality, and brotherhood;[11] on the other hand, his thinking feeds on motives that have racialized features: the theological status of the human is, teleologically speaking, the extension of some peoples, not others. It was only in the culture and mythos of the Nordic people that Grundtvig found the potential to merge eschatology and common popular culture.[12] In one of the most potent examples of the decolonization of theology in Scandinavian theological discourse, Johnsen juxtaposes Grundtvig's theology and that of his Norwegian mediators like Christoffer Bruun to the so-called *manifest destiny* imaginations of white settlers. In manifest destiny theology, the enterprise of colonizing North America is seen as a divinely ordained task bestowed by God on white settlers.[13] The question that Johnsen argues that needs to be researched further is: if and to what extent did Grundtvig's theology become a Scandinavian manifest destiny theology for the majority state churches in Scandinavia at the expense of the indigenous cultures?

This last point becomes even more acute when Johnsen displays how Grundtvig's theology was translated into state policies and the administration of Sámi affairs. An example of this is the work of priest, politician, bishop, and minister of church affairs Vilhelm Wexselsen (1849–1909),

10. Johnsen, "Menneske først, så Kristen," 304–11.
11. Johnsen, "Menneske først, så Kristen," 313.
12. Johnsen, "Menneske først, så Kristen," 312.
13. Johnsen, "Menneske først, så Kristen," 313.

who is regarded as the architect of the fiercest laws against Sámi culture and language. Wexselsen was highly influenced by Grundtvigianism, both through his upbringing and through his theological training. One of the intensely uncomfortable results of decolonizing Scandinavian theology is how to deal with one of the most severe policymakers against the Sámi people being fueled and nurtured by theological resources from a Grundtvigian theological program.

Johnsen also points out that, whereas the nineteenth-century Romantic discourse of transferring power from the king to the people had an emancipatory effect on the majority population of Norway, the opposite was true when it came to the Sámi population. In contrast, understanding the people—the common—as a source of both political authority and God's work on earth had devastating effects on Sámi culture. The conceptual conflation of the common majority culture and the church into some form of folk-church ecclesiology led to greater integration between the common culture and the church. However, due to a lack of critical awareness of the effect colonization had on the Sámi and a subsequent failure to include the Sámi in the notion of 'the common,' the marginalization of Sámi culture and privileging of Norwegian and political institutions gained a theological flair.[14]

Interrogating the Epistemological Dimension of Colonization: What Gets to be Counted as 'Human' in Contemporary SCT?

Johnsen's critique of SCT is extremely important in Scandinavian theological discourse for at least two reasons. On an apparent level, racializing seemingly liberal and 'innocent' theological statements like "first human, then Christian" exposes the complicity of liberal theological agents in colonization. This calls into question the often self-congratulatory identification of SCT as the guardian and guarantor of the 'human' in theological Scandinavian discourse.

The radical nature of Johnsen's perspective becomes apparent when considering two contemporary, state-of-the-art volumes on SCT: *Reformation Theology for a Post-Secular Age: Løgstrup, Prenter, Wingren* and *American Perspectives Meet Scandinavian Creation Theology*.[15] Notably, neither of these volumes includes contributions from Indigenous

---

14. Johnsen, *Folkekirke for hvilket folk?*, 76.
15. Gregersen, Uggla and Wyller, *Reconfiguring Reformation Theology*.

minorities from Scandinavia. In the introductory chapter to *Reformation Theology*, the editors spell out the aspiration of SCT to begin with universal human experience, positioning itself as the discursive antagonist of a theology rooted in revival pietist Christianity:

> It goes without saying that the search for universality cannot fit together with any claim that creation theology is an 'ethnic' theology particular to Scandinavians. Indeed, from the perspective of Scandinavian creation theology, there can be only a secondary interest in promoting any particular 'identity theology.' . . . there are also shared aspects of human existence, and these need to be taken seriously . . . Yet, just as Scandinavian creation theologians are not interested in describing Scandinavia in particular, they are not interested only in generic features of humanity either. Rather their theological concern is the shared conditions of human life.[16]

However, the question becomes: *Who has access to 'the shared condition of human life,' and what are the epistemological conditions for formulating the claim to reflect theologically from this position?* In addition, if the Scandinavian (male) editors discursively position access to 'the shared condition of human life' in opposition to the formulation of a contextual theology for Scandinavia, how do they ensure that SCT does not become another version of universalizing European life experiences disguised as articulating a theology from the 'shared conditions of human life'? Johnsen's critical reading of the 'first human, then Christian' maxim may be seen as a demonstration that—to put it bluntly—there is no such thing as a 'shared condition of human life,' only contextual accounts of what it means to be human under given political, cultural, and economic conditions. These conditions often involve processes of colonization. In these processes, or in their aftermath (as in contemporary Norway), it is not an arbitrary or innocent person who gets to formulate what 'the shared conditions of life' contain. Johnsen's critique summons SCT scholarship to understand 'the human' not as an empirical but as an epistemological and political category.

---

16. Gregersen, Uggla and Wyller, *Reconfiguring Reformation Theology*, 20–21.

Interrogating SCT on its Own Terms: How Do We Determine What Is Relevant to Theological Discourse, according to the Perspective of SCT?

The critique put forward by Johnsen also addresses a different level of SCT discourse. This level, paradoxically speaking, can be seen as having been inspired by a key element of SCT itself: the theological intertwining of—empirically speaking—the 'secular' and 'ecclesial.' This level is not so much a matter of establishing through historical analysis actual and new knowledge about the relationship between SCT and the colonization of the Sámi people (like the manifest destiny theology outlined above). This level is what one may tentatively call a *sociology of dogma*, by which I do not mean the ecclesiastically sanctioned propositional content of any dogma, motif, or practice, but rather the social and political potential meaning of dogma in various given contexts. From the perspective of a sociology of dogma, the propositional status of any given dogma, motif, ritual, or practice is always open-ended and equivocal. Dogma itself is not the root cause of ethically and politically problematic or even destructive theologies. The same sets of theological resources have been used to both suppress and liberate. A sociology of dogma interrogates the multiple—and often surprising—ways that dogma or motif functions in actual use. This also means to count as valid and relevant the use of dogma outside strict ecclesial contexts and to acknowledge that elements of the theological imagination travel across and settle in very different empirical contexts.

Geir Afdal has coined a term that may be helpful for creating an operationalized terminology for a sociology of dogma. In his *Religion som bevegelse* (*Religion as Movement*), Afdal establishes a vocabulary intended to rid theological statements and practices from the possession of a discursive claim to originality or possession by any ecclesial or theological agent. Rather, the meaning of religious and theological practices is found in their multiple uses: religion therefore consists of artifacts that are mediated through various processes.[17] Artifacts are concepts, discourses, buildings, and practices. However, the meaning of these artifacts is never 'a thing' in itself and can never be understood without interrogating the various contexts of meaning—the multiple processes—in which these artifacts are already and always embedded.

---

17. Afdal, *Religion som bevegelse*, 160.

Sociologically speaking, SCT has grown out of and flourished in a context where the state and church have been intimately connected through the merger of state and church with the coming of the Reformation to Denmark-Norway. SCT has supplied the Scandinavian majority churches with theological and ideological scripts that have enabled them to welcome and support social changes, such as changing norms for gender identity and social roles: if creation is understood *theologically* as dynamic and ever-changing, then it cannot be used as a guarantor of static gender roles and sexual identities. Theological institutions, milieus, and individuals who adhere to SCT have, historically speaking, been in favor of female religious leadership and queer liberation. It is fair to say that, from the perspective of the sociology of dogma, SCT has been a theological script for deconstructing heteropatriarchal sexual norms and has fueled feminist and queer liberation in Scandinavian societies.

However, Johnsen's work challenges SCT theologians—like myself—to revisit this story. The ontological blurriness of what is 'inside' and 'outside' the ecclesial contexts may also include a more problematic—even destructive—dimension. In the discussion on the dual role of Wexselsen as both an ecclesial agent and top state bureaucrat, Johnsen investigates how theological resources and motives may have inspired practices and people who acted not only in their capacities as ecclesial agents but also in other capacities and offices, such as policymakers. Using Afdal's terminology, SCT theologians are guilty of self-congratulatory hubris when they promote the 'human first, then Christian' maxim as an inherently emancipatory idea. Rather, the maxim should be seen as an artifact that is at work in various contextual and historical contexts (processes). For some social groups, the theological consequence of the maxim has served the purpose of dispossessing pietistic Christianity of its self-claimed role as the revelation and guardian of the Christian faith in the secular world. For other social groups, it has had devastating effects by theologically legitimizing the need to 'humanize' Indigenous populations. Hence, the maxim is not emancipatory in itself; rather, it is an artifact that is mediated in various processes and has served to both liberate and oppress.

This insight may be seen as a call for what Althaus-Reid calls "serious doubting" in theologies that view themselves as philosophical partners of social movements with an emancipatory aim (which theologies of liberation and SCT theologians may understand themselves as). Althaus-Reid's "serious doubling" means to see that for some social groups, SCT's theology on the dynamic role of creation serves as a source of attesting theological validity to social change, such as changing gender roles. However, for colonized peoples living in Scandinavia, the emphasis on and the conceptualization of 'creation' in SCT is much more ambivalent. Integrating 'serious doubting' into the very core of SCT means formulating from within the discourse a highly uncomfortable question: *What factors or imaginations—political or epistemological—allowed SCT-theologians to be indifferent to the ambivalent potential of 'first human, then Christian' in the first place?*

It is important to underline that a sociology of dogma should not be tempted into a static binary between 'theologies of liberation' and 'other theologies.' Johnsen's critique exemplifies that reality is far more complicated and complex than static binaries. An example of this complexity is the Exodus motif, which, in liberation theology from both Latin America and the United States, has been deployed as a paradigmatic representation of the path from oppression to freedom. However, as Native American theologian Robert Allen Warrior points out, the Exodus is a story about liberation for those who identify with and see themselves as represented by the enslaved Israelites. Given the multiple contextual political landscapes of colonization in different regions and countries (including Scandinavia), though, one cannot take for granted that liberation for colonized people always occurs as a departure from one location in geography to another. For Native Americans, liberation comes with the process of reclaiming and returning to stolen land, not departing from it. In such cases, the Exodus becomes an ambivalent story because the primary agent with which one identifies is not the Israelites, but the Canaanites, whose voices and experiences are absent from the biblical narrative. The biblical story relies on the voicelessness of those who were already living on the land and thus mirror the worldview of the colonizer.[18] Warrior's insight points to the fact that no theological motif, practice, or dogma—Afdal's *artifact*—holds an inherent ethical or political normative status. This insight, however, is not only a challenge to theologies that do not understand themselves as liberation theologies and that have not been ready or forced to epistemologically reflect on contextuality (such as SCT). Rather, the challenge of the equivocal nature of any theological artifact is also a challenge to theologies of liberation. Thus, as Althaus-Reid argues, even liberation theology must submit itself

---

18. Catelli and Phillips, *The Postmodern Bible*, 272–301.

to 'serious doubting,'[19] a continuing process of questioning one's own normative position.

A sociology of dogma—what one operationalized by the vocabulary of Afdal and Althaus-Reid (as outlined above) may use as an overall term—is not merely an epistemological enterprise; it has political consequences. An example is Johnsen's critique of the 'White Book Project' of the Swedish Lutheran church. According to Johnsen, in this project, the responsibility of the Lutheran church in the Sámi cultural genocide is understood strictly as practices that were authorized and executed by the Swedish Lutheran church as an empirical institution. Johnsen argues that this perspective is far too narrow and overlooks and under-communicates the role of the Lutheran church in Scandinavia in ideologically and religiously legitimizing the policies that were implemented by secular authorities. A sociology of dogma thus points to theopolitics—that is, the sanctification of political decision-making and the structural and legal interdependence of state and church that may exist in any given society. A perspective of the sociology of dogma operationalizes decolonization by offering an epistemological awareness of what seems self-evident: establishment of the empirical material that is subject to decolonizing scrutiny is never given a priori. Rather, as in any other scientific inquiry, it is a matter of a social construction, informed by certain values and ontologies. When Johnsen chooses to include Wexselsen as a *bureaucratic agent* in a *theological* investigation of colonization, this presupposes an ontology of the interrelated nature of the secular and the religious. Such an ontology also recognizes, *as theologically relevant,* interventions and practices that empirically were not identified as theological or ecclesial, and which the empirical church today may not see itself as responsible for executing. In this regard, one may argue that Johnsen holds SCT accountable on its own terms: the church is both 'visible' (empirical church) and 'invisible' (where God acts in everyday life) as a supplier of ideological resources that legitimize the practices of governmental bodies in presecularized Norway. This empirical awareness is of great importance in societies where the majority culture, political power, and the church converge, because it points to the power of the overlapping space between theopolitics and the political role and involvement of ecclesial institutions.

---

19. Althaus-Reid, *Indecent Theology*, 5. See also Althaus-Reid, *The Queer God*; Althaus-Reid and Isherwood, *The Sexual Theologian*.

CONCLUSION:
IS THERE SUCH A THING AS DECOLONIZED SCT?

My starting point in this chapter was Labba's call to envision what a fabric of Scandinavian master narratives, encompassing both minority and majority voices, might look like in theological discourse. I highlighted two different strategies for incorporating Sámi narratives. One strategy is to carve out a space for Sámi experiences in the form of contextual theologies, both academic and popular. Tore Johnsen has contributed to both categories with his catechism and his dissertation.

With the aid of Althaus-Reid, I explored how inclusion might also have a more critical dimension that more actively interacts with the theological tradition of the majority population. In his critique of the key features of SCT, Johnsen also advocates a different understanding of the inclusion of Sámi voices in the master narratives of the majority population. This kind of understanding of inclusion calls even the most positive and innocent of theological artifacts—'first human, then Christian'—to account for its role in the colonizing project. This kind of inclusion is thus far more uncomfortable and provocative for the majority population than the first kind of inclusion. It is, however, important to underline that the two strategies intertwine and overlap.

Returning to the core of Johnsen's critique of SCT, one is left with a question: *Is there such a thing as a constructive dimension in a decolonized SCT, or is the term so tainted in colonial legacy and majority legacy that it is beyond rescue?* One may argue that Johnsen's critique does not entail the abandonment of SCT as a constructive theological resource in contemporary Scandinavian theology but that its historical legacy must be approached with hermeneutics characterized by greater critical awareness of its potential zones of structural invisibility. Examples of such zones could be the question of race in the thinking of Grundtvig and his nineteenth-century mediators. Indeed, other Sámi theologians have embraced the conceptual framework of SCT, especially its ontological starting point in creation.[20]

However, if the process of decolonizing Scandinavian theology aspires to go beyond the purely rhetorical stage, it is vital that it—and especially the discourse of SCT—be willing to consider the underlying racialized nature of the epistemological scripts of Grundtvig, Wexselsen, and Brun. I will argue that this means not to abandon SCT but rather to

---

20. Webber, "Creation and Relations," 155–60.

historicize and contextualize it and be aware that in theology, like anywhere else, there is no such thing as an innocent epistemological position.

In the coming years, as Norway is approaching the celebration of the millennium of the Battle of Stiklestad—which, according to legend, marked the beginning of the triumph of Christianity in Norway—it is vitally important that the epistemological awareness of both theologians and church officials be sensitized to questions of the political potential in theological and religious imaginations. An important dialogue partner for SCT in the coming years may be the flourishing theological research on the relationships between religions and the politics and representation of 'folk' in populism and right-wing extremism. Such a conversation partner may challenge the intra-Scandinavian vocabulary of SCT and supply SCT theologians with more critical analytical tools.[21]

BIBLIOGRAPHY

Afdal, Geir. *Religion som bevegelse*. Oslo: Universitetsforlaget, 2013.

Althaus-Reid. Marcella, *Indecent Theology: Theological Perversions in Sex, Gender and Politics*. London: Routledge, 2000.

———. *The Queer God*. London: Routledge, 2003.

Althaus-Reid, Marcella, and Isherwood, Lisa. *The Sexual Theologian: Essays on Sex. God and Politics*. London: T&T Clark, 2004.

Catelli, Elizabeth, and Gary Phillips, eds. *The Postmodern Bible*. New Haven: Yale University Press, 1995.

Fur, Gunlög. "Colonial Fantasies: American Indians, Indigenous Peoples, and a Swedish Discourse of Innocence." *National Identities* 18 (2016) 11–33. https://doi.org/10.1080/14608944.2016.1095489.

Gerle, Elisabeth, and Michael Schelde. *American Perspectives Meet Scandinavian Creation Theology*. Uppsala: Church of Sweden Research Department, 2019.

Gregersen, Niels-Henrik, Bernd Uggla, and Trygve Wyller, eds. *Reformation Theology for a Post-Secular Age: Løgstrup, Prenter, Wingren*. Göttingen: Vandenhoeck & Ruprecht, 2017.

Gunnes, Gyrid. "Hvem Skjuler Seg Bak 'Det Allmenne'?." In *Populisme Og Kristendom*, edited by Sturla Stålsett, Kristin Graff-Kallevåg and Svein Tore Kloster, 165–84. Oslo: Cappelen Damm Akademisk, 2022.

Höglund, Johan, and Linda Andersson Burnett. "Introduction: Nordic Colonialisms and Scandinavian Studies." *Scandinavian Studies* 91 (2019) 1–12. https://doi.org/10.5406/scanstud.91.1-2.0001.

Johnsen, Tore. "The Contribution of North Sami Everyday Christianity to a Cosmologically-Oriented Christian Theology." PhD diss., University of Edinburgh, 2020.

---

21. Strømmen and Schmiedel, *Claims to Christianity*; Schmiedel and Ralston, *The Spirit of Populism*.

———. "Folkekirke for Hvilket Folk? Et Samisk Perspektiv På Folkekirkedebatten." In *Folkekirke Nå*, edited by Stephanie Dietrich, Hallgeir Elstad, Beate Fagerli, and Vidar Haanes, 72–81. Oslo: Verbum Akademiske, 2015.
———. *Jordens barn, solens barn, vindens barn. Kristen tro i et samisk landskap.* Oslo: Verbum, 2007.
———. "Menneske Først, Kristen Så: Om Teologi, Rasisme Mot Samer Og Behovet for Avkolonisering." *Kirke og kultur* 126 (2021) 299–325. https://doi.org/10.18261/issn.1504-3002-2021-04-02.
———. "Urfolk Og Folkekirke: Et Samisk Perspektiv På Folkekirkedebatten." Vor kristne og humanistiske arv: betraktninger ved 200-årsjubileet for Grunnloven». Edited by Øystein Ekroll, Søren Hjorth, and Einar Vegge, 239–55. Trondheim: Nidarosdomens Restaureringsarbeid, 2014.
Labba, Elin A. *Herrene sendte oss hit [The Lords Sent Us Here].* Oslo: Pax, 2021.
Schmiedel, Ulrich, and Joshua Ralston. *The Spirit of Populism: Political Theologies in Polarized Times.* Political and Public Theologies, 1 vol. Leiden: Brill, 2022.
Skum, Line M. *Diakoni i et urfolksperspektiv.* Oslo: Den norske diakonforbund, 2006.
———. "En åpen kirke i forsoningens tjeneste." *Kirke og Kultur* 11 (2006) 355–59.
Strømmen, Hannah M. and Ulrich Schmiedel, "Claims to Christianity: Responding to the Far Right." London: SCM, 2020.
Webber, Torbjørn B. "Creation and Relations: A Sami Perspective on Scandinavian Creation Theology." *Dialog: A Journal of Theology* 60 (2021) 155–60. https://doi.org/10.1111/dial.12666/.

7

Truth and Reconciliation in Sápmi and Lebanon
Messianism of Decolonization

HELGE HIRAM ABDELNOOR JENSEN
*Department of Organization, Leadership and Management,
Inland School of Business and Social Sciences, Rena, Norway*

INTRODUCTION: PREMISES AND PROMISES

Peacemaking must be conflictual: Since conflict is the *reason* to seek truth and reconciliation, conflict is the *condition* under which truth and reconciliation are being sought. 'Truth' is contested, with competing public memories offering conflicting versions of the past.[1] 'Reconciliation' is contested too, with conflicting versions of the past giving rise to differing prescriptions for the future.[2] This chapter grapples with these questions by offering a *philosophical framework* for transitional justice: an *epistemology* for *truth*, and an *ethics* for *reconciliation*. How may civil society

---

1. Solomons et al., "Introduction," 6; De Brito et al., *The Politics of Memory*; Mendes, "Delayed Transitional Justice."

2. Solomons et al., "Introduction," 2; Karim and Baser, "Collective Memory"; Zamponi, "Collective Memory."

contribute to truth and reconciliation by moving somewhat closer to The Good and The True as universal ideals?

The chapter is conceptual and empirical: First, it sketches the framework with a *philosophical analysis* of Walter Benjamin's 'millenarist' philosophy of history (part 2). Philosophical questions of *epistemology* and *ethics* are being related to ongoing debates, within *human rights law* and *conflict research*, regarding the *method* and *theory* of transitional justice.

Thereafter, the chapter proceeds to develop the framework on empirical grounds, conducting *historical-anthropological analyses* of two cases (parts 3–5). Comparing Lebanon, known for its violent conflicts, with Sápmi, which has a comparatively less violent history, uncovers patterns across manifest and latent conflicts.[3] The *historical analysis* of (anti)colonial relations in these two cases (parts 3–4) demonstrates how Lebanon and Sápmi were both subject to 'internal colonization' under early modern regional empires with theocratic legitimation during the seventeenth and eighteenth centuries, but also, how the transnational revolutionary moment of 1848 translated into millennial anti-colonial movements in both cases.

Thereafter, the *anthropological analysis* turns to public memory in the present (part 5). Analyzing literary primary sources and ethnographic travel memories, this part inquires how social conflicts in the recent past influence contentions regarding long-term historical memory. What kind of colonization has taken place? What kind of wounds has it left? What does civil society do to heal the wounds? In this chapter, the anthropological analysis of public memory is based on a historical analysis of the factual past. It approaches the problem through the lens of *materialistic decolonial* research,[4] which aims to be more empiricist than *culturalist postcolonial* studies,[5] with the goal of contributing to evidence-based decolonization.

Theoretically, the chapter compares experiences of 'internal colonialism'[6] within processes of transitional justice.[7] The Norwegian Truth and

3. The empirical research behind this article was funded by the Research Council Norway and the European Commission 2008–2010.

4. Arguments for materialistic decolonial research are found in Sarkar, "The Decline"; see also: Fanon, *Les damnés de la terre*.

5. See, e.g. Ponzanesi and Colpani, *Postcolonial Transitions*.

6. Hechter, "Internal Colonialism"; Tinker, "Colonial Empires."

7. One should note that this chapter compares colonial experiences, not Indigenous peoples. The only Indigenous people of the Middle East are the Negev Bedouins of Israel/Palestine. Comparing Negev Bedouins with the Sámi People would have been a

Reconciliation Commission (TRC), in its official report, refers to academic debates regarding 'internal colonialism', and 'settler colonialism' within the traditional livelihoods of the Sámi, Kvens, and Norwegian-Finns,[8] seemingly defining the context for the report's frequent references to 'agricultural colonization'.[9] Hence, the official report is clearer regarding the fact that colonization has taken place, than what was expected by it from the previous volume from the ReconTrans project.[10] Lebanese historians have similar discussions about 'internal colonialism': Which of the imperial conquests throughout history are relevant for decolonization and transitional justice in the present?[11] Should the anti-colonial critique be directed only towards non-Arab colonizers in Lebanon, or also towards Arab authoritarianism?[12]

Methodologically, the chapter *oscillates* between philosophical analysis and historical-anthropological analyses—in other words, a *dialectic* approach that bridges the conceptual and the empirical. According to Mahdi Amel, such a confrontation of thought with reality reflects a method of 'fearless self-criticism' characteristic of Heretic Marxism.[13] Criticizing Orthodox Marxism, the chapter applies a family of Heretic Marxists, starting with Walter Benjamin, including thinkers that are related to him, either *diachronically*, by being his later critics, such as Jürgen Habermas, or *synchronously*, by being his contemporary heretics, such as Antonio Gramsci and the Ukrainian Communist Party (UCP).

Heretic Marxism, as a transdisciplinary tradition within the humanities and the social sciences, *opens transdisciplinary relevance*, but also *defines disciplinary belonging*. Regarding transdisciplinary relevance, this chapter operates from the midst of the historical-philosophical tradition, aiming at relevance for theology, history, peace studies, and other disciplines in this volume.

---

different project. (See Hall, "Bedouins' politics"; OHCHR. "The Arab Bedouin").

8. Truth and Reconciliation Commission in Norway, "Report to the Norwegian Parliament," 562. (The text box uses the terms "intern kolonialisme" and "kolonisering som bosetningekspansjon.")

9. Truth and Reconciliation Commission in Norway, "Report to the Norwegian Parliament." (The report uses the term "jordbrukskolonisering.")

10. Solomons et al., "Introduction," 5.

11. Salibi, *A House of Many Mansions*.

12. Kassab, *Contemporary Arabic Thought*, 5, 11, 14–15.

13. Amel, *Arab Marxism*, 17.

Regarding disciplinary belonging, the chapter itself belongs to International Relations (IR), or World Politics,[14] more specifically, the intersection of two sub-fields: Conflict Research[15] and Social Movement Studies.[16] Operating from within the Clausewitzean tradition,[17] the aim is to enhance practical competence[18] by mapping unique facts on the ground during individual wars or crises, applying insights from history[19], anthropology,[20] and philosophy.[21]

14. The term "World Politics" refers to IR that is *not state-centric* (see Evans and Newnham, *The Penguin Dictionary*, 578; Birnbaum, "Religion"). That is the case for the present chapter, since it compares *Sápmi*, a cross-border territorial homeland, and *Lebanon*, a sovereign state with contested borders (see Sjöberg and Sara, "When Justice"; Solomons et al., "Introduction," 2; Gharbieh, *Lebanese Confessionalism*). Thus, the chapter does *not take for granted* that *de jure* state sovereignty automatically translates into *de facto* authority on the ground. Instead, the force of *historical anthropology* is utilized for *empirical tracing* of material social forces that constitute hegemonic formations at multiple geographical levels of analysis (see Marchi, "Molecular Transformations"; Werner and Zimmermann, "Beyond Comparison"; Marcus, "Ethnography").

15. Conflict Research, as a sub-discipline of IR, was itself created by a fusion of the sub-disciplines Peace Research and Strategic Studies, thus analyzing *peace* and *reconciliation* in the context of *war* and *deterrence* (see Evans and Newnham, *The Penguin Dictionary*, 94).

16. "Social Movement Studies" refers to transversal social science study of the contentious politics of non-state actors: social, political, and religious movements. This research field takes interest in topics like political violence, civil society, public spheres, and democratic innovation (see della Porta et al., *Social Movements*; Malthaner et al., "The Social Science"; Birnbaum, "Religion"; Itçaina, "Une médiation invisible?"; O'Connor and Oikonomakis, "Preconflict Mobilization Strategies"; Kutmanaliev, "Public and Communal Spaces"; Froio et al., *CasaPound Italia*; Dorot, "Media Influence"; della Porta, *Can Democracy*; Jensen and Valaker, "Social Movement Communication"; Cini, *Societá civile*; Habermas, *Strukturwandel*; Mouffe, "Deliberative Democracy"; Habermas, *Ein neuer Strukturwandel*; Habermas, *Den nye offentligheten*).

17. "*Clausewitzean*" refers to the tradition within intellectual history which follows the military strategist Carl von Clausewitz (1780–1831). Though seen largely as conservative and "realist," the tradition is entangled with the Marxist tradition (see Gallie, *Philosophers*, Chpt. 4; Balibar, "Marxism and War"; Waever and Neumann, *The Future*, Chpt. 1. For methodological aspects, see Jensen, *State Transformation*, 147, 546).

18. Heier, *Kompetanseforvaltning i forsvaret*.

19. Venesson, "Case Studies"; Malthaner et al., "The Social Science."

20. Høiback and Ydstebø, *Krigens vitenskap*, 39; Çubukçu, "Vorwort."

21. Gallie, "Essentially Contested Concepts"; Gallie, *Philosophers*.

THEORY AND METHOD
FOR TRUTH AND RECONCILIATION

> The issue of Sámi Rights is quite uncomplicated
> It is only a matter of three rights
> The right to a past
> The right to a presence
> The right to a future
> —Ánde Somby[22]

The poem suggests that legal scholars, in response to *contemporary* inquiries, are striving to establish new legal evidence from the past to clarify rights that will inform *future* decisions.[23] Efforts toward truth and reconciliation take place within the current *"now-time,"* where the *retrospective descriptions* are being rediscovered, and through that, *prospective prescriptions* are being redefined. The ongoing process of rediscovering evidence and redefining rights challenges conventional perceptions of what is true and good. Does this imply that all versions of the good and the true are equally valid, a concept known as epistemological and ethical relativism or skepticism? Not at all.[24] However, transitional justice might need philosophical clarification of its epistemological and ethical foundations.

Walter Benjamin's essay 'The Concept of History' (*Über den Begriff der Geschichte*) from 1940 provides a critical analysis of *historicity,* existing within the continuum of history.[25] In alignment with the argument above, it offers philosophical guidelines on *retrospective descriptions* of the past and *prospective prescriptions* for the future. In more traditional philosophical terms: epistemology and ethics, or how to approach the concepts of 'The True' and 'The Good.' This duality of historicity comes from the task of not only interpreting the world, but also changing it.[26] Benjamin's concept of history explicitly criticizes the Orthodox Marxism of the Second and Third Internationals, with their assumptions about *progress* as a *teleological evolutionary process,* leading to ever more universal *truth* and

---

22. Somby, "The Issue of Sámi Rights." For a contextualization of the poem within legal theory, see Somby, "Statement at UNWGIP."
23. Jensen, *State Transformation*, Chpt. 1.1.1 and 2.1.2.
24. Jensen, *State Transformation*, Chpt. 1.2.2.
25. Benjamin, "Über den Begriff."
26. Marx, "Theses on Feuerbach," thesis 11.

justice.²⁷ Such 'positivist determinism,' according to Benjamin's Heretic Marxism, should be understood as secularized *crypto- eschatology*.²⁸ Thus, Benjamin returns to the question of how to interpret the eschatological philosophy of history presented in *Phenomenology of Spirit* by Hegel, from where Marx took his dialectic—either as *belief in predetermined progress* or as *hope of an open promise*.²⁹ The translation from philosophical to theological terms enables Benjamin to mobilize conceptual resources from a *less banal* philosophy of eschatology, and thus of *hope*, the Kabbalah, introducing the neologism 'now-time' (*Jetztzeit*).³⁰

If we attempt a 'reverse translation'—back from Kabbalah to philosophical terminology—the essay presents, in my view, two 'rival hypotheses' regarding the hope for truth and justice: *determinism* versus *possibilism*. The *deterministic* hypothesis of progress, found in the Orthodox Marxism of Benjamin's time, had been *falsified* by progress bringing Nazism and the Shoah³¹—undermining the validity of Orthodox Marxism as a wider 'research program.' By contrast, Benjamin suggests a *possibilistic* hypothesis of progress, as part of his Heretic Marxism. In part, the purpose was to restore a philosophy of science for his own ongoing social research, funded by the Institute for Social Research, the famous 'Frankfurt School.'³² Partly, the purpose of the text was also an existential expression of the situation for a Marxist Judaist on the run from the Gestapo—shortly before choosing suicide as the last way out from the Shoah.³³ Benjamin's essay can find resonance with other experiences of racialized suppression, beyond the viewpoint of an Ashkenazi during the Shoah.

For *colonization* as a political-economic phenomenon,³⁴ assumptions regarding progress as a *teleological evolutionary process* or a *secularized crypto eschatology,* according to Benjamin's critique, have

---

27. For a parallel, but separate critique, see Fiori, *Vita di Antonio Gramsci*, 92, 95, 111.

28. Benjamin, "Über den Begriff," theses IV, XI–XIII.

29. Berthold-Bond, "Hegel's Eschatological Vision," Hegel, *Phänomenologie des Geistes*.

30. Benjamin, "Über den Begriff," thesis XIV, XVIII.

31. Benjamin, "Über den Begriff," thesis IX.

32. Beiner, "Walter Benjamin's Philosophy."

33. Beiner, "Walter Benjamin's Philosophy."

34. Hechter, "Internal colonialism"; Smith, "Decolonization"; Tinker "Colonial Empires"; Casanova "Imperialism."

served an ideological function by promoting biased conceptualizations of The Good and The True: During the Cold War, the competing structure-functionalist and Marxist-Leninist theories of modernization both assumed 'unilineal' concepts of progress, functioning to legitimize economic neo-colonialism.[35] In a less secularized form, deterministic *messianism,* which combined 'hierarchical cosmologies' inherited from the Church Fathers, functioned to legitimize hierarchical subordination of Sámi people.[36] In colonized territories, such as Sápmi and Lebanon, missionaries, development workers, and revolutionaries have imposed domination legitimized as universalism.

Secularized 'crypto-eschatology' is just less obvious—and less accountable—than the explicitly theological version. With his essay, Benjamin found hope in the mystical concept of judgment and redemption as phenomena located *outside history,* but also, within any moment of existence, what he calls "now-time" (*Jetztzeit*).[37] This could be interpreted in post-Kantian terms as The True and The Good being "*Dinge an Sich,*" thus, real and universal, but impossible to fully actualize in material practice. Reading Benjamin this way spells out some specific philosophical consequences for the understanding of *retrospective descriptions* of The True as well as *proscriptive prescriptions* of The Good.

The True, or the *epistemology of historical science,* is a central topic in 'The Concept of History.' The essay urges the historian to uncover the less known facts about the less influential classes,[38] but also keeps in mind that this effort necessarily must remain unfinished, giving up the ambition of ever completing the truthful and reconciled historiography. That seems compatible with the methodology of E.H. Carr, a classical realist within IR, who sees historical research as a dialogue between empirical fact-finding, and theory-driven selection and arrangements of facts.[39] Carr built on Gramsci's rejection of the Orthodox Marxism of the 1920s, a debate in Italian[40] which seems parallel to, but separate from, the German debate where Benjamin contributed. A continuation of the Gramscian critique is found in the methodological debate within Indian subaltern studies, where Sarkar rejects the relativistic tendencies

---

35. Hulme and Turner, *Sociology and Development.*
36. Johnsen, *Sámi Nature-Centered Christianity.*
37. Benjamin, "Über den Begriff," thesis IX.
38. Benjamin, "Über den Begriff," theses VI–VIII, X.
39. Carr, *What is History?*
40. Fiori, *Vita di Antonio Gramsci.*

of cultural studies,[41] while Chakrabarty claims that a truly decolonial history is the ideal goal of a laborious empirical endeavor.[42] Applying this to the Lebanese case, Mahdi Amel[43] may be correct to argue that Edward Saïd,[44] while being sensitive to semiotic issues, is taking a wrong turn away from materialistic empiricism. Regarding Sápmi, this approach questions Tuhiwai Smith's portrait of a dichotomic situation between positivism and indigenous research.[45] Instead, the Sámi philosopher Nils Oskal may be more correct when he reminds that it is epistemologically uncontroversial to overcome bias from the past.[46] If the decolonization of knowledge, following Oskal, is not at all epistemologically controversial, then what is the controversy? Firstly, it is a question of rights, as for example, the collective copyright of Indigenous people to their local and traditional knowledge.[47] Secondly, it is a question about research dissemination and history didactics.[48]

The Good, or the *ethics of reconciliation*, on the other hand, is more indirectly present in 'The Concept of History.' Benjamin's essay uses terminology from Marxism and Judaism, evoking connotations towards the concept of the 'classless society' as a synthesis of antagonisms, but also towards the Torah and its prophecies of a Prince of Peace. Let us relate this to Legal Theory and then to Conflict Research.

In terms of *Legal Theory*, this suggests a form of natural law, like the distinction between *human rights* (a universal ethical good beyond language) and *human rights law* (the preliminary embodiment in law).[49] This distinction helps to grasp the gap that will always remain between written human rights law and ideal human rights. Some scholars claim that the development of United Nations (UN) certified human rights law since the Second World War has been strongly influenced by postcolonial states and indigenous rights movements.[50] There is an open-ended

41. Sarkar, "The Decline of the Subaltern."
42. Chakrabarty, *Provincializing Europe*.
43. Amel, *Arab Marxism*.
44. Saïd, *Orientalism*.
45. Smith, *Decolonizing Methodologies*.
46. Oskal, "The Question of Methodology."
47. Solbakk, *Árbevirolaš máhttu*.
48. Solomons et al., "Introduction."
49. Piechowiak, "What Are Human Rights?," 3.
50. Cismas "The Intersection," 452–53; Vasek, "A 30-Year Old Struggle," 29; Jensen, "State Transformation," 45.

decolonization of human rights law going on. How does this apply to the selected cases? Lebanese legal pluralism includes a cohabitation between international human rights law, French secular law, and various religious laws, with much legal scholarship regarding the complex relation between human rights law and Islamic law within "the Islamicate" world.[51] Sámi legal scholars build upon indigenous human rights, which explicitly emphasize the right of the individual to protection against racial discrimination and similar group discrimination.[52] Minority rights should not be perceived as privileges or a form of 'positive discrimination' but rather as a means to safeguard minority communities against undue privileges held by the majority.

If we approach this from the perspective of 'Conflict Research,' the essay reveals evident intertextual connections to both Hegel and the Torah. Implicitly, it aligns itself with a particular concept of peace: neither the Roman concept *pax* as 'deterrence,' nor the Indian concept of *ahimsa* as 'ethical pacifism,' but the Semitic concept of *shalom/salaam* as 'just peace.'[53] While Hegel and Marx might have promised a conclusive synthesis to bring an end to all conflict, presumed to occur at the end of history, Benjamin, in contrast, envisions no conclusion to history but an *everlasting struggle for just peace*. He clearly rejects the authoritarian state, but his lack of clarity regarding insurrectional violence has been an issue of debate: 'The Concept of History' boldly states that the 'state of exception' is the rule rather than the exception, using the word *Ausnahmezustand*.[54] The word is borrowed from the Nazi-affiliated lawyer and political theorist Carl Schmitt, known for his theory of 'antagonism' as a foundational element of politics.[55] Benjamin shows sympathy for the opposite side of that 'antagonism.' Would Benjamin have seen the Warsaw Ghetto Uprising as the ideal example of emancipatory struggle in peacetime? Maybe.[56]

51. Shahid, "Islamic Law and Human Rights."
52. Anaya, *Indigenous Peoples*.
53. For definitions, see Galtung, "Peace"; Bobbio, *Pace*.
54. Benjamin "Über den Begriff," Thesis VIII.
55. Schmitt, *Der Begriff des Politischen*.
56. The "permanent state of exception" (*Ausnahmenzustand*) in Thesis VIII may—or may not—be interpreted in the context of Benjamin's texts on political violence, written twenty years earlier, before becoming a Marxist. One such text, "Critique of Violence," from 1920, would become an object of controversy during the 1960s, when Habermas and Arendt would frame it as a justification of insurrectional violence. Habermas' and Arendt's critique might seem slightly justified if we interpret the mentioned text in

For a *contemporary* application, however, we may equally well reinterpret the concept of 'permanent state of exception' in the light of *post-war* theoretical developments about 'agonistic' non-violence as an alternative to 'antagonistic' violence.[57] This belongs to 'radical democratic' political research on topics like civil disobedience as 'communicative action,'[58] and social movement communication as 'democratic innovation.'[59] How does this translate to the selected cases? In Lebanon, the Semitic concept of *shalom/salaam* is clearly at home, including the usage of political violence to obtain just peace, or the usage of the concept of just peace to legitimize political violence. But as we will see, the 'agonist' and non-violent pathway to 'just peace' has gained relevance. In Sápmi, the Semitic concept *shalom* has been implanted by the Lutheran church, but for common believers, the Sámi concept of peace—*ráfi*—may be more relevant, with its connotations towards non-violence and sacred sites.[60] Within such a context, the 'agonist' and non-violent pathway to

the light of another text from the same period, "Theological-Political Fragment," also from 1920, with its positive words about "Nihilism." The political tendency known as "Nihilism" during the time of the Russian Revolution is more or less what we now know as "Insurrectionary Anarchism," however, we must keep in mind other parts of the historical context as well: during the 1920s, when Benjamin wrote those texts, the revolutionary violence of the working classes was more proportional to the institutional violence of the proprietary classes, compared to the 1960s, when Habermas and Arendt criticized insurrectionary tendencies within the student movement. (See Benjamin, "Über den Begriff"; Benjamin, "Zur kritik der Gewalt"; Benjamin, "Theologisch-politisches Fragment"; Moran and Saltzani, "On the Actuality"; Bojanić, *Violence and Messianism*; Khatib, "The Messianic").

57. In fact, we may also find interesting *reflections on non-violence* in Benjamin's "Critique of Violence," not only the power of *strikes* (which is non-violent direct action according to a contemporary classification), but, even more interesting, also regarding the *public sphere*. The latter opens for a potential reconciliation with Jürgen Habermas, especially in combination with Chantal Mouffe, who sees informal participatory-deliberative democracy within social movements as an "agonistic" practice, and an alternative to Schmitt's "antagonism." When reading Benjamin in retrospect, his writings seem compatible with such a contemporary discursive context. Thus, for a present-day application, we should interpret the "permanent state of exception" (*Ausnahmezustand*) in Thesis VIII of "The Concept of History" in line with Mouffe's and Habermas' *agonism*, rather than Schmitt's *antagonism*, and then, the guiding norm would be that the endless struggle for just peace is to be fought with peaceful—but contentious—means. (See Benjamin, "Über den Begriff"; Benjamin, "Zur kritik der Gewalt"; Schmitt, *Der Begriff*; Mouffe, "Deliberative Democracy." For Habermas' answer to Mouffe, see Habermas, *Ein neuer Strukturwandel*, 19, 51, 47–48, 63–64, or alternatively, the Norwegian translation: Habermas, *Den nye offentligheten*, 22–23, 51–53, 60, 64–66.)

58. Habermas "Civil Disobedience."

59. della Porta, *Can Democracy be Saved?*

60. Johnsen, "Luthersk teologi"; Johnsen, *Sámi Nature-Centred Christianity*, 194–95.

'just peace' may be more compatible than the 'antagonistic' and violent pathway.

All in all, 'The Concept of History' reveals a strong universalist ideal: As an *epistemological* philosophy, it suggests that we should not remain with what seems dogmatically 'true' for *someone*, but instead, strive towards the unattainable goal of obtaining The True for *everyone*. As an *ethical* philosophy, the essay says that we should not remain with what seems dogmatically 'good' for *someone*, but instead, strive towards an unattainable goal of obtaining The Good for *everyone*. Such strong, but unattainable, universalism, might be a philosophy for transitional justice.

Furthermore, Benjamin's 'Concept of History' exemplifies an *aesthetic* philosophy through its writing style. Like poetry and fiction, 'The Concept of History' demonstrates the standpoint that *aesthetics*, or sensuous perception, can enrich the epistemological and ethical endeavors. The Beautiful is entangled with The True and The Good. It makes me associate music as a universal language. From Lebanon, an enlightening example is *Ensemble De Musique Classique Arabe*, whose album *L'annonciation* embodies a dialogue of Christian and Muslim traditional chanting of the story of Virgin Mary. From Sápmi, a powerful example is the artist Mari Boine, who has spread awareness of the indigenous cause, and, within a World Music genre, has entered into dialogue with different musical cultures. This topic reactualizes the poem at the start of the paragraph. It was written by a legal scholar who made his doctorate about *law as rhetoric*.[61] Rhetoric invites sensitivity to an *aesthetic*, or sensuous, dimension of *epistemology* and *ethics*.

TRANSNATIONAL ANTICOLONIAL HISTORY

Lebanon and Sápmi both have had historical-geographical locations at the borders between the Western European colonial empires and non-Western regional empires. They reveal a multi-polar colonial history, which is of relevance to today's multi-polar world.

Both cases were certainly subject to Western European colonialism. Lebanon was a part of the French Mandate for Syria and Lebanon 1923–1946. Sápmi includes Finnmark County, which became explicitly administered as a "colony" from 1848.[62] Economically, both were 'developed'

---

61. Somby, *Juss som retorikk*.
62. Pedersen, "Statens eiendomsrett," 18.

for the benefit of the colonial metropoles as sources of raw materials and markets for industrial products. As a result, both became dependent and underdeveloped. Sápmi was a colony *internal* to the colonizing states,[63] but subject to similar colonization as Greenland, which was outside the colonizing state.[64] Furthermore, Sápmi became an outlet for population surplus from the metropole, through settler colonialist policy.[65] These findings challenge conventional IR theory, which sees the provinces of the Russian Empire as the only example of a modern 'colonial empire' internal to the colonial state.[66]

However, both cases were also subject to non-Western regional empires. These empires can also be called colonial in direct terms, not as a metaphor. A large part of Sápmi was initially under the Russian Empire, as well as the Swedish and Danish Kingdoms, which all had indistinct boundaries. While there is an established practice to analyze the Russian Empire as having a colonial relation to its peripheral provinces,[67] the same lens can also be used to consider the subjugation of Sápmi under early modern Swedish and Danish Kingdoms.

The territory that comprises modern-day Lebanon was made up of several provinces within the Ottoman Empire. Within the field of Ottoman history, an ongoing debate persists regarding whether this empire had a colonial relationship with its provinces, particularly towards its later years when it began to contend with Western European colonial empires.[68] It is true that the Ottoman and the Russian Empires had different policies for their provinces, with the Russian provinces being assimilated into the imperial mode of production, whereas the Ottoman provinces paid taxes.[69] In any case, from the viewpoint of global history, the Ottoman and Russian 'world empires' became integrated within the Western European 'world economy' during the nineteenth century.[70] We may distinguish *politically* between empires and colonialism, but in

63. Otnes, "Retrospect."

64. Truth and Reconciliation Commission in Norway, "Report to the Norwegian Parliament," 562.

65. Kalberg, "Norsk bureiserkolonialisme"; Pedersen, "Statens eiendomsrett."

66. Tinker, "Colonial Empires."

67. Amel, *Arab Marxism*, 48; Wallerstein, *The Capitalist World*, 26; Tinker, "Colonial Empires."

68. Türesay, "The Ottoman Empire."

69. Amel, *Arab Marxism*, 52; Marx, *Grundrisse*, §2, B1.

70. Wallerstein, *The Capitalist World*, 188–89.

economic terms, there is a continuity between them. This implies that the term 'colonial empire,' previously used to describe Russian internal provinces and Western European external acquisitions,[71] is a valid label for the internal provinces of a regionally grown Islamic empire.

Early modern time was a period marked by the presence of several regional empires with theocratic ideologies spanning the western part of the Eurasian landmass. In Western Europe, competition existed between the Habsburg Empire and smaller regional empires, such as the Swedish one. Further to the east, two large empires emerged: the Russian Empire to the north and the Ottoman Empire to the south. Such empires often had indistinct boundaries, with the largest of them enduring until the end of the First World War.

In the Levantine region, the Ottoman Empire presented itself as an Islamic Caliphate while retaining the Byzantine Church as an imperial institution. Through the *millet* system, which was based on religious divisions, the Sunni Muslims and Greek Orthodox religious groups had highly institutionalized functions. Despite this, the Maronites maintained their affiliation with the Vatican after the end of the crusade empires,[72] while the Shia remained connected with Najaf and Tehran.[73] After Lebanon's national independence in 1923, this system underwent transformation into consociationalism to accommodate all religious groups.[74] However, the ethno-religious divisions persist, leading different ethno-religious groups to align themselves with various foreign powers, as they become involved in competing imperial projects.[75] In the later centuries of the Ottoman Empire, a *Pax Ottomania* was established, characterized by a hierarchical dichotomy between urban civilization, known as *medeniyet*, which primarily applied to the metropolis of Istanbul, and tribal culture, referred to as *bedeviyet*, which was associated with provincial cities such as Beirut.[76] However, increased centralization provoked resistance.

In the Nordic region, three early modern empires competed for sovereignty in Sápmi and Kvenland: the expansive Russian Empire, along with the smaller Swedish and Danish kingdoms. Certain peripheral

71. Tinker, "Colonial Empires."
72. Mahfouz, *Short History of the Maronite Church*.
73. Abisaab, "The Cleric."
74. Swiss is another famous example of 'consociationalist' power sharing but based on language rather than religion.
75. Traboulsi, *A Modern History of Lebanon*, iix–3.
76. Türesay, "The Ottoman Empire," IV.

areas were subjected to tax collectors from two or three states, indicating a degree of relative autonomy for these subjugated areas. The empires executed a missionary zeal, grafting Christianity onto local shamanistic traditions.[77] Eastern Sápmi was colonized by Russian Orthodox monasteries, while in Northern and Southern Sápmi and Kvenland, a harsher approach was taken as Lutheran Protestantism was imposed by the rulers of Sweden and Denmark. This imposition occurred through a combination of witchcraft trials and monopolization of violence.[78] Cosmologically, this Lutheran imperial policy imposed a hierarchical worldview[79] that subordinated traditional spirituality.[80] Historian Steinar Pedersen has suggested that Sámi sorcery may have been a reason why, in the seventeenth century, Norwegian settlements were limited to the outer coast, leaving the fjords and the inland regions to the Sámi.[81] This is supported by a letter from King Christian IV in 1609.[82] Witchcraft trials facilitated the expansion of the sovereign's authority.[83] However, those who demonstrated loyalty to the church and the king within the "Lappiske Nation" also enjoyed certain minority rights, which were codified in the Swedish-Danish border treaty of 1751.[84] This situation changed after the Napoleonic War when the concept of popular sovereignty became a device not only for democratization but also for ethno-nationalism. Norway gained partial independence in 1814, and in 1848, the government redefined the northernmost county as having always been a colony ('Colonie').[85] In 1852, the border with Finland was closed, breaching the minority rights established in the Danish-Swedish treaty of 1751.

77. Myrvoll, "'Bare gudsordet duger.'"

78. Johnsen, *Sámi Nature-Centred Christianity*; Sjöberg and Sara, "When Justice Has Borders"; Jensen, "Monokulturalismens etiologi."

79. Johnsen, *Sámi Nature-Centred Christianity*.

80. Pollan, *For Djevelen*; Myrvoll, "'Bare gudsordet duger.'"

81. Pedersen, "Statens eiendomsrett," 21.

82. King Christian 4, "Kong Kristian 4.s befaling." (Thanks to Mikkel Berg-Nordlie for the reference.)

83. The social anthropologist David Graeber argues that historical anthropology ought to classify "violence" in agreement with the emic understanding of the historical actors (Graeber, *Fragments*). Consequently, the mentioned letter from King Christian 4 indicates that, in Sápmi 1609, *witchcraft* was *defense* and *Christianization* was *occupation* (see also Jensen, *State Transformation*, 251).

84. Jensen, "Monokulturalismens etiologi," 64–65.

85. Pedersen, "Statens eiendomsrett," 21.

In 1848, a series of revolutions in Western Europe ignited a global wave of anti-imperial resistance. In peripheral regions, this movement manifested itself as religious upheaval. *At the Lebanese shores*, this movement arrived between 1858 and 1860, taking shape as the *Kisrwan peasant republic*. The revolutionary impulse spread through an eastern Mediterranean network of socialist and anarchist organizations[86] and was channeled through regional forms of organization. In reaction to the centralization of the Ottoman Empire, *al-harakat al-fellahiyya* ("the peasant movement") had been sporadically active since the 1820s. In the Kisrwan area of Mount Lebanon, the peasant resistance was particularly facilitated by Maronite Parish Life—an organizational structure that also constrained the potential expansion of the rebellion. When Maronite peasants in Mount Lebanon attempted to liberate their Druze counterparts in neighboring Mount Chouf, what began as a class revolt transformed into an interreligious war, and in 1860, Maronite peasants found themselves in conflict with Druze peasants, a pattern that is rather typical for social movements in the region. Nonetheless, the Kisrwan peasant republic played a role in shaping the *tanzimat*, the process of liberalization that occurred toward the end of the Ottoman Empire.[87]

In the Sámi territory, the movement arrived in 1852, taking the form of the *Guovdageaidnu* rebellion. During that year, the government made the decision to close the border at the northernmost part of the country, which was a violation of the Sámi immemorial rights codified in 1751, but consistent with the explicitly colonial policy adopted after 1848.[88] The border closure had devastating consequences for the livelihoods of the Sámi people who depended on the land in the border area. Around the same time, a form of lay Lutheranism known as Læstadianism had taken root among the Sámis and Kvens. The movement preached a reversal of the ethnic hierarchies defined by the state church and practiced devout communal self-help with a degree of autonomy from the state apparatus.

Further south on the peninsula, similar movements had already become politicized. Haugianism, another lay Lutheran movement, had provided a social basis for the Thranite Rebellion in 1850,[89] a movement that merged the ideas of Proudhon with Christian socialism.[90] While

86. Khuri-Makdisi, *The Eastern Mediterranean*.
87. Traboulsi, *A Modern History of Lebanon*, 29–33.
88. Zorgdrager, *De rettferdiges strid*.
89. Gundersen, *Haugianerne*, 59.
90. Seip, *Utsikt over Norges historie*, 194–98.

the *Guovdageaidnu* rebellion had no direct causal link to the 1848 revolution,[91] it nonetheless played a role in a broader structural transformation in the political economy,[92] where class struggle in the center translated into anti-imperial and anti-colonial mobilization in the peripheries. The rebellion turned violent and was subsequently suppressed by the state's institutional violence. Nevertheless, it underscored the potential to defend ancient rights against imperialism and colonialism.

Thus, both the *Guovdageaidnu* rebellion and the Kisrwan peasant republic can be viewed as examples of how the revolutionary wave of 1848 was locally *embraced* by *adapting* to two peripheries in the capitalist world economy. In both of these peripheries, *religious millenarism* was the well-established way of doing politics. In both cases, lay religious movements resisted official religious law, reflecting a dialectical tension similar to the one pointed out by Mahdi Amal: *theocratic law* versus *mystical anarchy*,[93] or, alternatively, in terms of Spinoza's political theology: *constituted* order versus *constituent* practice.[94] In both cases, the ruling order was supported by a 'hierarchical world-making,'[95] but it faced challenges from an egalitarian cosmology. Furthermore, the official millenarism of the *afterlife* was contested by a revolutionary millenarism focused on the 'now-time' (*Jetztzeit*).[96]

If we define colonialism solely in political terms, the *Guovdageaidnu* rebellion can be considered anti-colonial, whereas the *Kisrwan* peasant republic can be seen as anti-imperial. However, if we define colonialism in economic terms, both movements were forms of anti-colonial resistance. Habermas viewed the 1848 wave of movements as a failed attempt by 'radical-democratic' revolutionaries to expand the 'bourgeois public sphere' by establishing a "plebeian public sphere" for proletarians, women, and people of color.[97] The events in *Guovdageaidnu* and *Kisrwan* can be seen as attempts at expanding universal rights to include colonial subjects.

91. Magga, "Hva forsårsaket opprøret?"
92. Otnes, "Retrospect on 'The Sámi Nation.'"
93. Amel, *Arab Marxism*, 111–19.
94. Negri, *Spinoza*.
95. Johnsen, *Sámi Nature-Centred Christianity*.
96. For a less sympathetic view, see Cohn, *In Pursuit of the Millennium*, especially the final chapter.
97. For "plebeian public sphere," see Habermas, *Strukturwandel*, §14–15. For the contemporary Habermas' view on "agonism," see Habermas, *Ein neuer Strukturwandel*, 19, 51, 47–48, 63–64 (Norwegian translation: Habermas, *Den nye offentligheten*, 22–23, 51–53, 60, 64–66.)

INTERNAL COLONIALISM?

The transnational history mentioned above illustrates how the events in *Guovdageaidnu* and *Kisrwan*, which followed the 1848 revolt in Paris, can both be analyzed as forms of resistance against internal colonization. This term refers to situations of geographically uneven development when both *center* and *periphery* are located within one and *the same state formation*.[98] This is not only a conceptual exercise; it has significant consequences for understanding history over *the long term*, from early modern times to the present day.

The term 'internal colonization' has emerged as a means of resolving dialectical tensions between materialist theory and empirical facts. The process illustrates what Mahdi Amel understands as a *methodology* of self-critique.[99] Initially, Lenin used the term to describe Ireland under British rule and Ukraine under the Russian Empire. Later, following clashes between the Red Army and Anarchist Cossacks, the UCP adopted the term for national independence from Moscow.[100]

At the same time, Antonio Gramsci employed the term to address the subordination of Southern Italian peasants and pastoralists during the *risorgimento*, the unification of Italy.[101] While, on a practical level, this was a (failed) attempt to break the cycle of reproducing a colonial economy,[102] the development of the term was on a theoretical level an effort to internally *decolonize* materialist social theory.

If we define colonialism in economic terms, it also applies to the Lebanese provinces of the Ottoman Empire, at least during its centralization. The Lebanese writer Mahdi Amel argues that it is fruitful to understand

98. Hechter, "Internal Colonialism."

99. Amel, *Arab Marxism*, 17–18.

100. UCP (Ukapists) gave in 1920 a Memorandum to the 2'nd World Congress of the Comintern. The party requested independence for the Ukrainian Soviet Socialist Republic, and hence, that this republic should be represented within the Comintern by the UCP, not by the Russian Bolsheviks (UCP, "Memorandum"; Ford, *UKAPISME*; Kowalewski, *L'Indépendence*; Kowalewski, *For the Independence*). See also Wikipedia, *Colonialisme interne*.

101. Gramsci, *La questione meridionale*, is a fine selection of Gramsci's texts on this issue. "Colonialism" is explicitly mentioned in the following places:

a) Gramsci, "Operai e contadini" from 1920 (p. 91 in the anthology).

b) Gramsci, *Alcune temi della quistione meridionale* from 1930 (p. 108 in the anthology).

c) Gramsci, *Quaderni del carcere*, Q19, §26 "Il rapporto città-campagna. . ." (184–85 in the anthology).

102. Wallerstein, *The Capitalist World*, 189.

colonialism economically, thus not distinguishing between colonialism and neo-colonialism.[103] Lebanon gained *formal* independence from *political* colonization in 1943. However, in 1975, the outbreak of war was spurred on by a leftist avant-garde seeking liberation from both *informal and economic colonization*, driven by their hope in Arab nationalism Nevertheless, if the term 'colonialism', defined in economic terms, applies to the Ottoman Empire, it raises questions about its applicability to other regionally rooted entities, such as Arab nationalist regimes. Franz Fanon, a teacher of Mahdi Amel, warned against the potential of postcolonial bourgeoisie to reproduce colonial patterns of domination.[104] Contemporary Arab thought calls for cultural resistance *not only* against *external* colonization, *but also* against *internal* authoritarianism.[105] The Lebanese left is divided between those who see Hezbollah's 'axis of resistance' as a force *against colonialism*, and those who see it as just *another colonialism*. Anti-colonial thought wishes a liberation from Eurocentrism[106]—will that lead to the discovery of regionally homegrown colonialism? Are Iran and Saudi Arabia exercising colonialism at a regional level, *autonomously* of global neocolonial players? Should we reconsider the Zionist project as not only the colonizer of Palestine, but, at the same time, as resistance to colonization by Pan Arab armies?

A model of 'conflict dynamics' at various geographical levels, originally developed to describe conflict in the Horn of Africa,[107] offers a valuable framework for addressing these intricate questions. In Lebanon, a layered colonialism framework becomes apparent: Firstly, there's *local colonialism*, where political figures known as "zuama" wield authority over the subaltern classes in specific locales. Moving up the scale, we encounter *national colonialism*, with Beirut's central powers exerting control over both urban suburbs and provincial areas. Beyond this, *macro-regional colonization* comes into play, featuring influential non-governmental organizations (NGOs) funded by external actors like Iran or Saudi Arabia. Finally, *global colonialism* is evident as France and the United States of America (USA) interfere in Lebanon's internal affairs. These factors collectively shape a 'multi-level' political opportunity structure for subaltern classes seeking empowerment.

103. Amel, *Arab Marxism*.
104. Fanon, *Les damnées de la terre*, Chpt. 3.
105. Kassab, *Contemporary Arab Thought*.
106. Amin, *Eurosentrismen*.
107. McGinnis, "Conflict Dynamics."

The Israeli *Anarchists Against the Wall* advocate for 'joint resistance' alongside occupied Palestinians as a practical means to achieve truth and reconciliation.[108] On the Lebanese side, a notable movement emerged during the 1970s, comprising ecumenical Christian and Islamic liberation theologians who worked for just peace.[109] Today, both Lebanese and Zionist state entities grapple with legitimacy crises, and the Syrian War, which followed the Arab Spring, serves as a stark illustration of the dire consequences that can unfold when equilibrium is disrupted.

The description provided highlights the applicability of the concept of 'internal colonization' to Sápmi, a region that experienced conquest by three early modern regional empires. This usage of the term 'colonization' finds resonance outside the mainstream of IR and has been explored in the context of Western European regionalism and minority nationalism.[110] Per Otnes,[111] in his 1970 book, was inspired to use this term concerning Sápmi[112] and Steinar Pederen in 1999[113] presented definitive historical evidence in support of this perspective. Additionally, the official report from the Norwegian TRC extensively addresses settler colonialism.[114]

By applying the concept of 'internal colonization' to Sápmi, one can argue that Indigenous peoples and national minorities within the region can be seen as *subaltern classes* engaged in a struggle to change their position against *cultural hegemonies*. These cultural hegemonies were initially established by national romanticist state-builders in Russia, Sweden, Norway, and Finland. While Russia operates as a multi-national federation, the colonizing states were established as uni-national nation states. The combined effects of the Norwegian assimilation policy, Swedish segregation policy, and informal Finnish settlements contributed to ethnic discrimination against Sámis, Kvens, and Finnish migrants.

Ketil Zachariassen conducted a pioneering study that delved into the concept of 'cultural hegemony' within the Nordic context. Specifically, his research focused on a notable but unsuccessful effort by 'Sámi

108. Gordon, *Anarchy Alive*.
109. Traboulsi, *A Modern History of Lebanon*, 176–80.
110. Lafont, *Décoloniser en France*.
111. Otnes, "Retrospect on 'The Sámi Nation'."
112. Otnes, *Den samiske nasjon*.
113. Pedersen, "Statens eiendomsrett."
114. Truth and Reconciliation Commission in Norway, "Report to the Norwegian Parliament." (The report uses the term "jordbrukskolonisering").

national strategists' to influence the trajectory of Norwegian nation-building, aiming for a more inclusive and less ethnically chauvinistic historical account.[115] Following in the true spirit of Gramsci, founder of the term 'cultural hegemony,'[116] Zachariassen analyzes minority mobilization within the context of majority nationalism. However, he departs from the path of the master when his history of ideas overlooks the contexts of economic and political history. These were exactly the dimensions observed by Steinar Pedersen in his analysis of 'internal colonization.'[117] Thus, for a valid historical analysis of 'cultural hegemony' in the Nordic area, it is necessary to take into account the political-economic phenomenon of internal colonization.

Both *Lebanon* and *Sápmi* find themselves in complex colonial relations, including internal colonialism. The question of how subaltern classes can challenge and change prevailing hegemonies in these contexts is critical. In both cases, achieving truth and reconciliation often hinges on *subaltern classes* maintaining a united front.[118] However, they also need to be cautious not to be stigmatized as disloyal to their respective states, as this can hinder their efforts. Radical-democratic theory on non-violent "agonism" sees the *public sphere* as a *theater of operation* for liberation struggles.[119] However: According to proponents of agonistic pluralism, an inclusive public sphere is a prerequisite of non-violent political contention. Whenever the public sphere is less inclusive, political violence is more prevalent.[120] The potential escalation of such political violence is demonstrated in the modern history of Lebanon, as well as the even more recent history of Syria.

115. Zachariassen, *Samiske nasjonale strateger*.

116. Fiori, *Vita di Antonio Gramsci*, 242–46, 276–78.

117. Pedersen, "Statens eiendomsrett."

118. For example, the Sámi people need to maintain unity across state borders, not only between four states, but also between two military alliances, the North Atlantic Treaty Organization (NATO) and Collective Security Treaty Organization (CSTO). Furthermore, subalterns need to keep some level of unified front across the legal distinctions between "Indigenous people" and "national minorities," to be able to be steadfast against hegemonical majority nationalism. Finally, political groups like Norgga Sámiid Riikkasearvi/ Norske Samers Riksforbund (NSR) may see the utility to accommodate a party like *Nordkalottfolket*, to avoid increased support to anti-Sámi NGOs, such as the so-called Etnisk og demokratisk likeverd (EDL). (For a discussion of the dangers of alienating subaltern groups, see also Nordquist, "Reconciliation Recommended").

119. Cini, *Societá civile*.

120. Laclau and Mouffe, *Hegemony and Socialist Strategy*, Chpt. 2.

The inclusivity of public spheres varies significantly across different regions and contexts, and it plays a critical role in enabling subalterns to participate in participatory-deliberative democracy. In many parts of the Arab world, contemporary intellectuals have expressed concerns about the limitations of public spheres due to issues like widespread illiteracy and censorship. These factors have indeed hindered open public debate and the development of social movements.[121] However, the Arab Spring did empower organizational culture,[122] and within an Arab context, the Lebanese public sphere is relatively inclusive. In Sápmi, regional newspapers have cultivated a notably inclusive and "carnivalesque public sphere,"[123] which has recently extended its presence online through the platform *Nordnorsk debatt*. These platforms may provide suitable arenas for engaging in contentious dialogues and practicing non-violent agonism.

PUBLIC MEMORY AS PUBLIC CONTENTION

After thirty years of war in Lebanon and a decade of discrimination in Sápmi, the issue of public memory becomes highly contested, as is often the case in transitional justice contexts. The practice of disseminating historical knowledge, known as history didactics, plays a crucial role in bridging the gap between academic historical research and public memory. One area where the struggle over cultural hegemony is particularly evident is in school history. School history curricula are inherently selective, and this selectivity can serve the interests of one social class or ethnic group over another. Does that imply that history didactics is merely a battlefield for memory wars, or does it promise a path towards truth and reconciliation? Now, transitioning to a more subjective style for an anthropological analysis of public memory, based on literary primary sources and ethnographic travel memories, allows for a more 'subjective' exploration, enabling ethnographic 'reflexivity.'[124]

    121. Kassab, *Contemporary Arab Thought*, 347–63.

    122. Bayat, *Revolutionary Life*.

    123. Jensen, *State Transformation*, 362. For Habermas' view on "plebeien public sphere," see Habermas, *Strukturwandel*, §14–15. For Habermas' view on "agonism," see Habermas, *Ein neuer Strukturwandel*, 19, 51, 47–48, 63–4 (Norwegian translation: Habermas, *Den nye offentligheten*, 22–23, 51–3, 60, 64–6).

    124. About ethnographic "reflexivity," it should be noted that "[t]he point of getting to know 'you, the ethnographer' better, getting to know the way you influence your research, is to create a more reliable portrait, argument or theory about 'them, the participants,'" as written in Madden, *Being Ethnographic*, 23.

"*[I]n Lebanon's case*, not even school textbooks could agree on a basic frame for the common historical narrative. Indeed, the two opposing versions of 'national memory' building appear in even the earliest history textbooks."[125] It is quite common for textbooks covering the history of the same country to emphasize different facts and consider various historical contexts. On one hand, there are 'Pan-Arab nationalist' accounts that situate the country's history within the context of South-West Asian history. This historiography finds strong support among Sunni Muslims and Greek Orthodox religious groups, which were the most established communities during the Ottoman Empire. On the other hand, 'Lebanese nationalist' accounts frame the country within the context of Mediterranean history[126] and are particularly favored by Maronite Christians, who have maintained their loyalty to Rome since the time of the Crusader states.

The tensions between the two forms of nationalist belonging, the Pan-Arab and the Lebanese, played a significant role in shaping the Lebanese Constitution. Originally drafted in 1926 during the French Mandate, the Constitution was fundamentally amended during the country's national independence in 1943. The post-independence Constitution, known as the "national pact," explicitly recognized both Lebanese and Pan-Arab nationalism. This included a "consociationalist" political system with separate political representation for each ethno-religious group, based upon the Ottoman *millet* system. However, the national pact faced challenges and was considered weak due to several factors. Firstly, the system was perceived as favoring the Maronites, one of several minorities, but protected by the French. Additionally, the national pact's fragility stemmed from the fact that the 'postcolonial' state maintained the territorial borders and economic structure established during the French mandate period.

The tension became a manifest conflict when war broke out in 1975. On the one hand, Pan-Arab nationalists were discontent with the borders of the existing 'Greater Lebanon,' emphasizing a shared economic and political history between Southern Lebanon and former Mandate Palestine. Among Pan-Arab nationalists, socialists and communists framed the French Mandate as pure colonialism, which had hampered the earlier eastward trade routes.[127] Lebanese nationalists, in contrast to Pan-Arabists,

125. Ziadeh, *Sectarianism*, 31 (emphasis is added).
126. Ziadeh, *Sectarianism*.
127. Amel, *Arab Marxism*.

emphasized a different historical perspective. They focused on the core areas of the Lebanese state, with their westward trade routes, and from this perspective, they viewed historical Arabization and Islamization as a form of colonization of Aramaic Christians.[128] However, as new military front lines emerged within each of these two groups, especially between Sunni and Shia Muslims, new historiographies also emerged. This was especially the case concerning Shia Muslims of Jabal Amel, or South Lebanon.[129]

After the civil war, the prominent historian Kamal Salibi, a Protestant Christian, changed his mind. Before the war, he had written *A Modern History of Lebanon*, a classic of Christian-centric Lebanese historiography. However, towards the end of the war, he penned *A House of Many Mansions*, in which he advocated for historians to engage in the essential task of disentangling myths from facts amidst the historiographical battles that had emerged during the civil war.[130] That certainly was a call for truth and reconciliation.

One answer to that call was Fawwaz Traboulsi's overview of Lebanese history, a Marxian *synthesis* of the various ethnocentric histories.[131] Another answer was offered by Hussein Gharbieh, who aimed at further scientific empowerment of an empirical *counter-history* for the deprived Shiite sect.[132] Thus, after the civil war, historians have been pursuing various paths towards truth and reconciliation. In such a situation, it is no wonder that during my fieldwork in Lebanon between 2009 and 2011, some of my Christian Lebanese family members raised their eyebrows at me for reading Palestine Liberation Organization (PLO)-influenced books with a Pan-Arab perspective. In response, they politely introduced me to Lebanese nationalist literature influenced by Force Libanaise.

Furthermore, the school system remains fragmented, newspapers are affiliated with sectarian parties, and public memory remains divided. But public and private dialogues stretch out towards potential truth.[133]

In *Sápmi's case*, historiography faces division along two significant factors. Firstly, the Sápmi territory is split among four different states, each with its own language, national historiographies, and public school

128. Ziadeh, *Sectarianism*, 35.
129. Ziadeh, *Sectarianism*, 36.
130. Salibi, *A Modern History of Lebanon*; Salibi, *A House of Many Mansions*.
131. Traboulsi, *A History of Modern Lebanon*.
132. Gharbieh, *Lebanese Confessionalism*.
133. For a similar "dialogical" view, see Grung, "Moral Enrichment."

systems. Secondly, the official efforts towards truth and reconciliation for Indigenous peoples and national minorities have been somewhat half-hearted. Some of these states have taken steps to establish school systems in the Sámi language and incorporate a syllabus on Sámi history. However, there has been a lack of comprehensive reform in the majority school system syllabi. Additionally, the histories of the Kven and Norwegian-Finnish communities remain under-researched and are even less widely disseminated.

During my fieldwork along the Deatnu River from 2010 to 2012, I was hosted by *ČálliidLágádus* (meaning Authors' Publisher) and introduced to their school history textbooks.[134] It was enlightening to discover that children attending the school system in the Northern Sámi language were provided with a syllabus that included recent findings in colonial history. For instance, they learned about the Norwegian state administration's claim in 1848 that Finnmark County was considered a colony.[135] However, it became evident that various issues remain under-researched in the colonial history of Sápmi, particularly concerning the Kven and Finnish minorities.[136] This observation aligns with the fact that official efforts to restore the Kven and Finnish languages have been even weaker than those aimed at revitalizing the Sámi language.[137] Even more conspicuous is that for children attending the school system in the Norwegian language, a *colonial* encounter between Sápmi and Norway is not even mentioned. This omission left me perplexed.

As a former museum teacher at the Norwegian Folk Museum, I had received training in history didactics from museum conservators who recognized the necessity for contemporary museum education to address and overcome the ethnocentric bias present in "the Norwegian historical school"—which I now saw being criticized also from the perspective of Sámi history.[138] *ČálliidLágádus* made a lasting impression on me by actively taking practical steps toward fostering a more democratic nation-building process within the Norwegian polity. Their efforts aimed to counter ethnic assimilation and embrace the actual cultural pluralism of the territory. This was evident in their school textbooks written in the

134. Solbakk, *Sápmi ja Málbmi*, vols. 1–2.
135. Pedersen, "Statens eiendomsrett," 37.
136. Niemi, "Kvenit ya yhteiskunta"; Robertsen, *Den finske arven*.
137. Truth and Reconciliation Commission in Norway, "Report to the Norwegian Parliament."
138. Pedersen, "Samiske rettigheter."

Sámi language. Their practice was funded, in large part, by the Norwegian state through the *Sámidiggi* on the Norwegian side. By contributing to alternative nation-building, they resemble the past nation-builders described in some of the books they have published.[139]

However, I was most unimpressed by the Norwegian state buying itself *indulgence* by using a little of its 'petrodollars' to pay for a revised syllabus for one of the minorities, while refraining to update the syllabus for the majority. The Norwegian TRC has recognized that the knowledge that does exist about the past has not been well disseminated throughout the majority, which is an obstacle for reconciliation.[140] That should come as no surprise, as the school syllabus says nothing about Norway's internal history of colonization. This may explain why "there is public debate as to how the logic of colonialism fits the historical context, and whether the Sámi people and lands were ever colonized" on the Norwegian side of Sápmi.[141] This public contention may be a result of old nationalistic myths being reproduced by majority school and majority media, despite these myths having been *falsified* by scientific historical research.

In both cases, Lebanon and Sápmi, *civil society* is the terrain where public memory, historical research, and public policy interact, shaping perceptions of truth and reconciliation. This is not merely a memory war between entrenched positions. There is also hope for truth and reconciliation.

The debate surrounding 'cultural hegemony,' as envisioned by Gramsci, included a *messianic hope* that the liberation of the subaltern classes would bring a somewhat more universally true and just syllabus.[142] On the one hand, history as a *research discipline,* appears progressive as it strives to create a less fragmented archive and engage in research and writing that aims to provide a clearer demarcation between myth and fact in our understanding of the past. On the other hand, history as an *education discipline,* history, when viewed as an educational discipline, tends to lag behind, with school history textbooks conveying established historical narratives deemed acceptable for the intended audience. These two inclinations can be likened to the concepts of 'constituent and constituted

139. Zachariassen, *Samiske nasjonale strategar*; Solbakk and Solbakk, *Dasgo eallin gáibida min soahtái.*

140. Truth and Reconciliation Commission in Norway, "Report to the Norwegian Parliament," Chpt. 25–26.

141. Solomons et al., "Introduction," 5.

142. do Mar Castro Varela, *Hegemonie bilden,* 12–13.

power' at the societal level, or *potestas* and *potentia* in terms of Spinoza's political theology.¹⁴³

By engaging in 'agonistic' non-violent action, akin to the contemporary variety of the Benjaminean permanent state of exception (*Ausnahmezustand*), increasingly marginalized groups are able to assert themselves in the public sphere. In essence, these actions empower marginalized communities with the means to exercise freedom of speech as a positive liberty. As they gain the opportunity to share their own empirical experiences publicly, we may expand the 'bourgeois public sphere' into what Habermas called a "the plebeian public sphere." The endless effort towards such a situation is a Benjaminean "now-time" (*Jetztzeit*), which brings us closer to the ideal of truth and reconciliation. That is a messianism of decolonization.

CONCLUSION

This chapter, firstly, suggested a *philosophical framework* for transitional justice, taken from Walter Benjamin's philosophy of history, and, secondly, it showcased the *epistemological* and *ethical* significance of this framework through an empirical *historical-anthropological* study of two cases of decolonization: Lebanon and Sápmi. The choice of these cases enabled the discovery of potential conflict dynamics that bridge the divide between manifest and latent conflicts.

In part 1 of the chapter, a philosophical analysis of Walter Benjamin's essay 'The Concept of History' was conducted with the objective of extracting an epistemological and ethical foundation for truth and reconciliation. We found in Benjamin's philosophy of history an eagerness to engage in the *endless struggle* for social justice. That implies a clear rejection of Hegel's philosophy of history, at least regarding its conventional reading, as being teleological and predetermined. Instead, Benjamin's term "now-time" (*Jetztzeit*) was interpreted in neo-Kantian terms, a choice that was justified philosophically. What emerged was an *ideal* of 'strong universalism' both epistemologically and ethically. This was coupled with a strong sensitivity for the *practically unattainable* nature of The True and The Good per se, and finally, an urge to push 'small truths' and 'small goods' closer to the ideal True and Good. These two issues,

---

143. Negri, *Spinoza*; Negri, *Il potere costituente*. (For the connections between Spinoza, Hegel, Gramsci, and Negri, see Cini, *Societá civile*, 31–33 and 80–81).

the *epistemological* and the *ethical*, were intimately connected to ongoing debates within IR: firstly, they intersected with *epistemological* debates regarding historical research methods and the decolonization of history. Secondly, they engaged with *ethical* debates regarding the Semitic concept of *just peace*. Furthermore, both the *epistemological* and *ethical* aspects were related to *human rights law*, encompassing its *prescriptive* and *descriptive* dimensions, both internationally and in the cases of Lebanon and Sápmi.

Furthermore, the suggested philosophical framework was related to a public debate within *normative political theory*: Benjamin has been accused, especially by Jürgen Habermas, of having been a supporter of insurrectionist violence, especially because of his (un)famous usage of Carl Schmitt's term "permanent state of exception" (*Ausnahmezustand*). Instead of trying to answer the validity or anachronism of the accusation, we argued that a *contemporary application* of Benjamin's readings should *also* take *later* philosophical development into account. In the post-World War Two era, radical democratic theorists like Habermas and others have advanced empirically grounded critical theories that explore how social conflicts can manifest within the theater of civil society and the public sphere. Within this context, 'agonistic' non-violence is regarded as a viable alternative to 'antagonistic' violence, offering a potential path toward achieving 'just peace'.

Parts 2 and 3 of the chapter involved a *historical analysis* of colonization and decolonization (defined politically and economically) in Lebanon and Sápmi. The argument put forth was that the concept of 'internal colonialism' is relevant for these cases, challenging conventional IR theory, which typically identifies the Russian Empire as the sole example of a colonial empire within the borders of the colonizing state. In Part 2, the historical narrative was traced back to the theocratic regional empires of the early modern era, and it extended to the significance of the year 1848 as a transnational moment for revolution. The chapter analyzed both regimes and revolutions in Benjaminean terms of a millennial "now-time" (*Jetztzeit*), as well as Habermasean terms of "public sphere" (*Öffentlichkeit*). Part 3 transitioned into a more conceptual discussion centered around 'internal colonialism.' It drew connections between Benjamin's philosophy of history and parallel historical efforts by the UKP and the Italian communist Antonio Gramsci in their attempts to internally decolonize dialectical materialist social theory.

In Part 4 of the chapter, an *anthropological analysis* was conducted, focusing on the contested public memory in Sápmi and Lebanon. This analysis involved the examination of literary primary sources and ethnographic travel memories. The study demonstrated how, in both regions, conflicting approaches to history education have developed alongside competing nation-building endeavors. In Lebanon, these conflicts have been more overt, while in Sápmi, they have remained relatively concealed. However, in both cases, the persistence of contested public memory poses a significant challenge to achieving truth and reconciliation. So, what are the Benjaminean prospects for 'just peace,' and what kind of 'now-time' and what kind of 'permanent state of exception' is to be found?

The chapter concludes with a discussion of how *public spheres* in Lebanon and Sápmi are being made more *socially inclusive*, and thus might serve as theaters-of-operation for social conflict that is 'agonistic' and non-violent rather than 'antagonistic' and violent. In its final remarks, the chapter proposes that the struggle over 'cultural hegemony,' when viewed through the combined perspectives of Benjamin and Gramsci and their critiques of historical materialism during the interwar period, transcends being merely a 'memory war.' Instead, it signifies a concerted effort towards a broader form of universalism, encompassing both epistemological and ethical dimensions.

BIBLIOGRAPHY

Abisaab, Rula J. "The Cleric as Organic Intellectual: Revolutionary Shi'ism in the Lebanese Hawzas." In *Distant Relations, Iran and Lebanon in the Last 500 years*, edited by Houchang Chehabim 231–58. London: Tauris, 2006.

Amel, Mahdi. *Arab Marxism and National Liberation. Selected Writings of Mahdi Amel*. Chicago: Haymarket, 2022.

Amin, Samir. *Eurosentrismen. Kritikk av en ideologi*. Oslo: Oktober, 1992.

Anaya, James. *Indigenous Peoples in International Law*. Oxford: Oxford University Press, 2004.

Balibar, Étienne. "Marxism and War." Paper presented at the seminar "Los Pensadores de la Crisis Contemporanea: Marx, Weber, Keynes, Schmitt," Universidad Internacional Menéndez Pelayo, Valencia, December 2–4, 2009. https://www.radicalphilosophy.com/wp-content/files_mf/rp160_article1_marxismwar_balibar.pdf/.

Bayat, Asef. *Revolutionary Life. The Everyday of the Arab Spring*. Cambridge: Harvard University Press, 2021.

Beiner, Ronald. "Walter Benjamin's Philosophy of History." *Political Theory* 12 (1984) 423–34.

Benjamin, Walter. "Kapitalismus als Religion."[144] In *Gesammelte Schriften*, edited by Rolf Tiedemann and Hermann Scheppenhäuser, 100–103. 6 vols. Frankfurt: Suhrkamp, 1974.

———. "Theologisch-politisches Fragment."[145]

———. "Über den Begriff der Geschichte." Frankfurt: Institut für Sozialforschung, 1943.[146]

———. "Zur Kritik der Gewalt."[147]

Berthold-Bond, Daniel. "Hegel's Eschatological Vision: Does History Have a Future?" *History and Theory* 27 (1988) 14–29. https://doi.org/10.2307/2504959/.

Birnbaum, Maria. "Religion: Westphalia, the Colony and the Secular." In *Concepts in World Politics*, edited by Felix Berenskoetter. London: Sage, 2016.

Bobbio, Norberto. *Pace*. Roma: Treccani, 2022.

Bojanić, Petar. *Violence and Messianism Jewish Philosophy and the Great Conflicts of the Twentieth Century*. London: Routledge, 2018.

Carr, Edward H. *What is History?* London: Penguin, 1961.

Casanova, Pablo G. "Imperialism." In *The Oxford Companion to Politics of the World*, edited by Joel Krieger. 2nd ed. Oxford: Oxford University Press, 2001.

Chakrabarty, Dipesh. *Provincializing Europe: Postcolonial Thought and Historical Difference*. Princeton: Princeton University Press, 2007.

Cini, Lorenzo. *Società civile e democrazia radicale*. Florence: Florence University Press, 2012.

Cismas, Ioana. "The Intersection of Economic, Social, and Cultural Rights and Civil and Political Rights." In *Economic, Social, and Cultural Rights in International Law: Contemporary Issues and Challenges*, edited by Eibe Riedel et al., 448–72. Oxford: Oxford University Press, 2014.

Cohn, Norman. *In Pursuit of the Millennium: Revolutionary Millenarians and Mystical Anarchists of the Middle Ages*. 2nd ed. Oxford: Oxford University Press, 1970.

Çubukçu, Ayça. "Vorwort zu Fragmente einer anarchistischen Anthropologie." In *Fragmente einer anarchistischen Anthropologie*, edited by David Graeber. Berlin: Unrast, 2022.

De Brito, Alexandra B., et al., eds. *The Politics of Memory: Transitional Justice in Democratizing Societies*. Oxford: Oxford University Press, 2001.

della Porta, Donatella. *Can Democracy Be Saved? Participation, Deliberation, and Social Movements*. New York: Wiley-Blackwell, 2013.

della Porta, Donatella, et al. *Social Movements and Civil War: When Protests for Democratization Fail*. London: Routledge, 2018.

144. "Capitalism as Religion." Originally written in 1920.

145. Originally written 1920. Available in German original and Danish translation at *Fønix* (2019) 166–70: http://foenix1976.dk/2019/08/13/walter-benjamin-teologisk-politisk-fragment/?fbclid=IwAR1vegrGF5lsJryot_9fFAjxdpY6hw6HlYaOHJwRXI1Rlo_u64sN9HgSoOM

146. Originally written in 1940. Available online in German original: https://www.textlog.de/benjamin/abhandlungen/ueber-den-begriff-der-geschichte and English translation: https://www.marxists.org/reference/archive/benjamin/1940/history.htm

147. Originally written in 1920. Available online in German original: https://musiclanguagethought.files.wordpress.com/2011/02/benjamin-zur-kritik-der-gewalt.pdf and in English translation: https://fswg.files.wordpress.com/2015/04/benjamin-critique-of-violence-new-translation.pdf Last accessed, 5. June 2023.

della Porta, Donatella, et al., eds. *Social Movements in a Globalizing World*. New York: Macmillan, 1999.
do Mar Castro Varela, María, et al., eds. *Hegemonie bilden: Pädagogische Anschlüsse an Antonio Gramsci*. Basel: Beltz, 2023.
Dorot, Roni. "Media Influence Matrix. Technology, Public Sphere and Journalism: Israel," Central European University; CDU Democracy Institute; Center for Media, Data and Society, 2021.
Evans, Graham, and Jeffrey Newnham. *The Penguin Dictionary of International Relations*. London: Penguin, 1998
Fanon, Franz. *Les damnés de la terre*. Paris: Maspero, 1961.
Fiori, Giuseppe. *Vita di Antonio Gramsci*. Nuoro: Ilissio, 2006.
Ford, Christopher, and Vincent Présumey. *UKAPISME—Une Gauche perdue : Le marxisme anti-colonial dans la révolution ukrainienne 1917—1925*. Stuttgart: Ibidem, 2021.
Froio, Caterina, et al. *CasaPound Italia: Contemporary Extreme-Right Politics*. London: Routledge, 2020.
Gallie, Walter B. "Essentially Contested Concepts." *Proceedings of the Aristotelian Society* 56 (1956) 167–98.
———. *Philosophers of Peace and War: Kant, Clausewitz, Marx, Engles and Tolstoy*. Cambridge: Cambridge University Press, 1978. https://doi.org/10.1017/CBO9780511558450
Galtung, Johan. "Peace." In *The Oxford Companion to Politics of the World*, edited by Joel Krieger. 2nd ed. Oxford: Oxford University Press, 20s01.
Gharbieh, Hussein. *Lebanese Confessionalism and the Creation of the Shi'i Identity*. Beirut: Dar al-Manhal al-Lubnani, 2010.
Gordon, Uri. *Anarchy Alive. Anti-Authoritarian Politics from Practice to Theory*. London: Pluto, 2008.
Graeber, David. *Fragments of an Anarchist Anthropology*. Chicago: Prickley Para-digm, 2004.
Gramsci, Antonio. "Alcune temi della quistione meridionale." In *La questione meridionale,* by Aantonio Gramsci. Milano: Editore Melampo, 2014 (1930).
———. *La questione meridionale. Nuova antologia a cura e con introduzione di Nando dalla Chiesa*. Milano: Editore Melampo, 2014.
———. "Operai e contadini." In *La questione meridionale,* by Antonio Gramsci. Milano: Editore Melampo, 2014 (1930).
———. *Quaderni del carcere. Edizione critica dell'Istituto Gramsci. A cura di Valentino Garretana*. Roma: Enaudi, 2021.
Grung, Anne H. "Moral Enrichment and Moral Critique of Texts from the Bible and the Koran: Towards an Interreligious Feminism?" *Islamochristiana* 37 (2011) 67–75.
Gundersen, Trygve R. *Haugianerne. 1: Enevelde og undergrunn 1795-1799*. Oslo: Cappelen Damm, 2022.
Habermas, Jürgen. "Civil Disobedience." *Berkeley Journal of Sociology* 30 (1985) 95–116. https://www.jstor.org/stable/pdf/41035345.pdf/.
———. *Den nye offentligheten. Strukturendring og deliberativ politikk*. Oslo: Cappelen Damm, 2023.
———. *Ein neuer Strukturwandel der Öffentlichkeit und die Deliberative Politik*. Berlin: Suhrkamp, 2023.
———. *Strukturwandel der Öffentlichkeit*. Berlin: Luchterhand, Neuwied, 1962.

Hall, Bogumila. "Bedouins' Politics of Place and Memory: A Case of Unrecognised Villages in the Negev." *Nomadic Peoples* 18 (2014) 147–64. https://doi.org/10.3197/np.2014.

Hechter, Michael. "Internal Colonialism." In *The Oxford Companion to Politics of the World*, edited by Joel Krieger. 2nd ed. Oxford: Oxford University Press, 2001.

Hegel, Georg Wilhelm Friedrich. *Phänomenologie des Geistes*. Norwegian translation. *Åndens fenomenologi*. Oslo: Pax 2009 (1807).[148]

Heier, Tormod. *Kompetanseforvaltning i forsvaret*. Bergen: Fagbokforlaget, 2017.

Høiback, Harald and Palle Ydstebø. *Krigens vitenskap*. Oslo: Abstrakt, 2013.

Hulme, David, and Mark Turner. *Sociology and Development: Theories, Policies and Practices*. London: Harvester Wheatsheaf, 1990.

Itçaina, Xabier. "Une médiation invisible ? Le travail de paix de l'Église catholique dans le conflit basque." In *Études internationales*, 53 (2022) 13–37. https://doi.org/10.7202/1090707ar.

Jensen, Helge H. "Monokulturalismens etiologi. Norske nasjonale strateger mot arbeids-folk og urfolk." *Sosiologisk årbok* 1 (2013).

———. "State Transformation in the High North: Cases of Environmental Movement Struggles." PhD diss., European University Institute, 2015. https://cadmus.eui.eu/handle/1814/35918/.

Jensen, Helge H., and Sigmund Valaker. "Social Movement Communication as Democratic Innovation: The Alta Conflict 1970–1982." In *Communication Crosswise: Contemporary Perspectives on Strategic Communication*, edited by Sharam Alghasi et al. Oslo: Cappelen Damm, 2023.

Johnsen, Tore. "Luthersk teologi, kolonial makt og samisk tradisjon—utkast til en dekolonial teologi." *Kirke og Kultur* 128 (2023) 5–26. https://doi.org/10.18261/kok.128.1.2/.

———. *Sámi Nature-Centred Christianity. Indigenous Theology beyond Hierarchical Worldmaking*. Lanham, MD: Lexington, 2022.

Kalberg, Thorbjørn. "Norsk bureiserkolonialisme." *Nytt norsk tidsskrift* 40 (2023).

Karim, Hawraman F., and Baser Bahar. "Collective Memory in Post-Genocide Societies: Rethinking Enduring Trauma and Resilience in Halabja." *Review of Middle East Studies* 56 (2022) 56–72. DOI: https://doi.org/10.1017/rms.2022.25/.

Kassab, Suzanne K. *Contemporary Arabic Thought. Cultural Critique in Comparative Perspective*. New York: Columbia University Press, 2010.

Khatib, Sami. "The Messianic without Messianism: Walter Benjamin's Materialist Theology" / "Le messianique sans messianisme. La théologie matérialiste de Walter Benjamin" / "Lo mesiánico sin mesianismo. La teología materialista de Walter Benjamin" *Anthropology and Materialism* 1 (2013). https://doi.org/10.4000/am.159/.

Khuri-Makdisi, Ilham. *The Eastern Mediterranean and the Making of Global Radicalism, 1860–1914*. Berkeley: University of California Press, 2013.

King Christian 4. "Kong Kristian 4.s befaling om trolldomsforfølgelse av samer, 1609. Published at *Norgeshistorie.no*, "Forfølgelse av samiske trollmenn i Finnmark." https://www.norgeshistorie.no/kilder/kirkestat/K1110-Forf%C3%B8lgelse-av-samiske-trollmenn-i-Finnmark.html?fbclid=IwAR3ZoHA55hAE-w3GthnMcBxrtyiv_maPg_JKJNdDpqdhe7xvC3U7-s68nkE/.

---

148. German original online at: https://www.gutenberg.org/cache/epub/6698/pg6698.html

Kowalewski, Zbigniew M. "For the Independence of Soviet Ukraine." *International Marxist Review* 4 (1989) 85–106.

———. "L'indépendance de l'Ukraine : préhistoire d'un mot d'ordre de Trotski." *Quatrième Internationale* 32/33 (1989). https://www.europe-solidaire.org/spip.php?article61474.

Kutmanaliev, Joldon. "Public and Communal Spaces and Their Relation to the Spatial Dynamics of Ethnic Riots: Violence and Non-Violence in the City of Osh." *International Journal of Sociology and Social Policy* 35 (2018) 449–77. https://doi.org/10.1108/IJSSP-02-2015-0027/.

Laclau, Ernesto, and Chantal Mouffe. *Hegemony and Socialist Strategy. Towards a Radical Democratic Politics*. 2nd ed. London: Verso, 2001.

Lafont, Robert. *Décoloniser en France: Les Régions face à L'Europe*. Paris: Idées Gallimard, 1971.

Madden, Raymond. *Being Ethnographic. A Guide to the Theory and Practice of Ethnography*. London: Sage, 2010.

Magga, Ole H. "Hva forårsaket opprøret?" *Klassekampen*, January 8, 2008.

Mahfouz, Joseph. *Short History of the Maronite Church*. Jounieh: Saint Paul, 2009.

Malthaner, Stefan, et al. "The Social Science of Political Violence." In *Contemporary Terrorism Studies*, edited by Diego Muro and Tim Wilson, 94–112. Oxford: Oxford University Press, 2022.

Marchi, Alessandra. "Molecular Transformations: Reading the Arab Uprisings with and Beyond Gramsci." *Middle East Critique* 30 (2021) 67–85.

Marcus, George. "Ethnography in/of the World System: The Emergence of Multi-Sited Ethnography." *Annual Review of Ethnography* 24 (1995) 95–117.

Marx, Karl. *Grundrisse. Foundations of the Critique of Political Economy (Rough Draft)*. London: Penguin with New Left Review, 1973. https://www.marxists.org/archive/marx/works/1857/grundrisse/.

———. "Theses on Feuerbach." Moscow, USSR: Progress, 1969. https://www.marxists.org/archive/marx/works/1845/theses/theses.htm/.

McGinnis, Michael. "Conflict Dynamics in a Three-Level Game: Local, National, and International Conflict in the Horn of Africa." Working paper 4, October 1999, from the Vincent and Elinor Ostrom Workshop in Political Theory and Policy Analysis, Indiana University.

Mendes, Maria. "Delayed Transitional Justice: Accounting for Timing and Cross-Country Variation in Transitional Justice Trajectories." PhD diss, European University Institute, 2019.

Moran, Brendan, and Carlo Saltzani. "On the Actuality of the 'Critique of Violence.'" In *Towards the Critique of Violence: Walter Benjamin and Giorgio Agamben*, edited by Brendan Moran and Carlo Saltzani, 1–15. London: Bloomsbury, 2015.

Mouffe, Chantal. "Deliberative Democracy or Agonistic Pluralism?" *Social Research* 66 (1999) 745–58. https://www.jstor.org/stable/40971349/.

Myrvoll, Marit "'Bare gudsordet duger': om kontinuitet og brudd i samisk virkelighetsforståelse." PhD diss., University of Tromsø, 2011.

Negri, Antonio. *Il potere costituente. Saggio sulle alternative del moderno*. Roma: Manifestolibri, 2000.

———. *Spinoza*. 2nd ed. Rome: DeriveApprodi, 2006.

Niemi, Einar. "Kvenit ya yhteiskunta: Kulttuurien kohtaamisia ja vähemmistöpolitiikkaa." / "Kvenene og storsamfunnet: Kulturmøter og minoritetspolitikk." In *Tunturin ja meren kansa / Fjellets og havets folk*, edited by Sonja Siltala. Vadsø: Trane, 2008.

Nordquist, Kjell-Åke. "Reconciliation Recommended: On the Anchoring of TRC Proposals." In *Trading Justice for Peace? Reframing Reconciliation in TRC Processes in South Africa and Nordic Countries*, edited by Sigrun Gudmarsdottir et al. Cape Town: AOSIS, 2021.

O'Connor, Francis, and Leonidas Oikonomakis. "Preconflict Mobilization Strategies and Urban-Rural Transition: The Cases of the PKK and the FLN/EZLN." *Mobilization* 20 (2015) 379–99.

OHCHR. "The Arab Bedouin Indigenous People." https://www.ohchr.org/sites/default/files/Documents/Issues/Housing/IndigenousPeoples/CSO/National_Coexistance_Forum_for_Civil_Equality.pdf/.

Oskal, Nils. "The Question of Methodology in Indigenous Research." In *Indigenous Peoples Self-Determination, Knowledge, Indigeneity*, edited by Henry Minde, 331–46. Delft: Eburon Academic, 2008.

Otnes, Per. *Den samiske nasjon. Interesseorganisasjoner i samenes politiske historie.* Oslo: Pax, 1970.

———. "Retrospect On 'The Sami Nation'. Text, Context, Field, Symbolic Violence. Confessions of a Bordering Actor." *Dieđut* 3 (2006).

Pedersen, Steinar. "Samiske rettigheter i lys av norsk nasjonalisme på 1800-tallet." In *Fortidsforestillinger. Bruk og misbruk av norsk historie*, edited by Bård A. Berg and Einar Niemi, 83–102. Romssa: University of Romssa, 2004.

———. "Statens eiendomsrett til grunnen in Finnmark—en del av den interne «kolonihistorie»." In *Samer og nordmenn. Temaer i jus, hisorie og sosialantropologi*, edited by Harald Eidheim. Oslo: Cappelen, 1999.

Piechowiak, Marek. "What Are Human Rights? The Concept of Human Rights and Their Extra-Legal Justification." In *An Introduction to the International Protection of Human Rights*, edited by Raja Hanski and Markku Suksi, 3–14. Åbo: Institute of Human Rights, 1999. https://philarchive.org/archive/PIEWAH/.

Pollan, Brita. *For Djevelen er alt mulig. Kristne Historier om Samene.* Oslo: Høyskoleforlaget, 2007.

Ponzanesi, Sandra, and Gianmaria Colpani. *Postcolonial Transitions in Europe. Contexts, Practices and Politics.* Lanham: Rowman & Littlefield, 2015.

Robertsen, Thor, ed. *Den finske arven. En antologi om det finske Finnmark.* Vadsø: Norwegian-Finnish Association, 2009.

Saïd, Edward. *Orientalism*. New York: Pantheon, 1978.

Salibi, Kamal. *A House of Many Mansions: The History of Lebanon Reconsidered.* Berkeley: University of California Press, 1990.

———. *A Modern History of Lebanon.* The Prager, 1956.

Sarkar, S. "The Decline of the Subaltern in *Subaltern Studies*." In *Mapping Subaltern Studies and the Postcolonial*, edited by Vinayak Chaturvedi. London: Verso, 2000.

Schmitt, Carl. *Der Begriff des Politischen.* Norwegian translation: *Begrepet om det politiske.* Oslo: Vidarforlaget, 2007.

Seip, Jens A. *Utsikt over Norges historie. Bind 1: Tidsrommet 1814— ca. 1860.* Oslo: Gyldendal, 1974.

Shahid, Ayesha. "Islamic Law and Human Rights." https://www.oxfordbibliographies.com/display/document/obo-9780199796953/obo-9780199796953-0129.xml/.

Sjöberg, Lovisa M., and Mikkel N. Sara. "When Justice Has Borders: Some Reflections On National Borders in Relation to the TRC in Norway." In *Trading Justice for Peace? Reframing Reconciliation in TRC Processes in South Africa and Nordic Countries*, edited by Sigríður Guðmarsdóttir et al. Cape Town: AOSIS, 2021. https://books.aosis.co.za/index.php/ob/catalog/book/174/.

Smith, Linda T. *Decolonizing Methodologies. Research and Indigenous Peoples*. 2nd ed. London: Zed, 2012.

Smith, Tony. "Decolonization." In *The Oxford Companion to Politics of the World*, edited by Joel Krieger, 2nd ed. Oxford: Oxford University Press, 2001.

Solbakk, Aage. *Sápmi & Málbmi*. 2 vols. Kárášjohka: Čálliid Lágádus, 2010.

Solbakk, John T., ed. *Árbevirolaš máhttu ja dahkkivuoigatvuohta / Tradisjonell kunnskap og opphavsrett / Traditional Knowledge and Copyright*. Kárášjohka: Sámikopiija, 2007.

Solbakk, John T. and Aage Solbakk. *Dasgo eallin gáibida min soahtái ja mii boahtit—mii boahtit dállan! / Selve livet kalder os til kamp og vi kommer—vi kommer straks!* Kárášjohka: Čálliid Lágádus, 1999.

Solomons, Demaine, et al. "Introduction: Trading Justice for Peace? Perils and Possibilities." In *Trading Justice for Peace? Reframing Reconciliation in TRC Processes in South Africa and Nordic Countries*, edited by Sigríður Guðmarsdóttir et al. Cape Town: AOSIS, 2021. https://books.aosis.co.za/index.php/ob/catalog/book/174.

Somby, Ánde. *Juss som retorikk*. Oslo: Tano Aschehoug, 1999.

———. "Statement at UNWGIP 2001 in Geneva." http://www.jus.uit.no/ansatte/somby/humrig01ENG.htm, 2001.

———. "The issue of Sami Rights." http://www.jus.uit.no/ansatte/somby/ivdni01ENG.htm/. 2001.

Tinker, Hugh. "Colonial Empires." In *The Oxford Companion to Politics of the World*. edited. by Joel Krieger, 2nd ed., Oxford: Oxford University Press, 2001.

Traboulsi, Fawwaz. *A Modern History of Lebanon*. London: Pluto, 2007.

Truth and Reconciliation Commission in Norway. "Report to the Norwegian Parliament." Dokument 19 (2022–20223) "Sannhet og forsoning: grunnlag for et oppgjør med fornorskingspolitikk og urett mot samer, kvener/norskfinner og skogfinner" Oslo: The Norwegian Parliament, June 1, 2023.

Türesay, Özgür. "The Ottoman Empire Seen through the Lens of Postcolonial Studies: A Recent Historiographical Turn." In *Revue d'histoire moderne & contemporaine* 60.2 (2013).

UCP. "Memorandum For The 2nd Congress of the Communist International, 1920." In *Oukraïns'ka souspilno-politychna doumka v 20 solitti: Dokumenty i materialy*, 1 vol, 456. New York: Soutchasnist, New York, 1938.

Vasek, Karel. "A 30-Year Struggle: The Sustained Efforts to Give Force of Law to the Universal Declaration of Human Rights." *The Unesco Courier* (1977).

Vennesson, Pascal. "Case Studies and Process Tracing: Theories and Practices." In *Approaches and Methodologies in the Social Sciences: A Pluralist Perspective*, edited by Donatella della Porta and Michael Keating. Cambridge: Cambridge University Press, 2008.

Waever, Ole and Iver B. Neumann, eds. *The Future of International Relations: Masters in the Making*. London: Routledge, 1997.

Wallerstein, Immaneuel. *The Capitalist World Economy*. Cambridge: Cambridge University Press, 1979.

Werner, Michael and Bénédicte Zimmermann. "Beyond Comparison: Histoire Croisée and the Challenge of Reflexivity." *History and Theory* 45 (2006) 30–50. https://www.jstor.org/stable/3590723.

Wikipedia. "Colonialisme interne." https://fi.wikipedia.org/wiki/Colonialisme_interne.

Zachariassen, Ketil. *Samiske nasjonale strategar. Samepolitikk og nasjonsbygging 1900-1940*. Kárášjohka: Čálliid Lágádus, 2012.

Zamponi, Lorenzo. "Collective Memory and Social Movements." In *The Wiley-Blackwell Encyclopedia of Social and Political Movements*, edited by David A. Snow et al. Malden: Wiley-Blackwell, 2022.

Ziadeh, Hanna. *Sectarianism and Intercommunal Nation-Building in Lebanon*. London: Hurst & Company, 2006.

Zorgdrager, Nellejet. *De rettferdiges strid: Kautokeino 1852: samisk motstand mot norsk kolonialisme*. Oslo: Norsk folkemuseum, 1997.

8

The Relation of Civil Society to the Norwegian TRC-Process in the Light of TRUCOM Research

A Reconciliation without the Majority?

KJELL OLSEN

*Department for Tourism and Northern studies,
UIT The Arctic University of Norway, Alta, Norway*

INTRODUCTION

In his analysis of the relationship between the Sámi minority and the national majorities in Fenno-Scandia, the Sámi philosopher Alf Isak Keskitalo asserted that this relationship has become a cognitive legacy found in Sámi folklore. According to Keskitalo, for the national majorities, the nation building process is a completed stage, while for the Sámi, it remains an ongoing and uncertain process without a final conclusion. Consequently, the Sámi must live with the pressure and awareness of this unfinished historical situation, while the majority population has no immediate connection to the process.[1] As Keskitalo puts it, "The stigma

---

1. Keskitalo, *Om möjligheten*, 99–100.

and consciousness of the fact rest with the Sámi. The majorities have no immediate contact with it."[2]

The development of political rights and the recognition of the Sámi as an Indigenous people, which occurred around the time of Keskitalo's writing, probably altered how those subsumed under the category of the majority in the northernmost parts of Norway are in touch with these still uncertain processes in the relationship between the Sámi and the Norwegian state. Hence, for the majority of the Norwegian population living in the southern part of the country, Keskitalo's analysis regarding the Indigenous Sámi, as well as for the two national minorities, the Kvens/Norwegian Finns[3] and the Forest Finns, still seems to be supported by the current situation. At least, this seems to be the case when assessing the level of interest exhibited by national media in The Commission to Investigate the Norwegianization Policy and Injustice against the Sámi and Kvens/Norwegian Finns (TRC). National media shows minimal interest in the TRC and its work, in contrast to media outlets targeting minority audiences.[4] Additionally, there is limited awareness among the Norwegian population, particularly regarding the minorities, especially the Kvens and the Forest Finns. This lack of awareness likely impacts the coverage by national media.[5] Nevertheless, as stated by Nagy and Gillespie in relation to the Canadian TRC, media coverage and the majority's understanding of the policies that have been implemented and their individual consequences do not necessarily lead the majority population to think "in expansive terms that frame reconciliation as requiring decolonization and systemic change."[6]

In this chapter, I discuss the little interest shown by national media in the TRC, which can be attributed to what appears as a territorialization of the three minorities under investigation by the TRC from a national perspective. To substantiate this territorialization, I conduct an analysis of two open local meetings conducted as part of the TRC's work process. Through an examination of the narratives shared during these meetings and an evaluation of what was presented—and equally important, what was omitted—by the local media that covered one of the meetings, my objective is to illustrate which issues and minority groups are considered significant

2. Keskitalo, *Om möjligheten*, 101.
3. Kvens/ Norwegian Finns are two different names officially used for the same group.
4. Vranic and Skogerbø, *Silence*, 8–9.
5. Norsk institusjon for menneskerettigheter (NIM), *Holdninger*, 46–54.
6. Nagy and Gillespie, *Representing*, 37.

by media outlets targeting their specific local audiences. It is worth noting that, despite the extensive number of open meetings organized by the TRC and their presence at 156 events up to the end of 2022, national media have provided coverage for only a small fraction of these events.[7]

Finally, drawing on Mahmood Mamdani's critique of the South African TRC,[8] I will discuss the potential consequences of this disconnect experienced by the majority population. This disconnect may lead to a majority population that can distance themselves from the policies and abuses that have taken place, as they may not have been aware of them or directly involved, viewing them as occurring 'elsewhere.' Consequently, it becomes challenging to bring about substantial changes in a political system that disadvantages minority groups. At a conference organized by VID Specialized University in May 2022, the experienced editor, journalist, and commentator Harald Stanghelle, to the best of my recollection, commented on the potential outcomes of the Norwegian TRC's work, suggesting that the predominant reaction among the southern Norwegian public could easily be: "Was it so bad? But what has this to do with us?"

Mamdani contends that there is a need for reconciliation between those who have been the beneficiaries of policies and those who have suffered as a result, rather than between victims and perpetrators. According to Mamdani, this approach would redirect attention towards a political system that favors certain groups.[9] Considering this perspective, it might be worthwhile to examine who has benefited and continues to benefit from the Norwegianization policy and who has suffered or may still be suffering from the political framework regulating the relationship between the majority and minorities in Norway. Such an analysis could potentially pique the interest of the majority population residing outside the geographical regions associated with the minorities within the TRC's mandate. This shift in focus would also blur the rigid distinctions between the majority and minorities, as it would start from the concrete impacts of policies.

Before delving further into this discussion, I will provide a brief introduction to the Norwegian TRC and its general media coverage.

---

7. Utsi, "En rapport."
8. Mandani, *Neither*, 180–88.
9. Mamdani, *Neither*, 182.

THE TRC, MINORITIES IN NORWAY, AND THE MEDIA

The Norwegian TRC had a mandate from the Parliament to:

> Perform a historical survey to map the Norwegian authorities' policy and activities towards the Sámi and Kvens/Norwegian Finns locally, regionally and nationally.
> Carry out an investigation of the effects of the Norwegianization policy. The Commission is to consider how the Norwegianization policy has affected the majority population's attitudes to the Sámi and Kvens/Norwegian Finns and will investigate the consequences of Norwegianization up until the present day.
> Propose measures to contribute to further reconciliation.[10]

A team of eleven experts, led by the prominent politician Dagfinn Høybråten, and supported by a rather modest secretariat, submitted their report on June 1, 2023. It is worth noting that the inclusion of the Forest Finns in the TRC's work occurred after the initiative was already underway. Consequently, they are neither included in the mandate nor explicitly mentioned in the full name of the TRC, which references only the Sámi and the Kvens/Norwegian Finns. There are also significant differences between the minorities. The Sámi hold a unique status as they are acknowledged as Indigenous people, and Norway ratified the Indigenous and Tribal Peoples Convention of 1989 (No. 169) in 1990. This positioning within the Norwegian political system sets the Sámi apart from the other two minorities. The Kvens and the Forest Finns, on the other hand, are recognized as national minorities according to the European Council's Framework Convention for the Protection of National Minorities, ratified by Norway in 1999.

What these groups have in common is that they were all targeted by the Norwegianization policy, which can perhaps best be understood as a reinterpretation of what Walter Mignolo describes as a universal claim at the heart of a regional European modernity/coloniality.[11] The aim of this policy was to culturally assimilate the entire population into Norwegian culture, with the later goal of integrating them into the welfare state—an integration that presupposed assimilation into the Norwegian culture.

A notable difference lies in the geographical distribution of the Sámi and the Kvens, who are predominantly situated within a culturally diverse population in Northern Norway. The Sámi have a 'core area' in the

---

10. Sannhets- og forsoningskommisjonen, *Sannhet og forsoning*, 14.
11. Mignolo, *Delinking*, 463–64.

northernmost county of Finnmark, while the Kvens are concentrated in specific regions known for their significant Kven cultural influence. In contrast, the Forest Finns are typically regarded as residing in specific border regions adjacent to Sweden in the southern part of Norway. This difference is also visible in the media coverage of the TRC. The media that exhibit the most interest in the TRC's work are primarily lesser-known to the majority population. These media outlets are situated in Northern Norway, with some catering to a Sámi or Kven audience, while others are local and regional newspapers, rarely mentioning the Forest Finns. This perpetuates the prevailing pattern of Kven, Sámi, and local and regional media in the northern regions being the primary sources for coverage of Kven and Sámi issues. This is likely due to the fact that minority politics has the most significant impact on the majority population in this area. Only a few media outlets, characterized as having a nationwide audience, albeit within relatively small niche markets, provide substantial coverage of the TRC.[12]

As demonstrated by Vranic and Skogerbø in their analysis of media coverage of the Norwegian TRC from 2016 to 2021, the process leading to the proposal of the TRC in 2017 garnered more attention than the TRC's subsequent work in the following years. According to these authors, this trend indicates both a "reduced news value" and mirrors "the work methods of the TRC,"[13] and likely reflects the level of knowledge about the different minorities among a nationwide audience mainly living in the southern parts of Norway.

TERRITORIALIZATION

Since its inception in the 1850s, a major goal of the Norwegianization policy was to make the population Norwegian-speaking. Preventing children from learning minority languages was considered a crucial aspect of fostering a Norwegian identity. In Finnmark, Norway's northernmost county, language shifts occurred in some areas as recently as around 1960, resulting in the Kven and Sámi languages being primarily spoken by the older generation. Today, the Sámi language is predominantly spoken in the 'Sámi core' areas, whereas there are no specific locations where the Kven language and Forest Finnish dialects remain vital everyday

---

12. Vranic and Skogerbø, *Silence*, 9.
13. Vranic and Skogerbø, *Silence*, 8.

languages. A committee appointed in 1957 also considered language preservation to be important and suggested major political changes for the Norwegian Sámi. They emphasized policies for the area where the Sámi language could still be 'saved,' which likely contributed to the establishment of the idea of a Sámi core and, consequently, a periphery.[14] The language issue remains relevant today and has even created a division within the Sámi Parliament. The second largest party, *Nordkalottfolket*, asserts that the Norwegian language is also a Sámi language.[15] Nevertheless, this territorialization is most evident in Norwegian language politics. Albury labels this a neo-traditionalist language policy where the minority language is an issue for the minority itself and not a concern for the majority.[16] This distinction likely arises because it was possible to establish geographical boundaries between Sámi-speaking communities and non-Sámi-speaking ones. Consequently, Sámi and other minority languages, except for those municipalities included in the *Administrative area for Sámi language*, become an individual right. However, due to their marginalized position in the Norwegian school system and society, students often struggle to achieve the level of fluency they desire.[17]

In political science, the Norwegian Sámi are often cited as a rare example of an Indigenous population that has achieved nonterritorial autonomy (NTA). Nevertheless, Spitzer and Selle argue that starting in the 2000s and continuing thereafter, the Sámi have been gaining increasing territorial autonomy. While the Sámi Parliament exemplifies Indigenous NTA, the Sámi have also achieved territorial autonomy, *de facto* and *de jur*, through other Sámi institutions.[18] In conclusion, they state, "It can be seen, then, that over the four decades of Sámi political mobilization in Norway, there has been a clear trend concerning the exercise of Indigenous territorial authority vis-à-vis NTA."[19] Without interfering in this discussion among political scientists, it is important to note that nearly all the territorial authority, "commonly seen as involving any one of three powers—jurisdiction, access control, and land-and-resource management,"[20] seems to be in areas in the north that until now have had a minor impact on

14. Andresen et al., *Samenes*, 340–41.
15. Bjørklund, *Society*, 30.
16. Albury, *Your*, 319–20.
17. Hermansen and Olsen, *Learning*, 74–75.
18. Spitzer and Selle, *Is Nonterritorial*, 558–63.
19. Spitzer and Selle, *Is Nonterritorial*, 563.
20. Spitzer and Selle, *Is Nonterritorial*, 564.

the lives of the dominant majority of the national population. This might change for the Sámi, if not for the Kvens and the Forest Finns, in particular because of Europe's current energy market, which craves new areas for mining, power plants, and transport, potentially conflicting with the interests of Sámi reindeer husbandry. But still, this territorialization can explain the lack of nationwide interest reflected by the national and local media the further one gets from Finnmark. The general attitude seems to be that the TRC's work is something happening "up there."[21]

LOCAL MEDIA AND THEIR COVERAGE OF THE TRC'S OPEN MEETINGS

As Plummer states, "[F]or stories to flourish there must be social worlds waiting to hear," since stories need an "interpretative community of support."[22] But a social world 'waiting to hear' necessitates that the people making up such a social world can relate to the story; it usually must have something to do with them. Furthermore, the way stories are supported may also depend on how they are framed, whether for creating goodwill and therapy, or for creating societal restructuring of a political system. Support for both framings by a national Norwegian majority is probably necessary for a reconciliation between minorities and the majority. Therefore, the questions of which stories are told and how they are framed, as well as what stories are omitted by the media, are essential to address. One way the media gains access to such stories is through narratives shared at open meetings arranged by the TRC or events where the TRC has been invited, primarily by voluntary organizations.

The data for this chapter is primarily based on the videos from two such meetings: one held in Lakselv on August 20, 2020, and the other in Mo i Rana on September 17 of the same year. Both videos were made public on YouTube.[23] These specific meetings were selected because Lakselv, located in the municipality of Porsáŋgu/Porsanki/Porsanger has a substantial population of both Sámi and Kvens and is situated close to what is considered the Sámi core area in Finnmark county. Mo i Rana, on the other hand, is an industrial town in the municipality of Rana, situated in the Ume and Southern Sámi area in Nordland.

21. See also Sønneland and Lingaas, *Righting*, 18–19.
22. Plummer, *Intimate*, 34.
23. The YouTube videos are no longer available to the public.

In addition, I also conducted two searches in two media databases, *Retriever* and *Infomedia*, using different search terms to find out what the media reported about the meetings. This was because I assumed that these events could provide an opportunity, especially for local and regional media, to highlight a local perspective on the TRC's work. One finding was in line with Vranic and Skogerbø's article, which indicated that the coverage of the TRC was mainly done by media outlets in Northern Norway.[24] Perhaps most important for my analysis, there was no media coverage of the meeting in Mo in Rana, whereas the meeting in Lakselv received extra coverage from Sámi and Kven media, including the newspapers *Ságat* and *Ruijan Kaiku*, the local branch of the national broadcasting *P1 Finnmark*, and the Sámi branch, *NRK Sápmi*.[25] This indicates a northern dominance, even within the context of what is considered Northern Norway.

Lakselv/Leavdnja/Lemmijoki

Lakselv, with approximately 2,200 inhabitants, serves as the administrative center for the municipality of Porsáŋgu/Porsanki/Porsanger in Finnmark. This municipality shares its borders with Kárášjoga gielda, a municipality where the Sámi language is spoken by the majority and where the Sámi Parliament is situated. The TRC organized the meeting, and on August 4, municipal authorities announced the event on Facebook.[26] In the days leading up to the meeting, there was brief coverage on national and regional radio.[27][28] *Ságat*, a newspaper with its main office in Lakselv, featured an article about the event on August 14.[29] Additionally, the regional paper *iFinnmark* reported about the meeting in advance.[30]

The meeting, which lasted for two and a half hours, was streamed and, as of April 30, 2023, has been viewed 1,023 times on YouTube.[31] The TRC's meetings follow a standardized structure. They begin with

---

24. Josefsen and Skogerbø, "An Indigenous," 72–72.

25. Retriever and Infomedia do not include Sámi language media, except for the bilingual Ságat, Ruijan Kaiku, and NRK Sápmi.

26. Facebook, Hva skjer i Porsanger.

27. NRK, *Sannhetskommisjonen*.

28. NRK-P1 Finnmark, "Forsoningskommisjonen."

29. Ságat, "Mange."

30. iFinnmark, "Sannhets," 1.

31. The YouTube videos are no longer available for the public.

a welcome from a representative of the TRC's administration, followed by a performance by an artist. The mayor or other local representatives then deliver speeches, followed by speeches from TRC members and representatives of various local organizations. Afterward, invited speakers share their stories, and at the end, there is an opportunity for others to contribute. Based on the video, there were no apparent spontaneous speakers at this meeting.

On the same day, both *Ságat* and the Kven newspaper *Ruijan Kaiku* published online reports from the meeting.[32][33] On August 24, the print version of *Ságat* featured an extensive report that referenced many stories shared during the meeting. A significant portion of these stories revolved around the losses caused by national policies. They described the 'silence' and lack of visibility, which many people perceive as part of Kven and Sámi heritage. Additionally, it touched on stories about the challenges and occasional joys experienced at the boarding school, the struggles faced by non-Norwegian-speaking Sámi individuals, and one narrator's grief over the Kven language not being passed down to her generation, born in the 1960s.[34]

The newspaper also mentioned a story that, due to its nuance and ambiguity, could be interpreted as countering the common perspective on Norwegianization. This story was shared by a man who, for various reasons, had been unable to attend the training for his Christian Confirmation in Lakselv. Therefore, in 1938, he had the opportunity to go to the closest larger settlement with a church, Kárášjohka, for a certain period to follow the teaching there. The result, in addition to his confirmation, was a lot of friends and being able to speak the Northern Sámi language. The story ends with the following sentence: "[I]n retrospect he has always been wondering about the policy of Norwegianization, because during his stay in Kárášjohka he experienced the opposite."[35]

Also, contemporary problems were highlighted and referred to by the newspaper. In other words, these delved more into the need for changes in terms of political rights and the Norwegian political system. One states, "[T]hat we talk about Norwegianization as if it was something that

32. Ságat, "På."

33. Ruijan Kaiku, "Imponert."

34. Some of the narrators spoke in the Northern Sámi language. For these, I have relied on the newspaper's article.

35. "at han i ettertid har lurt litt pådet der med fornorskningen, for han opplevde det motsatte den tiden i Karasjok" (Ságat, "På").

happened a long time ago, but it is not."³⁶ Another example is a narrator who tells that it is still difficult to get Sámi language education in school. For his children, it was a struggle every year to ensure that the school fulfilled this legal right. For those who have conducted some research on Sámi language teaching in Norwegian schools, this statement is recognizable: "It is individuals who take responsibility. There is no system[,] which means that there will be teaching in Sámi language or not . . ."³⁷

The chairman of the Porsanger Sámi Association is referred to as saying "that he thinks nature as the foundation for Sámi culture must be secured,"³⁸ probably introducing the issue of Sámi land rights. This opinion appears more strongly in the video on YouTube. In the meeting, the speaker emphasized that reconciliation means that Sámi rights must be taken seriously. This implies that the Sámi Parliament must have a right of veto against encroachments on nature, that rights must be granted to fjord and coastal fishermen, and there should be changes in school, language, and business policies. The need for changes in terms of rights and the Norwegian political system was something that, I would argue, also characterized the contributions at the meeting a little later in Mo i Rana.

References to the meeting in Lakselv also appeared in the media later in August, including a podcast interview in *Ságat* with the Head of the Commission in connection with a later meeting in Børselv.³⁹ Børselv is also located in the municipality of Porsáŋgu/Porsanki/Porsanger. *NRK P1-Finnmark* published an online story about the work of the health team from the *Sámi National Center for Mental Health Care (SANKS)*, which attends all meetings, and about the emotional burdens that everyone can experience from what is shared.⁴⁰

The general media coverage of the Norwegian TRC,⁴¹ including the meeting in Lakselv, demonstrates the lack of attention from national media. Nevertheless, regional and local media reported from the meeting, and media with a predominantly Kven and Sámi audience used it to tell stories about the TRC and its work. Comparing the video and what was

36. "at vi snakker om fornorskningen som om det er noe som har skjedd for lenge siden, men slik er det ikke," (Ságat, "På," 12–13).

37. "Det er enkeltpersoner som tar ansvaret. Det er ikke noe system som gjør at det blir Sámisk undervisning eller ikke . . ." (Ságat, "På," 12–13).

38. "at han synes naturgrunnlaget for Sámisk kultur må sikres" (Ságat, "På," 12–13).

39. Ságat, "Kaffemøte," 2–3.

40. NRK, "Terapeuter."

41. Vranic and Skogerbø, "Silence."

highlighted by the media, there seemed to be a tendency for the latter to emphasize individual stories and loss instead of speakers who were advocating for political change. One reason for this might be the relative prominence of the Kven population in Lakselv.

As a Norwegian national minority, the Kvens are situated quite differently in the Norwegian political context than the Indigenous Sámi, and these two groups do not necessarily have the same interests in a change of the political system. Another reason might be that Kven and Sámi media regularly publish on political structural issues, and therefore rather see the TRC as a platform for individual stories. As was pointed out regarding the Canadian TRC, reporting primarily centered around stories of individual victims and could serve as a viable approach for media reporting in Norway as well.[42] As Mamdani states, this emphasis on victims and perpetrators, even though in the work of the Norwegian TRC there are no individual perpetrators, only the abstract notion of the state, often overlooks the beneficiaries of the policies, in this case, those who benefitted from Norwegianization.[43] So why should the Norwegian majority and the mainstream media, as Niezen argues regarding the Canadian process, "go beyond the comfortable platitudes of goodwill and truth telling as therapy?"[44] And why should media with a majority readership bother at all?

Mo i Rana/Måhvie/Måehvie

The meeting in Mo i Rana was organized on October 17, 2020, at the local library by *Raanen Saemieh*, a politically independent Sámi association for northern Helgeland. As in Lakselv, the meeting was streamed live and published on YouTube. By April 30, 2023, a total of 367 people had already visited the site. The structure was quite similar to the meeting in Lakselv, with the exception of a brief introduction by a board member of *Raanen Saemieh*, who also led the meeting, as opposed to a representative from the TRC, as was the case in Lakselv. Additionally, in this meeting, I observed more spontaneous speakers from the audience.

42. Nagy and Gillespie, *Representing*, 8; Niezen, "Perpetration," 90.
43. Mamdani, *Neither*, 182.
44. Niezen, "Perpetration," 92.

As Johnsen writes, the local newspaper *Rana Blad* did not cover this meeting.⁴⁵ It is therefore somewhat ironic that Rana municipality's deputy mayor, in her address, highlighted the local newspaper's coverage of the bus accident on July 5, 1948, in which sixteen people died on their way home after attending a national meeting of the Sámi Reindeer Herder's Association of Norway (NRL). The accident, which in addition to the personal tragedies, had significance for Sámi political life and the reindeer herding industry, received extensive coverage in the local media. A regional paper, *Helgeland Arbeiderblad*, emphasized that it was a scandal that the national broadcasting, NRK, had no more than a short notice about this accident.

My searches in the databases show that, as far as the meeting with the TRC is concerned, the local and national media were in agreement this time. Two search engine searches yielded no media coverage of the meeting. The search on Infomedia revealed only one Facebook post from *Raanen Saemieh*, stating that the video will be available.⁴⁶ However, the editor of *Daerpies Dierie* (The *Southern Sámi Church Magazine*), Einar S. Bondevik, kindly informed me that they had covered the meeting. More accurately, their report focused on the lack of media coverage of the meeting. This lack of interest from the press had been a consistent trend in the nine meetings that had been held in the Southern Sámi area.⁴⁷ I will return to Bondevik's article later, but first, based on the YouTube video, what issues were not considered of interest by local, regional, and national media?

As Niezen describes the open Canadian hearings, the Norwegian hearings opened the possibility for stories that previously could not be told.⁴⁸ At the same time, some stories were erased because they did not fit into the expectations of a certain 'template' developed in the process of the TRC. The YouTube video of the meeting in Mo i Rana lasts for a little over two and a half hours. More than half of this time was used by invited speakers. To what extent these created templates or frameworks for later narrators is impossible to say. In any case, the narrators that came after the floor was free followed up on many of the topics that had been raised previously. Two themes that were raised early on were that, even though Rana was the third largest Sámi municipality in Norway in

45. Johnsen, "Negotiating," 23.
46. Facebook, "Raanen Saemieh."
47. Bondevik, "Lokalmedia," 5.
48. Niezen, "Perpetration," 58–59.

terms of population in the early twentieth century, the current invisibility and lack of knowledge among the majority population were problems. In addition, deficiencies in the school's teaching were highlighted early on and continued when the floor was open for input. The new themes were how the pressure for resource exploitation of nature was a danger to Sámi culture and how these conflicts caused harassment of people engaged in reindeer husbandry. In addition, two speakers also addressed the problem of reindeer herding's overriding role in the Sámi community.

It may appear somewhat perplexing that stories such as these, represented and embodied by the narrators themselves, did not pique the interest of regional, local, and even national media. Furthermore, these issues are readily connectable to broader challenges. For instance, the fact that statutory rights for language training in Sámi do not effectively function in many areas outside the Sámi administrative region, the individualization of the problem despite legal rights, and the students enduring months without a Sámi language teacher all seem to go unnoticed by the media. Even when stories recounting three generations' experiences of insufficient teaching in Sámi language classes are shared during the TRC meeting, they appear to hold little interest for media outlets targeting a general majority readership. The issues of invisibility and lack of knowledge are not unique to the Sámi community beyond so-called 'core areas' but are also prevalent among the Kvens.[49] Furthermore, conflicts over natural resources, with their clear dividing lines, should surely be able to be turned into a newspaper story with a local angle?

One of the reasons for the limited interest that *Daerpies Dierie* received from the local media was a lack of resources, a common challenge for many local newspapers. Additionally, some media outlets held the opinion that covering the meeting itself was not relevant. This lack of relevance was justified by the fact that "[i]n order to reach many people with information about, for example, the commission's work, the issue must be angled in a way that makes it interesting. Then covering of meetings is not the solution, says an editor in Rana Blad."[50]

It may appear somewhat perplexing that despite the deputy mayor's acknowledgement at the opening of the meeting that Rana was, in the early twentieth century, the third largest Sámi municipality in Norway

---

49. Olsen, "La," 80–81.

50. "For å nå ut til mange med informasjon om for eksempel kommisjonens arbeid, må saken vinkles på en måte som gjør den interessant. Da er ikke å dekke møter løsninga, sier redaktør i Rana Blad" (Bondevik, "Lokalmedia," 5).

in terms of population, there were no journalistic approaches that could make some of the following stories presented in the meeting interesting for the media:

- The invisibility and lack of knowledge about the Sámi among the majority continue to be a problem.
- There are still major shortcomings in the school's teaching of the Sámi language.
- The pressure to exploit natural resources poses a danger to the Sámi reindeer husbandry culture.
- Conflicts over the exploitation of natural resources lead to increasing harassment of the Sámi, particularly by those connected to the reindeer herding industry.
- The overriding role of reindeer herding in Sámi society is a problem for Sámi who do not engage in reindeer herding.

It is somewhat puzzling to me that themes like these, concretized and personified by the narrators themselves, could not be turned into articles that made them interesting for regional and local media, and even national media. These narratives might have been of interest both as individual stories that could make an emotional impression and, perhaps more importantly, as examples of general problems for minorities in Norway created by political structures. Such political structures will likely need to undergo significant changes that affect the majority population as well when the commission fulfills the third part of its mandate, which states, "Propose measures that contribute to further reconciliation." These measures may necessitate changes in both the national prioritization of education in minority languages in schools and, in alignment with the Supreme Court's judgment in the Fosen case where the government's issuance of permits for wind power plants was deemed a violation of human and Indigenous rights, a different understanding of Sámi rights to land use.[51] These are just two examples that are well covered by the second part of the mandate, which states, "The effects of the Norwegianization policy must be examined. If there are any after-effects today, these must appear in the report." However, local journalists seem to be missing the link between individual stories and their potential consequences for policies that also affect the majority.

51. Ravna, "The Fosen," 167–69.

The commission is capable of making such connections and generating media attention, as evidenced by national media coverage of the TRC's letter to the Ministry of Oil and Energy regarding the state's lack of action on the Fosen case. In this case, the Norwegian Supreme Court applied Article 27 of the International Covenant on Civil and Political Rights and ruled that the Norwegian government's granting of licenses for wind power plants in Fosen violated the human rights of reindeer herders.[52]

Another notable aspect of the meeting in Mo i Rana was that there was hardly any mentioning of the Kvens and the Forest Finns. This could be attributed to the fact that the meeting was organized by the local Sámi association, but it might also be because these two minority groups are not seen as having a significant connection to the issues discussed at the meeting. This contrast can be observed in Porsáŋgu/Porsanki/Porsanger, where discussions and media coverage included both Kven and Sámi issues, primarily by media outlets with audiences among the Sámi and Kven communities, as well as local media. However, even in these contexts, the Forest Finns received little to no attention.

DISCUSSION AND CONCLUDING REMARKS

The Norwegian TRC has faced criticism for its limited visibility in national media. In response to this criticism, the Head of the Commission, Dagfinn Høybråten, emphasized that having prior knowledge about the TRC is not a prerequisite for reconciliation. According to Høybråten, what truly matters is "that the truth about the history of Norwegianization becomes known, that the majority population is affected, and that the authorities show a will to right the wrong. Only then will the basis for reconciliation be present."[53] The Norwegian word "*berørt*" is translated here as "affected." In Norwegian, *berørt* can imply that people are emotionally touched, but it can also refer to those who are influenced by various factors, including political decisions. In the emotional meaning of the word, the Head of the TRC may be understood to emphasize the narratives of the individual victims. As pointed out by other scholars, this 'victim-oriented' genre has been prominent in other TRCs, like the

52. Sønneland and Lingaas, "Righting," 23–24.
53. "men at sannheten om fornorskingshistorien kommer frem, at majoritetsbefolkningen blir berørt og at myndighetene viser vilje til å rette opp i urett. Først da vil grunnlaget for forsoning være til stede" (Høybråten, "FORNORSKNINGEN," 14).

Canadian TRC. Nagy and Gillespie, in their analysis of Canadian media's coverage of the TRC, state that "reporting was primarily framed around survivor testimony and stories of individual abuse, forgiveness, and healing."[54] According to Niezen, "Witnessing, as part of the therapeutic paradigm of public confession, was seen as sufficient unto itself as a pathway towards reconciliation."[55] However, as Niezen describes in the context of the Canadian TRC process, "the media and their publics engaged in a refusal to go beyond the comfortable platitudes of goodwill and truth telling as therapy."[56] This approach alone is insufficient for bringing about societal restructuring of a political system.

Nevertheless, at this stage in the Norwegian TRC process, the national media in Norway seems to show little interest even in this victim-oriented framing. As summarized by Vranic and Skogerbø in their findings of media coverage from 2016 to 2021, "Throughout the entire period, stories from survivors, that is, personal stories of past injustices or current discrimination, were scarce."[57]

If "affected" should be understood as those affected by the proposed political changes made by the commission, which are likely a prerequisite for reconciliation involving both minorities and the majority, then we enter a perspective more in line with what Keskitalo wrote more than 40 years ago.[58] For the Norwegian national majority, the nation building process can then no longer be seen as a completed stage. Instead, the majority will need to join the Kvens, the Sámi, and the Forest Finns in an unfinished, ongoing, and uncertain process without a final conclusion. As I read Mamdani, such a perspective will necessitate a rethinking of the political community for all groups.[59]

In a political modernity where the nation-state constructs its minorities, it is possible to deconstruct them through a dedication to a shared future. To facilitate such a transformation, it becomes crucial to prioritize reconciliation between those who have benefited from national policies and those who have experienced losses due to them, rather than solely focusing on the dichotomy of victims and perpetrators. This is particularly important in the Norwegian case where the perpetrator is the

54. Nagy and Gillespie, "Representing," 8.
55. Niezen, "Perpetration," 90.
56. Niezen, "Perpetration," 92.
57. Vranic and Skogerbø, "Silence," 11.
58. Keskitalo, "Om möjligheten," 99–100.
59. Mamdani, *Neither*, 31–36.

abstract notion of the state. In this context, the media must engage with the political issues raised at the meetings in both Lakselv and in Mo i Rana. However, this does not seem to be the case in either place. Despite the relatively broad coverage of the meeting in Lakselv by Kven, Sámi, regional, and local media, there were few attempts to situate the individual narratives within the framework of political change.

The Norwegian TRC is set to deliver its report in June 2023. As Niezen pointed out regarding the Canadian commission, it "transcended the limits of its original terms of reference with a surprise ending: the ninety-four 'Calls to Action,' which refused the 'listening' orientation of its mandate and early hearings by wading deeply into the political."[60] It is possible that the Norwegian commission could follow a similar path, as demonstrated by its letter to the Ministry of Oil and Energy regarding the Norwegian government's inaction on the Fosen case. This letter garnered attention from national media and highlighted that, in a time when energy prices have reached unprecedented heights in Norway, reconciliation may indeed involve the majority population. However, most cases that can potentially involve the majority population are related to the Indigenous Sámi, rather than the Kvens and the Forest Finns. Therefore, the TRC faces an additional challenge in convincing a majority, mostly residing in the southern part of Norway, that they also have been among the beneficiaries.

BIBLIOGRAPHY

Albury, Nathan J. "Your Language or Ours? Inclusion and Exclusion of Non-Indigenous Majorities in Māori and Sámi Language Revitalization Policy." *Current Issues in Language Planning* 16 (2015) 315–34.

Andresen, Astrid, et al., eds. *Samenes historie fra 1751 til 2010*. Oslo: Cappelen Damm Akademisk, 2010.

Bjørklund, Ivar. "Society, Ethnicity and Knowledge Production—Changing Relations Between Norwegians and Sámi." In *Sámi Research in Transition. Knowledge, Politics and Social Change*, edited by Laura Junka-Aikio et al., 19–33. London: Routledge, 2022.

Bondevik, Einar S. "Lokalmedia tause om Sannhetskommisjonen." *Daerpies Dierie/Sørsámisk Kirkeblad* 4 (2020) 5.

Facebook. "Hva skjer i Porsanger. *Hva skjer i Porsanger*," August 4, 2020. https://www.facebook.com/iPorsanger/?locale=nb_NO/ .

---

60. Niezen, "Perpetration," 92.

Facebook. "Raanen Saemieh." *Raanen*, https://www.facebook.com/raanensaemieh/posts/2731529713756741/?paipv=0&eav=AfYYIWHoerxhA-8dPh2s2Jisb2s7RZspY6qni-MEHYCpooiXXU-Kuddx-_pTvzfUUrs&_rdr/.

Hermansen, Nina, and Kjell Olsen. "Learning the Sámi Language Outside of the Sámi Core Area in Norway." *Acta Borealia* 37 (2020) 63–77.

Huyhraten, Dagfinn. "FORNORSKNINGEN. For at vi skal komme videre mot et forsonet samfunn, må sannheten om fornorskningshistorien komme frem." *Vårt Land* 14 (2020).

iFinnmark. "*Sannhets- og forsoningskommisjonen: Åpent møte i Lakselv.*" August 20, 2020.

Johnsen, Tore. "Negotiating the Meaning of "TRC" in the Norwegian Context" In *Trading Justice for Peace? Reframing Reconciliation in TRC Processes in South Africa, Canada and Nordic Countries*, edited by Sigríður Guðmarsdóttir et al., 19–40. AOSIS, Cape Town, 2021.

Josefsen, Eva and Eli Skogerbø. "An Indigenous Public Sphere? The Media and the 2009 Sámediggi Election Campaign." *Arctic Review on Law and Politics* 4 (2013) 62–89.

Keskitalo, Alf I. "Om möjligheten av folklore som ett hinder i en etnisk inkorporasjonsprocess." [On the Negative Influence of Folklore on Ethnic Incorporation] *Tradisjon: Tidsskrift For Folkeminnevitskap* 10 (1980) 97–101.

Mamdani, Mahmood. *Neither Settler Nor Native: The Making and Unmaking of Permanent Minorities*. Cambridge: Harvard University Press, 2020.

Mignolo, Walter D. "Delinking: The Rhetoric of Modernity, the Logic of Coloniality and the Grammar of De-Coloniality." *Cultural Studies* 21 (2007) 449–514.

Nagy, Rosemary, and E. Gillespie. "Representing Reconciliation: A News Frame Analysis of Print Media Coverage of Indian Residential Schools." *Transitional Justice Review* 1 (2015) 30–40.

Niezen, Ronald. "Perpetration, Impunity, and Irreconciliation in Canada's Truth and Reconciliation Commission on Indian Residential Schools." *Journal of the Royal Anthropological Institute* 28 (2022) 79–94.

———. "*Truth and Indignation: Canada's Truth and Reconciliation Commission on Indian Residential Schools*." Toronto: University of Toronto Press, 2017.

Norsk institusjon for menneskerettigheter (NIM). "*Holdninger til samer og nasjonale minoriteter i Norge*." Oslo: NIM-R-2022-006, 2022.

NRK. *Sannhetskommisjonen til Porsanger*, August 18, 2020.

———. "Terapeuter bistår sannhetskommisjonen—granskingen vekker vonde minner." https://www.nrk.no/sapmi/psykiatrien-bistar-sannhetskommisjonen—granskingen-vekker-vonde-minner-1.15130382. August 26, 2020.

NRK-P1. "Forsoningskommisjonen." *Finnmark Distriktsprogram*. August 18, 2020.

Olsen, Kjell. "'La de usynlige bli synlige' Om kvenske steder og kvensk usynlighet." *Norsk Antropologisk Tidsskrift* 32 (2021) 72–86.

Plummer, Ken. *Intimate Citizenship: Private Decisions and Public Dialogues*. Seattle: University of Washington Press, 2003.

Ravna, Øyvind. "The Fosen Case and the Protection of Sámi Culture in Norway Pursuant to Article 27 ICCPR." *International Journal on Minority and Group Rights* 30 (2023) 156–75.

Ruijan Kaiku. "Imponert over engasjementet." https://www.ruijan-kaiku.no/takker-for-engasjementet/

Sannhets- og forsoningskommisjonen, *Sannhet og forsoning- grunnlag for et oppgjør med fornorskningspolitikk og urett mot samer, kvener/norskfinner og skogfinner*.

Rapport til Stortinger fra Sannhets- og forsoningskom-misjonen, 2023. https://www.stortinget.no/globalassets/pdf/sannhets—og-forsoningskommisjonen/rapport-til-stortinget-fra-sannhets—og-forsoningskommisjonen.pdf

Ságat. "*Kaffemøte i Børselv.*" August 24, 2020, 12–13.

———. "*Mange vil fortell.*" https://www.sagat.no/nyheter/. August 17, 2020.

———. "På søken etter sannhet." https://www.sagat.no/pa-soken-etter-sannhet/19.23375/.

Sønneland, Anne M. and Carola Lingaas. "Righting Injustices Towards the Sámi. A Critical Perspective on the Norwegian Truth and Reconciliation Commission." *International Journal on Minority and Group Rights* 30 (2023) 1–29.

Spitzer, Aron J., and Per Selle. "Is Nonterritorial Autonomy Wrong for Indigenous Rights? Examining the 'Territorialisation' of Sámi Power in Norway." *International Journal on Minority and Group Rights* 28 (2021) 544–67.

The Truth and Reconciliation Commission. https://uit.no/kommisjonen_en.

Utsi, Inger Elin Kristina. "En rapport som skal legge grunnlag for et oppgjør." https://uit.no/nyheter/artikkel?p_document_id=798854.

Vranic, Anja and Eli Skogerbø. "Silence, Voice, and Public Listening." *Journal of Global Indigeneity* 6 (2022) 1–17.

PART THREE

Transformative Reconciliation

The TRC Processes and Beyond

9

Between Performance and the Absurd
Evaluating Reconciliation at the South African TRC

DEMAINE SOLOMONS
Faculty of Theology, Stellenbosch University, South Africa

RECONCILIATION IN THE MIDST OF THE ABSURD

The societal importance of reconciliation in South Africa and its role in advocating for a just social order has been extensively examined in academic literature. Debates concerning the utility of reconciliation continue to elicit diverse reactions, oscillating between being highly esteemed and, at times, nothing more than a stale artifice. Two of the foremost scholars on the topic in South Africa, Du Toit and Doxtader's illuminating characterization of reconciliation as a 'prized idea or cheap deception,' beautifully captures the elusive nature of this ideal.[1] This is further compounded by the incongruence of the vision of a racial utopia and the reality of a country that continues to be separated along racial lines, an inherent contradiction entrenched in the socio-political fabric of a country grappling with the violence of colonialism and apartheid. The contested nature of reconciliation emerges from our innate desire for meaning and fulfillment and the world's insouciant refusal to provide

---
1. Du Toit and Doxtader, *In the Balance*, ix.

such assurances. I mention elsewhere that this conundrum bears a striking resemblance to philosophical absurdism, a concept that addresses the human inclination to seek intrinsic value and meaning in the face of the arbitrary, irrational, and at times nonsensical aspects of our existence.[2] Albert Camus, a prominent French philosopher renowned for his philosophical exploration of the concept of the 'absurd,' confronts this existential reality in his influential essay, *The Myth of Sisyphus*, first published in 1942.[3] For Camus, the absurdity of life is akin to the plight of Sisyphus, a figure from Greek mythology, who is condemned to endlessly repeat the grueling task of pushing a boulder up a mountain, only to have it cascade back down once he reaches the summit peak. This cycle of exertion is continued into the realms of eternity, illustrating the paradoxical and inescapable nature of the human condition.

Driven by the desire for meaning amid meaninglessness, South Africans embarked on a quest for reconciliation, a bold and romantic endeavor seeking to forge a new way of being in the wake of the brutality of apartheid. This audacious vision set in motion a sequence of events that culminated in the formation of the Truth and Reconciliation Commission (TRC), a process that, for better or worse, inscribed the dream of reconciliation in the hearts and minds of the people. Archbishop Desmond Tutu, the anti-apartheid stalwart and chairperson of the TRC, was at the center of the process. Along with his colleagues, including prominent church leaders (such as Alex Boraine, the deputy chairperson) and theologians (including Charles Villa-Vicencio and Piet Meiring) and others, they were entrusted with imbuing life into one of the most contentious notions shaping public discourses at the time. In this sense, reconciliation and its sometimes conflicting interpretations have always been contested. This is evident from the "Message to the People of South Africa" (1968), the "South African Leadership Assembly" (1979), the "Belhar Confession" (1982/1986), the "National Initiative for Reconciliation" (launched in 1985), and the "Rustenburg Declaration" (1990). However, it is worth noting that the term has also been the subject of much controversy, particularly in the "Kairos Document" (1985).

Within local congregations, the theme of reconciliation has engendered numerous debates, ranging from structures for unity to the need for a ministry of reconciliation that bridges cultural, racial, and class

---

2. Solomons, "The Absurdity of Reconciliation," 395.
3. Camus, *The Myth*.

divides. In this context, prominent South African theologian Dirkie Smit reminds us that reconciliation is intricately related to ideological conflict.[4] Moreover, the persistent uncertainty regarding its capacity to bring about societal transformation is a perennial issue. More than a decade after Smit's observation, the TRC became the stage upon which tension associated with reconciliation was enacted (or performed). This was a delicate affair, something that shed light on the beauty of the reconciliation ideal and the circumstances that made this ideal nearly impossible.

THE POLITICS OF RECONCILIATION: A NATIONAL INITIATIVE

The transitional period (1990–1994) in South Africa marks a pivotal moment when the discourse on reconciliation underwent a significant transformation from a predominantly theological endeavor to a matter that now occupied the national psyche. In this sense, it evolved from its traditional theological associations, which aimed to reconcile the different racial groupings within the church, to something that now focused on reconciliation on a societal level. While theologians and church leaders continued to shape the public debate, the concept gained increasing significance when political figures, including people like Nelson Mandela, started using it as a rallying call for social transformation. As a result, the discourse on reconciliation was incorporated into various spheres of inquiry, such as psychology, sociology, philosophy, and political science.[5] In essence, this period marks reconciliation's transcendence of the theological into something that was now part of the country's reconstruction and development process, underscoring its importance as a symbol of hope in the multiparty negotiating process, a crucial ingredient in what eventually became the democratic project.

An essential aspect of the political negotiations was the issue of an Interim Constitution that would replace the old Constitution that formed the basis of apartheid legislation. Among other things, one of the more controversial aspects of the Interim Constitution was the issue of whether the advent of democracy would include the possibility of amnesty. The lack of an amnesty provision in the Interim Constitution posed a particular problem, especially to those on opposite sides of the political

4. Smit, "The Symbol," 88.
5. Van der Borght, "Reconciliation," 413.

spectrum. Nevertheless, the issue of amnesty was temporarily "solved" by allocating a place for it in the postamble of the Interim Constitution and by framing it within the context of reconciliation on the road to national unity. In Doxtader's[6] words:

> The pursuit of national unity, the well-being of all South African citizens and peace require *reconciliation* between the people of South Africa and the *reconstruction* of society. The adoption of this constitution lays the secure foundation for the people of South Africa to transcend the division and the strife of the past, which generated gross violations of human rights, the transgression of humanitarian principles in violent conflicts and a legacy of hatred, fear, guilt, and revenge. These can now be addressed on the basis that there is need for understanding not for violence, need for reparation but not retaliation, a need for ubuntu not for victimization.

On this basis, an amnesty provision was announced. Doxtader highlights that:

> In order to advance such reconciliation and reconstruction, amnesty shall be granted in all respect of acts, omissions, and offences associated with political objectives and committed in the course of past conflicts. To this end, Parliament under this constitution shall adopt a law determining a firm cut-off date ..., and providing for the mechanisms, criteria, and procedures, including tribunals, if any, through which such amnesty shall be dealt with at any time after the law has been passed.[7]

Van der Borght observes that the inclusion of the amnesty provision in the postamble did not satisfy the various stakeholders.[8] The representatives of the apartheid government understood this as "forgive and forget," and accordingly, they wanted to "close the books on the past." On the other hand, the victims of gross human rights violations opposed the amnesty provision because they were not prepared to consider immunity to prosecution. Moreover, some were convinced that to prevent the explicit risk of forgetting the past, a process was necessary to help facilitate the transition from a violent past to a more sustainable future. The main issue was that the postamble did not provide the tools for such

---

6. Doxtader, *With Faith*, 213.

7. Doxtader, *With Faith*, 211–17. See Doxtader (Doxtader, *With Faith*, 211–17) for the full text and the interpretation of the postamble to the Interim Constitution.

8. Van der Borght, "Reconciliation," 417.

a procedure. Due to the uniqueness of the situation, it would be fair to suggest that at this stage, such tools had not yet been developed.

In the context of this negotiated settlement, Kader Asmal, in his inaugural lecture as Professor of Human Rights Law at the University of the Western Cape in 1992, had already explained why and how the past needed to be opened. Asmal explained that "we must take the past seriously as it holds the key to the future. The issues of structural violence, unjust and inequitable economic and social arrangements, of balanced development in the future cannot be properly dealt with unless there is a conscious understanding of the past."[9] In this context, Asmal was convinced that in order to come to terms with the problematic history of South Africa, something more than a Nuremberg-style trial was needed. He argued that such an approach would lack the capacity to deal with the humiliation, brutality, deprivation, and degradation of the past. In his view, South Africa needed a truth commission (TC) because the harm done by apartheid simply exceeded the law's grasp.

For this reason, South Africa needed to embrace the mode of reconciliation that carefully considered the past, located accountability, and supported the revival of moral conscience. Doxtader notes that the reconciliation envisioned entailed more than merely creating new structures and arrangements; instead, for reconciliation's potential to be realized, it needed to serve at least three ends: Firstly, it required a demonstration of apartheid's illegitimacy. The process needed to illuminate the past to better grasp the current predicament. Secondly, reconciliation's potential to enact change largely depended on its capacity to broker disputes and disputation. This would forge consensus and deter denials about the evils of apartheid. Finally, reconciliation offered the chance for cathartic truth-telling, a process in which South Africans could hear the experiences of fellow citizens, stories that set the stage for the 'justice' of acknowledgement, 'restitution,' and 'atonement.'[10]

After adopting the Interim Constitution, the organization Justice in Transition, headed by Alex Boraine, organized an international conference in February 1994 to reflect on dealing with the past in the context of a negotiated transition. Through these deliberations, it became apparent that amnesty without history and truth-telling would not yield the intended aim of reconciliation. Doxtader further explains that "the

---

9. Doxtader, *With Faith*, 230.
10. Doxtader, *With Faith*, 229–32.

spirit of transition called for the constitution of individual and collective identity while emphasizing that apartheid's violent identitarian logic was precisely why citizens needed to remember the past in the name of creating the identifications of reconciliation."[11]

The end of the political negotiations reached its symbolic climax with the inauguration of Nelson Mandela as the country's first democratically elected president on May 11, 1994.[12] The passing of the Promotion of National Unity and Reconciliation Act in mid–1995 followed this. According to Van der Borght, this legislation gave birth to the TRC. Chapter 2, section 3:1 (a-d) of the Act, spells out the commission's mandate.[13] Here the commission is tasked with (a) establishing a picture of the gross violations of human rights in the period between March 1, 1960, and May 10, 1994, through investigations and hearings; (b) facilitating the granting of amnesty to those who made full disclosure of all the relevant facts to acts associated with political objectives; (c) establishing and making known the fate or whereabouts of victims, restoring dignity by allowing victims to relate their own accounts, and recommending reparations; and (d) compiling a comprehensive report with findings and recommendations. De Gruchy observes that through the Promotion of National Unity and Reconciliation Act, reconciliation was crucial in trying to uncover the truth, also in terms of how the country should deal with the past as well as define the future.[14] Moreover, reconciliation was now seen as part of defining the national goals of democratic transformation and reconstruction.

THE MANDATE OF THE TRC

The 17-member commission, headed by Desmond Tutu, was inaugurated in December 1995. Tshaka notes that the commissioners were nominated by a representative panel appointed by President Nelson Mandela.[15] The commissioners included people from diverse backgrounds, with a notable presence of Christian leaders. Alongside Archbishop Tutu, the commissioners featured Deputy Chairperson Alex Boraine, an accomplished

11. Doxtader, *With Faith*, 239.
12. South Africa's first democratic elections (including all racial groupings) took place on April 27, 1994.
13. Van der Borght, "Reconciliation," 419.
14. De Gruchy, *Reconciliation*, 25, 41.
15. Tshaka, "The Black Church."

theologian and former Methodist Church leader in South Africa. Other church leaders included Khoza Mgojo (a theologian and former president of the South African Council of Churches [SACC]), Charles Villa-Vicencio (a theologian), Bongani Finca (a respected church leader and prominent ecumenist), Tom Manthata (a former employee of the Justice and Reconciliation division in the SACC), Rev Xundu (a church leader), and Piet Meiring (a theologian and prominent figure in the Dutch Reformed Church [DRC]).

It is well documented that the idea of a TC is not unique to South Africa. There are other examples, particularly in Latin America, where similar ventures have been undertaken in post-conflict situations.[16] However, these commissions differed in their approaches. Elsewhere they tended to opt for approaches focused on providing 'blanket amnesty' or for 'Nuremberg-style trials' to deal with past atrocities.[17] In contrast, the South African TRC attempted to balance the two approaches. In Tinyiko Maluleke's words:

> On the one hand, the plan aims to grant amnesty 'at a price'—the price being the requirement for those applying for amnesty to make 'full disclosure of all the relevant facts' regarding their activities. On the other hand, through its processes of public and private 'hearings,' the TRC hopes to give the victims of 'gross human rights violations' a chance to tell their story, not only to the TRC but also to the nation as a whole, with some prospect of possible reparations.[18]

Furthermore, central to the TRC process are the notions of 'reconciliation' and 'reconstruction' rather than retribution or justice in a judicial sense. Cole underscores this 'balancing act,' stating that "the TRC was neither here nor there, located somewhere between the islands of the past

---

16. Hayner, U*nspeakable Truths*.

17. Jennifer Harvey (*Dear White Christians*, 91) posits that: "In the challenge coming out of apartheid and birthing a new civic society, (a) it was not feasible to imagine one could prosecute and punish all the perpetrators for their gross participation in human rights violations; (b) layers of secrecy and lies made getting to the truth of the past virtually impossible without significant cooperation from perpetrators; (c) learning such truth was perceived as one of the most important needs of victims if they were to become full participants in a new civic community; and (d) the possibility of massive social violence (civil war even) threatened at every turn in the transition to a 'new South Africa' such that some type of honest, collective, and public contending with the past had to take place if nationhood was to have any hope of success."

18. Maluleke, "Truth, National Unity," 60. Also see Boraine, Levy, and Scheffer, *Dealing with the Past*, 11.

and an imagined future integration—integration for the races, of course, but also integration for South Africa itself within both the continent and the larger world from which it had been severed through years of cultural and economic boycotts."[19] With no template on how to proceed and what to expect, the TRC sprang from 'the morality as a people' and reflected a cultural interest in realizing the common humanity (ubuntu) of the people of South Africa.[20] Coupled with what is described as an international 'fetishization,' the South African TRC became one of the most ambitious projects of its sort ever undertaken.[21]

With much fanfare, skepticism, and notable opposition, the TRC started its work in 1996. The commission was divided into three distinct sub-committees: a) the Committee on Human Rights Violations, b) the Committee on Amnesty, and c) the Committee on Reparations and Rehabilitation. The initial plan envisioned these committees conducting simultaneous hearings nationwide throughout the two-year operational period. Notably, due to the public nature of its work, the Committee on Human Rights Violations attracted the most attention when it commenced its activities. This particular commission was tasked with listening to the accounts of victims to ascertain whether gross human rights violations had occurred. It recorded testimonies from over 21,000 victims and witnesses, with 2,000 selected to participate in public hearings. The hearings received extensive media coverage, with the weekly Truth Commission Special Report becoming South Africa's most-watched news show in the process.[22] Hendriksson notes that this was in line with the TRC's mandate to promote national reconciliation by providing ordinary South Africans, who were neither perpetrators nor victims of gross human rights violations, the opportunity to reflect on their past and future through the publicity surrounding the TRC.[23]

The most innovative yet controversial aspect of the TRC's work was its power to grant amnesty for gross human rights violations. The Promotion of National Unity and Reconciliation Act made provision for granting amnesty to persons who fully disclosed all the relevant facts.

In his critical assessment of the amnesty provision, Wilson argues that the postamble's "amnesty provisions were the only indispensable

19. Cole, *Performing South Africa's* (see the Preface and Acknowledgments).
20. Moodley, "African Renaissance," 3.
21. Doxtader, *With Faith*, 5.
22. Hayner, *Dear White Christians*, 28.
23. Hendriksson, *A Journey with a Status*, 147.

and necessary part of the process of national unity and reconciliation."[24] In his words, "reconciliation was the Trojan horse used to smuggle an unpleasant aspect of the past (that is, impunity) into the present political order, to transform political compromises into transcendental moral principles." For this reason, the legal framework of the TRC was often described as weak, in some ways favoring the perpetrators at the expense of victims.[25] Following the granting of amnesty to prominent political and military figures, many perpetrators began to experience a diminished fear of prosecution and condemnation. Instead of stepping forward to confess their actions, many opted not to pursue amnesty. As a result, a substantial number of crimes committed during apartheid remained undisclosed. A total of 7,115 amnesty applications were submitted; of these, 4,500 were rejected, and an additional 145 were granted partial amnesty.[26]

The Committee on Reparations and Rehabilitation was tasked with determining how each victim should be compensated and making recommendations to the president to restore the human and civil dignity of such victims. Whereas the Committee on Amnesty had the power to grant amnesty, the Committee on Reparations and Rehabilitation, which dealt with reparations for victims, could only make recommendations to the president or a parliamentary standing committee. In this context, the TRC had the mandate to provide amnesty to perpetrators but was only mandated to make recommendations for the provision of reparations for victims. According to Maluleke, beyond the complex arguments about whether the TRC ought to have been given more judicial "teeth" so that it could adopt a prosecution-centered approach, a blanket amnesty approach, etcetera, there was the feeling that as things stood, the scales were tilted slightly in favor of the perpetrators of apartheid atrocities.[27] Indeed, the very clause of the Interim Constitution that gave rise to the TRC referred mainly to amnesty and not reparations.

24. Wilson, *The Politics of Truth*, 97, 99.
25. Maluleke, "Truth, National Unity," 63; see also 59–86.
26. Van der Borght, *Reconciliation*, 420.
27. Maluleke, "Truth, National Unity," 67.

THE PERFORMATIVE ASPECT OF RECONCILIATION AT THE TRC

A comprehensive understanding of reconciliation during TRC proceedings necessitates acknowledging the concept's multifaceted interpretations and highlighting the event-based nature of reconciliation as a performative act. Van der Borght alludes to Christian liturgical elements that were an ever-present reality at the TRC proceedings.[28] For example, the hearings were imbued with a ceremonial quality, whereby the opening remarks of the chairperson—whomever they may have been on a given day—were frequently preceded by rituals such as prayer, the lighting of a memorial candle, and the singing of hymns. When Archbishop Tutu was in attendance, his distinctive presence was further enhanced by wearing his purple liturgical robes, among other things. While the religious element of the hearings was occasionally criticized, particularly for its emphasis on the Christian faith, it was deemed appropriate given the reality that the majority of the people were members of this religious tradition. In instances when Archbishop Tutu was not present, other religious leaders were often invited to lead the prayer. Furthermore, it was not uncommon for communities to introduce their unique songs and ceremonial practices during the proceedings. In this sense, the religious aspects of the TRC were observed to serve a specific performative function.

The perspective that the TRC encompassed far more than a mere legal process warrants serious consideration. While the TRC was undoubtedly a legal mechanism established to investigate and address human rights violations perpetrated during the apartheid era, its scope was far-reaching and multifaceted. The TRC aimed not only to uncover the truth about past atrocities but also to promote national healing, reconciliation, and unity. To achieve this goal, it employed a range of approaches that extended beyond the confines of the traditional legal framework. As a result, the TRC embodied the social, cultural, and spiritual aspects of the actors, actions, symbols, and narratives, all of which encapsulated the evolving nature of the reconciliation process. By incorporating Christian liturgical elements, the TRC invoked a religious dimension that underscored the event's moral, spiritual, and communal significance. This involved recognizing the harm caused by past wrongs, the admission of guilt and responsibility, the expression of remorse and apology, the granting of

---

28. Van der Borght, *Reconciliation*, 422.

forgiveness, and the restoration of broken relationships. Through this enactment of the past and present, the TRC sought to create a space for healing, transformation, and renewal, where individuals, communities, and the nation could come to terms with their history, confront their current reality, and envision a new and different future.

In this context, reconciliation played a cathartic role in what Moosa describes as the birth of a newborn nation.[29] Reconciliation functioned as an "event," prefiguring all other events, utilizing past events to anticipate a new future.

> Any event of this magnitude is actually a performance. A performance is when the actors have already configured the purpose of the play and there is hope that other participants and viewers will also understand its message. World history, especially sacred history, has a long record of narratives of performance: the Genesis story, Abraham's sacrifice of this son, and the crucifixion of Jesus. It is as performance that the TRC event has greater value as symbol, myth and spectacle.[30]

For Moosa, the performance of the TRC event carried significant meaning as the symbolic atonement for the sins of apartheid. In other words, the experience of suffering and oppression endured by the disenfranchised was portrayed or enacted twice in the lives of many individuals.[31] Firstly, it was experienced during the injury or trauma suffered by the victims or their dependents. Secondly, it was re-enacted in the theater of the TRC itself, where these transgressions were revisited to the benefit of numerous parties, including commissioners, the media, observers, the aggrieved, archivists, psychologists, and politicians, to name but a few. In this context, the TRC event turned the suffering of liberation heroes into a gift of sacrifice for the new South Africa. The sacrifices of the victims of gross human rights violations became a conduit for reconciliation. And whilst justice remained elusive, the theater of the reconciliation act provided the impetus to work towards the realization of a more humane society. So even though reconciliation remained distant, for many, it represented the most viable option in a context plagued by incompleteness, incoherence, and the coexistence of opposing forces.

---

29. Moosa, "Truth and Reconciliation," 113–22.
30. Moosa, "Truth and Reconciliation," 114.
31. Moosa, "Truth and Reconciliation," 119.

OVERCOMING THE ABSURD

As one might expect, the vision of reconciliation is not without its detractors. Some have argued that prominent figures like Archbishop Tutu set the bar too high by imbuing the concept of reconciliation with theological significance instead of political significance. They caution against the potential misrepresentation of the South African project as a spiritual quest rather than a secular political agreement.[32] Nevertheless, nearly thirty years after establishing the TRC, the elusive nature of reconciliation in South Africa remains as evident as ever. The democratic dispensation has brought an array of new challenges, leading to a departure from reconciliation as the primary driver of social transformation. Today, the discourse on reconciliation has the potential of being rendered esoteric and less appealing in comparison to other, more immediate societal issues.

Furthermore, the legacies of Desmond Tutu and Nelson Mandela have become subject to increasing debate. Some perspectives argue that their leadership placed an undue emphasis on reconciliation, which did not adequately address the socio-economic vestiges of apartheid. This skepticism is grounded in the conviction that reconciliation, without a concerted effort to address the root causes of injustice, is inadequate. The tension between the TRC's endeavors and the stark reality of South Africa having one of the world's highest rates of persistent income inequality exemplifies this concern. The nation's profound social divisions, marked by factors such as race, class, gender, and ethnicity, among others, only exacerbate the problem.

In this context, the pursuit of the reconciliation ideal remains perplexing for those in search of quick solutions to what could be described as a wicked problem.[33] In this regard, one could easily assert that the quest for reconciliation has, to some extent, become an exercise in absurdity, given the lack of a rational or concise way of articulating what is truly at stake. So while there may be a general agreement on the essence of reconciliation, disagreements over how to actualize this ideal signify differing interpretations of its value and significance. For this reason, reconciliation is often perceived as enigmatic, something that surpasses our urge for mastery and comprehension. For this reason, it may sometimes appear unfathomable and unattainable. This is within the context of our

---

32. Gerwel, "National Reconciliation," 277–86.
33. Solomons, "Overcoming Reconciliation," 198–211.

proclivity to continually seek for meaning, despite the discrepancy between the ideal and the absurdity that defines our disordered, irrational, and occasionally meaningless existence.

Often criticized for its inadequacies, the South African TRC represents the audacity to dream of a world beyond meaninglessness by invoking the dream of reconciliation. In doing so, it resists the temptation of complete hopelessness. Camus' conception of the absurd provides a glimmer of hope, reminding us that our efforts may seem futile, but we must persevere, nonetheless. Much like Sisyphus, we are tasked with pushing the boulder up the mountain, only to see it roll down over and over again. This cyclic and seemingly futile labor becomes a metaphor for the struggles of our existence, where we must continuously strive for meaning and purpose despite the inevitability of obstacles and setbacks. As Camus poignantly reminds us, the struggle itself towards the heights of this ideal is enough to fill one's heart.[34] And despite all the obstacles, 'one must imagine Sisyphus happy.' The South African TRC is a reminder of why certain difficulties are worth enduring in the face of our precarious reality.

BIBLIOGRAPHY

Asmal, Kader, et al. *Reconciliation through Truth: A Reckoning of Apartheid's Criminal Governance.* Cape Town: Philip, 1996.

Boraine, Alex, et al., eds. *Dealing with the Past: Truth and Reconciliation in South Africa.* Cape Town: Idasa, 1993.

Camus, Albert. *The Myth of Sisyphus.* Translated by Justin O'Brien. Harmondsworth: Penguin, 2000.

Cole, Catherine M. *Performing South Africa's Truth Commission: Stages of Transition.* Indianapolis, IN: Indiana University Press, 2010.

De Gruchy, John W. *Reconciliation: Restoring Justice.* London: SCM, 2002.

Doxtader, Eric. *With Faith in the Works of Words: The Beginnings of Reconciliation in South Africa, 1985–1995.* Cape Town: Philip, 2009.

Du Toit, Fanie, and Erik Doxtader, eds. *In the Balance: South Africans Debate Reconciliation.* Johannesburg: Jacana Media, 2010.

Gerwel, Jakes. "National Reconciliation: Holy Grail or Secular Pact?" In *Looking Back, Reaching Forward: Reflections on the Truth and Reconciliation Commission of South Africa*, edited by Charles Villa-Vicencio and Wilhelm Verwoerd. Cape Town: Cape Town University Press, 2000.

Harvey, Jennifer. *Dear White Christians: For Those Still Longing for Racial Reconciliation.* Grand Rapids: Eerdmans, 2014.

---

34. Camus, *The Myth*, 119.

Hayner, Priscilla B. *Unspeakable Truths: Transitional Justice and the Challenge of Truth Commissions.* New York: Routledge, 2001.

Hendriksson, Lennart. *A Journey with a Status Confessionis: Analysis of an Apartheid Related Conflict Between the Dutch Reformed Church in South Africa and the World Alliance of Reformed Churches, 1982–1998.* Uppsala: Swedish Institute of Missionary Research, 2010.

Maluleke, Tinyiko S. "Truth, National Unity and Reconciliation in South Africa: Aspects of the Emerging Theological Agenda." *Missionalia* 25 (1997) 59–86.

Moodley, Kogila. "African Renaissance and Language Policies in Comparative Perspective." *Politikon* 271 (2000) 103–15.

Moosa, Ebrahim. "Truth and Reconciliation as Performance: Spectres of Eucharist Redemption." In *Looking Back, Reaching Forward: Reflections on the Truth and Reconciliation Commission of South Africa,* edited by Charles Villia-Vicencio and Wilhelm Verwoerd, 113–22. Cape Town: Cape Town University Press, 2000.

Smit, Dirk J. "The Symbol of Reconciliation and Ideological Conflict." In *Reconciliation and Construction,* edited by W. S. Vorster. Pretoria: Unisa, 1986.

Solomons, Demaine J. "The Absurdity of Reconciliation. What We (Should) Learn From Rustenburg and the Implications for South Africa." *Stellenbosch Theological Journal* 6 (2020) 393–412.

———. "Overcoming Reconciliation as a Wicked Problem. A Theological Response to the Dominant Split Between Heaven and Earth in South Africa." *Philosophia Reformata* 85 (2020) 198–211.

Tshaka, Rothney S. "The Black Church as the Womb of Black Liberation Theology?: Why the Uniting Reformed Church in Southern Africa (URCSA) is Not a Genuine Black Church?" *HTS Teologiese Studies/Theological Studies* 71 (2015).

Van der Borght, Eduardus A. J. G. "Reconciliation in the Public Domain: The South African Case." *International Journal of Public Theology* 9 (2015) 412–27.

Wilson, Richard A. *The Politics of Truth and Reconciliation in South Africa.* Cambridge: Cambridge University Press, 2001.

10

Small Stories Challenging Large Narratives

The Contribution of Personal Accounts to Transformative Reconciliation in Post-TRC Norway

TORE JOHNSEN

*Faculty of Theology and Social Sciences,
VID Specialized University, Tromsø, Norway*

INTRODUCTION

In what ways are personal accounts shared by Sámi and Kven individuals at public Truth and Reconciliation Commission (TRC) meetings in Norway contributing to the understanding of reconciliation in post-TRC Norway? In this chapter, I explore this question based on a qualitative analysis of personal accounts shared at sixteen public TRC meetings in Norway between 2019 and 2021.[1]

The question posed is topical as the Norwegian TRC investigating the Norwegianization policy recently (June 1, 2023) submitted its final

---

1. Having processed personal data on ethnicity, this study is registered with and approved by Sikt- Norwegian Agency for Shared Services in Education and Research.

report to the Norwegian Parliament, after almost five years of extensive work.² As the truth and reconciliation process enters its political post-TRC phase, it is relevant to consider whether there is a risk of losing essential aspects of these stories when they are documented in a formal report and eventually discussed as 'issues' in public debates. Therefore, moving beyond the task of conveying pertinent information about the historical and lasting impact of the Norwegianization policy, what can be articulated more concretely regarding the added value of personal stories to the discourse of reconciliation in post-TRC Norway?

In this chapter, my aim is to provide preliminary insights into this question by developing a bottom-up argument structured in two main parts. The first part involves a qualitative analysis of personal accounts shared at sixteen public TRC meetings, where the key features emerging are presented as six narratives. In the second part, I discuss the findings of the qualitative analysis in light of relevant transitional justice, theological, and Indigenous research literature. In the conclusion, I recapitulate contributions identified in a forward-looking reflection including brief references to the TRC report.

THE NORWEGIANIZATION POLICY, THE PEOPLES AFFECTED, AND THE CALLS FOR A TRC

What is the Norwegian TRC process about? While the commission's short name—'TRC'—situates the Norwegian inquiry in a broad international field,³ its full name—The Commission Investigating the Norwegianization Policy and Injustice against the Sámi and Kvens/Norwegian Finns'—suggests the specific questions investigated.⁴ The Norwegianization policy, spanning over a century, was a state-run assimilation policy that specifically targeted two distinct minorities: the Indigenous Sámi and the national minority known as Kvens/Norwegian Finns.⁵ This policy,

---

2. Sannhets- og forsoningskommisjonen, *Sannhet og Forsoning*.

3. While somewhat inspired by the transitional model of the South African TRC and the non-transitional model of the Canadian TRC related to Indigenous peoples, Skaar ("When Truth Commission Models Travel") considers the Norwegian TRC as a new TC model tailored to the Nordic context.

4. Johnsen, "Negotiating the Meaning."

5. "Kvens" and "Norwegian Finns" are used interchangeably, reflecting disagreements within the group about preferred self-designation. In this chapter, I primarily use "Kven" which is increasingly more common.

however, also had repercussions on a third group known as Forest Finns. While the two former groups are associated with northern Norway, the traditional Sámi territory also encompasses large parts of mid-Norway. The Forest Finns, in turn, are associated with south-eastern Norway.

The Norwegianization policy, having its beginnings around 1850, reached its most powerful implementation phase between 1900 and 1950 (when, inter alia, residential schools were introduced), and the policy was gradually dismantled in the decades that followed.[6] That is, the latter view, locating the Norwegianization policy firmly in the past, was the established story until a growing number of Sámi and Kvens in the early 2010s argued that the Norwegianization is still ongoing, giving rise to demands for a truth commission (TC). While the minority government at the time opposed the idea, a majority vote in Parliament in June 2017 eventually secured a public inquiry. The following year, the Parliament unanimously appointed the commission, endorsing its name and mandate.[7]

The TRC's mandate encompassed three primary tasks: to document the policies and actions of Norwegian authorities toward the Sámi and the Kvens/Norwegian Finns from 1800 onward; investigate the ongoing effects and consequences of the Norwegianization policy; and put forth recommendations aimed at advancing reconciliation.[8] Although the initial mandate explicitly referred to the Sámi and the Kvens/Norwegian Finns, in 2019, the TRC decided to expand its scope to include the Forest Finns in the inquiry. In this chapter, the discussion is delimited to the Sámi and Kvens, for reasons further explained below.

"HISTORICAL NARRATIVES" AS AN OVERARCHING PERSPECTIVE

The title of this chapter, 'Small Stories Challenging Large Narratives,' suggests the overarching theoretical approach informing the analysis. By 'large narratives,' I mean dominant narratives about Norway as a nation, shaping the circumstances under which Indigenous and national minorities live in contemporary Norway. This resonates with Romero-Amaya's critical discussion of three types of 'historical narratives' in post-conflict

6. Minde, "Assimilation of the Sami."

7. For an elaborate analysis of these developments, see Johnsen, "Negotiating the Meaning."

8. See the adopted mandate in "Innst. 408 S (2017–2018)."

societies, namely: "narratives of nationhood," "narratives of silence," and "narratives of resistance."[9] Given that injustices are neither self-explanatory nor isolated events, Romero-Amaya draws attention to how historical narratives "set the moral compass and the explanatory framework of the conflict."[10] TCs play a pivotal role in this context, considering that historical narratives function as "memory frameworks connecting past, present, and future *to sustain political agendas*."[11] Grounded in these assumptions, Romero-Amaya discusses how two types of historical narratives, namely 'narratives of nationhood' and 'narratives of silence,' serve to justify and mask injustices, while 'narratives of resistance' typically emerge as counter-narratives from below.[12]

This offers a relevant perspective for discussing the question of the contribution of personal narratives to reconciliation in post-TRC Norway. Motivated by Norwegian nationalism, racist ideas, and national security policy, the Norwegianization policy cultivated a master narrative about Norway as a mono-ethnic and mono-cultural nation.[13] Such 'large narratives' are now being challenged by what I call 'small stories'—the personal stories told by Sámi, Kvens, and Forest Finns to the Norwegian TRC. Until now, these stories have had limited reach within the broader Norwegian public, largely staying confined to the private and social circles of minority communities or, in many cases, remaining untold.[14] Therefore, as individuals now opt to share these 'small stories' on a profoundly new stage—the TRC authorized by the Norwegian Parliament—the agency involved should be acknowledged.

PART I: QUALITATIVE ANALYSIS OF PERSONAL ACCOUNTS AT PUBLIC TRC MEETINGS: SIX NARRATIVES

Material, Method, and Narrative Theory

So, in what ways are personal accounts shared by Sámi and Kven individuals at public TRC meetings in Norway contributing to the understanding of reconciliation in post-TRC Norway? The material used to

9. Romero-Amaya, "Historical Narratives."
10. Romero-Amaya, "Historical Narratives," 114.
11. Romero-Amaya, "Historical Narratives," 113; my emphasis.
12. Romero-Amaya, "Historical Narratives," 115–18.
13. Andersen et al., *Samenes historie*, 17–18, 20, 157.
14. Nergård, *Det skjulte Nord-Norge*; Minde, "Assimilation of the Sami."

explore this question is generated through observing a large part of the public TRC meetings.

From 2019 to 2022, the Norwegian TRC convened twenty-eight physical 'public meetings.'[15] These meetings, typically lasting for 2 to 2.5 hours, were designed as a hybrid between informational sessions and a platform for people to start sharing their concerns and experiences. I personally observed sixteen of these meetings; four meetings physically, complemented with the fifteen[16] fully recorded meetings made available on YouTube.[17] All observed meetings have been transcribed verbatim by the author, and personal accounts have been labelled and interpreted in line with thematic analysis as suggested by Spencer et al.[18] All quotes from personal accounts in this chapter are my translations from Norwegian, or in rare occasions from North Sámi.

The analyzed material consists of 180 accounts or shorter inputs from 169 individuals.[19] With few exceptions, the speakers positioned themselves in relation to the groups addressed in the inquiry, a few with a double affiliation. Among the participants, 123 individuals are identified as Sámi, 19 individuals as Kvens/Norwegian Finns, 24 individuals as majority Norwegians, and 2 individuals as Forest Finns. Due to their minor representation, the Forest Finns are barely mentioned in the analysis. The overall gender distribution in the material is 56 percent women and 44 percent men, a distribution which has insignificant variations among the groups. The observed meetings have a good geographical distribution, comprising two larger Norwegian cities and fourteen smaller cities, towns, and communities distributed across South, Ume, Pite, Lule, and North Sámi areas, including a few locations with a significant Kven presence.[20]

15. It is worth noting that the TRC also organized a single digital "public meeting" and held eight informal "coffee meetings" characterized by their conversational nature. This additional context helps explain why the TRC's official count includes a total of 37 "open meetings" convened by the commission. Sannhets- og Forsoningskommisjonen, *Sannhet og Forsoning*, 14, 121.

16. Note that three meetings were observed both physically and on YouTube (explaining the total number of sixteen), whereas one physically observed meeting lacked videorecording.

17. Note that the TRC's YouTube channel was terminated in mid-June 2023. Consequently, this chapter lacks references to any videos from this source.

18. Spencer et al., "Analysis: Principles and Processes."

19. A precaution regarding the number of 169 must be taken. In a few instances, the YouTube videos do not show the person speaking. This makes it occasionally hard to say whether a new person has the floor or that a person speaks a second time.

20. The locations represented are Oslo, Tråante/Trondheim, Plaassja/Røros,

To convey the voice of the individual accounts, my qualitative analysis has stayed close to the original accounts. The value of doing that can be appreciated in light of South African theologian John Klaasen, who has used narrative methodology to explain the contribution of individual stories in the context of the South African TRC.²¹ Mindful of the asymmetrical power relations between individual stories and dominant meta-narratives, Klaasen argues that including the stories of ordinary people into TRC hearings makes a hole in the fence surrounding the privileged space where the national narrative is usually defined.²² The significance of this is not merely about "*whose truth* is being told," according to Klaasen, since personal stories additionally convey a different kind of truth—a "*moral truth* that demands an ethical response from society."²³ Beyond conveying mere *information about events and life conditions*, personal stories additionally provide *criteria for their interpretation*, not least in the ways the past, present, and future are interlinked.²⁴ Mindful of these observations, we now turn to the personal accounts shared at public TRC meetings.

Six Narratives of Personal Accounts Shared at Public TRC Meetings

In the qualitative analysis undertaken, six narrative types are identified in the personal accounts. I call them 'narratives of discovery and reconnecting,' 'narratives of revitalization,' 'narratives of invisibility and silence,' 'narratives of land and conflict,' 'narratives of hate speech,' and 'narratives of harm and communal healing.' While not claiming that this typology captures everything, I have endeavored to provide a balanced picture of key features emerging in the material. Beyond reflecting a distinct set of positions, concerns, and relations, each narrative also offers valuable insight into various relevant processes involved, including existential, social, intergenerational, and historical processes. While some narratives

---

Mearohke/Meråker, Maajehjaevrie/Majavatn, Måefie/Mo i Rana, Bådåddjo/Bodø, Ájluokta/Drag, Loabák/Lavangen, Dielddanuorri/Tjeldsund, Málatvuopmi/Målselv, Romsa/Tromssa/Tromsø, Guovdageaidnu/Kautokeino, Kárášjohka/Karasjok, Leavdjna/Lemmijoki/Lakselv, and Deatnu/Tana.

21. Klaasen, "Narrative and Truth."
22. Klaasen, "Narrative and Truth," 158–59.
23. Klaasen, "Narrative and Truth," 160.
24. Klaasen, "Narrative and Truth," 163.

may intertwine and mutually inform one another, others do not exhibit such a connection. Therefore, this typology serves as a framework for discussing commonalities and differences across the material.

Narratives of Discovery and Reconnecting

What I call 'narratives of discovery and reconnecting' are told by individuals from families who have lost their connection to a Sámi or Kven collective at some point. Thus, starting from a position of having little or no awareness of one's own ethnic background, these narratives tell stories of uncovering one's genealogy, family history, and local history, processes which may lead to reclaiming and reconnecting.[25]

At the TRC meeting in Tråante/Trondheim, an older woman told that "*[t]he Norwegianization policy and [its impact on] the Sámi people has been a terribly deep abuse that [continues] to spread across generations.*"[26] Her father had been married to her mom for over fifty years without knowing that he was married to a Sámi, she said. Standing on the platform, she underscored how her Sámi inspired dress symbolized the "*long shadows the Norwegianization policy has thrown on us who have lost our culture and identity*":

> *Because it is no proper Sámi traditional dress. It doesn't belong anywhere. But dressed in it here, I stand vulnerable, clothed in my own longing. And without it, I wouldn't have stood here. Because without it, I wouldn't have started asking my mother, and she would not have told me stories about my grandparents and the life they lived. . . . I am deeply grateful to my mom, who at her very old age was brave enough to admit that we are of Sámi ancestry, and in that way breaking through [the shame].*

A descendant of a South Sámi family group, a victim of so-called *finnjaging* ("chasing of the Sámi") three generations ago, spoke from the floor at the same TRC meeting.[27] "*[M]y family . . . was slaughtered down*" and "*wiped away*," he said, referring to the forced slaughtering of the family herd of his great grandfather, ending up as a poverty-stricken Sámi in the mining town of Plaassja/Røros. The Norwegian state "*tore to pieces*

---

25. This was exemplified by several stories shared in Målselv, *Public TRC meeting in Málatvuopmi/Målselv*.
26. First speaker at *Public TRC meeting in Tråante/Trondheim*.
27. Eighth speaker at *Public TRC meeting Tråante/Trondheim*.

everything we had," he said. *"We have no other Sámi family left, other than history."* This had confronted this man with an identity challenge: *"What my family and I have struggled with is the following: Am I Sámi, or am I not Sámi? Do I want to hide it? Where should I go? I have descendants."* Yet, the man's tireless efforts to uncover his family history eventually provided a means for 'reconnecting' with the Sámi community. *"I search, and I search; and before Christmas, I found a new [Sámi] family, and we are relatives."* Despite the dark sides of this history, the man emphasized the positive of uncovering his *Sámi* history.

> *I have become more and more happy with the good history I have, and I am proud. . . . I am grateful that I have discovered the place where I should be, and that is my Sámi connection. So, to you that are searching, be happy and joyful, because there is much to find.*

In some accounts, references to the activity of local history associations or museums unveil the ambiguous social context of processes of discovery and reconnecting. Local history associations or museums may be a tool, an ally, or even an obstacle to reclaiming the past. A woman told how the overlooked Kven presence in Troms Interior popped up as soon as she, a historian external to the local museum, looked for it in the sources.[28] A man shared a story about a local museum pioneer who came across an old Sámi man who owned a *gákti* (a traditional Sámi jacket) unique to the community but assumed to be lost. Stopping by the next time to borrow his *gákti* for the exhibition, the old man had burned it.[29]

A few narratives of discovery lack an element of reconnecting. Despite curiosity and an undefined feeling of loss, some remain observing at a distance.[30] On the opposite end, narratives of discovery may also push beyond 'reconnection,' translating into 'narratives of revitalization' (the next narrative), exemplified by the account of a young woman speaking at the TRC meeting in Tråante/Trondheim:

> *I am the leader of Norwegian Kven Association Mid-Norway. I am raised here in Trondheim without any knowledge of my Kven background. Becoming aware of it a few years ago, it became important to me to find out as much as possible about the Kvens and the Kven history. As I became more involved in the Kven issues,*

---

28. Third speaker at *Public TRC meeting Málatvuopmi/Målselv*.
29. Fourth speaker at *Public TRC meeting in Loabák/Lavangen*.
30. Fifth speaker at *Public TRC meeting Málatvuopmi/Målselv*.

leaning more about the Kven history, I have also started to experience myself as a Kven.[31]

Narratives of Revitalization

The most common narrative type in the material is 'narratives of revitalization.' Common among Kven and Sámi accounts alike, this type occurs in two narrative settings that at times intertwine. The first concerns the communal and organizational dimension of these narratives, evident in the last quote. Local mobilization through Sámi or Kven associations, initiatives, and networks is obviously instrumental to ongoing culture and language revitalization.

The second setting concerns the deeply existential, intergenerational processes involved in culture and language revitalization. A Lule Sámi father recounted how his life took a transformative turn when his teenage daughter confronted him with the question, "Dad, why haven't you said that we are Sámi?" This moment changed his life path toward reclamation, revitalization, and embracing his heritage with pride.[32] In another instance, an elderly Kven woman, who now plays a key role in the 'Kven revival' in Porsáŋgu/Porsanki/Porsanger, revealed how the passing of her husband, who was a fluent Kven speaker, marked a significant turning point in her life.[33] A few Sámi parents shared their experiences of how parenthood presented them with an existential choice. It gave them the courage to overcome the shame they felt for not speaking the language sufficiently.[34] They spoke of the pride and restored sense of self-worth that came with their efforts to reclaim and preserve their language.[35]

Many frame their revitalization efforts as a deliberate response to the Norwegianization policy. At the TRC meeting in Romsa/Tromssa/Tromsø, a North Sámi mother said that *"[t]he Norwegianization and the efforts to reverse it, that is my life. That's what I spend my time on. Norwegianization and de-Norwegianization and taking back the language":*[36]

31. Fourth speaker at *Public TRC meeting Tråante/Trondheim.*
32. Eleventh speaker at *Public TRC meeting in Bodø/Bådåddjo.*
33. Third speaker at *Public TRC meeting in Leavdnja/Lemmijoki/Lakselv.*
34. Cf. Fifth and sixth speakers at *Public TRC meeting in Ájluokta/Drag.*
35. Sixth speaker at *Public TRC meeting Ájluokta/Drag.* Ninth speaker at *Public TRC meeting in Deatnu/Tana.*
36. Eighth speaker at *Public TRC meeting Romsa/Tromssa/Tromsø.*

> *All the evenings where I've been very tired making that glossary so that I can read to my girls in the evenings afterwards. And feeling the pain and the guilt when you become silent when not being able to explain the world to your child in Sámi. So, Truth Commission, you must listen to the stories and acknowledge them, ensuring that this report is not just a report about pain, but that it can do something about it.*[37]

The vulnerability of local language revitalization efforts is evident in many accounts. During numerous TRC meetings, Sámi parents expressed their deep frustrations with a public school system that consistently fails to implement adopted Sámi language rights.[38] One poignant example is the account of a Lule Sámi mother struggling for her children's language education:

> *I have had the feeling of powerlessness, the feeling of anger, the feeling of despair, the feeling of sadness, the feeling of hope, the feeling of pride, the feeling of lack of understanding. I feel insufficient as a mother. Most of all I feel injustice. . . . I have felt a sense of powerlessness faced with a school system that constantly blames someone else, either up or down the system.*[39]

As in this case, the question of justice (or injustice) often surfaces in the narratives of revitalization, yet it is framed somewhat differently across Kven and Sámi accounts. The Sámi typically view the injustice as a failure to *implement* their established rights,[40] while the Kvens tend to perceive it as a lack of or insufficient *recognition* of their rights as an old minority in Norway. In both cases, reconciliation tends to be framed as a call for political will to support the revitalization of their language and culture, structurally and financially.

> *Reconciliation is not just listening to the stories we tell . . . The Norwegianization policy was, after all, a deliberate policy with budgets and salary increases for teachers. There was also a salary increase for the teachers who were good Norwegianizers.*

---

37. Eighth speaker at *Public TRC meeting Romsa/Tromssa/Tromsø*.

38. Eighth speaker at *Public TRC meeting Leavdnja/Lemmijoki/Lakselv*. Third, tenth and eleventh speakers at *Public TRC meeting in Måefie/Mo i Rana*. Eighth speaker at *Public TRC meeting in Oslo*. Ninth speaker at *Public TRC meeting Bådåddjo/Bodø*. Second speaker at *Public TRC meeting Loabák/Lavangen*.

39. Eighth speaker at *Public TRC meeting Bådåddjo/Bodø*.

40. Third speaker at the *Public TRC meeting Ájluokta/Drag*. Second speaker at *Public TRC meeting Loabák/Lavangen*.

Therefore, the de-Norwegianization must be the same. That must also be a conscious and deliberate policy with a budget.[41]

Narratives of Invisibility and Silence

'Narratives of invisibility and silence' are prevalent in a considerable number of both Kven and Sámi accounts. When viewed through Romero-Amaya's typology, the rationale of this narrative is that the Norwegianization policy has created a national 'narrative of silence,' perpetuating injustices in contemporary society.[42] This narrative is particularly pronounced in the accounts of the Kvens, as exemplified by the story of an elderly man who spoke at the TRC meeting in Oslo.

> *While proactive Norwegianization was abandoned some decades ago, other measures than prohibition and coercion are today slowly strangling the Kven culture. Silence, ignorance, trivialization may today turn out to be just as effective a policy as prohibition and coercion were before. From silence and ignorance grows a collective amnesia; not only in other parts of the population, but also among the Kvens themselves. In this way, the collective awareness about the Kven people and the Kven culture is slowly wiped away.*[43]

Many Kven accounts suggest an interlocked dynamic between invisibility and non-recognition, explaining the obstacles the Kven revitalization is confronted with. Some individuals point to the absence of a public apology recognizing the historical hardships endured by the Kvens.[44] Additionally, many emphasize the importance of a package of 'reconciliatory measures,' which is typically emphasized, either in its entirety or partially, by numerous voices. This includes proper arrangements supporting the revitalization of the Kven language; professionalizing the field of Kven culture through institution building; proper funding and allocation systems for such measures and initiatives; and strengthening the Kven participation and co-determination in society by establishing a Kven council.[45]

41. Eighth speaker at *Public TRC meeting Romsa/Tromssa/Tromsø*.
42. Romero-Amaya, "Historical Narratives."
43. Seventh speaker at *Public TRC meeting Oslo*.
44. Third speaker at *Public TRC meeting Oslo*. Ninth speaker at *Public TRC meeting Romsa/Tromssa/Tromsø*.
45. See third speaker at *Public TRC meeting Oslo*. Tenth speaker at *Public TRC*

Furthermore, when discussing matters of 'justice,' the Kvens, who are officially recognized as a 'national minority' but not classified as 'Indigenous,' often draw comparisons with the Indigenous Sámi.⁴⁶ Many Kvens seem to feel that their non-Indigenous status has been unfairly used to hinder their culture and language revitalization efforts. For instance, there is nothing in the European Minority Language Charter that prevents Norwegian authorities from elevating the Kven language from level 2 to level 3, the implementation level adopted for official Sámi languages in Norway.⁴⁷ So when Kvens talk about 'equality' and 'discrimination' (*forskjellsbehandling*), the context is typically a Sámi/Kven comparison, rather than a Kven/Norwegian one.⁴⁸

Although the concept of Sámi Indigenous rights emerges as a common theme, it is apparent that the actual stances on this issue may vary significantly among the Kven accounts. This assumption finds support in the consultative responses regarding a potential inquiry submitted to the Norwegian Parliament in 2017. Here, the Norwegian Kven Association, being the largest Kven organization, centered its argument on the status of the *Kvens as a national minority*, whereas the smaller Kven Land Association (later renamed as the Kven-Finnish National Association) framed its argument as a critique of *Sámi Indigenous rights*, challenging the legitimacy of the established Indigenous/national minority distinction.⁴⁹ During the public TRC meetings, a minority of Kven accounts likely

---

meeting Bådåddjo/Bodø. Third and ninth speakers at *Public TRC meeting Romsa/Tromssa/Tromsø*.

46. Such comparative references were explicit in the accounts of the sixth and tenth speakers at *Public TRC meeting Oslo*. Third, fifth, and ninth speakers at *Public TRC meeting Romsa/Tromssa/Tromsø*. And tenth speaker at *Public TRC meeting Deatnu/Tana*.

47. Elevating the Kven language to level three was a topic at TRC meetings in Oslo, Bodø, and Tromsø. Cf. Sixth speaker at *Public TRC meeting Oslo*. Ninth speaker at *Public TRC meeting Romsa/Tromssa/Tromsø*. Tenth speaker at *Public TRC meeting Bådåddjo/Bodø*.

48. One exception is found in the account of the third speaker at *Public TRC meeting Oslo*.

49. This difference is explicit in the consultation responses submitted by the two above-mentioned Kven organizations to the Norwegian Parliament in 2017. See attachments 3 and 4 in Stortinget, "Innst. 408 S (2017–2018)." In a recent master's thesis analyzing the Presidency's negotiations with the Sámi Parliament and the Kven organizations on the commission mandate, Habbestad has substantiated that this dynamic explains why all references to rights were removed from the final version of the adopted TRC mandate. See Habbestad, "From Ideas to Final Mandate."

conveyed the latter position through euphemisms, using terms such as "structural discrimination" and "equal treatment."[50]

Also, several Sámi accounts pinpointed the connection between invisibility and injustice, but in the context of Sámi-*Norwegian* relationships. At the TRC meeting in Måefie/Mo i Rana, a young South Sámi woman elaborated on the link between 'silence' and the 'indifference' of majority Norwegian approaches to the Sámi.[51]

> *And now as I speak to official authorities, it cannot pass unnoticed the silence surrounding the Sámi today, both concerning modern Sámi societal conditions and the traditional and historical events that have occurred. It is quite ugly to stand up against the indifference from those who should promote our well-being. . . . That the authorities are indifferent, not taking things seriously, and that indifference and silence is put into system. We can talk about Norwegianization that has been. But what about the Norwegianization that is?*

Many Sámi accounts suggested that a connection between silence, invisibility, and indifference reproduces injustices in two regards: First, the ongoing effects of former Norwegianization measures are not acknowledged and thus not properly reversed. Second, adopted Sámi language, culture, land, and fishing rights are oftentimes poorly understood, respected, and implemented by both authorities, public administration, industrial actors, etc.[52]

Regarding the two Forest Finn accounts found in the material, these basically reflect the three types of narratives rendered so far, by dwelling on processes of discovery and reconnecting, revitalization, and invisibility and silence.[53]

Narratives of Land and Conflict

What I call 'narratives of land and conflict' are exclusive to the Sámi accounts. Here they are many, occurring with a considerable geographical distribution, and conveying historical depth. Centered on safeguarding traditional Sámi livelihoods and ways of life, these narratives are

50. See, for example, the tenth speaker at *Public TRC meeting Oslo*.
51. Ninth speaker at *Public TRC meeting Måefie/Mo i Rana*.
52. Fourth and ninth speakers at *Public TRC meeting Måefie/Mo i Rana*.
53. Fourth and ninth speakers at *Public TRC meeting Oslo*.

characterized by references to "(neo-)colonialism," "ongoing Norwegianization," and the fundamental questioning of whether discussions about "reconciliation" hold any significance in the face of ongoing encroachments on their land.

At the TRC meeting in Plaassja/Røros, a representative of Norway's Reindeer Herders Association provided an overview of historical developments up to the present day.[54] He recounted instances of forced slaughtering of reindeer herds and entire *siiddat* being chased away (cf. the reference to *finn-jaging* in narrative one). He also highlighted racially biased laws and regulations that favored Norwegian settlers at the expense of South Sámi reindeer herders. Decades of legal battles, falsified administrative maps, and individuals providing false testimony in court were also mentioned. He argued that if these lawsuits were conducted today, the Sámi would likely never have lost them, expressing a legitimate hope of reclaiming lost reindeer herding lands. At the same TRC meeting, an elderly reindeer herder spoke about his lifelong struggle in the courts, a struggle depicted from an intergenerational perspective:

> *We have fought for our existence our entire life. I cannot praise my ancestors enough, who resisted this pressure against the Sámi, the reindeer herding, and the nomadic culture; despite the policy of the majority society putting our nomadic culture in conflict with an agriculture regarded to be a better and more advanced culture.*[55]

At the TRC meeting in Tråante/Trondheim, an elderly South Sámi reindeer herder shared his experience of being impacted by the massive wind turbine plant at the Fosen peninsula.[56] He recounted how his small reindeer herding community had struggled for nineteen years against this industry project, a fight that came with personal costs.[57] "*In my mind, it is this neocolonialism going on, taking my land piece by piece*," he said, asking the TRC to investigate the matter.[58]

54. Second speaker at *Public TRC meeting in Plaassja/Røros*.
55. Fourth speaker at *Public TRC meeting Plaassja/Røros*.
56. The Storheia and Roan wind power plants, completed in 2019 and consisting of 151 turbines, were built in the winter grazing area of two South Sámi reindeer herding communities at Fosen, despite consistent protests.
57. Seventh speaker at *Public TRC meeting Tråante/Trondheim*.
58. Note that on October 11th, 2021 (19 months after this man spoke to the TRC), Norway's Supreme Court ruled unanimously that the wind power plants at Storheia and Roan violate the rights of the South Sámi reindeer herders according to the

At the TRC meeting in Mearohke/Meråker, a reindeer herding woman expressed the collective sentiment, stating, "*Many of us are of the opinion that in some areas the state wants to remove the reindeer herding.*" She described it as an ongoing Norwegianization process that seems to be firmly entrenched.[59] Similar stories have been told all the way to the north. A North Sámi reindeer herding woman, speaking at the TRC meeting in Guovdageaidnu/Kautokeino, added to this narrative:

> *The reindeer herders are now in the situation where they must fight the state to save their own land to be able to work with reindeer, as well as complying with all other laws and regulations. And that can be quite difficult. Big money powers take and buy land.*[60]

In Romsa/Tromssa/Tromsø, an elderly woman made a connection between the struggle in her South Sámi homeland and the struggle of coastal (North) Sámi against big rich trawlers ruining the base of their sea Sámi culture. "*Colonialization continues with unabated force,*" she argued.[61] In Leavdnja/Lemmijoki/Lakselv, a North Sámi man explained the challenge faced by the sea Sámi culture of his community, arguing that "*reconciling ourselves*" with what has happened would "*cement the injustice of the past, bringing it into the future.*"[62] Similar concerns have been brought to attention regarding traditional Sámi salmon fishing in the river of Deatnu/Tana, and regarding traditional land uses of settled Sámi in Guovdageaidnu/Kautokeino.[63]

While the narratives of land and conflict are closely associated with reindeer herding, they also extend to encompass the traditional land uses of locally settled Sámi.[64] Moreover, the frustration over the current

---

International Covenant on Civil and Political Rights, Article 27. The verdict implies that the expropriation permits and licenses granted by Norwegian authorities are invalid. As this chapter was written, almost 2 years had passed without any follow-up of the Supreme Court verdict. The failure of the Government to respect the Supreme Court, led to huge demonstrations in Oslo Feb/March 2023, involving a peaceful blockade of several ministries. See Fjellheim, "Wind energy on trial."

59. Speaker at *Public TRC meeting in Mearohke/Meråker.*
60. Eighth speaker at *Public TRC meeting in Guovdageaidnu/Kautokeino.*
61. Eleventh speaker at *Public TRC meeting Romsa/Tromssa/Tromsø.*
62. Fourth speaker at *Public TRC meeting Leavdnja/Lemmijoki/Lakselv.*
63. Second, seventh, and twelfth speakers at *Public TRC meeting Deatnu/Tana.* Second, fourth, and fifth speakers at *Public TRC meeting Guovdageaidnu/Kautokeino.*
64. Exemplified in the claim that the ownership to the land of the Sámi municipality of Kárášjohka belongs to the local people. Cf. Tenth speaker at *Public TRC meeting in Kárášjohka/Karasjok.*

national policy on these matters has an even broader distribution in the Sámi society, as exemplified in the account of a Sámi woman not affiliated with reindeer herding, speaking from the floor at the TRC meeting in Måefie/Mo i Rana:

> *How are we supposed to reconcile ... when, in parallel, the colonization is in full swing throughout Sápmi? ... We have Øyfjellet. We will soon have Sjomfjellet. We have Repparfjorden. We have Davvi [Rásttigáisá]. We have Fosen. In other words, there is an endless list of betrayals and a colonialization taking place at a pace that has not existed before, by means of larger machines, computer technology and, not least, foreign capital. A prime minister who says yes, we see that it can be a disadvantage for reindeer herding, but for society as a whole it is a gain. Who holds the defining power? ... Here are important matters for the Commission to consider. You are appointed by those in power. And concerning the way forward, two brutal processes run parallel. Anyway, I don't feel like laying down, reconciling myself to the current situation.*[65]

Alongside the land intrusions listed, the second 'brutal process' referred to is the *reconciliation process* associated with the TRC. The underlying assumption seems to be that reconciliation is *brutalized* when reduced to a tool for making people conform to injustice. A similar point was made in Ájluokta/Drag, where a man pinpointed the "*paradox that the authorities set up a commission to deal with injustice and reconciliation at the same time as they pursue a policy that is so unjust.*" The one hand of the state does good, while the other does wrong, he said.[66]

Narratives of Hate Speech

The fifth narrative type I call 'narratives of hate speech.' These tend to link up with the previous narrative, as pointed out by a middle-aged Sámi woman at the TRC meeting in Oslo: "*Breakthroughs or demands for [Sámi] rights are all too often met with new flourishing of hate speech.*"[67] A South Sámi woman told how this dynamic can be experienced on the ground.

---

65. Fifth speaker at *Public TRC meeting Måefie/Mo i Rana*.
66. Tenth speaker at *Public TRC meeting Ájluokta/Drag*.
67. Seventh speaker at *Public TRC meeting Oslo*.

> *But we also get a lot of other correspondence that is very aggressive. We also receive phone calls. Our young people are harassed and attacked when visiting town in the evenings. And much of this has become much, much worse with Øyfjellet wind. And with this [wind turbine] construction, we are experiencing enormous aggression from the local population. This morning, what we experience is unbridled racism.*[68]

The fact that Sámi Indigenous rights trigger hate speech directed toward the Sámi in contemporary Norway, particularly in Mid- and Northern Norway, is confirmed by a recent population survey conducted by the Norwegian Institute for Human Rights.[69] Hate speech and bullying refer to a rather broad social phenomenon, particularly evident today in media comment sections and social media.[70] However, they also surface in other public spaces such as football arenas, schools, etc. This phenomenon can be understood as a reflection of the historical legacy of both popular and scientific racism, which characterized the Sámi people as a primitive race.[71]

Many Sámi individuals have addressed the topic of hate speech at open TRC meetings, drawing on past and contemporary experiences. A significant milestone in addressing this problem was achieved in 2019 when the first verdict in Norway on hate speech against the Sámi was handed down. This legal action stemmed from a Northern Norwegian man who had posted harassing comments about the Sámi on a media site.[72] At the TRC meeting in Bodø/Bådåddjo, the Sámi man who initiated this case shared his concerns. He expressed his dismay at the lawyer's argument that the Sámi should endure such hate speech, justifying it as a part of Northern Norwegian language.[73] "*Here, the TRC has a job to do,*" he said.

At the same meeting, his young daughter spoke to the TRC about her own experiences of being bullied daily at secondary school. She recounted hurtful name-calling such as "Lapp devil" and "Sámi devil," along

---

68. Seventh speaker at *Public TRC meeting Måefie/Mo i Rana*.
69. Norges institusjon for menneskerettigheter, *Holdninger til samer*.
70. A recent governmental report from The Commission on Freedom of Expression draws attention to the problem, observing that this makes many Sámi hesitant to engage in public debates. See Ytringsfrihetskommisjonen, *En åpen og opplyst offentlig samtale*, 16, 25, 27, 71–72, 108–9.
71. See Lingaas, "Hate Speech."
72. Utsi and Boine Verstad, "Mann dømt for hatefulle ytringer."
73. Utsi and Verstad, "Mann dømt for hatefulle ytringer."

with recurring comments about her body.⁷⁴ In another account from Ájluokta/Drag, a relatively young Sámi woman recounted a humiliating experience from her youth. She described how an entire arena began ridiculing her and her Sámi football teammates during an away match by mockingly singing a *joik*, a traditional Sámi song.⁷⁵ She was emotionally moved as she shared that no one, including the referee, the managers, the organizers, nor the parents, intervened to stop this offensive behavior. The incident had been buried in silence for years, and it took a long time before she felt comfortable sharing this painful experience with anyone.

While generally agreeing that things were worse before, the Sámi accounts affirm a continuity between past and present experiences.⁷⁶ This foregrounds a difference between the Sámi and Kven accounts. As noted, it is *invisibility* and lack of recognition (cf. narrative three) that emerges as the core problem in the Kven accounts, with no references to being bullied on ethnic grounds.⁷⁷ The following comment by an elderly Kven, speaking at the TRC meeting in Romsa/Tromssa/Tromsø, is likely rather representative: "*I have not . . . been . . . discriminated against or bullied with or anything like that . . . [I]t's more about making it [the Kven identity and culture] invisible, and about hiding and not bringing it up.*"⁷⁸ In the Sámi accounts, however, experiences of invisibility co-exist with experiences of a negative-laden *visibility*. The personal experiences shared at public TRC meetings thus reflect the fact that the Sámi historically are a far more racialized population than the Kvens.⁷⁹

Due to the prominent role residential schools hold as a symbol of the Norwegianization policy, the few occurrences of residential school survivor stories in the material are somewhat surprising.⁸⁰ One possible explanation may be that such stories, to begin with, tend to be buried in

---

74. Fifth speaker at *Public TRC meeting Bodø/Bådåddjo*.

75. Thirteenth speaker at *Public TRC meeting Ájluokta/Drag*.

76. Beyond the examples already mentioned, the topic was particularly foregrounded at the TRC meetings in Lavangen and Tjeldsund. *Public TRC meeting Dielddanuorri/Tjeldsund*; *Public TRC meeting Loabák/Lavangen*.

77. This difference in the dissemination of experiences of hate speech and bullying among Sámi and Kvens is supported by recent population surveys. See Norges institusjon for menneskerettigheter, *Holdninger til samer*.

78. Third speaker at *Public TRC meeting Romsa/Tromssa/Tromsø*.

79. See Kyllingstad, *Rase*.

80. I have found only two exceptions, the first and sixth speaker at *Public TRC meeting Leavdnja/Lemmijoki/Lakselv*.

silence by those having experienced it. This observation is supported by an older Sámi woman at the TRC meeting in Loabák/Lavangen:

> There are quite a few people gathered here today, but I miss the flock of all those who should have been here. All those who didn't get anything out of schooling. Sorry [moved, holding back tears]. It's such a pain to remember all those who didn't make it at school.... But that oppression all the time there. That you are nothing. And there were words like Lapp-devil. Always commenting where you came from.[81]

The context of this story was not a residential school, but experiences at a local school. Beyond undermining the self-esteem of Sámi individuals, the imprint of this history has also generated disintegration and conflict within the Sámi community, as evident in the story of a middle-aged Sámi speaking at the TRC meeting in Ájluokta/Drag.

> [W]hen you [my cousin's family] came to Narvik, I didn't want to meet you. You looked so typically Sámi. Meeting you in downtown Narvik was a shame. I apologize for the betrayal. That shame is old. It is the history of our people. It is our shared history—also the Norwegian history.... One effect was that I—when attending confirmation school and was about to be confirmed in the church of Narvik—then I wondered: How much does a surgery removing my cheekbones cost? That was what I was going to spend the confirmation money on. It was the fear of being discovered.[82]

The story of this man sheds light on a related phenomenon mentioned by a few others: the realization that some of the worst instances of bullying against the Sámi have, at times, been perpetuated by Norwegianized Sámi individuals who conceal their own identity.[83] The latter illustrates how narratives of hate speech, initially external phenomena imposed from the outside, can eventually transform into social harms that manifest *within* the group itself. This points us to the last narrative.

Narratives of Harm and Communal Healing

The Sámi stories, being more numerous and varied, encompass a broader range of topics compared to the Kven accounts. This includes a focus on

---

81. Ninth speaker at *Public TRC meeting Loabák/Lavangen.*
82. Third speaker at *Public TRC meeting Ájluokta/Drag.*
83. Eighth and ninth speakers at *Public TRC meeting Dielddanuorri/Tjeldsund.*

ethnic in-group relations within the context of 'narratives of harm and communal healing.' Two topics emerge as particularly relevant.

The first topic concerns sexual abuse and intergenerational trauma. While briefly mentioned at other meetings, this was a dominant theme at the TRC meeting in Ájluokta/Drag in Divtasvuodna/Tysfjord. This was not unexpected, given the explosive nature of the "Tysfjord case," which gained significant media attention in Norway in 2016 when eleven individuals came forward with their stories.[84] The case eventually involved 151 cases of sexual abuse of children primarily belonging to the local Lule Sámi community. At this TRC meeting, a young woman shared the heartbreaking story of her mother, who was one of the eleven who came forward but tragically took her own life before the media coverage was published.[85] A memorial fund was established in her mother's name to support preventive measures against sexual abuse, violations, and suicide, as well as to promote greater openness and awareness surrounding these critical issues.

The Lule Sámi community in recent years has played a leading role in breaking the silence surrounding the problem of sexual abuse. They have also been instrumental in raising awareness about the connection between sexual abuse and the intergenerational trauma stemming from the Norwegianization policy. At the TRC meeting, some individuals expressed a sense of pride and relief that the "silence was broken" and that people had the strength to come forward and share their experiences.[86] Emphasizing that the truth and reconciliation process must also be about the responsibility of the Norwegian majority society, a Sámi man underscored the importance that *"we who tell this ... don't have to bear responsibility for our history, for the situation we have found ourselves in."*[87]

A second prominent topic that emerged in the narratives of harm and communal healing pertains to the challenge of embracing Sámi diversity in the wake of the Norwegianization policy. Due to this policy, individuals today may hold very different resources for claiming a Sámi identity and for participating in a Sámi society. For this reason, Sámi revitalization and community-building efforts are confronted with certain internal tensions. Several leaders of Sámi associations/centers in Northern Norwegian cities have emphasized the necessity of creating safe and

84. Berglund et al., "Den mørke hemmeligheten."
85. First speaker at *Public TRC meeting Ájluokta/Drag.*
86. Fourth and seventh speakers at *Public TRC meeting Ájluokta/Drag.*
87. Eighth speaker at *Public TRC meeting Ájluokta/Drag.*

inclusive spaces that can accommodate Sámi diversity.[88] A Sámi woman in a leadership role within a regional Sámi association described their efforts in this context as a form of "small scale reconciliation work":

> People have backgrounds from various Sámi groups. Moreover, due to the Norwegianization policy, people may be placed quite differently in terms of knowledge of history, culture, and language. For such reasons, Sámi issues are not always easy. At times, one must negotiate internal misunderstandings, suspicion, since people are hurt by experiences of being overlooked or not understood, carrying different experiences and relations of being Sámi. Running a local association may serve a welcoming space.[89]

Accommodating these types of tensions is, however, not only an issue in urban areas where people have relocated from a large geographical area. The legacy of the Norwegianization policy has also generated tensions within individual municipalities. This issue was discussed at the TRC meeting in Deatnu/Tana. Two elderly Sámi women from lower Deatnu (historically a separate municipality subjected to more forceful Norwegianization measures than the upper part of Deatnu/Tana) expressed their regrets about how the Sámi further up the valley tended to regard their Sámi village as part of the Norwegian part of the municipality and referred to them as "destroyed Sámi."[90] The women wanted to put an end to this prejudice, calling for a stronger *local* recognition of their Sámi community, despite having lost far more of the Sámi language.

At the TRC meeting in Kárášjohka/Karasjok, two elderly women recounted somewhat similar experiences, but from the opposite end. They had been dedicated to preserving the Sámi language and advocating for Sámi political rights during a period when the Norwegianization policy had taken root in their community. However, they found themselves accused of excluding other Sámi and labeled as "super Sámi." They considered these accusations to be untrue and unfair.[91] Their shared sentiment was that the pain and challenges they faced due to these accusations are often overlooked or not fully acknowledged.[92]

---

88. Third speaker at *Public TRC meeting Bodø/Bådåddjo*. Third and twelfth speakers at *Public TRC meeting Mo*. Sixth account at *Public TRC meeting Romsa/Tromssa/Tromsø*.
89. Sixth speaker at *Public TRC meeting Bodø/Bådåddjo*.
90. Fifth and thirteenth speakers at *Public TRC meeting Deatnu/Tana*.
91. Fourth and seventh speaker at *Public TRC meeting Kárášjohka/Karasjok*.
92. Fourth and seventh speakers at *Public TRC meeting Kárášjohka/Karasjok*.

Another tension arising from the Norwegianization policy has a significant impact on the young. While the stigma and shame associated with being Sámi is gradually diminishing in Norway, they are being replaced by a new type of shame—the shame of not being Sámi enough.[93] This concern was expressed by several younger individuals at TRC meetings.[94] A somewhat related topic, the issue of multiple identities, may inform this type of question,[95] or simply be framed as a wish of not having to defend one's "right to be Kven and Sámi."[96] The latter suggests overcoming oppositional identities as a concern for both in-group and inter-group healing.

PART II: DISCUSSION OF CONTRIBUTIONS TO POLITICAL RECONCILIATION IN POST-TRC NORWAY

Having outlined the basic features of the Sámi and Kven accounts shared at public TRC meetings in six narratives, we are ready to discuss the main question: In what ways are these personal accounts contributing to the understanding of reconciliation in post-TRC Norway? In this section, this question is deliberated in light of relevant transitional justice, theological, and Indigenous research literature discussing aspects of political reconciliation.

Political Reconciliation as a Priority: The Human Face of Political Issues

It is evident that while explicit references to 'reconciliation' may be limited in the personal accounts, the material indeed provides a fertile ground for discussing this concept. The notion of reconciliation was far from absent in the observed TRC meetings,[97] suggesting that most attendees speak-

---

93. Hansen and Skaar have elaborated on this challenge in a recent report on the psychosocial health among Sámi youth. Hansen and Skaar, "Unge samers psykiske helse, 86–87, 93.

94. Third and fifth speakers at *Public TRC meeting Bodø/Bådåddjo*. Twelfth speaker at *Public TRC meeting Måefie/Mo i Rana*.

95. Twelfth speaker at *Public TRC meeting Måefie/Mo i Rana*.

96. Fifth and sixth speakers at *Public TRC meeting Romsa/Tromssa/Tromsø*.

97. These meetings were convened by the TRC. In each of these meetings, at least one commissioner elaborated on the notion of reconciliation, and attendees were invited to suggest "measures for further reconciliation."

ing were fully aware that they were engaging in a public discourse on the meaning of reconciliation in the aftermath of the Norwegianization policy. Therefore, our discussion should be attentive to both the underlying assumptions of reconciliation as well as explicit references to it.

The South African theologian John W. de Gruchy's differentiation between 'political reconciliation' (reconciliation processes involving political authorities), 'social reconciliation' (intergroup reconciliation), and 'interpersonal reconciliation' (reconciliation between individuals) is helpful for identifying pivotal points in the reconciliation discourse reflected in the personal accounts.[98] While concerns of political and social reconciliation are well represented in our material, issues of interpersonal reconciliation are barely mentioned, except for sporadic occurrences in the context of ethnic in-group healing concerns. I have, for this reason, replaced de Gruchy's category of 'interpersonal reconciliation' with what I denote 'communal reconciliation.' This provides us with a three-fold typology differentiating between national authority related (political), intergroup related (social), and in-group related (communal) aspects of reconciliation.

While not all accounts fit easily into these categories, a majority resonate with one or two. Concerns of social reconciliation (such as ignorance, prejudice, negative attitudes, bullying, hate speech, and other discriminatory practices) and concerns of communal reconciliation (such as breaking the silence around sexual abuse and historical trauma, being good enough, and accommodating Sámi diversity in a situation where individuals are hurt in various ways by the Norwegianization policy) are relatively evenly distributed among the personal accounts. The most dominant feature, however, concerns the extent to which people engage in a discourse on political reconciliation. Many individuals have addressed the Norwegianization policy as a state-driven initiative that continues to have a profound impact on their lives, as well as that of their families, communities, and the broader population, formulating expectations to Norwegian authorities about positive change for the Sámi and the Kvens. A first observation regarding the contribution of personal accounts to reconciliation thus concerns the extent to which they foreground political reconciliation as a priority in post-TRC Norway.

In the book *Reconciliation as Politics*, the Swedish peace researcher Kjell-Åke Nordquist argues that the key contribution of 'reconciliation'

---

98. de Gruchy, *Reconciliation*, 26–27.

to the political vocabulary concerns the way this concept "recognizes the social and human dimensions of political processes."[99] Being a concept with "direct reference to human experience," political reconciliation is about the "restoration of *human dignity* that has been violated in political conflict."[100] An added value of the personal accounts shared with the TRC thus concerns the way they contribute with a thick description of the complex personal, social, existential, intergenerational, cultural, economic, and political conditions constituting the matrix for experiencing human dignity (or the lack thereof) among Sámi and Kvens in contemporary Norway. Furthermore, reflecting a communitarian view of truth, these accounts are not easily reduced to a series of individualized stories of pain.[101] Rather, in the words of Nordquist, they reflect "[a] communitarian view [that] would argue that restoring human dignity is a community-based process, where reconciliation is a tool for the wider conception of identity and dignity." People have shared stories where "hurting the individual is hurting a community" and "restoring human dignity is a community-based process."[102]

An additional communitarian characteristic concerns a striking temporal feature, namely, the way the past and the present are interwoven in intergenerational modes of experience. The significance of these observations can be appreciated considering Klaasen's point that the contribution of personal stories to TRC processes goes beyond conveying relevant information about events and life conditions. They also provide *criteria* for their interpretation.[103]

However, beyond contributing to the discourse of political reconciliation in the ways emphasized above, what can be said about the particular approach to reconciliation reflected in these accounts?

---

99. Nordquist, *Reconciliation as Politics*, 45.

100. My emphasis. Nordquist, *Reconciliation as Politics*, 93, 148.

101. Nordquist (*Reconciliation as Politics*, 41–43) has discussed the significance of differentiating between 'liberal' versus 'communitarian' perspectives on truth in the context of political reconciliation. While a liberal view on truth refers to the objective, fact-based, scoped, and individualized truth-seeking logic typically applied in courts, a communitarian view on truth implies that shared knowledge, shared experiences, and shared values and practices emerge as key to what is considered truth, both at an individual and a social level.

102. Nordquist, *Reconciliation as Politics*, 43.

103. Klaasen, "Narrative and Truth," 163, 60.

Overarching Reconciliation Approach: Truth, Justice, and Freedom

A debated topic in the research literature concerns the way 'reconciliation' serves as an umbrella concept integrating and negotiating other key aspects, such as truth, justice, peace, apologies, forgiveness, etc.[104] Focusing on the actual negotiation of such aspects, American theologian Leah Robinson has proposed a theoretical model for analyzing contextual approaches to political reconciliation.[105] The model holds explanatory power beyond the theological discourse Robinson engages in, justifying my use of it here.

Synthesizing previous debates, Robinson identifies 'truth,' 'justice,' 'repentance,' and 'forgiveness' as the four broad dimensions ideally (but not necessarily) informing a *process* of political reconciliation.[106] Depending on the context and how it is responded to, Robinson argues that every reconciliation approach has its unique contextual profile, which is reflected in the way emphases and priorities are made among these four dimensions.[107] This observation is associated with an additional conceptual layer in Robinson's model, namely, the way 'freedom' and 'peace' represent the two *goals* that reconciliation processes typically steer toward and prioritize amongst. While reconciliation ideally orients itself towards both goals, concrete reconciliation approaches (referred to as "reconciliation theologies" in Robinson's vocabulary) generally tend to emphasize one of the two, aligning with what is deemed most relevant and pressing in the actual situation. Based on this framework, two basic reconciliation approaches (or "reconciliation theologies" in Robinson's vocabulary) are identified. The first type refers to reconciliation approaches with "liberating tendencies." These emphasize *truth* and *justice*, with *freedom* as a primary goal. The second type is reconciliation approaches with 'atoning tendencies,' which emphasize *repentance* and *forgiveness,* with *peace* as its primary goal.[108]

I have categorized the personal accounts I observed using Robinson's framework, which includes the dimensions of 'truth,' 'justice,'

---

104. Nordquist, *Reconciliation as Politics*, 1, 12. See also Llewellyn and Philpott, "Introduction."
105. Robinson, *Embodied Peacebuilding*, 37–53.
106. Robinson, *Embodied Peacebuilding*, 44–45.
107. Robinson, *Embodied Peacebuilding*, 45–50.
108. Robinson, *Embodied Peacebuilding*, 44–50.

'repentance,' and 'forgiveness.' The pattern that emerges is quite evident. The majority of both Sámi and Kvens accounts place a strong emphasis on 'truth,' often coupled with a concern for 'justice.' Relatively fewer accounts delve into aspects of "repentance," such as references to apologies or the need for attitudinal change. 'Forgiveness' is barely mentioned. In light of Robinson's model, it becomes apparent that the speakers from both the Sámi and Kvens communities have essentially advocated for a reconciliatory approach that leans toward liberation, with the central focus being on the question of justice.

Reconciliation, Justice, and Human Rights: The Hard Rights/Soft Rights Dynamic

The role of justice in truth and reconciliation processes is a widely debated topic in the research literature on TCs.[109] In transitional states, such as South Africa, where TRCs typically have addressed histories of authoritarian rule or internal armed conflict, the discourse has primarily revolved around concerns related to criminal justice.[110] However, in Norway, calls for justice typically implicate references to human rights in the form of Indigenous or minority rights,[111] a situation resonating more with Canadian debates.[112] Nordquist considers human rights as a substantive category providing content to the process-oriented concept of reconciliation, acknowledging that both concepts are rooted in an emphasis on 'human dignity.'[113] So, how is this relevant for unpacking the contribution of personal accounts to reconciliation in post-TRC Norway?

---

109. Llewellyn and Philpott, "Introduction," 10.

110. Hayner, "Unspeakable Truths," 91–109. Note that the South African TRC's emphasis on restorative justice in the spirit of *Ubuntu*, to a large extent centered around criminal justice concerns in the context of granting amnesties. In hindsight, the limitations of the South African TRC process regarding addressing socio-economic justice have been pointed out. See, for instance, the chapters of Henkeman, Verwoerd, and Thesnaar in Guðmarsdóttir et al., *Trading Justice for Peace?*

111. The ways human rights are relevant to the work of the Norwegian TRC is discussed in Haugen, "Any Role."

112. See Lightfoot, "Truth and Reconciliation Commission."

113. Human rights are "an interpretation and operationalization of human dignity," while political reconciliation concerns the "restoration of human dignity that is violated by political conflict," according to Nordquist. Nordquist, *Reconciliation as Politics*, 97, 92, 93.

The hard rights/soft rights distinction introduced by Indigenous rights expert and Anishinaabe scholar Sheryl Lightfoot is relevant for discussing this, as it highlights a striking difference between narratives of revitalization and narratives of land and conflict in our material. Lightfoot's hard/soft distinction is based on her observation that states are far more hesitant to implementing Indigenous rights to land and self-determination (thus 'hard' rights to the states) than to accommodating Indigenous rights to culture, language, education, etc. (thus 'soft' rights).[114] We have seen that the calls for justice in the revitalization narratives concern the 'soft' rights to culture, language, and education. Neither these rights are easily implemented, according to Lightfoot,[115] something that both Sámi and Kven accounts affirm. However, it is in narratives of land and conflict that the "hard" rights dynamic surfaces, powerfully demonstrated in the Norwegian government's hesitation to follow up on the Supreme Court verdict in the Fosen case.[116]

Interesting for our discussion is the fact that it is exactly in the hard rights discourse of narratives of land and conflict that the most numerous, explicit, and critical references to 'reconciliation' occur in all the material. Some have commented critically on the felt expectation to reconcile in a situation where the state continues to pursue its policy as if nothing has happened.[117] Foregrounding trust as a precondition to reconciliation, a crisis of confidence is reflected in several stories. "How can we trust a prime minister or a government that does this to us? And then we are the ones supposed to reconcile with what they do."[118]

The Risks of Politics of Reconciliation: Towards Transformative Reconciliation

The skepticism regarding the authenticity of current reconciliation politics in Norway finds resonance in a Canadian debate. In his 2014

---

114. Lightfoot, "Truth and Reconciliation," 13–14.

115. Lightfoot, *Global Indigenous Politics*, 14.

116. Eva Fjellheim's ethnographic study of the legal proceedings in the Fosen case, demonstrates how such hard rights dynamic has been at play in the entire process. See Fjellheim, "Wind energy on trial."

117. Beyond the speakers cited in the section on "Narratives of land and conflict," this concern was also underscored by the third, fifth, and seventh speakers at *Public TRC meeting in Maajhjaevrie/Majavatn*.

118. Fifth speaker at *Public TRC meeting Måefie/Mo i Rana*.

publication, *Red Skin, White Masks*, Dene scholar Glen Coulthard put forth the argument that Canadian politics of reconciliation, which essentially mirrors the politics of recognition, effectively served to domesticate Indigenous resistance against oppressive colonial structures. Coulthard's critique can be summarized as follows: the politics of reconciliation tends to relegate colonial violence to the past, implying that contemporary injustices are seen as a 'legacy'; it centers on Indigenous individuals and communities, while masking settler-colonial structures; its emphasis on forgiveness pathologizes justified Indigenous harm and resentment to the colonial situation; and it represents a pacifying discourse inviting Indigenous people to reconcile to the settler-colonial situation.[119] Coulthard contends that Indigenous people should instead commit themselves to "Indigenous resurgence." This approach involves "re-creating the cultural and political flourishing of the [Indigenous] past to support the well-being of our contemporary citizens."[120]

Discussing the Sámi-related TRC process in Finland, Sámi scholar Rauna Kuokkanen argues that "without a commitment to a structural approach to justice, reconciliation in Finland will indeed mark an extension of ongoing settler colonialism." Coulthard's critique thus alerts us to obvious risks of political reconciliation also in Norway, Sweden, and Finland.[121] Yet, Coulthard's argument is at the same time resting on a biased description of the broader phenomenon of political reconciliation. With reference to Robinson's model, we see that Coulthard's critique is targeting the second peace-oriented reconciliation type with atoning tendencies.[122] This suggests that there is space for negotiating the reconciliation approach in other directions.[123] *Resurgence and Reconciliation*, published in 2018, shows that the discussion about reconciliation in Canada today is taken beyond Coulthard's approach. Instead of treating them as two different projects, Anishinaabe legal scholar John Borrows and Canadian philosopher James Tully argue that resurgence and reconciliation can be combined in approaches of 'transformative reconciliation.'[124] I argue that the concept of *transformative reconciliation* captures the liberating type

---

119. Coulthard, *Red Skin, White Masks*, 22, 106–9, 26–27.
120. Here, Coulthard (*Red Skin, White Masks*, 156) is quoting Simpson.
121. Kuokkanen, "Reconciliation as a Threat," 294.
122. Robinson, *Embodied Peacebuilding*, 44.
123. Note that Coulthard is not fully rejecting this possibility.
124. Borrows and Tully, "Introduction," 10.

of reconciliation called for in the personal accounts shared at public TRC meetings in Norway.

CONCLUSION: SMALL STORIES CHALLENGING LARGE NARRATIVES

Considering the discussion above, the contributions of personal accounts to the understanding of reconciliation in post-TRC Norway can be summarized in six points. First, informed by concerns for social (intergroup) and communal (in-group) reconciliation, the personal stories point out political reconciliation as a priority. Second, the contribution of personal stories in this context concerns the way they foreground the human face of political issues. Grounded in communitarian accounts of reality, the personal stories contribute to a thick description of the conditions for experiencing human dignity among Sámi and Kvens in contemporary Norway. Third, reflecting a liberating type of reconciliation, the Sámi and Kven accounts implicate calls for justice. In the Norwegian context, this emphasis on justice translates into a focus on human rights, specifically Indigenous/minority rights. Fourth, taken together, the personal accounts suggest that the state-related dynamic implicated in Lightfoot's hard rights/soft rights distinction is in full play in Norway, which is particularly evident in the narratives of land and conflict. The significant skepticism expressed regarding the meaningfulness of reconciliation with the state in this context highlights the extent of conflicting positions that will likely inform the public debate about reconciliation in post-TRC Norway that is about to start. Fifth, the overarching picture emerging in the personal accounts suggests that there is a risk that the politics of reconciliation in post-TRC Norway may be used to domesticate resistance to remaining colonial structures. Sixth, in this context, the Sámi and Kven accounts implicate a notion of reconciliation as 'transformative,' in which both relational and structural aspects of reconciliation must be considered.

While there is a risk that essential aspects of personal stories shared at public TRC meetings are lost when domesticated in a report and discussed as 'issues' in post-TRC public debates, the bottom-up argument of this chapter suggests that these accounts resist being reduced to a series of isolated individual stories of pain. Emerging as "small stories challenging large narratives," they contribute with rich communitarian counter-narratives about Norway as an *interethnic nation*, providing content and depth to the meaning of reconciliation in post-TRC Norway.[125] In the words of Romero-Amaya, these stories form "narratives of resistance" challenging dominant majority-Norwegian "narratives of nation-building" and their affiliated "narrative of silence" regarding Indigenous and national minorities.[126]

We have seen that the personal accounts convey a concern for transformative reconciliation. Here, Romero-Amaya's perspective underscores the notion that the perception of sociopolitical conditions as just or unjust is often shaped by the *narratives* that define them.[127] If Romero-Amaya is correct that historical narratives "set the moral compass and the explanatory framework" of a conflict,[128] and that historical narratives function as "memory frameworks connecting past, present, and future to sustain political agendas,"[129] then it is relevant to raise the following question: To what extent are large narratives about Norway hindering the possibilities for transformative reconciliation in post-TRC Norway?

It goes beyond the scope of this chapter to discuss the 700-page TRC report from this perspective. Thus, a few preliminary observations will suffice. The TRC report has undoubtedly offered a thorough analysis of the Norwegianization policy and injustices against the Sámi, Kvens, and Forest Finns. Generally speaking, the TRC report both affirms and conveys the basic concerns foregrounded in the personal accounts analyzed in this chapter. Yet, two limitations may be commented on, relevant to the questions discussed in this chapter.

The first concerns the insufficient attention given to structural reconciliation in the recommended measures of the TRC report. This critique was articulated by Sámi researchers Else Grete Broderstad and Eva Josefsen in a debate article shortly after the release of the TRC report.[130] While commending the TRC report for its focus on "closing the implementation

---

125. This view finds support in the TRC report: "The commission believes that recognizing that Norway has been and is a multicultural society must be the basis for reconciliation." Sannhets- og forsoningskommisjonen, *Sannhet og Forsoning*, 655.

126. Romero-Amaya, "Historical Narratives."

127. My emphasis. Romero-Amaya, "Historical Narratives," 114.

128. Romero-Amaya, "Historical Narratives," 114.

129. My emphasis. Romero-Amaya, "Historical Narratives," 113.

130. Broderstad and Josefsen, "Hva kan føre til forsoning." Note that the section in the TRC report on measures for further reconciliation is organized around five pillars: knowledge and communication; language; culture; preventing conflict; and implementation of regulations.

gap between adopted policy and actual implementation,"[131] they pointed out a need for a more thorough analysis of how public administration contributes to perpetuating this problem, which they referred to as "the Norwegianization and injustice 'sticking to the walls.'" Due to this, the TRC report fails in proposing concrete solutions for addressing these implementation gaps. They contend that merely filling knowledge gaps is inadequate[132] because the issue of implementation deficiencies is intricately linked to the individuals and entities who hold the power to define 'relevant knowledge' in decision-making processes. To further this argument, it is worth noting that dominant national narratives likely serve as a tool for defining 'relevant knowledge' in this context.

Broderstad and Josefsen's critique resonates with Coulthard's warning that the politics of reconciliation tend to mask unjust (colonial) structures,[133] something which leads me to my last point. Considering recurrent references to 'colonialism' in the personal accounts, and the fact that Scandinavian colonialism constitutes an emerging historical field,[134] it is striking (if not surprising) that the Norwegian TRC report fully avoids colonialism as a relevant perspective for discussing historical and contemporary injustices.[135] It is a fair assumption that there were internal disagreements in the commission on the matter, and that the approach taken is assumedly reflective of a dominant historical interpretation in the Norwegian commission. A different outcome may be

---

131. This refers to the fifth pillar of proposed follow-up measures. See Sannhets- og Forsoningskommisjonen, *Sannhet og Forsoning*, 657–68.

132. This refers to the first pillar of proposed follow-up measures. See Sannhets- og Forsoningskommisjonen, *Sannhet og Forsoning*, 652–53. Broderstad and Josefsen elaborated on this critique in a later research article. See Broderstad and Josefsen, "The Norwegian TRC."

133. Coulthard, *Red Skin, White Masks*.

134. See Höglund and Burnett, "Introduction."

135. The recurring term of *jordbrukskolonisering* (agricultural colonization) in the TRC report is defined broadly as "new cultivation, establishing farms and new settlements" (pinpointed in footnote 168) without any explicit reference to 'colonialism.' In the contemporary section, the report disowns the latter term by locating it in a small textbox on 'Colony, colonialism, and colonization' in the section on the conditions of reindeer husbandry. Here, it is said that this constitutes an extensive debate, that the latest standard work on Sámi history (cf. Andersen, Evjen and Ryymin) primarily uses 'colonization' in the same way as the TRC report, and that reindeer herding Sámi have referred to the concept of 'colony' in the general sense. See Sannhets- og forsoningskommisjonen, *Sannhet og Forsoning*, 183, 562. However, as my qualitative analysis shows, the latter references have both a broader dissemination in the Sámi society and are referring to colonialism more specifically than suggested in the TRC report.

expected in the final report from the Swedish TC related to the Sámi, since one of the leading historians here, Gunlög Fur, has Scandinavian colonialism as her field of expertise.[136] By delimiting its analytic lens to the policy of assimilation (Norwegianization), the key question in the TRC report becomes whether contemporary injustices can be labelled as 'Norwegianization', and whether such Norwegianization is the outcome of an *intentional* assimilation policy in the contemporary context.[137] However, what if assimilation is an insufficient perspective for unveiling the dynamic of injustice at play, as suggested in the context of narratives of land and conflict? As I have argued in a previous publication on the Norwegian TRC process, the role of the policy of assimilation in Wolfe's settler colonial theory suggests that it could have offered a relevant complementary lens for unveiling a "more hidden colonial *realpolitik* at work in the Norwegianization policy."[138] In Wolfe's theory, the policy of assimilation is not the goal itself, but rather a means to a different end: the dispossession of Indigenous land.[139] Here, the policy of assimilation is seen as a late phase of settler colonial histories, which in the contemporary context primarily manifest themselves as a *structural reality*.[140] The Norwegian TRC has avoided delving into these types of questions. Despite its obvious strengths, it is therefore relevant to ask whether the TRC report, by sticking more or less solely to the interpretive horizon of "Norwegianization," inadvertently contributes to reinforcing a large narrative that continues to mask relevant aspects of ongoing injustices in contemporary Norway.

These concluding reflections have a bearing on the question about the contribution of personal accounts to the understanding of reconciliation in post-TRC Norway. As the analysis of this chapter suggests, the Sámi and Kven accounts shared at public TRC meetings in Norway may inform, complement, and expand the reading or the TRC report, alerting the public to concerns and dimensions that are vital to reconciliation in post-TRC Norway.

---

136. Sanningskommissionen för det samiska folket, "Kommissionens ledamöter och sekretariat."

137. See Sannhets- og forsoningskommisjonen, *Sannhet og Forsoning*, 560, 66.

138. Johnsen, "Negotiating the meaning of 'TRC,'" 39–40.

139. Wolfe, *Settler Colonialism*, 3, 34.

140. Wolfe, *Settler Colonialism*, 2, 27–33.

BIBLIOGRAPHY

Berglund, Eirik L., et al. "Den Mørke Hemmeligheten." *VG Helg* (2016) 18–29.

Borrows, John, and James Tully. "Introduction." In *Resurgence and Reconciliation: Indigenous-Settler Relations and Earth Teachings*, edited by Michael Ash et al., 3–25. London: University of Toronto Press, 2018.

Broderstad, Else G., and Eva Josefsen. "Hva Kan Føre Til Forsoning." https://www.nordnorskdebatt.no/hva-kan-fore-til-forsoning/o/5-124-252446.

———. "The Norwegian TRC: Truth, Reconciliation, and Public Engagement", *International Journal on Minority and Group Rights 31*, no. 2 (2023): 205–232. https://doi.org/10.1163/15718115-BJA10120.

Coulthard, Glen S. *Red Skin, White Masks: Rejecting the Colonial Politics of Recognition*. Minneapolis, MN: University of Minnesota Press, 2014.

de Gruchy, John W. *Reconciliation: Restoring Justice*. Minneapolis: Fortress Press, 2002.

Fjellheim, Eva Maria. "Wind Energy on Trial in Saepmie: Epistemic Controversies and Strategic Ignorance in Norway's Green Energy Transition." *Arctic Review on Law and Politics* 14 (2023): 140–68. https://doi.org/https://doi.org/10.23865/arctic.v14.5586.

Guðmarsdóttir, Sigríður, et al., eds. *Trading Justice for Peace? Reframing Reconciliation in Trc Processes in South Africa, Canada and Nordic Countries*. Cape Town: AOSIS, 2021.

Habbestad, Amalie D. "From Ideas to Final Mandate: An Analysis of the Process of Formulating the Norwegian TRC Mandate and the Idea." Master's thesis, UiT Norges arktiske universitet, 2023. https://munin.uit.no/handle/10037/29449.

Hansen, Ketil L., and Sara W. Skaar. *Unge samers psykiske helse: En kvalitativ og kvantitativ studie av unge samers psykososiale helse* (Mental Helse Ungdom, 2021). https://uit.no/Content/721559/cache=20210403160302/Miha_Unge_samer_rapport_digital.pdf.

Haugen, Hans M. "Any Role for Human Rights in the Norwegian Truth and Reconciliation Commission Addressing Forced Assimilation?" *International Journal on Minority and Group Rights* 29 (2021) 205–29. https://doi.org/https://doi.org/10.1163/15718115-bja10059.

Hayner, Priscilla B. *Unspeakable Truths: Transitional Justice and the Challenge of Truth Commissions*. 2nd ed. New York: Routledge, 2011.

Höglund, Johan, and Linda A. Burnett. "Introduction: Nordic Colonialisms and Scandinavian Studies." *Scandinavian Studies* 91 (2019) 1–12. https://www.jstor.org/stable/pdf/10.5406/scanstud.91.1–2.0001.pdf.

Johnsen, Tore. "Negotiating the Meaning of 'TRC' in the Norwegian Context." In *Trading Justice for Peace? Reframing Reconciliation in TRC Processes in South Africa, Canada and Nordic Countries*, edited by Sigríður Guðmarsdóttir et al., 19–40. Cape Town: AOSIS, 2021.

Klaasen, John. "Narrative and Truth and Reconciliation." In *Trading Justice for Peace? Reframing Reconciliation in TRC processes in South Africa, Canada and Nordic Countries*, edited by Sigríður Guðmarsdóttir, et al. Cape Town: AOSIS, 2021. https://books.aosis.co.za/index.php/ob/catalog/book/174.

Kuokkanen, Rauna. "Reconciliation as a Threat or Structural Change? The Truth and Reconciliation Process and Settler Colonial Policy Making in Finland." *Human Rights Review* 21 (2020) 293–312. https://doi.org/10.1007/s12142-020-00594-x.

Kyllingstad, Jon R. *Rase: En Vitenskapshistorie.* Oslo: Cappelen Damm, 2023.
Lightfoot, Sheryl. *Global Indigenous Politics: A Subtle Revolution.* New York, NY.: Routledge, 2016. https://doi.org/https://doi.org/10.4324/9781315670669.
———. "Truth and Reconciliation Commission of Canada: An Invitation to Boldness." In *Trading Justice for Peace? Reframing Reconciliation in TRC Processes in South Africa, Canada and Northern Ireland*, edited by Olga Ulturgasheva et al., 141–53. Cape Town: AOSIS, 2021.
Lingaas, Carola. "Hate Speech and Racialised Discrimination of the Norwegian Sámi: Legal Responses and Responsibility." *Oslo Law Review* 8 (2021) 88–107. https://doi.org/10.18261/issn.2387-3299-2021-02-02.
Llewellyn, Jennifer. J., and Daniel Philpott. "Introduction." In *Restorative Justice, Reconciliation, and Peacebuilding: Studies in Strategic Peacebuilding*, edited by Jennifer J. Llewellyn and Daniel Philpott, 1–12. New York: Oxford University Press, 2014.
Minde, Henry. "Assimilation of the Sami—Implementation and Consequences." *Acta Borealia* 20 (2003) 121–46. https://doi.org/10.1080/08003830310002877.
Nergård, Jens-Ivar. *Det Skjulte Nord-Norge.* Oslo: Ad notam Gyldendal, 1994.
Norges insititusjon for menneskerettigheter. *Holdninger Til Samer Og Nasjonale Minoriteter I Norge.* (nhri.no: 2022). https://www.nhri.no/wp-content/uploads/2022/08/NIM-R-2022-006-web.pdf.
Nordquist, Kjell Å. *Reconciliation as Politics: A Concept and Its Practice.* Eugene, OR: Pickwick Publications, 2017.
Robinson, Leah. *Embodied Peacebuilding: Reconciliation as Practical Theology.* Bern: Lang, 2015.
Public TRC Meeting in Ájluokta/Drag, 30 June 2021. (2021).
Public TRC Meeting in Bådåddjo/Bodø, 10 June 2020. (2020).
Public TRC Meeting in Guovdageaidnu/Kautokeino, 12 October 2021. (2021).
Public TRC Meeting in Kárášjohka/Karasjok, 13 October 2021. (2021).
Public TRC Meeting in Leavdnja/Lemmijoki/Lakselv, 20 August 2020. (2020).
Public TRC Meeting in Loabák/Lavangen, 22 September 2021. (2021).
Public TRC Meeting in Maajehjaevrie/Majavatn, 27 August 2021. (2021).
Public TRC Meeting in Mearohke/Meråker, 9 November 2020. (2020).
Public TRC Meeting in Måefie/Mo i Rana, 17 September 2020. (2020).
Public TRC Meeting in Málatvuopmi/Målselv, 23 September 2021. (2021).
Public TRC Meeting in Oslo, 22 November 2019. (2019).
Public TRC Meeting in Plaassja/Røros, 11 March 2020. (2020).
Public TRC Meeting in Deatnu/Tana, 2 June 2021. (2021).
Public TRC Meeting in Dielddanuorri/Tjeldsund, 22 October 2020. (2020).
Public TRC Meeting in Romsa/Tromssa/Tromsø, 3 December 2020. (2020).
Public TRC Meeting in Tråante/Trondheim, 25 January 2020. (2020).
Robinson, Leah. *Embodied Peacebuilding: Reconciliation as Practical Theology.* Bern: Peter Lang, 2015.
Romero-Amaya, Daniela. "Historical Narratives and Civic Subjectification in the Aftermath of Conflict." In *Historical Justice and History Education*, edited by Matilda Keynes et al., 107–29. Cham: Springer International, 2021.
Sannhets- og forsoningskommisjonen, *Sannhet og forsoning- grunnlag for et oppgjør med fornorskningspolitikk og urett mot samer, kvener/norskfinner og skogfinner. Rapport til Stortinger fra Sannhets- og forsoningskommisjonen,* 2023. https://www.

stortinget.no/globalassets/pdf/sannhets—og-forsoningskommisjonen/rapport-til-stortinget-fra-sannhets—og-forsoningskommisjonen.pdf/.

Sanningskommissionen för det samiska folket, "Kommissionens ledamöter och sekretariat." Sanningskommissionen för det samiska folket, accessed 06.09.2023, https://sanningskommissionensamer.se/om-kommisionen/kommissionens-medlemmar/.

Skaar, Elin. "When Truth Commission Models Travel: Explaining the Norwegian Case." *International Journal of Transitional Justice* 17 (2023) 123–40. https://doi.org/10.1093/ijtj/ijac027.

Spencer, Liz, et al. "Analysis: Principles and Processes." In *Qualitative Research Practice: A Guide for Social Science Students and Researchers*, edited by Jane Ritchie et al., 269–93. Los Angeles, London, New Delhi, Singapore and Washington, DC: Sage, 2014.

"Innst. 408 S (2017–2018): "Innstilling Fra Stortingets Presidentskap Om Mandat for Og Sammensetning Av Kommisjonen Som Skal Granske Fornorskingspolitikk Og Urett Overfor Samer, Kvener Og Norskfinner." https://www.stortinget.no/no/Saker-og-publikasjoner/Publikasjoner/Innstillinger/Stortinget/2017–2018/inns-201718-408s/#m9/.

Utsi, Johan A., and Anders B. Verstad. "Mann Dømt for Hatefulle Ytringer:—Han Kalte Dette for Klovnedrakt." *NRK Sápmi* (nrk.no), 15.05.2019, 2019. https://www.nrk.no/sapmi/mann-domt-for-hatefulle-ytringer_-_-han-kalte-dette-for-klovnedrakt-1.14563099/.

Wolfe, Patrick. *Settler Colonialism and the Transformation of Anthropology: The Politics and Poetics of an Ethnographic Event*. London: Cassell, 1999.

Ytringsfrihetskommisjonen. *Nou 2022: 9 En Åpen Og Opplyst Offentlig Samtale—Ytringsfrihetskommisjonens Utredning*. Oslo: DepMedia, 2022.

11

Narrative as Interlocutor of Identity and Reconciliation

JOHN KLAASEN

Faculty of Theology and Religion, University of the Free State, South Africa;
Faculty of Theology and Social Sciences,
VID Specialized University, Oslo, Norway

INTRODUCTION

"Who are we?" remains a decisive question within processes of truth and reconciliation. This question engenders several interconnected issues that can either impede or promote reconciliation. The fundamental issue that arises from the question is about identity. Truth and reconciliation processes are typically initiated in response to various forms of suppression or oppression, which, at their core, violate individuals' fundamental human rights, including their inherent right to maintain and express their social, cultural, political, or religious identities.

During oppressive and suppressive acts, people are coerced into conforming to and adopting foreign cultural practices, social acts, symbols, languages, traditions, histories, and authorities. These foreign practices lead to alienation, assimilation, domination, and marginalization.

The successful Truth and Reconciliation Commission (TRC) in South Africa is a prime example of a process that highlighted the loss of identity inflicted by institutional racism. The commission brought to light the systematic segregation of people based on categories, with the privileged group placed above the rest of the population.

Identity is a complex phenomenon with many layers. The geography of origin, residence, family history, tradition, cultural practices, language, and symbols are some of the phenomena that constitute identity. There is also the complexity of the different identities such as individual, group, national, and international identities that exist within constant tension of each other. In the Norwegian context, the Norwegianization policy implemented a cohesive nationalization strategy that effectively detached the Kven and Sámi communities from their ancestral identities. Similarly, in Canada, residential schools enforced policies that forcibly cast Indigenous peoples as inferior to the rest of the Canadian society.

Commissions such as the South African TRC applied a restorative justice model that looks at the individual beyond the deed that was committed. Narratives were used to give voice to individual experiences, and the commission's focus transcended the individual person. The pain caused and suffered was the central focus for restorative justice, national reconciliation, and unity. The interest of this contribution lies with the role that narratives played in the identity of the fragmented and divided nation. The division that the TRC had to deal with was based on systemic racist policies that were executed through unimaginable brutality, violence, psychological breakdown, and deprivation.

Individual stories were listened to, broadcasted on radio and television, translated, documented, analyzed, and interpreted by both the commissioners, researchers, the media, and a large portion of the South African society. Individual stories are one of the single most important factors that formed part of the reconciliation process. When racism is a systemic and structural social and political phenomenon that deprives certain groups of their identity, what effect can individual stories have on the dismantling of such a widespread oppressive and suppressive system and the construction of reconciliation and national unity?

THE BACKGROUND OF THE TRC

The dimensions of the TRC can be summarized in four interrelated aspects.[1] Firstly, the TRC was a legal instrument aimed at facilitating constitutional democracy. The structure of the hearings followed a specific format, including swearing in, taking of statements, cross-examination, and determining the truth. While the commission's primary task was to listen to gross human rights violations occurring from March 1960 to December 1993, its limited duration prevented it from listening to lesser abuses, such as those related to pass laws.[2]

Secondly, the TRC was political. The legal aspect of the TRC was positioned within a broader political context, representing the transition from a racially based system to a democratic society. Political reconciliation was the undergirding value of the process, committee members, government authorities, and main political parties.

Thirdly, the TRC had a robust theological element, notably reflected in the chairperson[3] leading the commission. The frequent appearance of clerical attire during hearings, coupled with deliberate religious practices such as prayers, retreats, and religious symbols, are visible signs of explicit religious conduct and actions during, before, and after the hearings.

Fourthly, the TRC was a public investigative and media event that connected perpetrators and victims, past and present, visible and invisible, friend and foe. Personal stories that were broadcasted reached remote rural areas, allowing the entire South African nation to engage in the process. The media played a crucial role in exposing brutality, suffering, pain, loss, as well as hope, opportunities, potential, and closure.

The multidimensional nature of the TRC process set it apart from other reconciliation processes, such as those in Canada, Sweden, and Norway. The four distinct dimensions made the South African process both complex and complete. Its complexity lay in the fact that it brought together diverse and historically separated groups of people, ideologies, positions, and beliefs within a confined space, all with the aim of forging national reconciliation and unity. The four dimensions—law, politics, theology, and media—brought their own contradictions and variances.

---

1. Corry and Terre Blanche, "Where Does the Blood," 6–17.

2. The Pass Laws was a system used to control the movement of Black, Indian and Colored people in South Africa, see https://www.sahistory.org.za/article/pass-laws-south-africa.

3. Archbishop Desmond Tutu.

It was complete in its openness to the retelling of the different perspectives of the experiences of both those who were victims and those who caused gross human rights violations. The goal of the TRC was not to give blanket amnesty nor to be punitive, but to seek the truth by uncovering the underlying moral causes of these acts. Nordquist rightly asserts that political reconciliation includes

> the need for an individual or group to realize that its own picture of truth, or its own view of its place in society, may not be the only relevant one for that individual, or for that group. Instead, to realize the importance of the Other also for me, or for us, who used to be in conflict, that is the first and necessary element in reconciliation.[4]

Nordquist's assertion implies that identity and related issues are central to reconciliation. The Other becomes indispensable for uncovering the truth, and subsequently, achieving restoration and unity. It is within this antagonism or perceived opposites, that the quest for restoration is expressed through enactment, retelling, and reliving personal stories. Stories provide a safe space to expose the past as a means for healing, (w)holeness, and holiness. It serves as the mechanism to see each Other for who they truly are, transcending the perceptions that acts and deeds of violation may have created. The Other becomes a necessary reflection or mirror of one's identity. This reflection or mirroring analyzes the relationship between victim and perpetrator in an interdependent movement. This movement is eschatological. The boundaries of violence and violation of rights are transcended.

The success of the TRC to keep the volatile process in creative tension can be attributed to the specific rationale and the structure of the commission. Three committees—on human rights violations, on amnesty, and on reparation and rehabilitation—embed the objective to:

> Provide for investigation and the establishment of as complete a picture as possible of the nature, causes and extent of gross violations of human rights committed during the period from 1 March 1960 to the cut-off date contemplated in the Constitution, within or outside the Republic, emanating from the conflicts of the past, and the fate or whereabouts of the victims of such violations; granting of amnesty to persons who make full disclosure of all the relevant facts relating to acts associated with

---

4. Nordquist, *Reconciliation as Politics*, 145.

a political objective committed in the course of the conflicts of the past during the said period.[5]

The three committees represent integral components of the commission's structure, each interrelated with the others. The three components link the exposition of the nature, context, and motivation of the gross human rights violations through the lenses of the perpetrator and the victim, what acts of mercy will unite persons from the different spectrums, and how best to compensate towards the healing of the victims. While these committees did possess the authority to grant reparation, they provided a safe space for the victims and perpetrators to discover Otherness as a relational phenomenon for unveiling the self.

At the core of the unveiling of the self is the telling of personal stories, as demonstrated in the following testimony of one of the victims at the TRC hearings:

> Ms Gobodo-Madikizela: Baba is going to present us what he says is the work of the man who came to be known as the Rambo of the Peninsula . . . Could you please tell us, Baba, what happened on that day of this incident, could you please explain to us.
>
> Mr Sekwepere: . . . I heard we are now being attacked. I ran. Now that place was between Crossroads and KTC. While we were still there, a van approached—it was a white van and it was driven by Barnard. When he had just passed, he asked us all to disperse within five minutes. Now the communities asked, 'How can you ask us to disperse, because this is just a small meeting?'—we were just 20 to 25.
>
> . . . The white man said this in Afrikaans—'You are going to get eventuality what you are looking for. And I am going to shoot you'. 'I was shocked at what this white man said to me. He said in Afrikaans, 'Ek gaan jou kry'. . . . But during that time shootings were going on. . . . I felt somebody stepping on my right shoulder. And saying 'I thought this dog has died already'.
>
> . . .Ms Gobodo-Madikizela: Baba, do you have any bullets in you as we speak?
>
> Mr Sekwepere: Yes, there are several of them. Some are here in my neck. Now on my face you can really see them, but my face

---

5. Republic of South Africa, Promotion of National Unity and Reconciliation ACT, No. 34 of 1995.

feels quite rough, it feels like rough salt. I usually have terrible headaches.

Ms Bobodo-Madikizela: Thank you, Baba.

Mr Sekwepere: Yes, usually I have a fat body, but after that I lost all my body, now I am thin, as you can see me now.

Ms Gobodo-Madikizela: How do you feel, Baba, about coming here to tell us your story?

Mr Sekwepere: I feel what—what has brought my sight back, my eyesight back is to come back here and tell my story. But I feel what has been making me sick all the time is the fact I couldn't tell my story. But now I—it feels like I got my sight back by coming here and telling my story.[6]

Mr. Sekwepere did not seek to replace his identity; rather, he sought to make sense of it amidst the pain and suffering inflicted by a systemic, violent institution. It is the space and time to tell his story that unmasked the identity that he had lost, both physically and emotionally, at the hands of the white policeman. The process of assembling a truthful and personal account of events provided the moment of meaning-making.

This process finds support in Joy's recollection of the narratives of three women who discovered their identities after experiencing incest. Joy claims that Ricoeur challenges identity as a timeless abstract phenomenon. Instead of modernity's abstract individualism, a person is in a state of flux and develops while still remaining constant. Narrative provides that duality in which different plots *(mythos)* of a person's life are constructed in specific contexts. Through this process, individuals construct a coherent and cohesive story that imparts meaning to their identity without becoming the author of their own lives. Within this duality, there are aspects of identity that are objective *(idem)* and others that are existential *(ipse)*.[7]

TRC processes, such as the one that took place in South Africa, are multilayered and encompass so much more than objective facts that can be retrieved through instrumental reasoning. The multiplicity requires a multidimensional approach that goes beyond what is immediately evident and accessible through abstract reasoning. Narratives serve as a

---

6. Krog, *Country of My Skull*, 30–31.
7. Morny, *Paul Ricoeur*, xxix.

valuable source of knowledge capable of constructing an account of the past. Narratives, like the one of Mr. Sekwepere, construct a lived reality that reveals insights that elude abstract rationality.

Mr. Sekwepere's retelling of his experience through a story weaves together both emotions and reason, involving a process that engages both logic and imagination. The reconstruction of the events of that fateful day is presented from the perspective of the victim and forms the basis of the truth upon which his identity is built. The events of that day altered both the physical and emotional identity of Mr. Sekwepere, and the act of retelling the story provided him with the opportunity, knowledge, and tools necessary to face his identity.

NARRATIVE AND TRUTH-TELLING

In 1997, the TRC convened a special hearing conducted by the Human Rights Violation Committee. During this hearing, Oboe recalled women's experiences of violence and suffering under the apartheid regime. The opening words of the hearing, delivered by oral artist Gcina Mhlope, vividly illustrate the central role that narratives would later play in national reconciliation, unity, and the transition to democracy. Oboe quotes Mhlope: "Watch my eyes, hear my voice, I tell you true," asserting that this statement encapsulates the idea of merging "body, voice and truth-telling, or the idea of story as public testimony grounded in the flesh."[8]

Storytelling is a common and essential part of the African worldview, and at the TRC, it emerged as the most pertinent and relevant means of uncovering the truth. From the perspective of the victims, storytelling held particular importance due to the traditional forms of communication among the oppressed people of South Africa.

Oral history carried more weight than written tales about experiences. Written texts were limited to English and required interpretation, which lacked the familiar symbols, rituals, and forms of expression that the victims intended to convey. In contrast, oral presentations featured familiar expressions and meanings that represented the victims' intended and authoritative messages above all else. Oral testimony is also not only limited to the individual experience but contributes to a common

---

8. Oboe, "The TRC," 60–76.

memory. The symbols, expressions, rituals, idioms, and gestures are identifiable by groups, societies, and even nations.[9]

Both victims and perpetrators' oral stories represented a common history, common communities, common experience, and common memory. The testimony of a perpetrator of gross human rights violations, Jeffrey Benzien, was later quoted by a commissioner, Dumisa Ntsebeza, who recalls:

> Even a Benzien was able to say, 'I asked myself continually what sort of a person I am.' And that does not come easily from the lips of a person who for years and years was brought up to believe that he belongs to a super race and what he was fighting for was sanctified by the Bible... Benzien came to symbolize to a lot of people that there is hope.[10]

Narrative is broadly defined as "a way of presenting or understanding a situation or series of events that reflects and promotes a particular point of view or set of values."[11] Within the social science narrative, it is "defined as a story that includes characters engaged in emplotted events to project some sort of future condition (Polletta et al. 2011). Narratives are structures of meaning used by social actors to make sense of their worlds (Polkinghorne 1988)."[12]

These definitions of narrative position the individual at the heart of the meaning-making process in a manner distinct from the prevalent Western, modern paradigm, where the rational, absolute, and independent individual employs reason to construct meaning. In contrast to reason serving as the sole determinant of identity, narrative encompasses elements such as tradition, symbol, imagination, and community for sense and sensibility. The past is important for the present, and the future can be determined by the recalling of the past.

Symbols and signs are connecting points of the visible and invisible, the physical and imaginable, the reality and lived reality, and the actual and potential. Symbols and signs represent both what is and what ought to be. Viewed through the lens of the heart, the actual, physical, and lived experience becomes the tangible whole that makes aspirations and visions concrete. Symbols represent in a concrete manner the desired

---

9. Wüstenberg, *The Political Dimension*, 87.
10. Wüstenberg, *The Political Dimension*, 87.
11. Merriam Webster Online Dictionary, "Narrative."
12. Barcelos and Gubrium. "Reproducing Stories," 466–81.

future. Witnessing the hearing at Paarl Town Hall, Wüstenberg makes the following observations about symbols: The city hall, once reserved exclusively for whites, was now decorated, and the victims of abuse were strategically positioned to occupy the central focus. The symbolic significance is that the once prohibited space now became the place of the victims. The people were ushered by the police. The significance of this kind of entrance dispels the brutality of the police and replaces it with service (servanthood) to protect those who were labeled outcasts. The victims were positioned at the elevated table of the commissioners so that the audience had to look up to the once downtrodden and marginalized. The horseshoe shape of the table symbolized togetherness and openness to one another's stories. The stories were told in the language of the storyteller with translations in different languages. This symbolized both the originality of the storyteller and the equality of the rest of the audience and the vision of a democracy.[13]

Narratives are also functional and perform a variety of roles within the scope of meaning-making.

> Narratives have various functions, such as to construct individual and group identities, encourage others to act, mobilize others for social change, and/or provide a way for individuals to make sense of an experience or engage others in that experience. They can also entertain, argue, mislead, and persuade, and are often present in the 'ruling regimes' of schools, welfare offices, workplaces, hospitals, and governments.[14]

Narrative 'makes' and 'does' identity. "That is, it creates a person's sense of self and communicates it to others in particular ways. . . . Through the work of narrative, storytellers convey meaning about how they perceive themselves to be in the world, and how they desire others to see them."[15]

These functions cannot be executed as abstract and universal, but they take place within a set of rules. These rules are not determined by the storyteller, but the storyteller is part of a community, part of a history, and part of a thought process. Within the narrative tradition, as opposed to the abstract reason tradition, the storyteller is a person within a community. In this case, the victims of human rights violations are part of a bigger narrative with Other individuals. These individuals

---

13. Wüstenberg, *The Political Dimension*, 83.
14. Barcelos and Gubrium. "Reproducing Stories," 2.
15. Barcelos and Gubrium. "Reproducing Stories," 2.

can include both those who have the same culture and background, and those who have a different culture, language, and beliefs. Narratives make it possible for persons with differences to connect beyond similarity or sameness. Persons can also discover connecting points or the blurring spaces of certain parts of histories and transcend the historical lines that divide and separate into victim and perpetrator. These blurring spaces are the interactions between different histories. Niebuhr[16] refers to such histories as internal and external history. The internal history is the known and specifics of an individual's or group's identity, while the external history refers to the bigger picture that transcends the known and specifics. Reason is not instrumental reason, but critical engagement with the experience of persons. This implies that rationality is not discarded, but that it is not limited to abstract reasoning that leaves no room for tradition or history. Instead, critically engaged reason is embedded in the experiences of the victims of gross violations of human rights.

Dullah Omar, the then Minister of Justice, refers to the initial consideration of a truth commission (TC) at a National Executive meeting while the African National Congress (ANC) was still banned. In an interview with Krog, Minister Dullah Omar recalls:

> There was strong feeling that some mechanism must be found to deal with all violations in a way which would ensure that we put our country on a sound moral basis. And so, a view developed that what South Africa needs is a mechanism which would open up the truth for public scrutiny. But to humanize our society, we had to put across the idea of moral responsibility—that is why I suggested a combination of the amnesty process with the process of victims' stories.[17]

Truth that is discovered through narrative is not only about historical facts. Within the context of the TRC, the question of "*How* and *why* the events happened," is as important as *when* and *where* the events happened. History meets morality. A fundamental aspect of the truth that the TRC had to uncover was teleological. The goal of uncovering the truth was to bring about change. The stories of the victims had to be seen within the metanarrative of apartheid.

Wüstenberg distinguishes between two facets of truth within social reconciliation: "factual truth" and "healing truth." The former

---

16. Niebuhr, *The Responsible Self*.
17. Krog, *Country of My Skull*, 5.

pertains to the period from 1960 to 1994, during which the National Party (NP) ruled South Africa under apartheid, and which encompasses the era of gross human rights violations examined by the TRC. These facts were determined through investigations and research. "Healing truth," on the other hand, was about the testimonies of political parties, state institutions, religious institutions, communities, and individual stories.[18] These testimonies and statements provide the lenses for reconciliation and national unity.

The TRC was not established to bring about reconciliation and national unity. Its mandate was to provide the necessary truth that would facilitate healing, reconciliation, and unity. In the final report,[19] truth is categorized as "forensic truth," "narrative truth," "social or dialogue truth," and "healing or restorative truth." These four kinds of truth are evidence of the dual goal of remembering and healing.

IDENTITY AS THE CATALYST FOR RECONCILIATION

The TRC had about 2,000 hearings in different parts of South Africa that included urban, rural, traditional, and modern communities. The hearings were attended by commissioners, the media, victims, perpetrators, families, and the general public. It also had the virtual participation of the general public via radio or television. Approximately 21,400 people appeared before the commission. At the time, this amount was about 0.05 percent of the population.[20][21]

Individual stories revolved around individuals grappling with the loss of their identities, a circumstance applicable to both victims and perpetrators. The act of storytelling marked the beginning of the healing process. While these narratives may not have immediately led to reconciliation and unity, they served as a catalyst for nurturing both reconciliation and national unity. The retelling of these narratives helped establish a sense of "who we are" and "who we ought to be." This dual inquiry encompasses the two-fold truth inherent in both the scientific and historical facts surrounding the metanarrative representing gross human

---

18. Wüstenberg, *The Political Dimension*, 98–99.

19. The final report of the Truth and Reconciliation Commission of South Africa (1998).

20. Andrews, *Shaping History*, 155.

21. Klaasen, "Narrative and Truth," 160.

rights violations and the loss of identity experienced by both victims and perpetrators. The narrative provides healing truth that calls people to take responsibility for change.

According to Ganzevoort, narrative consists of four interconnected components: the storyteller, the story, the audience, and a purpose.[22] The author holds a significant position in both their physical placement (on the podium, visible to the entire audience) and their role as the storyteller. The storyteller also wields control over the narrative's direction, determining what is revealed and how it is presented. However, the storyteller does not always have control over the symbols, rituals, setting of the scene, language, signs, and images that are part of the metanarrative.

In the case of Mr. Sekwepere, he recounted his story in his own language, employing metaphors such as 'sight,' 'rough salt,' 'dog,' 'white,' 'Rambo,' 'Afrikaans,' and 'fat body.' These symbols and signs provide us with insights into Mr. Sekwepere's identity. 'Rough salt,' 'dog,' and 'fat body' depict how he felt during and after the incident, symbolizing his sense of insignificance in comparison to the broader society and the freedom and power he experienced with those advocating for justice and equality. 'Sight' is a powerful symbol, representing a transformation from captivity to freedom and signifying the transition from anger, resentment, regret, loss, and defeat to healing, control, and dignity.

Mr. Sekwepere opens the opportunity for reconciliation when he puts together the story by emplotment. The entire story is constructed by the storyteller (author) by linking the episodes into a coherent whole. This process involves pauses that allow for interaction, such as when commissioners ask questions, and it considers the impact of the audience's responses, whether they are tears or expressions of astonishment. Additionally, the roles assigned to other individuals, including the perpetrator, and the content being narrated collectively shape the story. This story portrays loyalty to a racist and oppressive system that perpetrated cruel acts of violence. It includes elements such as stepping on the shoulder, gunfire, insults, and death threats as some of the plots integral to Mr. Sekwepere's narrative.

The audience comprises a diverse group of individuals, including the counselors, family members, friends, and those who were affected by Mr. Sekwepere's story. These individuals constitute the primary audience, having been directly impacted by the order of events narrated. The

---

22. Ganzevoort, "Religious Coping," 2.

secondary audience consists of those who are not physically present or do not actively participate but engage with the narrative through imagination. In other words, they are the people watching on television, or listening on the radio, and the crowds during the event. "It is also important that the distant listeners understand his story so that there is space for his story in the plurality of stories that form the storyscape."[23]

The fourth part of the narrative is the purpose or goal of storytelling, i.e., the significance of telling the story. Ganzevoort used the reference "significance" instead of "meaning" to avoid the misinterpretation of the story by different translators or listeners. Significance has a direct bearing on the *telos*. This approach places the direction of the story on the storyteller and moves the storyteller to the center from the margins. This positioning of the storyteller, Mr. Sekwepere, contributes to the successful influence of the former to impact the audience. Ganzevoort claims that,

> Given the weight of the audience, the author tries to convince his or her public of the legitimacy and plausibility of the narrative construction. The aim of this is that every author (i.e. every human being) is consequently seeking to be accepted, affirmed and loved. For that reason, the actors in the story play their role according to how the author wishes to be seen by the audience.[24]

Mr. Sekwepere tells his story to find the truth and ultimately to be healed. For him, healing means finding an identity. His new identity is a sign of his willingness to deal with the memory of the past in order to construct a new future. In defining 'recollection,' Freeman explains:

> The 're' refers to the past, 'collection' refers to the present act, and act . . . of gathering together what might have been dispersed or lost. Framed another way, the word recollection holds within it a reference to the two distinct ways we often speak about history: as the trail of past events or 'past presents' that have culminated in now and as the act of writing, the act of gathering them together, selectively and imaginatively, into a followable story.[25]

Mr. Sekwepere uses symbolic language such as "Afrikaans" and "white" to identify the Other. Within the construction of identity, the Other is mirroring or reflecting the experience of Mr. Sekwepere. The Other, the perpetrator, is part of the recollection and gathering of information to

23. Klaasen, "Narrative and Truth," 157–68.
24. Ganzevoort, "Religious Coping," 276–86.
25. Ganzevoort, "Religious Coping," 276–86.

construct a story for the purpose of identity. Identity is a precondition for reconciliation. In a recent interview on SABC[26] news, the nephew of an anti-apartheid activist applauded the decision by the National Prosecution Authority of South Africa to reopen the sixty-four cases of gross human rights violations that were referred to by the TRC. In the interview, the family member of the victim made a passionate call for the disclosure of information that identifies the perpetrators of those who committed these atrocities, so that the family members of the victims can find closure.[27]

CONCLUDING REMARKS

The TRC's narrative approach placed the victims at the center of the process, and their positioning influenced the truths and ultimately the future. The identity of the victims, as portrayed through the recollection of the past, became the determining factor in the decisions of the commission. The final report clearly gave preference to the knowledge compiled through the oral and written narratives. Borraine, who served as the Deputy Chairperson of the commission, recalls: "The generosity of spirit by the majority of the victims/survivors was one of the remarkable experiences of those of us who sat on the Commission, and this feeling spilled over into the wider community."[28]

Narrative knowledge contributed to perpetrators acknowledging human rights violations. Within the narrative setting, actors were assigned roles by the storyteller, including perpetrators who became entangled in knowledge production and the acknowledgment of facts and information that could corroborate the storyteller's account. (Ac)knowledgment through storytelling contributes to moral truth and fosters a moral climate that compels the acceptance of wrongdoing and the violations of the dignity and identity of those at the margins.[29] Narrative transforms the broken, disfigured, misconstructed, and coercive identity into a personal identity that embraces the Other as meaningful for a mature identity. The Other forms part of a community of reciprocal and mutually enriching encounters, from strangers to independent persons.

26. SABC stands for South African Broadcasting Corporation.
27. SABC, "NPA to Investigate."
28. Boraine, "Truth and Reconciliation."
29. Sachs, "His Name," 296.

Narrative unfolds closed and factual history. Notwithstanding the scientific knowledge that external history contributes to information, the interpretation of this knowledge and the discovery of its moral truths are most effectively achieved through the storytelling of those who have been directly affected. What significance does this knowledge hold for the individual sharing their experience during the hearings? How do they choose to convey it, and what impact does it have on them? Furthermore, how can this knowledge drive change? These are some of the insights that a narrative approach to knowledge brings to the processes of reconciliation and unity.

BIBLIOGRAPHY

Andrews, Molly. *Shaping History: Narratives of Political Change.* Cambridge: Cambridge University Press, 2007.

Barcelos, Christine A. and Aline C. Gubrium. "Reproducing Stories: Strategic Narratives of Teen Pregnancy and Motherhood." *Social Problems* 61 (2014) 466–81.

Boraine, Alex, "Truth and Reconciliation in South Africa: The Third Way." In *Truth and Justice: The Morality of Truth Commissions,* edited by Robert I. Rotberg and Dennis Thompson, 141–57. Princeton: Princeton University Press, 2000.

Corry, Wendy, and Martin Terre Blanche. "Where Does the Blood Come From: True Stories and Real Selves at the TRC Hearings." *PINS* 26 (2000) 6–17.

Freeman, M. *Rewriting the Self: History, Memory, Narrative.* London: Routledge, 1993.

Ganzevoort, Ruard R. "Religious Coping Considered, Part Two: A Narrative Reformulation." *Journal of Psychology and Theology* 26 (1998) 276–86.

Klaasen, John. "Narrative and Truth and Reconciliation." In *Trading Justice for Peace: Reframing Reconciliation in TRC Processes in South Africa, Canada and Nordic Countries,* edited by Demaine Solomons et al., 157–68. Durbanville: AOSIS, 2022.

Krog, Antjie. *Country of My Skull.* Johannesburg: Random House, 1998.

Merriam Webster Online Dictionary. "Narrative." https://www.merriam-webster.com/dictionary/.

Morny, Joy, ed. *Paul Ricoeur and Narrative.* Calgary: University of Calgary Press, 1997.

Niebuhr, Richard. *The Responsible Self.* London: Macmillan, 1941.

Nordquist, Kjell-Ake. *Reconciliation as Politics: A Concept and its Practice.* Oregon: Pickwick Publications, 2009.

Oboe, Annalisa. "The TRC Women's Hearings as Performance and Protest in the New South Africa." *Research in African Literatures* 38 (2007) 60–76.

Republic of South Africa. "Promotion of National Unity and Reconciliation ACT, No. 34 of 1995." https://www.gov.za/documents/promotion-national-unity-and-reconciliation-act.

Sachs, Albie. "His Name Was Henry." In *After the TRC: Reflections on Truth and Reconciliation in South Africa,* edited by Wilmot James and Linda van de Vijver. Cape Town: David Philip, 2000.

South African Broadcasting Corporation (SABC). "NPA to Investigate 64 Apartheid-era Cases Emanating from TRC." *SABC,* January 15, 2023.

Truth and Reconciliation Commission. "The final report of the Truth and Reconciliation Commission of South Africa," 1998. https://www.justice.gov.za/trc/report/

Wüstenberg, Ralf. *The Political Dimension of Reconciliation: A Theological Analysis of Ways of Dealing with Guilt During the Transition to Democracy in South Africa and (East) Germany.* Cambridge: Eerdmans, 2009.

12

Remembering
A Pathway to Unburden Our Present?

BONITA BENNETT

District Six Museum, Cape Town, South Africa

INTRODUCTION

High dwellings are the peace and harmony of our descendants. Remember the calamity of the great tsunamis. Do not build any homes below this point.[1]

These words are carved into a stone tablet along the coast of Aneyoshi, a village in Japan. 'Tsunami stones' are ancient stone markers. They are trans-generational warnings strategically positioned along the Japanese coastline by a previous generation who wished to pass on their collective memory of disasters to their descendants. Writing about the potential for a collective memory of the COVID-19 pandemic to aid both current and future generations in preparing for the next one, Sean Donahue draws inspiration from the Aneyoshi stone. He poses a thought-provoking question: "When the last wave of the coronavirus recedes, what kind of guide stone will exist for future generations?"[2]

---

1. Patowary, "Ancient Tsunami" (italics added).
2. Donahue, "As Collective Memory."

The global pursuit of understanding how we might learn from the past, to mitigate the impact of disasters, both natural and human-instigated, continues to occupy our minds. We have come to realize that knowing about the past and making a commitment to non-recurrence of violent atrocities, is no guarantee that they will not happen. The 'never, never again' utterance is in danger of becoming a well-worn and meaningless slogan in situations involving state-sponsored atrocities such as ethnic cleansing, genocide, and apartheid, and for those who act with impunity, outside of the law.

We need not look further than our own country, South Africa, where the words of our dearly beloved Nelson Rolihlahla Mandela, echo with a disheartening hollowness in our current context: "Never, never and never again shall it be that this beautiful land will again experience the oppression of one by another, and suffer the indignity of being the skunk of the world."[3] These words, originally spoken with genuine sincerity and profound aspiration, now resonate differently in the current context. However, the scourge of extreme poverty, unemployment, gender-based violence, endemic state and corporate corruption, and the widespread disregard by corporates for the environmental and social consequences of extractive industries have all emerged as stark indicators of ongoing oppression and exclusion.

The promises of the Constitution, and especially the Bill of Rights, have not rung true for the many individuals who struggle daily to access their rights as full citizens in this free, rights-based constitutional democracy. These include those forced to endure long queues under inhumane conditions to receive meagre poverty relief grants during the COVID-19 pandemic[4]; individuals living in fear in their homes because of intimate partner violence and a lack of legal protection; brave whistle-blowers who face threats and even assassination for exposing state capture and corruption; and communities whose drinking water has been compromised by industrial pollution. Additionally, many have lost their food security because their once-fertile lands have been depleted of nutrients, tainted with pesticides, harmed by carbon emissions, and subjected to

3. Mandela, "Inauguration Speech," 2.

4. On December 31, 2019, the World Health Organization (WHO) China country office reported a cluster of pneumonia cases in Wuhan, Hubei Province of China. On January 7, 2020, the causative pathogen was identified as a novel coronavirus (SARS-CoV-2). By March 11, 2020, 114 countries had reported nearly 120,000 cases and the WHO declared COVID-19 the first pandemic caused by a coronavirus (National Institute for Communicable Diseases, "Guidelines for Case-Finding").

other chemical interventions. While these oppressions may not always be direct outcomes of specific legal statutes, they are experienced as consequences of an uncaring and incompetent state, as well as a relentless pursuit by individuals and cabals to secure and protect unwarranted privileges and power.

In this chapter, I will address some of these issues using the lens of memory. I will explore the role of memory as a tool for raising awareness of the past and its impact on our present, particularly in the aftermath of national trauma. Furthermore, I will reflect on the role that memory has played as part of the country's restorative justice regimen, and as a crucial component of the Truth and Reconciliation Commission (TRC).[5] The latter created a supportive yet challenging public platform where individuals' stories became an integral part of public memory, allowing some to piece together fragments of the untold stories of their lost loved ones and filling gaps in their own recollections, ultimately offering a degree of closure. Beyond its collective and public facets, memory also possesses an intensely personal dimension. I will contemplate the potential for healing and recovery that memory affords, always mindful of its inherent limitations and what it can realistically achieve.

In the context of reflecting on the role that personal, collective, and public memory can play in the journey towards reconciliation, I will examine the profound impact of land dispossession during the eras of colonialism and apartheid. Additionally, I will assess the possibilities for achieving a measure of social cohesion through land restitution and the valorizing of the memory of land dispossession, particularly as far as it still exists in living memory. Even though the new regime has in its restitution arsenal an array of tools, which include the Restitution of Land Rights Act (RLRA), Regional Land Claims Commissioners, and Land Courts, matters relating to land reform, land development, and ownership remain fraught with difficulty and unresolved.

Fay and James[6] write: "Legacies of dispossession persist: loss of land is not a onetime event, but an ongoing process that continues to shape the life chances of those affected and their descendants." Embedded, I argue, in our personal and collective memories.

---

5. The Truth and Reconciliation Commission (TRC) in South Africa was established by the Promotion of National Unity and Reconciliation Act, No.4 of 1995.

6. Fay and James, "Giving Land Back," 32.

THE PROMISE OF MEMORY

It is sometimes suggested that a new order cannot be served by dwelling on a painful past. The problem is that there is no zero hour for starting anew. History lives on, shapes the present, and will threaten the future. Unspoken memory cries out to be heard. It needs to be dealt with, not only to uncover the truth about the past, but also as a way of dealing with the future.[7]

In the pursuit of a just and dignified future on a national scale, memory emerges as a potent instrument. For numerous displaced individuals, it often stands as the sole tether linking them to the land from which they were uprooted, fostering a deep connection even in the absence of a formal title deed.

Approaching the act of sharing memories requires recognizing its inherent value, one that transcends the mere recounting of historical events along a linear temporal plane. There are several inner processes of sense-making and recovery that take place in the individual engaged in active remembering. During this process, they scour their minds to retrieve specific details of past actions and reawaken the feelings associated with those actions, which may be joyful or traumatic. Often, individuals selectively omit experiences that elicit shame or prove difficult to articulate. Instead, they prioritize memories that hold significance in the given moment, whether it pertains to recalling specifics to support a land claim, constructing a comprehensive family narrative to preserve the family's history and legacy, or simply providing an outlet for narratives that were previously suppressed. In the wake of the truth-telling context provided by the TRC, acts of remembering gained prevalence and validity.

Thinking of memory as a fluid and malleable process, rather than as a finished product, helps to illuminate its true nature. Maurice Halbwachs[8] refers to all thoughts, events, and experiences as leaving some form of residual trace within the mind as they merge into the realm of memory. At times, these imprints are distinctly clear and detailed, while at other moments, they may manifest as vague recollections that become more defined through various memory triggers. These triggers can include interactions with people, visits to specific places, exposure to particular smells, sights, or sounds, as well as the act of viewing photographs or reading documents.

7. Villa-Vicencio, "Reconciliation," 7.
8. Halbwachs, *The Collective Memory*.

Scholarship about the humanizing role that memory work can play in countries emerging from state-led violence has grown substantially over the last while.[9] Beyond what the TRC has been able to achieve in South Africa in terms of supporting truth-telling in public, several memory initiatives have emerged in the period following the end of apartheid. These initiatives grew out of the recognition that a range of opportunities and platforms were needed for people to deal with their own traumatic memories. This is crucial in our national journey of healing and restoration. Among these are organizations such as the Institute for the Healing of Memories, the Institute for Justice and Reconciliation, *Khulumani*,[10] and the District Six Museum, as just some examples.

Numerous individuals opt not to, or find themselves unable to, discuss experiences in which their dignity and humanity were gravely violated. For instance, they might have been subjected to degrading racial classification tests to comply with the race-based Population Registration Act of 1950. Others may have been forced to flee their homes as bulldozers approached, threatening to reduce everything to rubble. Some have had to painstakingly search through debris to salvage remnants of their lost homes. For many, the indescribable loss of home remains beyond words, and they may never attain the capacity to articulate it, as Ben Okri describes in *Birds of Heaven*: "When we have made an experience or a chaos into a story, we have transformed it, made sense of it, transmuted it, domesticated the chaos."[11] They might never have tamed their internal mental chaos sufficiently to craft a coherent narrative. "There may be no words to make sense of the moments and fragments that surface in dreams and nightmares which are experienced not only in the dark recesses of the night, but also in flashes of light in the day."[12]

While museums diligently focus on preserving archives and narrating stories, an important question arises: How can we effectively capture the meaningful silences that shroud the pain of loss? Karen Till[13] introduces the concept of a "place-based ethics of care" that is needed in wounded cities. By this she means engagements with physical landscapes as markers that can evoke memories of pain and loss in ways that are not

---

9. See Casey, *Remembering*; Grunebaum, "Spectres of the Untold"; Till, "Waiting for the City"; Till, "Wounded Cities"; Whigham, "Constructing Prevention."

10. *Khulumani* means 'speak out' in Zulu.

11. Okri, *Birds of Heaven*.

12. O'Connell, *Impossible Return*, 31–32.

13. Till, "Waiting for the City," 4.

always verbal. They can be ritualistic and performative, such as traversing the contours of a battered landscape; acknowledging (whether through acceptance or contestation) that the past has been layered over and something else now exists in its place; or engaging in some other expressive way where no words are needed or expected.

Art has also been used to great effect in working with memory in organizations such as the District Six Museum in Cape Town. Mapping, mural-making, inscription, and performance, form part of their memory strategies and have been embraced by many for whom the experiences of displacement have not been easy to verbalize. In instances such as these, the intention is to provide scaffolding to the individuals who need it to rebuild their own sense of self, rather than to build an archive of recorded oral histories.

THE PROMISE OF HEALING, JUSTICE, AND RECONCILIATION

In the euphoria created by the birth of the 'new' South Africa,[14] there seems to have been great haste to move on to the next celebratory step after the first free and democratic elections took place in 1994. To this day, many untold realities remain hidden, unhealed, and festering, hindering the process of engaging with full dignity, which includes self-belief, agency, and hope.

Healing is a complex and multilayered process, one that may, in some respects, never be complete. Telling stories of past traumas in a safe, non-judgmental space, is but one of many healing tools. Thandi Shezi, testifying at the TRC about her experience of being arrested, tortured, and gang-raped by apartheid police, says: "But of course, I needed more than talking to feel whole again."[15] It was the first time that she spoke of this ordeal, ten years after it had happened. She acknowledged that her experience at the TRC had helped her to confront her past trauma, but it was not enough. A sense of justice, a dignified life, and experiencing some form of restitution are equally critical.

---

14. South Africans regard the start of the 'new' South Africa as being April 27, 1994—the day of the country's first democratic elections.

15. Dube, "Story of Thandi Shezi," 129.

Justice is central to achieving reconciliation. Charles Villa-Vicencio[16] believes that it is not reasonable to ask victims and survivors of human rights abuses to be reconciliatory in the absence of justice. He refers to the need for "the building of civic trust, the promotion of a human rights culture and the pursuit of economic transformation" as being essential parts of this package. This draws attention to Thandi Shezi's sentiments that she needed more than the telling of her story so that she could feel whole again.

In celebrating the achievements of the TRC in creating spaces for breaking silences, and for the valuing of people's experiences, there have been occasions when too much emphasis was placed on the healing impact of personal narrative and truth-telling, and too little attention paid to the other components to achieve deeper healing. Adequate resources were not made available to improve people's life circumstances in substantial and sustainable ways. This is even more disturbing given our current awareness of the cost of state capture[17] and government corruption, issues that have been so shockingly foregrounded in the South African public eye. An estimate of 500 billion ZAR[18] has reportedly been looted from state coffers, while "6.5 million South Africans go hungry every day."[19] This alone impacts on the above three conditions specified by Villa-Vicencio: there has been a substantial breakdown in *civic trust*, in the *culture of human rights*, and *economic transformation* has not taken place except in the case of a small group of black elites. This can be seen as a consequence of the country's compromise on the revolutionary ideals embedded in the struggle to overcome apartheid, in favor of a negotiated settlement. Any progress made by the TRC in terms of personal and national healing has been significantly undermined by the present state of affairs in South Africa.

---

16. Villa-Vicencio, "Reconciliation," 3.

17. The Judicial Commission of Inquiry into Allegations of State Capture, Corruption and Fraud in the Public Sector including Organs of State was established in August 2018 by President Cyril Ramaphosa, after being signed into existence by former President Zuma in February of the same year. The Commission was chaired by Deputy Chief Justice Raymond Zondo and is commonly referred to as the Zondo Commission. The Commission handed over the last of its five-part final report in June 2022.

18. This amounts to approximately $2,769,195,000.00 USD.

19. Ryan, "State Capture Scorecard."

NOSTALGIA: 'THE TIME OF OUR CHILDHOOD, THE SLOWER RHYTHMS OF OUR DREAMS'[20]

Individuals who engage in reminiscing about the past are frequently criticized for romanticizing it and perceiving it through rose-tinted glasses, potentially distorting the true nature of historical events. There is, of course, always the danger that recollections might be tinged with nostalgia, with the past being idealized and hankered after.

But is nostalgia all bad? Being stuck in a perpetual state of nostalgia can be debilitating. However, I do believe that it has a necessary role to play in the need to assuage the deep pain of past loss, especially when the present and future seem uncertain. It is often a coping mechanism. Speaking about a character in his book *Love in the Time of Cholera*, Gabriel Garcia Márquez[21] writes profoundly and poetically: "He was still too young to know that the heart's memory eliminates the bad and magnifies the good, and that thanks to this artifice we manage to endure the burden of the past." In this he beautifully conveys the power—the necessity, even—of nostalgia.

Svetlana Boym defines nostalgia as "longing for a home that no longer exists or has never existed."[22] She goes on to say that nostalgia seems to be a longing for a different place but in actual fact is a longing for a time that is different from now—"the time of our childhood, the slower rhythms of our dreams."[23] Boym delineates two distinct nostalgic tendencies: reflective and restorative. *Reflective nostalgia* finds its essence in the *algia*—the longing, while the *nostos* attempts a "trans historical construction of the lost home."[24] She posits that *restorative nostalgia* addresses both the ache of temporal distance and displacement. "Distance is compensated by intimate experiences and the availability of the desired objects. Displacement is cured by a return, preferably a collective one."[25] This return can take on symbolic forms, such as engaging with a memorial landscape. Alternatively, it can manifest as a practical return within a land restitution process. In the latter case, it involves a complex interplay of documented history, remembered past,

20. Boym, *Future of Nostalgia*, 8.
21. Márquez, *Love in the Time of Cholera*, 106.
22. Boym, *Future Nostalgia*, 9.
23. Boym, *Future Nostalgia*, 8.
24. Boym, *Future Nostalgia*, 4.
25. Boym, *Future Nostalgia*, 44.

elements of nostalgia, legal frameworks, and sensitive processes that facilitate restoration and healing.

LONGING FOR A RETURN

The land question has always been at the center of the South African struggle. In some ways, land dispossession can be viewed as the 'original sin' of colonialism. It is significant that the RLRA of 1994 was one of the first laws of the new South Africa and was in place even before the Constitution of the Republic was finalized, demonstrating the commitment of the Government of National Unity to ensuring that the restoration of land rights was central to the country's restorative processes. The RLRA has as its aim:

> *To provide for the restitution of rights in land in respect of which persons or communities were dispossessed under or for the purpose of furthering the objects of any racially based discriminatory law; to establish a Commission on Restitution of Land Rights and a Land Claims Court; and to provide for matters connected therewith.*[26]

In the new South Africa inaugurated in 1994, citizens gained access to their land and heritage rights through the provisions of the RLRA. Together with other Acts promulgated in this fledgling democracy, it acknowledged the trauma of land dispossession that had been part of the country's colonial and apartheid legacy. It heralded that it was time for the language of nation-building centered around narratives of freedom, democracy, equality, and all that it implied, to triumph. The three main tenets of South Africa's land reform program are (i) restitution, (ii) redistribution, and (iii) tenure reform.[27]

District Six stands out as one of the most renowned urban areas associated with forced removals, known not only locally but also nationally and globally. However, it is important to note that there are numerous lesser-known sites of displacement from the apartheid era across South Africa. While there is no way of knowing the exact number of people who were displaced, it is estimated that well over 3.5 million people were affected between 1960 and 1982.[28] This is a conservative estimate,

---

26. Republic of South Africa, *Restitution of Land Rights Act*, 3.
27. South African Government, "Land Reform."
28. Surplus People Project, *Forced Removals*.

and Elaine Unterhalter,[29] a researcher, suggests that this total does not encompass the significant number of individuals residing in informal settlements who were repeatedly uprooted as their homes were demolished by authorities time and time again. Some researchers even propose a figure as high as 10 million.

District Six, located in Cape Town, was a culturally diverse inner-city neighborhood that was completely demolished as part of the legally sanctioned forced removals during the apartheid era. In 1966, it was declared for 'whites only' under the Group Areas Act (GAA).[30] Even though the majority of its residents were tenants and not property owners, the loss of their homes and connection to the land was no less profound. Its value as a place representing 'home' was derived over several generations by connections to significant others and by the *genius loci*[31] of the area, not by title deed or its real estate value. The RLRA takes into account that black people under apartheid were prohibited either by law or economics from owning property, so it makes allowance for claims to be made not only for property lost, but for loss of a right to land.

In an article titled "Grieving for a Lost Home: Psychological Costs of Relocation," Marc Fried writes about his research concerning the impact of urban renewal on a residential area in the West End of Boston. While any relocation can be potentially unsettling and disruptive, a forced move, one that lacks personal agency and emphasizes one's oppression, is even more profoundly distressing. He refers to feelings experienced in such situations as akin to grief, which manifest as "feelings of painful loss, the continued longing, the general depressive tone, frequent symptoms of psychological or social or somatic stress . . . the sense of helplessness, the occasional expressions of both direct and displaced anger, and tendencies to idealize the lost place."[32]

Fueled by the hope of restitution and the opportunity to reclaim the land from which they had been forcibly uprooted, numerous former residents of District Six, along with their descendants, joined forces with those from other areas of displacement. They embarked on an arduous quest to uncover documents that could substantiate their past residency. When such documents proved elusive, they sought out neighbors who

29. Unterhalter, *Forced Removal*, 3.

30. O'Malley—The Heart of Hope, "1950. The Group Areas Act."

31. In current usage it refers to the 'spirit of place,' said to have its origins in Roman mythology in which it referred to the protective spirit of a place.

32. Fried, "Grieving," 360.

could vouch for their previous residence. They diligently completed the necessary forms and attended a series of information meetings. They actively participated in events such as land handover ceremonies and groundbreaking rituals and joyously commemorated 'The Return of the Elders' alongside the first wave of returnees.

February 11, 2004, took on a new meaning for the residents of District Six when the first two returnees were handed the keys to their new homes by the then president, the late Nelson Mandela. The commemorated day had an added dimension: in addition to marking the day that District Six was declared a 'whites only' area in 1966 and Mandela's release from prison in 1990, it now also stood as a marker for the success of the restitution process. Amidst much celebration and with hundreds of people gathered in the streets, the two eldest claimants, Mr. Dan Dali Ndzabela and Mr. Ebrahim Murat, were handed the keys to their new homes. While the atmosphere was filled with joy and hope at the visible signs of progress, there was an underlying critique whispered among some attendees. Six years had passed since the deadline for lodging claims in 1998, yet only 24 houses had been constructed, with just two of them ready for handover. The meager achievement, though masked by the grand event, also exposed the limited headway made in the restitution process.[33] Although the government had envisioned the restitution of land rights as a means to contribute to the healing of the nation, the experiences of the claimants proved to be frustrating and disheartening, and some would even describe it as having been re-traumatizing.

Ruth Hall writes: "Public ceremonies around the settlement of land claims have acquired iconic status in the democratic South Africa. They have brought into the public eye images of . . . dispersed urban communities returning from the periphery to the site of their demolished homes—handshakes, speeches, singing, and dancing. This is part of a healing process. It is generally a happy but transitory moment that marks the culmination of the claiming process and the start of the work of reconstructing communities and livelihoods—and possibly signals reconciliation."[34] Unfortunately, for these returnees and others in a similar situation, the act of moving into their homes appeared to mark the conclusion of official support, when, in reality, it should have signaled the beginning of the process of rebuilding their lives and livelihoods.

33. Bennett, "Memory," 156.
34. Hall, "Land," 20.

The hope of restitution was palpable, though complicated from the start. Over time, dreams were dashed, and people became disillusioned as the reality of return became more remote: a seemingly impenetrable bureaucracy, cynicism, incompetence, and the understandable 'teething pains' associated with implementing new legislation, littered the way to restitution. The downward spiraling of the dashed restitution dream has been acutely apparent.

Another great celebratory land restitution process that has been marred by disappointment, is a rural town located approximately 200 km outside of Cape Town. The story of Elandskloof, a community located in the Cederberg area of the Western Cape, is documented in a film titled *Uitgesmyt*.[35] The film begins with one of the residents declaring, "Elandskloof is 'n restitusie plek" (*Elandskloof is a place of restitution*), referencing the fact that this small community was hailed as the first successful land restitution claim in the new South Africa, an achievement realized in 1996. Having been forcibly removed from the farmland where they had lived and supported their livelihoods in 1962 due to the GAA, they were now communal landowners able to participate in shaping its future. Hope and dreams for a better future dominated.

With great pomp and ceremony, the success of the Elandskloof land claim was celebrated on Reconciliation Day in 1996. The selection of this specific day was symbolic of the reconciliatory purpose that this accomplishment was intended to serve. The event was marked by spirited singing, exuberant dancing, and an outpouring of hope and joy. It reached its climax when the title deed to the Elandskloof Farm was officially handed over to the community by the then Minister of Land Affairs, Derek Hanekom.

By the time this film was produced in 2018, twenty-two years after the initial celebration of their successful land claim, the sense of euphoria had faded into meaninglessness for the Elandskloof community. A longstanding resident described their situation as a 'pitsweer' (a festering boil). Land expert and researcher Ben Cousins, interviewed in the film, refers to Elandskloof as a "poverty trap." Regrettably, not much had changed in the lives of the residents since the land had been handed over; in fact, their circumstances appeared to have deteriorated. Cousins pointed to

---

35. *Uitgesmyt* is the Afrikaans word for 'thrown out.' The film was produced by Siona O'Connell for the Department of Historical and Heritage Studies at the University of Pretoria in partnership with the Centre for Curating the Archive at the University of Cape Town.

the shortcomings in the long-term planning of land reform and the lack of support provided to the community for the subsequent steps. External consultants had been brought in to develop business plans, which were largely ill-suited as they lacked familiarity with the specific contextual issues faced by the community.

In a master's thesis addressing the absence of post-settlement support for the claimant community in Elandskloof, Andries Titus[36] identifies several other gaps in the process that have contributed to escalating community conflict. These include dissatisfaction about the 308 claimants who have been named as beneficiaries in The Consumer Protection Act (CPA), ongoing disputes over who the rightful claimants are, the community's perception that the government has not fulfilled its commitments to provide financial and other resources, and a lack of expertise to develop the land commercially to support the livelihoods of the beneficiaries. Additionally, the impact of climate change on the land's ability to sustain traditional crops and the challenge of limited access to water further exacerbate their disillusionment. These residents had initially anticipated significant improvements after enduring impoverishment during the 1962 removals, which saw them lose their possessions to bulldozers and witness the burning of their homes, crops, and livestock. They had hoped that the opportunity to return to the land and revive a way of life deeply rooted in their connection to the land, still vivid in living memory, would bring about positive change. However, much like the case of District Six, the restorative aspect of being reconnected to the land has been fragmented and unfulfilled.

It would appear that ceremonies that overstate achievements and underplay the challenges have had a detrimental impact rather than fostering a culture of civic trust and reconciliation. These are just two examples among many that illustrate how processes originally intended to promote healing and restorative justice have, in practice, generated environments in which the opposite has been experienced.

---

36. Titus, "A Public Participation," 18, 20.

VULNERABLE COMMUNITIES, CLIMATE CHANGE AND ENVIRONMENTAL DEGRADATION: ANOTHER CHALLENGE TO RECONCILIATION AND JUSTICE

For the first time on a global scale, we have felt the impact of living in the age of the Anthropocene,[37] the geological epoch which dates to the start of significant human impact on the earth's geology and ecosystems. Land restitution, and all other developments in South Africa, are compelled to consider how the related processes will impact on the earth's finite natural resources and how they will minimize the degrading impact on the environment. Post-settlement support provided to claimants needs to make allowance for the changed ways in which we need to live in relation to both the human and non-human world.

It is no longer speculation that climate change can exacerbate existing conflicts. At the same time, the frequency of what used to be regarded as natural disasters has increased, with clear indications that human actions continue to have adverse consequences for planetary health. Flooding, air and water pollution, earthquakes, and tornados are likely to be experienced as several times more severe in places that have already been ravaged by conflicts.

In September 2022, a mining dam wall collapsed in Jagersfontein, a mining town in the Free State province, unleashing water and mine waste. This tragic event resulted in the loss of one life and forced more than 300 residents in the small town to evacuate. "While the provincial government has described the flooding as an 'unexpected disaster', it's understood that the mine had come under scrutiny in the past for its environmental impact."[38] The owners had been warned several times that the site was unsafe.

In April 2022, the city of Durban experienced devastating floods, described as the "most catastrophic natural disaster yet recorded in KwaZulu Natal (Province) in collective terms of lives lost, homes and infrastructure damaged or destroyed, and economic impact."[39] Research has indicated that flooding in the province has doubled in the last century.

---

37. "COVID-19 is a paradigmatic example of an Anthropocene disease. It follows a complex sequence involving disruption of the natural, social, economic and governance systems" (O'Callaghan-Gordo and Anto, "COVID-19").

38. Mokhoali, "Owners of Jagersfontein."

39. Wits University, "The 2022 Durban Floods."

These are two different catastrophes, but both have had dire consequences for those directly affected. The first example is not a natural disaster but a result of corporate neglect of a facility located in a poor community. The long-term impact on the environment and on the people who had to continue living in close proximity to the sludge is not yet known. In the case of the floods, they are a consequence of changes in weather patterns. In both instances, the most vulnerable were the hardest hit—the poorest of the poor, those unlikely to have insurance for their homes and possessions, those whose earthly belongings and financial resources were likely all lost in their destroyed homes. These are the people who have been denied both access to economic resources and restorative justice.

According to the United Nations Environment Programme, the world is almost certainly heading for a temperature rise of 2.6°C by the end of this century.[40] Higher temperatures will have an impact on water available for domestic and agricultural consumption, which will affect food production and security. Overuse, climate change, and related factors have resulted in more than 90 percent of Lake Chad drying up, for example. Some direct impacts of this shrinking water source have been conflicts between the border communities in Cameroon and Chad over fishing rights, access to grazing, and water for human use.[41] It is anticipated that such conflicts will increase in different places across the globe over time. Furthermore, these conflicts are likely to be exacerbated by lingering, unaddressed pain in places like South Africa and other societies currently grappling with the process of recovery from historical trauma.

In 2018, Cape Town was faced with the possibility of 'Day Zero,' a situation in which the city's taps were expected to run dry. This crisis arose due to a combination of factors, including an outdated water management system, rising demand for water, and a shift in rainfall patterns over several years. Dam levels reached alarmingly low levels. In a city known for its artesian streams, which emerge as springs in various locations around the lower slopes of the Table Mountain range, these springs became highly sought-after sources for collecting water during this time.

The queues that formed around the taps were generally orderly, starting as early as 4 am and extending late into the night. Occasionally, remarks made in these situations provided insights into underlying tensions within different communities of Cape Town. In particular, residents

---

40. United Nations Environment Programme (2022). *Emissions Gap Report 2022*.
41. Ikubaye and Odun, *Envisioning a Transitional*, 4.

of the predominantly white leafy suburbs, where the springs offered cool mountain water, sometimes expressed irritation that people from other areas were coming to access 'their' water. 'From other areas' would be a coded way of referring to the black people present, who would remind them that they (current residents) lived in areas from which black people had been displaced. They would recall that collecting water from these streams had been part of their daily routines before they were forced to relocate to other areas by the apartheid government. There were several tense moments that were, for the most part, averted from escalating to high levels of confrontation by interventions of others present, who reminded all parties that everyone was affected by the crisis and should deal with each other empathetically. However, the underlying issues of who belongs where, who is entitled to the city's resources, together with the untransformed residential and economic demographic of the city, lurk just below the surface of daily life, emerging as discontent and conflict at different times.

CONCLUSION

While there is no way to turn back the clock on wrongs that were inflicted in the past, there have to be better and more substantially transformative ways that we can learn valuable lessons from this past. I believe that we have not yet missed that moment, but we are close to doing so.

The common adage is that those who do not remember or know the past, are condemned to repeat it.[42] Reality has shown us that this is not entirely true, and neither is its opposite—that those who remember the past are not likely to repeat it. We know a lot about the past, yet histories continue to repeat themselves. Mobilizing the past constructively is not likely to solve all of the issues that we as human beings in different parts of the globe have to confront, but there are several clues to strategies that have helped communities to survive and live coherently, despite substantial challenges. There is a planetary project that awaits us.

How might we engage with knowledge of the past differently, and honor people as knowledge-carriers which has nothing to do with levels of formal education? How can we elevate the role and meaning of memory? A District Six story comes to mind. As new houses were being built as part of the process of restitution, attempts were made to restore

---

42. This saying is attributed to Spanish-American philosopher George Santayana.

the street grid along the contours that they had followed before being destroyed. One of the streets was named Aspeling Street, and on a walk through the area by former residents, Mrs. Smith[43] pointed out that it was incorrectly named. She knew that because she had lived in the area, and she remembered that when she stood in the old Aspeling Street, the view that she had of Table Mountain was not the view that she got when she stood in the newly named street. She placed her body in several positions in relation to the mountain but could not get the view that she remembered. Based on her bodily experience and somatic memory of the landscape, she was convinced that it was Rutger Street but was not taken seriously. As part of a next phase of development when additional maps were cross-referenced, it was discovered that it was indeed Rutger Street, and the street name has been changed. The information provided by Mrs. Smith was not even considered to be valid, and if it had not been for a different map being consulted, it would have been rejected.

While it is a good and desirable practice to verify information from any source, the lesson that I take from this simple story is that different ways of knowing have validity and should be able to intersect with each other in ways which, in the academy, would be referred to as being interdisciplinary. Feminist philosopher Noëlle McAfee[44] refers to the inherent value of community knowledge. She emphasizes that situatedness provides a strong context for knowing, and that values commonly held by a group give rise to active solidarity and involvement. In this way, communities can become rich repositories of lessons that can serve as a catalyst for community development, growth, and learning. While scholarly endeavors require support and recognition, McAfee criticizes the tendency for such knowledge to be elevated to the point where it is equated with expertise, while public opinion is often dismissed as error. She critiques the manner in which "the everyday knowledge of regular people—call it common sense—is disparaged."[45]

In South Africa, the Indigenous Khoekhoe people were dispossessed of their land and annihilated on a large scale with the arrival of European colonists. Their knowledge of the land, derived from living in close proximity to the rhythms of nature, was interrupted, and the natural environment was ravaged to serve the needs of the colonizing powers. As Indigenous people, they had cultivated a sustainable way of life rooted

43. A pseudonym.
44. McAfee, "Ways of Knowing," 32.
45. McAfee, "Ways of Knowing," 39.

in their understanding of their environment and their connection to the land to which they belonged.⁴⁶ Indigenous people "hold an informational structure that makes space for geological and cosmic time—and creates ways of knowing and seeing the world at multiple scales,"⁴⁷ but this indigenous epistemology was replaced with a Eurocentric one which engaged with the non-human world as 'the Other.' Yvette Abrahams, writing about the importance of attending to indigenous knowledge systems as one of the ways to restore the planet, speaks of indigenous epistemologies as being "experiential, situated and contextual," reflecting a sense of "balance and harmony with the ecosystem."⁴⁸

In the previously mentioned film, *Uitgesmyt,* an elderly resident reflects on life in the past. She describes the community as having been rich, but it becomes evident that she is not referring to monetary wealth. She speaks of the community's close connection to nature and their harmonious coexistence. They practiced a form of subsistence farming, with different community members cultivating a variety of crops and raising various types of livestock. This arrangement allowed for the exchange of food through sales or barter among community members. The diversity of crops also prevented the depletion of nutrients from the soil all at once.⁴⁹ Excess produce could be sold for extra income. Specifically, she mentions the harvesting of *buchu,* a local medicinal herb that they currently cannot access because the pathways have changed, and it is now protected flora. Additionally, the traditional *rooibos* (red bush) tea was also much more freely available for harvesting in the past.

These everyday stories reflect a traditional knowledge that was refined through close attentiveness to the environment. They are just two examples from a much larger repository of knowledge that remains largely untapped.

---

46. 'We belong to the land' refers to an understanding by Indigenous people of the relationship between land and humans. ". . . many indigenous people, land relates to all aspects of existence—culture, spirituality, language, law, family and identity. Rather than owning land, each person belongs to a piece of land which they're related to through the kinship system" (Australians Together, "The Importance of Land").

47. Chattarjee, "The Arts."

48. Abrahams, "Forgive them Lord," 61.

49. For example, crops such as beets, spinach, and potatoes require a high nitrogen content in the soil, whereas other crops do not. Plants such as *rooibos* and green beans put nitrogen back in the soil. Communities using traditional farming methods developed intuitive knowledge about how to plant crops symbiotically.

Throughout its development, the District Six Museum has gained valuable insights from the materials contributed to its archive, including photographs, documents, and artifacts, as well as the narratives crafted from memory. This information extends beyond mere facts and forensics, it delves into the ways in which people forged a sense of community, surmounted obstacles, preserved their spirits, and practiced an ethics of care toward one another and the land. It recognizes the knowledge and expertise of community members in their own right, "tied to a place and community through mapping, photographs, stories, street signs, landscape markers and oral histories drawing on citizen activism, public exchange, artistic practice, story-telling and research to question the power relations inherent in colonial and postcolonial productions of knowledge."[50]

We may not be able to reverse time, but we can heed the call of the Sankofa exhortation, that "it is not taboo to go back for what you forgot (or left behind)."[51] We need to significantly scale up our efforts to learn from—and not only about—the past. This requires collaborative initiatives between government and non-governmental actors that are not ego-driven but truly people-centric. It necessitates a new approach to listening and engaging with custodians of traditional knowledge, signaling to them that their voices truly matter and are being heard. In the words of Arundhati Roy: "There's really no such thing as the 'voiceless'. There are only the deliberately silenced, or the preferably unheard."[52]

District Six and Elandskloof, the two examples I discussed in this chapter, continue to face challenges akin to *pitswere*. As has been alluded to, in addition to the problems with the process of post-restitution support, some of the troubles stem from differing perceptions held by various community members and groups regarding the best way forward. Some of these differences are driven by self-interest born out of a sense of desperation, primarily fueled by the fear of being left behind. Others arise from a lack of access to comprehensive information required for making well-informed decisions and statements.

McAfee strongly advocates for the positive harnessing of subjectivity and vested interests within processes to foster a shared understanding of

---

50. Bennett, "Memory," 174–75.

51. *Sankofa* is a Twi word from the Akan tribe in Ghana. Literally translated it means "It is not taboo to go back for what you forgot (or left behind)." The loose translation is: "go back and get it."

52. Roy, "Peace."

the long-term public interest. She critiques those who exclusively pursue objective solutions and hold the belief that subjective perspectives are inherently limited. She contends that partial perspectives are only problematic if they remain as such: "Through deliberation, partial perspectives can be woven into a new whole."[53] She appeals for allies in this venture of engaging with different forms and sources of knowledge, particularly conscious that "the public sphere and contextual understanding (solidarity) have been so denigrated." These processes demand "interpretation, judgement, imagination and expression."[54] It is crucial to form alliances and seek allies who can collaborate with individuals on the ground, especially those who perceive that laws and regulations threaten their land and rights. People who feel invisible and unheard must be listened to in a more meaningful manner, and the knowledge they contribute should be validated beyond mere folklore. In a manner reminiscent of Sankofa, we must recognize the imperfections of the recent past and revisit the shortcuts we have taken on the path to reconciliation.

In my view, the core elements of our path toward reconciliation, restorative justice, and lasting peace revolve around the reclamation of dignity, self-esteem, self-love, visibility, and the restoration of land. There are many voices not yet listened to. In concluding his biography, aptly titled *Memory is the Weapon*, the late Don Mattera writes: "I knew deep down inside of me, in that place where laws and guns cannot reach nor jackboots trample, that there had been no defeat. In another day, another time, we would emerge to reclaim our dignity and our land."[55]

We possess a remarkable Constitution and Bill of Rights, an array of rights-based laws, and a wealth of expertise in the various spheres of civil society, including faith-based organizations and social movements. Our history is rich with struggles that have empowered and dignified us. However, time may be running short. May Don Mattera's "another day, another time"[56] come to pass in our lifetime, and may we actively contribute to its realization.

---

53. McAfee, "Ways of Knowing," 48.
54. McAfee, "Ways of Knowing," 49.
55. Mattera, *Memory is the Weapon*, 173.
56. Mattera, *Memory is the Weapon*.

BIBLIOGRAPHY

Abrahams, Y. "Forgive them Lord, for they know not what they do." In *Racism, Violence, Betrayals and New Imaginaries*, edited by Nadia Sanger and Benita Moolman, 54–74. Pietermaritzburg: University of Kwazulu-Natal Press, 2022.

Australians Together. "The Importance of Land." https://australianstogether.org.za/

Bennett, Bonita. "Memory, Heritage and the Spaces Between: A District Six Biography." PhD diss., University of Pretoria, 2021.

Boym, Svetlana. *The Future of Nostalgia*. New York: Basic Books, 2001.

Casey, Edward. *Remembering: A Phenomenological Study*. Bloomington: Indiana University Press, 2000.

Chatterjee, Sria. "The Arts, Environmental Justice, and the Ecological Crisis: A Provocation." https://www.britishartstudies.ac.uk/issues/issue-index/issue-18/arts-environmental-justice-ecological-crisis/.

Donahue, Sean. "As Collective Memory Fades, So Will Our Ability to Prepare for the Next Pandemic." https://theconversation.com/as-collective-memory-fades-so-will-our-ability-to-prepare-for-the-next-pandemic-137370/.

Doxtader, Eric. "Amnesty." In *Pieces of the Puzzle*, edited by Charles Villa-Vicencio, et al., 39–45. Rondebosch: Institute for Justice and Reconciliation, 2005.

Dube, Pamela S. "The story of Thandi Shezi." In *Commissioning the Past: Understanding South Africa's Truth and Reconciliation Commission*, edited by Deborah Posel and Graeme Simpson, 117–30. Johannesburg: Witwatersrand University Press, 2002

Fay, Derick, and Deborah James. "Giving Land Back or Righting Wrongs? Comparative Issues in the Study of Land Restitution." In *Land, Memory, Reconstruction and Justice*, edited by Cheryl Walker et al., 41–60. Ohio: Ohio University Press, 2010.

Fried, Marc, "Grieving for a Lost Home." In *Urban Renewal: The Record and the Controversy*, edited by James Wilson. Boston: Massachusetts Institute of Technology Press, 1966.

Grunebaum, Heidi. "Spectres of the Untold: Memory and History in South Africa after the Truth and Reconciliation Commission." PhD diss., University of the Western Cape, 2006.

Halbwachs, Maurice. *The Collective Memory*. New York: Harper & Row, 1980.

Hall, R. "Reconciling the Past, Present and Future: the Parameters and Practices of land Restitution in South Africa." In *Land, Memory, Reconstruction and Justice: Perspectives of Land Claims in South Africa*, edited by Ruth Hall, et al, 17–44. Athens: Ohio University Press, 2010.

Ikubaje, John G., and Usani Odum. *Envisioning a Transitional Justice-Based Approach to Climate-Induced Conflicts in Africa*. Uppsala: Life & Peace Institute, 2023.

Mandela, "Inauguration Speech." 1994. https://www.africa.upenn.edu/Articles_Gen/Inaugural_Speech_17984.html/.

Márquez, Gabriel G. *Love in the Time of Cholera*. Translated by Edith Grossman. London: Penguin, 1988.

Mattera, Don. *Memory Is the Weapon*. Gauteng: African Perspectives, 2007.

McAfee, Noëlle. "Ways of Knowing." In *Standing with the Public*, edited by James Veninga et al., 29–50. Dayton: Kettering Foundation, 1997.

Mokhoali, Veronica. "Owners of Jagersfontein Mine Dam Were Warned to Stabilise Wall—FS GOVT." *EWN,* September 12, 2022. https://ewn.co.za/2022/09/12/owners-of-jagersfontein-mine-dam-were-warned-to-stabilise-wall-fs-govt/.
Moore, Jason. "Who Is Responsible for the Climate Crisis." https://www.maize.io/magazine/what-is-capitalocene/.
National Institute for Communicable Diseases. "Guidelines for case-finding, diagnosis, management and public health response." 2020. https://www.nicd.ac.za/
O'Callaghan-Gordo, Cristina, and Joseph M. Anto "COVID-19: The Disease of the Anthropocene." *Environmental Research* 187 (2020) 109683. DOI: 10.1016/j.envres.2020.109683/.
O'Connell, Siona. *Uitgesmyt.* University of Pretoria and University of Cape Town, 2018.
———. *Impossible Return: Cape Town's Forced Removals.* Cape Town: Kwela, 2019.
Okri, Ben. *Birds of Heaven.* London: Orion, 1995.
O'Malley—The Heart of Hope. "1950. Group Areas Act No. 41." https://omalley.nelsonmandela.org/index.php/site/q/03lv01538/04lv01828/05lv01829/06lv01839.htm/.
Patoway, Kaushik. "Ancient Tsunami Warnings Carved in Stones in Japan." https://www.amusingplanet.com/2015/03/ancient-tsunami-warnings-carved-in.html/.
Republic of South Africa. *Promotion of National Unity and Reconciliation Act, No. 35 of 1995.* Vol 361. No. 16579. https://www.justice.gov.za/legislation/acts/1995-034.pdf.
———. *Restitution of Land Rights Act (RLRA), No. 22 of 1994.* Vol 353. No. 16106. Government Gazette. Cape Town. https://www.gov.za/documents/restitution-land-rights-act.
Roy, Arundhati. 2004. "Peace and the New Corporate Liberation Theology." Transcript of speech delivered at the University of Sydney, November 3, 2004. https://sydneypeacefoundation.org.au/peace-prize-recipients/2004-arundhati-roy/#:~:text=Today%2C%20in%20a%20world%20convulsed,will%20rid%20us%20of%20both.
Ryan, Ciaran. "State Capture Scorecard: R500bn looted, Zero Assets Recovered." *Moneyweb,* July 5, 2022. https://www.moneyweb.co.za/news/south-africa/state-capture-scorecard-r500bn-looted-zero-assets-recovered/.
South African Government. "Land Reform." https://www.gov.za/issues/land-reform.
Surplus People Project. *Forced removals in South Africa.* Volume 1. Cape Town: Surplus Peoples Project, 1983.
Till, Karen. "'Waiting for the City to Remember': Archive and Repertoire in ANU Productions and CoisCéim Dance Theatre's 'These Rooms.'" *The Irish Review* 54 (2018) 34–51.
———. "Wounded Cities: Memory-Work and a Place-Based Ethics of Care." *Political Geography* 31 (2012) 3–14.
Titus, Andries. "A Public Participation Perspective of the Process of Post-Settlement Support in Elandskloof." Master's thesis, University of the Western Cape.
United Nations Environment Programme (2022). *Emissions Gap Report 2022: The Closing Window—Climate Crisis Calls for Rapid Transformation of Societies.* Nairobi. https://www.unep.org/emissions-gap-report-2022.
Unterhalter, Elaine. *Forced Removal.* London: International Defence and Aid Fund for Southern Africa, 1987.

Villa-Vicencio, Charles. "Reconciliation." In *Pieces of the Puzzle*, edited by Charles Villa-Vicencio and Erik Doxtader, 3–9. Rondebosch: Institute for Justice and Reconciliation, 2005.

Villa-Vicencio, Charles, and Erik Doxtader, eds. *Pieces of the Puzzle*. Rondebosch: Institute for Justice and Reconciliation, 2005.

Whigham, Kerry. "Constructing Prevention: An Exploration in Building Memorials That Prevent Atrocity." In *Societies Emerging from Conflict: The Aftermath of Atrocity*, edited by Dennis B. Klein, 104–28. Cambridge: Cambridge Scholars, 2017.

———. "Remembering to Prevent: The Preventive Capacity of Public Memory." *Genocide Studies and Prevention: An International Journal* 11 (2007) 51–71.

Wits University. 2023. "The 2022 Durban Floods Were the Most Catastrophic Yet Recorded in KwaZulu-Natal." https://www.wits.ac.za/news/latest-news/general-news/2023/2023-04/the-2022-durban-floods-were-the-most-catastrophic-yet-recorded-in-kwazulu-natal.html/.

Appendix
Elin Skaar's article

Table 1: The Nordic truth commissions focusing on the assimilation of the Indigenous Sámi and national minorities

Name of commission	NORWEGIAN TRC (2018–2023)	SWEDISH TC (2021–2025)	SWEDISH TRC (2020–2023)	FINNISH TRC (2021–2023)
Focus of TC	Sámi, Kvens, Norwegian Finns, and Forest Finns	Sámi	Tornedalians, Kvens, and Lantalaiset	Sámi
Full name of TC	"Kommisjonen for å granske fornorskings-spolitikk og urett overfor samer, kvener og norskfinner" (Sannhets- og forsoningskom-misjonen) (in Norwegian)	"Sannings-kom-missionen för det samiska folket" (in Swedish)	"Sannings- och försoningskom-missionen för tornedalingar, kväner och lantalaiset" (in Swedish)	"Saamelaisten totuus- ja so-vintokomissio jatkaa työtään" (in Finnish)

Name of commission	NORWEGIAN TRC (2018–2023)	SWEDISH TC (2021–2025)	SWEDISH TRC (2020–2023)	FINNISH TRC (2021–2023)
Short name English	Norwegian Truth and Reconciliation Commission (TRC)	The Swedish Truth Commission for the Sámi People (TC)	The Swedish Truth and Reconciliation Commission for Tornedalians, Kvens and Lantalaiset (TRC)	The Finnish Sámi Truth and Reconciliation Commission (TRC)
Established	June 14, 2018	November 3, 2021	March 19, 2020	October 28, 2021
Background for TC	Claims for TRC from Sámi Parliament, forwarded to the Norwegian Parliament by two political parties.	Sámi Parliament	Claims for TRC forwarded by National Association of Swedish Tornedalians supported by Ministry of Culture.	Sámi Parliament
Overall objective of TC	Reconciliation (between the Norwegian state and the Indigenous people and minority groups, and between these groups and the majority population).	Investigate the Swedish state's historical relationship with and abuses of the Sámi people.	(1) Contribute to the collective reparation for the minorities; (2) Promote reconciliation, and (3) Prevent similar acts in the future.	Identify and assess historical and current discrimination and fascilitate reconciliation between the Sámi and the State of Finland.

APPENDIX 285

Name of commission	NORWEGIAN TRC (2018–2023)	SWEDISH TC (2021–2025)	SWEDISH TRC (2020–2023)	FINNISH TRC (2021–2023)
Focus of mandate	Norwegianization and its effects on individuals and groups/collectives in four specified ethnic groups: Sámi, Kvens, Norwegian-Finns and Forest Finns. Propose measures for reconciliation.	(1) Document assimilation policies against the Sámi and their consequences; (2) Increase public understanding of the Sámi experience; and (3) Propose measures for reconciliation.	(1) Map and review the assimilation policy and its consequences for the minority (Tornedalians, Kvens and Lantalaiset); (2) Disseminate information to increase knowledge about the minority and its historical experiences; and (3) Submit proposals for further efforts to contribute to redress and promote reconciliation.	(1) Identify and evaluate discrimination against the Sámi people and the historical and present violations of their rights, including assimilation policies; (2) Research how these policies affect the Sámi and their community today; (3) Present proposals on how to promote contact between the Sámi people and the Finnish state, as well as between Sámi groups; (4) Increase awareness in the country of the Sámi people's status as Finland's Indigenous population. Propose measures for reconciliation.

Name of commission	NORWEGIAN TRC (2018–2023)	SWEDISH TC (2021–2025)	SWEDISH TRC (2020–2023)	FINNISH TRC (2021–2023)
Time for Investigation	Not defined. Period of Norwegianization and its effects on individuals and groups/collectives *up to the present.*	Sámi history and policy dating back to the 1500s.	Not defined. Historical analysis of assimilation policies of Sámi (Swedification).	NA
Final TC report due	June 1, 2023 (originally due June 2022. Due date extended 12 months due to covid).	December 1, 2025	May 15, 2023 (originally due May 2022. Due date extended 12 months).	December 1, 2025 (Originally due November 2023. Due date extended 24 months).
Number of commissioners	12	13	8	5
Gender balance in TC	5 women, 7 men	7 women, 6 men	4 women, 4 men	4 women, 1 man
Ethnic representation among commissioners	Ethnic representation included, though not formally	Ethnic representation included, though not formally	Ethnic representation included, though not formally	Currently all Finnish, but secretariat includes many Sámi

Index

academic, 21, 101, 106, 107, 122, 135
    debate, 77, 140
    discipline, 125
    endeavor, 15
    fashion, 122
    institution, 81
    literature, 45, 195
    research, 77, 108, 113, 158
    scholar/s, **107**
aesthetics, 148
African National Congress (ANC), 253
aggressors, 55, 59
analysis, 90, 111, 142, 157, 165, 173–75, 177, 180, 188, 213, 238–40
    anthropological, 139, 158, 165
    comparative, 76
    historical, 131, 139, 164, 286
    philosophical, 139, 140, 163
    qualitative, 209-12, 214, 239
    thematic, 213
Anarchists Against the Wall, 156
Aneyoshi, 260
    stone, 260
antagonism, 146, 147, 247
Anthropocene, 273
anthropology, 127, 141, 151
anti-colonial, 139, 140, 153, 155
anti-imperial, 152, 153
apartheid, 81, 82, 88–91, 109, 195–99, 201, 203–6, 250, 253, 254, 261, 262, 264–66, 268, 269, 275
artifact, 132, 133

Asmal, Kader, 87, 199
atrocities, 3, 17, 81, 83, 90, 201–4, 257, 261
Australia, 7, 8, 35
authoritarianism, 140, 155
axis of resistance, 155

bedeviyet, 150
Benjamin, Walter, 140, 143, 144, 146, 147, 164, 165
Berggrav, Eivind, 41
Bishop of Oslo, 41
body, 7, 8, 15, 43, 45–47, 54, 56, 75, 85, 226, 249, 250, 255, 276
Bosnia, 57
bullying, 84, 255-7, 231

Calls to Action, 78, 86, 189
Canada, 4, 7, 8, 18, 35, 77, 78, 85, 87, 91, 236, 245, 246
centralization, 150, 152, 154
Christian, 32, 34, 44, 123, 126, 127, 129, 130, 132, 133, 135, 148, 151, 156, 160, 181, 200, 204; faith 103, 204; socialism 152
Christianity, 9, 102, 123, 130, 132, 136, 151
church, 7, 13, 15, 17, 32–34, 41, 42, 78, 102, 106–108, 121, 124, 125, 127–29, 132, 134, 136, 147, 150–52, 181, 184, 197, 201, 227
    Fathers 144

287

INDEX

church (continued)
  Leaders, 78, 79, 196, 197, 201; life 42–47; Lutheran 14, 134
Church of Norway (CoN), 30, 31–35, 38, 40–47, 65, 121
Church of Sweden (CoS), 12, 14–16, 101, 102, 105, 106, 108, 110, 115
civilization, 105, 150
climate change, 272–74
colonial, 9, 39, 54, 75, 80, 82, 91, 92, 94, 103, 125, 126, 139, 148, 149, 152, 154, 155, 157, 161, 236, 237, 239, 240, 278
  empire/s, 149, 150, 164
  legacy, 95, 125, 135, 268
  powers, 8
  subjects, 153
  see settler
colonialism, 62, 74; 75, 82, 86, 90–94, 125, 139, 140, 148, 149, 153–57, 162, 164, 195, 222, 236, 239, 240, 262, 268; *see* settler
colonization, 8, 10, 30, 37, 45, 74, 94, 120–24, 129–31, 133, 134, 139, 140, 143, 149, 154, 155–57, 160, 162, 164, 224, 239
colonized, 66, 75, 93, 121, 125, 126, 133, 144, 151, 162
colonizer, 125, 126, 133, 155
colony, 90, 126, 148, 149, 151, 161, 239
commissions, 4–7, 18, 19, 20, 23–25, 55, 77, 87, 92, 93, 103, 105, 201, 245
  fact-finding, 3
  post-transitional, 6;
  see truth commissions (TCs)
  see truth and reconciliation commissions (TRCs)
communicative action, 147
conflict, 4, 6, 52, 55, 56, 61, 64, 74–77, 83, 87, 102, 138, 139, 146, 152, 155, 159, 163, 165, 197, 212, 214, 221–23, 227, 232, 234, 235, 237, 238, 240, 247, 272, 275
conflict research, 141, 145, 146
constructive critique, 119
Consumer Protection Act (CPA), 272
context, 4–7, 9, 11, 24, 38, 44, 45, 47, 52, 54, 56, 66, 74, 91, 109–12, 122, 125–28, 132, 140, 141, 146, 147, 156–159, 162, 164, 180, 183, 188, 189, 197–99, 203, 205, 206, 210, 212–14, 216, 220, 221, 227–29, 231–34, 237, 239, 240, 245, 246, 248, 253, 261–63, 276
contextual party, 124
corruption, 261, 266
cosmology, 153
counter, ethnic, 161
  history, 160
  see narratives, 212, 238
COVID-19, 16, 17, 260, 261, 273, 286
creation, 18, 67, 94, 119, 121, 123, 124, 127, 129, 130, 132, 133, 135
culture, 9, 32, 53, 62–65, 83, 84, 87, 91, 103, 125, 128, 129, 158, 176, 182, 185, 215, 217–23, 226, 229, 235, 238, 253, 272, 277
  affirming, 124
  of civic trust, 266, 272
  common, 127, 129, 128
  dominant, 35, 92
  historical, 104
  history, 112
  human, 127
  husbandry, 186
  mainstream, 4, 9
  majority, 125, 129, 134
  musical, 148
  popular, 128
  organizational, 158
  traditional, 105
  tribal, 150
  Western European, 128
  see human rights

Day Zero, 274
decolonial, 66, 139, 145
decolonization, 4, 5, 8, 10, 25, 45, 74–77, 80, 82, 92–95, 119–22, 124, 128, 134, 139, 140, 146, 163, 164, 174
  of history, 164
  of knowledge, 75, 145
  messianism of, 138, 163
decolonize, 75, 77, 91, 119, 154, 164

decolonizing, 77, 80, 102, 124–26, 129, 134, 135
de Klerk, Frederik Willem, 90
democracy, 6, 55, 59, 81, 85
    advent of, 197
    constitutional, 246, 261
    fledgling, 268
    participatory-deliberative, 147, 158
    transition to, 250
    vision of, 252
    see settler
Denmark, 105, 125, 126, 132, 151
determinism, 143
deterministic messianism, 144
deterrence, 141, 146
deterritorialization, forced, 119, 120, 125
dialectic approach, 140
dialectical tension, 153
dialogue, 23, 24, 33, 34, 44, 46, 75, 79, 92, 94, 95, 108, 109, 136, 144, 148, 254
diocese, 41–43, 45, 46
disciplinary belonging, 140, 141
discipline, 7
    academic, 125
    education, 162
    research, 162
discourse/s, 8, 58, 60, 65, 80, 81, 88, 120–24, 127, 128, 129, 131, 133, 135, 197, 206, 210, 231–36
discrimination, 20, 53, 61, 84, 85, 86, 103, 125, 156, 158, 188, 220, 221, 284, 285
    gender, 8
    positive; processes, 52
    racial, 88, 146
    structural, 221
displacement, 6, 265, 267–69
District Six, 260, 264, 265, 268–70, 272, 275, 278
District Six Museum, 260, 264, 265, 278
Diversity, 45, 88, 277, 228, 229, 231
dogma, 131
    sociology of, 131–34

economic transformation, 266

education, 10, 13, 61, 63, 75, 80, 114, 115, 120, 161, 162, 165, 182, 186, 218, 235, 275
    Christian, 32, 44
educational practices, 103
educationalization, 114
England, 125
environmental degradation, 273
epistemological, 119, 121, 123, 130, 133, 142, 163, 164
    awareness, 126, 134, 136
    category, conditions, 130
    dimension of, 129, 165
    enterprise, 134
    issue, 120
    lens, 120
    philosophy, 148
    position, 136
    scripts, 135
    starting point, 127
    traditions, 127
epistemology, 139, 142, 144, 148
    indigenous, 277
    for truth, 138
equality, 84, 86, 95, 128, 220, 252, 255, 268
eschatology, 128, 143, 144
ethical relativism, 142
ethics, 108, 109, 139, 142, 148
    of care, 264, 278
    for/of reconciliation, 138, 145
ethno-nationalism, 151
everlasting struggle for just peace, 146
Exodus, 133
    motif, 133
exploitation, 11, 65, 66, 67, 90, 185, 186
extrajudicial executions, 6

Finland, 4, 5, 7–9, 12–14, 16, 17, 19, 23, 24, 31, 36, 37, 41, 58, 151, 156, 236, 284
Finnish-cultural agitation, 41
Finnmark County, 148, 161, 179
folk, 34, 123–26, 129, 136, 161
food security, 261
forgiveness, 35, 75, 81, 83, 188, 205, 233, 234, 236
Fornljot, 36

Fosen, 63–65, 67, 186, 187, 189, 222, 224, 235
France, 125, 155
freedom, 107, 128, 133, 163, 225, 233, 255, 268

gender, 92, 124, 206, 213, 261, 286
    see discrimination identity 132
    see injustices, roles, 132, 133
genocide, 6, 103, 134, 261
Gordian Knot, 52, 53, 54, 68
Greenland, 7, 149
Group Areas Act (GAA), 269
Guovdageaidnu, 152–154, 223

Haugianism, 152
Healing, 59, 75–77, 79, 94, 109, 188, 204, 205, 214, 227, 228, 230, 231, 247, 248, 253–56, 262, 264–66, 268, 270, 272
hearings, 21, 23, 89, 90, 184, 189, 200–202, 204, 214, 246, 248, 254, 258
    public 15, 16, 56, 58, 81, 88
hegemonies, 157
    cultural, 156
hegemony, 156–58, 162, 165
heretics, 140
hermeneutical process, 120
Herzegovina, 57
hierarchical cosmologies, 144
hierarchization, 38
historicity, 142
history
    multi-polar colonial, 148
    oral, 250
    transnational anti-colonial, 148–53
hope, 87, 143–44, 162
    of an open promise, 143
human, 53, 109, 122, 124, 126–30, 132, 133, 135, 196, 237, 254
    beings, 126, 256, 275, 277
    dignity, 203, 230, 232, 234, 237, 261, 273, 274
human rights, 11, 56, 57, 59, 63–65, 68, 74, 85, 87, 90, 92, 125, 145, 186, 187, 198, 234, 237, 244, 247, 250

abuses, 6, 56, 91, 94, 266
culture, 266
indigenous, 186
law, 139, 146, 164, 199
profiles, 4
protection, 6
violations, 3, 6, 55, 59, 64, 75–77, 81, 83, 87, 198, 200, 202–5, 246–48, 251–54, 257
hypothesis/es, 143
    deterministic, 143
    possibilistic, 143
    rival, 143

identity, 8, 39, 53, 85, 123, 127, 130, 132, 177, 200, 215, 216, 226–28, 232, 244, 245, 247, 249–57, 277
identities, 83, 86, 245, 249, 252, 254
    ancestral, 245
    cultural, 10, 244
    linguistic, 10
    loss, multiple, 230
    oppositional, 230
    political, 244
    religious, 244
    sexual, 132
    social, 244
imperialism, 153
Indigenous, 47, 63, 66, 67, 74, 78–80, 83, 85, 91–93, 123, 145, 148, 174, 178, 210, 220, 225, 230, 234, 235, 236, 237, 240, 276, 277
    children, 86
    communities, 75, 79, 94
    epistemology, group/s, 4, 25, 54, 90
    minority/minorities, 4, 6, 52, 67, 90, 129, 210, 211, 220, 238
    people/s, 4, 5, 7–9, 11–14, 17, 25, 31, 33, 38–40, 46, 47, 54, 56, 65, 66, 74, 75, 78, 79, 80, 85, 86, 91–95, 119, 121, 139, 145, 156, 157, 161, 174, 176, 236, 245, 276, 277, 284
    population/s, 4, 17, 18, 20, 24, 61–63, 65, 68, 77, 132, 178, 285
    rights, 3, 11, 18, 25
    status, 31, 220

INDEX 291

Indian Residential School (IRS), 18, 75, 78, 80, 86
injustices, 55, 57, 58, 61, 67, 74, 77, 79, 80, 83, 86, 92, 95, 212, 219, 221, 236, 238, 239, 240
    gender/ed, 92
    historic/al, 4, 5, 11, 38, 68, 75–77, 94, 95, 239
    past, 20, 75, 80, 104, 188
    structural, 61
Institute for Justice and Reconciliation, 264
Institute for the Healing of Memories 264
interlocutor, 244
International Relations (IR), 141, 144, 149, 156, 164

Japan, 260
Johnsen, Tore, 83, 119, 120, 121, 124, 128, 129, 131, 132, 134, 135, 209
just peace; *see* peace
justice, 59, 62, 67, 76, 81, 87, 95, 121, 143, 199, 201, 205, 218, 220, 233–37, 253, 255, 264–66, 273
    historical, 101–5, 109, 113–15
    social, 88, 163
    restorative, 245, 262, 272, 274 279
    transitional 3–7, 76, 82, 92, 94, 95, 138–140, 142, 148, 158, 163, 210, 230

Khoekhoe, 276
Kisrwan, 152–54
knowledge, 8, 13, 19, 20, 23, 40, 58, 60, 70, 89, 103, 107, 114, 120, 124, 131, 145, 162, 177, 185, 187, 216, 229, 232, 238, 239, 250, 257–79, 285
    historical, 32, 104, 112, 114, 158
    scientific, 106, 258
    traditional, 145, 277, 278
Kven/s, 4, 5, 13, 21, 31, 32, 34, 36, 37, 39–47, 53, 83–85, 161, 180, 182, 183, 187, 189, 209, 212, 213, 215–20, 226, 227, 230, 235, 237, 240, 245

heritage, 181
language, 13, 14, 31, 32, 40–44, 46, 47, 161, 177, 219, 220
newspaper, 181
Kven Psalm booklet, 43, 47
Kvenland, 31, 36, 37, 150, 151

Labba, Elin Anna, 119
Lake Chad, 274
Lakselv, 179, 180, 181, 182, 183, 189, 223
Lantalaiset 4, 5, 10, 17, 19, 22, 23, 283–85
Lapp school system, 110, 111, 114
law, 12, 22, 66, 67, 76, 87, 90, 91, 145, 146, 148, 153, 198, 246, 261, 168, 269, 277
    see human rights
Lebanon, 138–41, 144, 147–49, 152, 155, 157–60, 162–65
legacy, 8, 86, 92, 93, 124, 126, 198, 229, 236, 263
    apartheid, 268
    cognitive 173
    historical, 225
    see colonial
    see colonialism
    see majority
Levantine region, 150
liberalization, 152
Love in the Time of Cholera, 267

majority, 58, 61, 66, 67, 91, 93, 112, 120, 124, 128, 135, 146, 157, 161, 162, 173, 175, 178–80, 183, 186, 188, 204, 211, 221, 222, 228, 231, 234, 238, 257, 269
    church/es, 33, 132, 174
    culture, 129, 134
    legacy, 135
    population/s, 19, 25, 53, 61, 66, 84, 120–24, 129, 135, 173–77, 185–87, 189, 284
    society/societies, 67, 102
    voices, 120, 121, 135
Mandela, Nelson Rolihlahla, 87, 197, 200, 206, 261, 270
manifest destiny, 128, 131

marginalization, 52, 53, 54, 61, 62, 63, 68, 92, 95, 129, 244
Marxism, 145
   Heretic, 140, 143
   Orthodox, 140, 142–44
Marxists, 140
materialistic empiricism, 145
meaningful silences, 264
medeniyet, 150
media, 81, 84, 85, 108, 162, 174–77, 179, 180, 182–89, 202, 205, 225, 228, 245, 246, 254,
memory, 88, 104, 112, 139, 158–60, 162, 165, 212, 238, 251, 256, 260, 262–65, 267, 272, 275, 276, 278, 279
memories, 88, 138, 139, 158, 165, 262–64
metanoia, 120
metaphor, 54, 121, 149, 207, 119; *see* weaving of a fabric 119
method, 122, 139, 140, 142, 212
millenarist, 139
millet system, 150, 159
minority/ies, 4–7, 9–15, 17, 19, 20, 24, 31, 34, 38, 40, 47, 84, 90, 120, 121, 125, 135, 146, 151, 156, 157, 174–79, 183, 186–88, 210–12, 218, 220, 238, 283–85
   also see indigenous
   see Sámi
misrecognition, 54, 55, 62, 85
missionaries, 41, 144
mobilization, 11, 40, 90, 153, 157, 178, 217
modernization, 144
monasteries, 151
motherland, 126
mountain/s, 36, 196, 207, 274, 275, 276
movement/s, 121, 131, 152, 156, 246, 247
   indigenous rights, 145
   liberation, 81
   millennial anti-colonial, 139
   peasant, 152
   revival, 85
   social, 141, 147
   student, 147
mystical anarchy, 153

narrative/s, 76, 81, 88, 102, 109, 119–21, 133, 135, 159, 162, 164, 174, 179, 186, 187, 189, 204, 205, 209–12, 214–19, 221–24, 226, 227, 228, 230, 235, 237, 238–40, 244, 245, 249–58, 263, 264, 266, 278
   counter, 212, 238
nationalism, 103, 155–57, 159, 212
   ethno-nationalism, 151
nation building, 4, 9, 24, 157, 161, 162, 165, 173, 188, 268
nation states, 8, 119, 121, 126, 156
National Party (NP), 89, 90, 254
neo-colonialism, 144, 155, 222
neologism, 143
   see now-time
non-governmental actors 278; organization/s (NGO) 89, 155
Nord-Hålogaland Diocese Commission for Kven Church Life 43, 46
Nord-Hålogaland Diocese Council 43
Nordkalotten 9
Norway, 4, 7–15, 17, 19, 21–24, 30, 31, 33–38, 41, 42, 47, 52–54, 57, 59, 63, 65, 66, 75, 77, 83–85, 90, 91, 103, 125, 126, 129, 130, 132, 134, 136, 151, 156, 161, 174, 175, 176–78, 180, 183–86, 188, 189, 209–12, 216, 218, 220, 225, 228, 230–32, 234–38, 240, 246
Norwegian Finns, 4, 9–11, 13, 19, 21, 30–32, 34–40, 42, 43, 45–48, 83, 84, 140, 174, 176, 210, 211, 213, 283, 285
Norwegianization policy, 13, 19, 40–42, 53, 174–77, 186, 209–12, 215, 217–19, 226, 228–31, 238, 240, 245
nostalgia, 267, 268
   reflective, 267
   restorative, 267
now-time, 142–44, 153, 163–65

Omar, Dullah, 253
original sin, 268

pacifism, ethical, 146

pain, 62, 63, 218, 227, 229, 232, 245, 246, 249, 264, 267, 274
pandemic, 16, 17, 260, 261; *see* Covid-19
Parliament, 3, 10, 13, 81, 176, 198, 211
   Norwegian, 15, 21, 57, 210, 211, 220, 284
   Sámi, 14–17, 20, 22, 31, 41, 64, 84, 178, 180, 182, 220, 284
pathway, 147, 148, 188, 260
peace, 77, 83, 87, 103, 140, 141, 145–48, 156, 164, 165, 198, 231, 233, 236, 260, 279
peasants, 152, 154; Druze 152; Maronite 152, 159
perpetrators, 55, 56, 59, 60, 78, 79, 81, 83, 88, 91, 175, 183, 188, 201, 202, 203, 246, 248, 251, 254, 255, 257
Peru, 52, 54, 61, 63, 65
pitswere, 278
place-based ethics of care, 264
policy, 10, 18, 19, 38, 53, 57, 58, 77, 78, 83, 108, 149, 156, 162, 176, 178, 181, 210–12, 218, 219, 224, 226, 228, 235, 239, 240, 285, 286
   assimilation, 11, 12, 19, 156, 210, 240
   Lutheran imperial, 151, 152
   see Norwegianization
political, 4, 6, 8, 11, 14–16, 18, 25, 31, 37–39, 52, 53, 60, 61, 64, 75, 81, 90, 91, 93, 104, 108, 109, 110, 112, 119, 124–26, 129–31, 133, 134, 136, 141, 143, 146, 147, 153, 155, 157, 159, 163, 164, 174–76, 178, 179, 181–84, 186–89, 195, 197, 198, 200, 203, 206, 210, 212, 218, 223, 229–33, 236, 237, 238, 244–48, 254, 284
poor, 62, 274
popular sovereignty, 151
possibilism, 143
postcolonial, 111, 112, 126, 139, 145, 155, 159, 278
post-TRC, 209, 210, 212, 230, 231, 234, 237, 238, 240
poverty trap, 271

power, 61, 64, 74, 76, 77, 79, 80, 82, 88–90, 92, 94, 102, 120, 122, 123, 126, 129, 134, 147, 150, 163, 179, 186, 187, 202, 203, 214, 222–24, 239, 255, 262, 267, 278
pre-colonial, 39, 68
pre-invasion, 39
priest/s, 40, 85, 111, 126, 128
Prince of Peace, 145
progress, 23, 45, 91, 142, 143, 144, 266, 270
   as a teleological evolutionary process, 142, 243
   predetermined 143
promises, 47, 138, 261
propaganda, 41
proscriptive prescriptions, 144
psalms, 34, 43, 44
public sphere, 147, 157, 158, 163, 164, 279
   as a theater of operation, 157, 165
   bourgeois, 153
   carnivalesque, 158
   plebeian, 153, 158
Protestantism, 151

racialized suppression, 143
racism, 13, 14, 56, 92, 128, 225, 245
rebellion, 152
   Guovdageaidnu 152, 153
   Thranite, 152
recommendation/s, 7, 19, 25, 47, 60, 76, 77, 79, 80, 86, 91–94, 115, 200, 203, 211
reconciliation, 6, 8, 19, 20, 25, 32–35, 41, 44–47, 52–54, 59, 60, 62, 64–68, 75–81, 83–86, 89–92, 94, 95, 101–3, 105–9, 111, 115, 138, 139, 142, 145, 156–58, 160–63, 165, 173–76, 179, 182, 186–89, 195–207, 209–12, 218, 222, 224, 228–40, 244, 245–47, 250, 253–55, 257, 258, 262, 265, 266, 270, 272, 273, 279, 285
   see theology

recognition, 8, 11–14, 31, 35, 37, 44, 45, 52–55, 60, 61, 65, 67, 68, 76, 84, 86, 88, 89, 93, 174, 218, 226, 229, 236, 264, 276
Reconciliation Day, 271
Recontrans, 104, 140
redistribution, 55, 268
regime 41, 56, 88, 250, 262
reindeer, 64, 85
   herder/s, 64, 187, 222, 223
   herds, 222
   herding, 9, 105, 184, 186, 222, 223, 224
   husbandry, 64, 179, 185, 186, 239
   see conflicts
religious millenarism, 153
remembering, 254, 260, 263
repentance, 35, 120, 233, 234
research 3, 4, 9, 20, 23, 32, 33, 38, 53, 78, 82, 85, 93, 102–4, 106–9, 110–15, 125, 136, 139, 141, 143, 145, 147, 156, 158, 162, 182, 233, 234, 254, 269, 273, 278, 285 academic 77, 108; see conflict; discipline 162; historical 101, 109, 115, 144, 158, 162, 164; history education 115, 165; indigenous 145, 210, 230; materialistic decolonial 139; TRUCOM 173
resistance, 8, 11, 41, 42, 88, 150–56, 212, 236, 237, 238
Restitution of Land Rights Act (RLRA), 262, 268, 269
retrospective descriptions, 142, 144
revolutionaries, 144
   radical-democratic, 153
right-wing extremism, 136
rights, 3, 4, 6–8, 11–14, 20, 25, 37, 38, 54, 58, 61, 64–68, 83, 84, 90, 93, 142, 145, 173, 181, 182, 185, 186, 198, 218, 220–22, 224, 229, 234, 235, 237, 247, 261, 268, 270, 274, 279, 285
   see human
   see Indigenous
   minority 125, 146, 151–53, 237
   see Sámi

risorgimento, 154
Romani people, 34
ruling order 153

sacred sites, 9, 147
Sagastallamat conference, 16, 105
Sámi Church Council (SCC), 31, 32, 43, 45, 46, 47, 121
Sámi, 4, 5, 8–22, 24, 30–36, 38, 40–42, 44–47, 53, 57, 58, 63–68, 75, 83–85, 91, 101–3, 105, 106, 108, 111, 115, 119–25, 128, 129, 131, 134, 135, 139, 140, 144–47, 151, 152, 156, 157, 161, 162, 173, 174, 176–89, 209, 211–13, 218–32, 234–40, 245, 283–85
   see indigenous; minority/minorities 11, 12, 14, 17, 24, 25, 173
   see Parliament
   rights 8, 14, 142, 186, 218, 220, 224, 225
SANKS, 182
Sápmi, 9, 31, 66, 110, 112, 138, 139, 141, 144, 145, 147–51, 156–58, 160, 161–65, 180
Scandinavia, 121, 124, 128, 130, 133, 134
Scandinavian, 119, 120, 123–25, 128, 129, 130, 132, 136, 239, 240
   see theology
   see narrative
Scandinavian folk church ecclesiology, 125
Scandinavian Lutheran churches, 121
school/s, 34, 105, 110–12, 114, 143, 158, 159–62, 178, 181, 182, 218, 225, 227
   see Indian Residential School (IRS)
   Lapp, 110, 111, 114
Sekwepere, Mr., 249, 250, 255, 256
self-organizing, 39
self-reflexivity, 120, 124
Serbia, 57
serious doubling, 132
settlements, 151, 156, 239, 269
settler, 102
   colonial governments, 92
   colonial histories, 240
   colonial perspective, 82

colonial situation, 236
colonial structures, 82, 236
colonial theory, 240
colonialism, 82, 140, 156, 236
colonialist policy, 149
democracy, 56
denial, 82
witnessing, 86
slower rhythms of our dreams, 267
social cohesion, 262
society, 15, 19, 53–55, 57, 60–62, 64, 67, 74, 75, 81, 83, 85–87, 89, 114, 134, 138, 139, 141, 145, 162, 164, 173, 178, 186, 198, 205, 214, 219, 222, 224, 228, 239, 245–47, 253, 255, 279
South Africa, 8, 77, 81, 82, 85, 87, 88, 91, 195–99, 201, 202, 205, 206, 234, 245, 249, 250, 254, 257, 261, 262, 264, 265, 267, 268, 270, 271, 273, 274, 276
speech, 58, 163, 214, 224, 225, 227, 231
  see narratives
spirituality, 9, 124, 151
state of exception, 146
stigma, 61, 62, 173, 230
stone, 260
  ancient markers, 260
  see Aneyoshi
  guide, 260
  tablet, 260
  tsunami, 260
stories, 179, 181–86, 188, 199, 209, 210–12, 214, 215, 218, 223, 226–28, 232, 235, 237, 238, 245–48, 251–54, 256, 262, 264, 265, 277, 278
storytelling, 250, 254–58
studies, 32, 94, 114, 139, 141, 144, 145; cultural 145; culturalist postcolonial 139; peace 140
study plan, 44
subaltern, 55, 144, 155–57, 162
subjugation, 149, 123
suffering, 6, 81, 89, 175, 205, 246, 249, 250
survivor, 188, 226

Sweden, 4, 8–10, 12–19, 22–24, 31, 36, 37, 58, 75, 125, 126, 151, 156, 177, 236, 246

tax, collection, 33
  collectors 37, 151
  jurisdiction 37
taxation, 36, 37
teleological evolutionary process, 142, 143
tension, 153, 159, 197, 206, 230, 245, 247
territorialization, 174, 177–79
testimony, 60, 88, 188, 222, 248, 250, 251
"The Concept of History," 142, 144–48, 163
The Good, 139, 142, 144, 145, 148, 163
"the time of our childhood," 267
The True, 139, 142, 144, 148, 163
theocratic law, 153
theologians, 123, 126, 127, 130, 135, 136, 156, 196, 197
  SCT, 132, 133, 136
Theologies, 132
  destructive, 131
  of liberation, 121, 122, 127, 133, 135; process 127; problematic 131; reconciliation 233
theology, 120, 123, 124, 127, 130; 136, 140, 246
  contextual, 122–24, 130
  eco, 127
  decolonized/decolonization of, 126, 128, 135
  Grundtvig, 128
  indecent, 122, 123, 124
  liberation, 33, 122, 133
  Lutheran, 123, 126
  manifest destiny, 128, 131
  normal, 124
  political, 153, 163
  practical, 44
  reconciliation, 108
  Reformation, 129
  Sámi contextual, 121, 123
  Scandinavian, 124, 129, 135
  Scandinavian creation (SCT) 119, 123–27, 129–36

INDEX

Torah, 145, 146
Tornedalians, 4, 5, 10, 17, 19, 22, 23, 283–85
torture, 6, 88, 89
tradition, 123, 127, 135, 140, 204, 245, 251–53
    Clausewitzean 141,
transdisciplinary relevance, 140
trauma, 86, 120, 205, 228, 231, 262, 265, 268, 274
Troms region, 119
TRUCOM, 3, 173
trust, 64–68, 235, 266, 272
truth, 3, 4, 6, 24, 52, 55, 57, 58, 61, 62, 67, 74, 86, 88, 89, 109; 110, 112, 120, 138, 139, 142, 143, 156, 160, 187, 200, 201, 204, 214, 232–34, 246, 247, 250, 253–57, 263
truth commission/s (TC/s), 3–8, 15, 17–19, 22–25, 53, 55–59, 61, 63, 75, 76, 78, 88, 90, 110, 199, 211, 212, 218, 234, 253, 284
truth-seeking, 77, 94, 232
truth-telling, 79, 80, 183, 188, 199, 250, 263, 264, 266
Truth and Reconciliation Commission/s (TRC/s), 8, 15–19, 21, 25, 30, 31, 52, 58–61, 67, 74, 75, 76, 78–90, 110, 174–77, 179–85, 196, 197, 200–206, 209, 210, 212–25, 227–30, 232, 234, 238–40, 245, 246, 247, 248, 250, 253, 254, 257, 262–66
    alternatives for, 93
    "early bird," 4
    Canada's/Canadian, 17, 18, 24, 54, 75, 77, 85, 183, 174, 188, 210
    Finland's/Finnish, 5, 20, 22–23, 59, 283–85
    Greenlandic, 54
    meetings, 209, 210, 212–14, 218, 220, 225, 226, 230, 237, 240
    model, 3, 5, 83
    Nordic, 3, 5, 7
    Norway's/Norwegian, 4, 5, 17, 18, 21, 23, 24, 30, 44, 52, 56–60, 63, 65, 67, 83–85, 90–91, 140, 156, 162, 173–77, 182, 183, 187–89, 209, 210, 211, 213, 283–85
    Peruvian, 56, 57, 60, 61
    South Africa/n, 81, 82, 87, 93, 109, 175, 195, 200, 207, 210, 214, 245
    Swedens/Swedish 22–23, 283–85
Tutu, Desmond (Archbishop), 87, 196, 200, 206

Uitgesmyt, 271, 277
Ukrainian Communist Party (UCP), 140, 154
United States of America (USA), 155
unity, 81, 157, 198, 203, 204–47, 250, 254, 258
universalism, 144, 148, 163, 165

victim/s, 62, 89, 113, 187, 188, 203, 215, 247, 248, 250, 253, 257
    voice of, 58
Vlok, Adriaan, 90
VID Specialized University, 44, 175
Villa-Vicencio, Charles, 196, 201, 266
violations, 6, 7, 20, 56, 57, 61, 228, 247, 253, 285
    ongoing, 3
    see human rights
violence, 6, 56, 61, 74, 75, 77, 87, 92, 146, 147, 164, 195, 198, 199, 201, 236, 245, 247, 250, 255
    apartheid, 88
    gender-based, 261
    intimate partner, 261
    past acts of, 89
    political, 141, 146, 147
    state-led, 264
    victims of, 60
voiceless, 278
voices, 88, 94, 108, 133, 219, 278, 279
    majority, 120, 121, 135
    minority, 120
    Sámi, 120, 121, 135
    unheard, 122
vulnerable communities, 273

war
    civil, 160, 201
    First World War, 150

Great Nordic War, 37
interreligious, 152
Napoleonic Wars, 151
post-war, 164
Second World War, 11, 103 145
Syrian War, 156
Warsaw Ghetto Uprising, 146
Water, 10, 53, 63, 65, 68, 261, 272, 273, 274, 275
  see Day Zero
  management system, 274
  pollution, 273
  rights, 25
Western European regionalism, 156
whistle-blowers, 261
White Book Project, 134
White Paper Project, 16, 101, 102, 104–15

windmill park/s, 63, 64, 66
world, 127, 142, 202, 205, 207, 218, 252, 261, 274
  Arab, 158
  economy, 149, 153
  empire/s, 149
  Islamic, 246
  multi-polar, 148
  music genre, 148
  non-human, 273, 277
  politics, 141
  secular, 132
  social, 179
  see war
World Council of Churches (WCC), 33
worldview, 102, 133, 250
wounds, 35

www.ingramcontent.com/pod-product-compliance
Lightning Source LLC
Chambersburg PA
CBHW070059020526
44112CB00034B/1640